A Moment of Peace

ROSE OTIS, EDITOR

REVIEW AND HERALD® PUBLISHING ASSOCIATION
HAGERSTOWN, MD 21740

Copyright © 1995 by
Review and Herald® Publishing Association

The author assumes full responsibility for the accuracy
of all facts and quotations as cited in this book.

This book was
Edited by Gerald Wheeler
Designed by Patricia S. Wegh
Cover illustration by Kim Jacobs/© 1991 Kim Jacobs.
                    Licensed by AMCAL Licensing.
Typeset: 10.5/11.5 Berkeley Book

PRINTED IN U.S.A.

00 99 98 97 96 95   10 9 8 7 6 5 4 3 2 1

Library of Congress Cataloging in Publication Data
A moment of peace : a daily devotional for women by women / Rose Otis,
    editor.
          p.   cm.

    1. Women—Prayer-books and devotions—English.   2. Devotional
calendars.   I. Otis, Rose Marie Niesen.
BV4844.M59   1996   95-33463
224'.2—dc20   CIP

ISBN 0-8280-0979-1

Biographical Sketches

Rondi Aastrup is an English and history teacher at Greater Boston Academy. She has been a member of the New England Youth Ensemble, touring Asia in 1992 and 1993. A freelance author, she currently writes for town newspapers and is working on a book for children. MAY 28.

Juliana Agboka was born in Ghana. She is a homemaker and pastor's wife writing from Côte d'Ivoire. Trained as a schoolteacher, she spends time organizing church women into ministry, helping them find and develop their talents. OCT. 6.

Ginny Allen lives in Vancouver, Washington, with her husband. They have two married sons. As a nurse in a public high school in Portland, Oregon, she has spoken for retreats, seminars, and church-sponsored weekends across the United States, Canada, Brazil, and Russia. A collection of raccoons is scattered throughout the Allen home. JUNE 26.

Ellen Anderson, Ph.D., is a licensed certified social worker and associate professor in the Department of Social Work at Oakwood College in Alabama. Well known for her untiring services to the college, community, and church, she has been cited numerous times for her meritorious service. FEB. 23.

Marlene Anderson is a first time writer for the women's devotional book project. She writes from Mississippi. FEB. 4, MAR. 6, SEPT. 8, OCT. 7, DEC. 16.

Ruth Anneke was raised in the Northwest. She is a widow and a mother of five sons. Before her retirement to north Idaho, she was an elementary teacher for 20 years and has an M.A. in counseling and guidance. Her hobbies include reading, writing, gardening, sewing, and cooking. MAY 27, JUNE 5, AUG. 7.

Indrani J. Ariyaratnam taught school before marrying her minister husband. Being a pastor's wife has been the joy of her life, for it has led to meeting many interesting people and experiencing exciting adventures. Originally from Sri Lanka, then from India, Indrani has lived in Pakistan for the past 10 years and is now the Women's Ministries director for the Pakistan Union of Seventh-day Adventists. JAN. 24, MAY 26.

Alma Atcheson, a mother of three children, presently serves as the communication secretary and assistant welfare leader in her church and is a community visitor for the Coffs Harbour Regional Volunteer Service in Australia. Her main interests are welfare work and gardening. OCT. 11.

Sylvia Atkins is a wife, mother of two teenage sons, literature evangelist, and licensed nurse. Her church offices include personal ministries director, adult Sabbath school teacher, social planner, pianist, and handbell choir director. Her hobbies are music, crafts, people, interior design, plants, and Bible study. APR. 9.

Wilma Atkinson, a retired elementary school teacher, taught 42 years and won the Zapara Award for excellence in teaching. She is married to a retired minister. Her articles have appeared in *Adventist Review, Insight, The Michigan Teacher,* and *Praxis.* JULY 22.

Dalal Aziz is a pastor's wife from the Middle East who enjoys team ministry, cooking, walking, sewing, and reading. She is currently serving as the executive office secretary for the Jordan Section of the East Mediterranean Field. Dalal has been a health correspondence course director and Bible teacher at the elementary level. She is her church's youth leader. JAN. 26.

Audrey Balderstone is the mother of two sons, and she and her husband operate a garden and landscaping company in England. She is completing her honors degree at the University of London, but still conducts her bimonthly Home Fellowship group meeting while maintaining her interest in community activities and flower arranging. MAY 25, JUNE 4, JULY 31, AUG. 8.

Jennifer Baldwin writes from Sydney, Australia, where she is an administrative assistant at Sydney Adventist Hospital. She has served in various capacities in her local church, including elder, teacher, and communication secretary. Enjoying writing, she is a regular contributor to *Signs of the Times* (Australian edition). SEPT. 9.

Paula C. Barnes has a Ph.D. in English and education and is a university professor in Virginia. Her current research is in the area of Black women writers' literary treatment of spirituality. She has been active in children's and women's ministries. SEPT. 28.

Mary Barrett is a pastor's wife and a mother of two young girls. She plays an active part in her husband's ministry, and writes for a variety of magazines. For relaxation she loves to be with friends, do crafts, read, and walk. **Feb. 2, Oct. 14, Dec. 27.**

Moira Barthle is a wife and mother/home school teacher of two active boys who likes walking, reading, studying, and entertaining. She has served as the Women's Ministries coordinator and on the executive planning committee in her church for two years. **May 24, July 21.**

Pamela Baumgartner, a missionary wife and mother of four children, is national coordinator for child evangelism in the Nicaragua Mission. She enjoys writing and counseling troubled young people. **Jan. 25, Feb. 24, Nov. 7.**

Jessie Beard and her husband live in Pennsylvania. The mother of three grown sons, she works as a customer service representative and serves as a superintendent in her local church. She enjoys writing, walking, bicycling, shopping, and public speaking. **Jan. 12.**

Dawna Beausoleil taught for 14 years on the elementary and college levels. She now lives in northern Ontario with her pastor husband. She assists him with visiting, seminars, and public speaking. Her hobbies include reading, writing, camping, and crafts. **Mar. 16.**

Elizabeth Bediako is a native of Ghana. She and her minister husband, four children, and one grandson live in Maryland. An office clerk at the General Conference of Seventh-day Adventists, she enjoys traveling, photography, cooking, and sewing. **Jan. 27.**

Deborah Bilby is a high school foreign language teacher in Palatka, Florida. She works with the youth and the music groups in her church. Her hobbies include reading, writing, and just about any form of needlework. **May 23, Aug. 9.**

Karen Birkett is an administrator in a financial planning firm in Toronto, Ontario. She has been involved in the children's and youth departments of her church. Her hobbies include reading, knitting, embroidery, and camping. **Jan. 5.**

Marjory Button Bodi is a nurse and birthing expert who loves babies, knitting, crocheting, and learning spiritual lessons from nature through her dirty log cabin windows in upper Michigan. She and her husband, Keith, have two grown daughters. **Dec. 11.**

Joan Bova and her husband are licensed foster parents caring for abused children in Florida. She is an enthusiastic and humorous orator, specializing in disability awareness. As a member of the NAD Commission for People With Disabilities, she is actively involved in developing disabilities ministries within local churches. **Mar. 18.**

Arlene Brathwaite is a wife of 48 years, a mother and grandmother, and great-grandmother of three; she also has foster children. An active church member, she has held every office in the church except one. Currently she is a Sabbath school pianist and teacher, a member of the church school board, and head of the flower committee. Gardening, knitting, crocheting, and sewing are her hobbies. Arlene has reached the blessed age of 76. **Mar. 20.**

Cheryl Bratton is a homemaker living in Spangle, Washington. She participates in church music activities and spends much of her spare time arranging and writing music and playing her various musical instruments. **Apr. 10.**

Carole Breckenridge is a freelance writer in Bethesda, Maryland. She enjoys visiting other countries, spending time with family, and nurturing young people. **Apr. 1.**

Ellen Bresee, recently retired coordinator of Shepherdess International, has served with her husband in pastoral and evangelistic team ministry for many years. She has taught elementary school, is the mother of four, is a marriage counselor, speaker, and a published writer. She and her husband have recently moved to Oregon. **Feb. 25.**

Delilah Briggs writes from her home in the mountains near Boulder, Colorado. She is happily married and has two teenage sons. **Apr. 2.**

Judy Broeckel rejoices in Jesus in Yreka, California, where she lives with her mountain-climbing, caving, pediatrician husband and their two children. **May 22.**

Marilyn Brown spent 27 years teaching and serving as a departmental chair in various colleges. Active in her church and other professional organizations, she also edits two large-print magazines for Christian Record Services. **Aug. 12.**

Suzanne Danforth Brozny, a widow of two years, is a retired nurse living in South Carolina. She has lived in Michigan and Illinois much of her life and has helped organize several new churches. In addition she enjoys freelance writing, organ and piano, and plays the organ for different churches on weekends. **Oct. 3.**

Darlene Burgeson, formerly a sales manager, enjoys reading, gardening, and working with creative family albums. She and her husband have both been involved with church leadership for years. **MAR. 17.**

Ann Burke is a full-time homemaker and the mother of young adults who has dabbled in tutoring and teaching over the years. She enjoys writing and usually has a writing project or two in the back of her mind. Her preferences are simple—a little music, a bit of verse, and a window view of the old elm tree in the front yard of her southern California home. **DEC. 24.**

Maureen O. Burke is a counselor at a private hospital in New York. In addition to serving her local church as an ordained elder and Women's Ministries coordinator, she conducts seminars and workshops for those who teach Bible classes, and singles, including "The Role of Female Elders." **JAN. 28, SEPT. 10.**

Betty Burnett, from "Charlevoix the Beautiful," Michigan, works for the Department of Agriculture, has been married for 37 years, and is a mother of five and grandmother of eight. She is active in her church and enjoys reading, crocheting, children, and walking in the fields and woods. **OCT. 9.**

Hazel Burns and her husband live in Ohio and have two grown children. She is a homemaker, church and neighborhood Bible study leader, lecturer, and seminar instructor. Her interests include baking, quilting, painting, hiking, skiing, and family outings. Hazel began a women's ministries program in her local church 12 years ago and is still actively involved in it. **DEC. 22.**

Ellie Lukens Calkins has been happily married to a minister for 54 years. She has been a counselor for the *Voice of Prophecy* and is now retired in Glendale, California. Her two sons have provided her with a lapful of grandchildren. **JAN. 29, MAR. 30, NOV. 8.**

Jeanne Calkins is a retired elementary school teacher living in Berrien Springs, Michigan. She has also been a pastor's wife and active in children's church work. Her hobbies are reading, flowers, cooking, shopping, Bible study, and elementary school volunteering. **NOV. 21.**

Margaret I. Campbell is a Canadian-born retired minister's wife, mother of two daughters, and grandmother of two girls. Having worked as a teacher, registrar, and accountant, she loves to gather material for scrapbooks and try new recipes. **MAY 9, JULY 26, AUG. 4.**

Pam Caruso is a mother of 10 grown children who loves to read, play the piano, and walk. She assists in the cradle roll and Community Services departments at her church and is currently writing a book. **MAR. 27.**

Virginia Cason and her doctor husband live in California and have four grown children. Virginia is a homemaker, public speaker, and writer of children's Bible lessons and a songbook. She teaches voice and is a radio DJ, a ham radio operator, and a private pilot. In addition, she is the daughter of H.M.S. Richards, Sr. **JUNE 20.**

Jan Chamberlain, a minister's wife with four children, has been an elementary teacher, writer, and editor of Ohio and Michigan's *Shepherdess Newsletter*. Also, Jan was a missionary at Ebeye, Marshall Islands, and Truk, Caroline Islands, before "semi-retiring" in Florida. **DEC. 26.**

Shari Chamberlain began her career as a health educator but has been an associate in pastoral care for 10 years and a chaplain for five years. She is currently a chaplain with Hospice of Napa Valley at St. Helena Hospital, in California. Shari enjoys mountain climbing, a good book, chatting with friends, and adventuresome travel. **MAR. 19.**

Lyndelle Chiomenti is an editor for Bible lesson materials. She is married and enjoys writing, reading, crocheting, antiques, history, water gardening, and biblical studies. **MAR. 28.**

Birol C. Christo lives with her husband in India. She is a retired teacher, the mother of five grown children, and the Shepherdess International coordinator for the Southern Asia Division. Birol spends all her spare time sewing and making craft items to sell as fund-raisers to help orphans. **OCT. 30, NOV. 16.**

Ginger Mostert Church, the mother of two grown sons, is a marketing representative for the Review and Herald Publishing Association. She teaches seminars on possibility thinking, and has had articles published in several magazines and local newspapers. She and her husband, Dennis, live in Maryland, where she enjoys cross-stitch, reading, writing, sharing ideas in seminars, and flowers of all kinds. **DEC. 30.**

Carel Clay lives in Napa, California, with her husband and daughter. She has two grown stepchildren. A nursing instructor at Napa Valley College, she is currently completing her master's degree in nursing. She has taught cradle roll, youth, and adult Bible classes. Carel enjoys quilting, sewing, writing, public speaking, cats, and being a mom. **MAR. 21, JUNE 16.**

Jacquelyn Cochran has been director of publications for a private corporation since June 1993. She has lived all her life in Washington, D.C., but has been on five continents. Her next conquests are Australia and Antarctica. **FEB. 26.**

Daphnie M. Corrodus hosts a weekly religious television program in Jamaica. A mother of three grown children, she also enjoys gardening, dressmaking, writing, and architecture. She is actively involved in Family Life ministries in her church. **APR. 25.**

Alice Covey was a schoolteacher before her marriage, and is now a widow living in Canada. She is the mother of six and grandmother of 15 and is a published writer. Alice enjoys writing, sewing, crocheting, playing the piano, and flower gardening, and has worked in various children's departments of her church. **FEB. 18.**

Faith Johnson Crumbly, *Celebration* magazine's managing editor, is the mother of five grown children and grandmother of five. She has been published in various magazines and two preschool devotional books. **MAY 21, SEPT. 27.**

Celia Mejia Cruz is the administrative secretary in the Office of Women's Ministries at the General Conference. A pastor's wife, local church elder, and mother of four adult children and one teenager, she enjoys people, her family, teaching the preteen Bible class at her church, presenting seminars, and preaching. Some of her interests are needlework, reading, writing, dogs, and ceramics. **JULY 2, DEC. 6.**

Jayne Doswell Darby, although retired after 37 years as an administrative secretary, still works as the Women's Ministries leader in her church. She keeps her fingers in shape by playing the piano and writing to her four children and seven grandchildren. **JUNE 19, AUG. 1.**

Lynn Marie Davis, a sign language interpreter in the Georgia school system, coordinates the disability services for her church. Facilitating "Finding Your Niche" workshops and seminars, walking, cooking, and writing are some of her favorite things to do. **FEB. 27.**

Liyda E. de Justiniano writes from Lima, Peru, where she and her minister-husband of 36 years are currently living. They have three grown children and one grandchild. Lidya taught school for 20 years and is currently employed as a secretary at a high school. She enjoys giving Bible studies, reading, presenting seminars on Christian hospitality, and working in her flower garden. **JAN. 4.**

Brenda Forbes Dickerson writes from Omaha, Nebraska, where she is a wife, mother, and homemaker. She enjoys writing, gardening, sewing, and teaching Bible stories to children at her church. **FEB. 28, NOV. 17.**

Sally Dillon is a registered nurse, mother of two boys, Sabbath school teacher, and freelance writer. She has been published in *Guide, Insight,* and other Christian magazines, as well as *Crossroads in Time,* an archaeology activity book for children. **APR. 11.**

Goldie Down and her husband are retired missionaries living in Australia. She teaches creative writing and, to date, has had 18 books and hundreds of stories and articles published. **JAN. 3, SEPT. 21.**

Laura Drown enjoys music, nature, reading, and writing letters. Now retired in Massachusetts, she has done secretarial, editorial, and accounting work in denominational organizations. **SEPT. 20, OCT. 12.**

Etta Maycock Dudley is a mother of three (and four "adopted") and grandmother of four (and four "adopted"). Now retired in Tennessee, she was her husband's secretary for 31 years while he was president of the South Central Conference of Seventh-day Adventists. She enjoys sewing, hiking, reading, gardening, and bringing sunshine to all her contacts. **DEC. 9.**

Rita Eisenhower Duncan is a wife, mother, and secretary in California. Formerly a teacher, she enjoys reading and browsing in libraries, bookstores, museums, stationery stores, and antique shops. She sings in the church choir and helps in planning Women's Ministry activities for her local church. **APR. 6.**

April Dunnett is working for the National Trust's Mottisfont Abbey in England as an assistant gardener, mainly with the Old and Ancestral Rose Collection. She has taught literature, fine arts, and communication in Nigeria and Kenya. Her interests range from arts and crafts to folk guitar and her own handbell choir, Forest Bells. **JUNE 15.**

Crystal Earnhardt is the author of *Will You Still Love Me Tomorrow?* She and her husband spend most of their time traveling in public evangelism. They recently returned from a series of meetings in the Philippines. She enjoys quilting and spending time with her new grandson. **MAR. 31.**

Sudlyn Elder lives in Trinidad, where she is an associate in Church Ministries, Sabbath school, and Community Services director for the South Caribbean Conference of Seventh-day Adventists. She is a dialect specialist and poet who has had numerous articles and poems published. **NOV. 20.**

Janet Evert is the editor of *Young Disciple* magazine. Involved in youth ministries for many years, she has written several Vacation Bible School manuals and Sabbath school materials. She has a special burden for the spiritual welfare of teenagers and has organized youth camps, mission trips, and overseas tours to minister especially to this age group. JULY 7.

Waloma Bennett Fehrenbach is a retired nurse and teacher who has worked as a nursing instructor and school nurse, and has been a former missionary to Ecuador and Peru. She grows fruit and berries and raises flowers that "beg" to go to church, shut-ins, and the sick. Her "play" is making the flower arrangements. NOV. 9.

Valerie Fidelia is the Health and Temperance and Women's Ministries director for the Middle East Union of Seventh-day Adventists in Cyprus. The music coordinator for her local church, she enjoys singing, cross-stitch, embroidery, knitting, and reading. Valerie and her pastor/administrator husband have three grown sons and one almost grown daughter. So far, they have two grandchildren. AUG. 25, SEPT. 19.

Heide Ford is the assistant editor of *Women of Spirit*, a new Christian magazine. A registered nurse, she holds a master's degree in counseling. Her interests include reading, writing, studying different cultures, and white water rafting. She and her pastor-husband make their home in Hagerstown, Maryland. FEB. 3, MAR. 22, JUNE 30, AUG. 11.

Carol Ann Fraser, a freelance writer from Silver Spring, Maryland, has previously written for *Cornerstone Connections*, the youth edition of *Steps to Christ, Adventist Woman*, and the *Adventist Review*. She loves people and someday hopes to practice law in the areas of civil rights, international relations, and personal injury. JAN. 13, FEB. 15, JUNE 10.

Edna Maye Gallington lives in Riverside, California, and works in communications. A graduate of La Sierra University, she has taken public relations studies at the University of California at Riverside. She enjoys playing the piano, creative writing, hiking, and working in her church. SEPT. 29.

Lila Lane George assists her minister husband in Arizona (and sometimes international) evangelism. She is an artist who likes to swim, hike, and play with her six grandchildren. Her articles have been published in previous women's devotional books. JUNE 29, AUG. 10.

Dawna Giem is the mother of Matthew, 9, and Jacob, 5, and wife of an OB-gyn physician. A part-time physical therapist, she is deeply involved in church school volunteering and enjoys crafts, camping, and traveling. Her family resides in Spokane, Washington, after living three years in England. DEC. 4.

Leila Gilhousen retired in Oregon after 36 years of denominational service in the Seventh-day Adventist Church. Her writings have been published in *Youth's Instructor, Life and Health, Adventist Review*, and *Signs* magazines. JUNE 28.

Evelyn Glass is a wife, mother, grandmother, and farmer. She heads the Women's Ministries Department for the Mid-America Union of Seventh-day Adventists and serves as an elder and clerk at her church. Her interests include folk painting, refinishing furniture, public speaking, and writing for local and state newspapers as well as Christian publications. FEB. 13, JUNE 8, SEPT. 23.

Judy Glass enjoys spending time with family and friends, reading, and doing cross-stitch and stained-glass work. She currently works as the assistant business manager of a group of private schools in Lincoln, Nebraska. APR. 18.

Carmen O. Gonzalez, a single mother of one adult son, is a teacher with the New York City public school system. She has held many church offices and is a singles ministries coordinator in New York. Her interests include praising God, praying, writing letters, walking, bicycling, people watching, and playing with her nephew, Danny. FEB. 5.

Carrol Grady is a minister's wife, a mother of three sons and two daughters-in-law, a grandmother of three granddaughters, and a secretary in the state of Washington. She has had a number of poems, articles, and stories published, and is seldom seen without a needle and quilt pieces in her hand. JAN. 16, FEB. 9, NOV. 22.

Mary Jane Graves retired with her husband after spending 21 years as an academy registrar, librarian, and/or secretary. Her stories have been published in *Youth's Instructor, Our Little Friend, Primary Treasure*, and *Guide*. She has two sons, two granddaughters, and likes gardening, reading, and collecting recipes. JUNE 27, AUG. 19.

Ramona Perez Greek, assistant director of Women's Ministries for the North American Division of Seventh-day Adventists, travels extensively, speaking on women's issues and concerns in the church. In recognition for her work and service, Andrews University presented her with an honorary degree, Doctor of Humane Letters, in 1993. She is the proud mother of 5-year-old James-Pierre. **Feb. 6, Sept. 13.**

Ellie Green is the president of Frederick Nursing Consultants. She's a prolific writer and full-time lecturer who enjoys speaking at Christian women's retreats; she enjoys oil, watercolor, and chalk painting, as well as crocheting and knitting. Her son is an attorney, her daughter is a nurse, and her husband is a rocket scientist for NASA. **Apr. 22, June 6, Dec. 23.**

Glenda-Mae Greene is the assistant vice president for student affairs at Andrews University in Berrien Springs, Michigan. She is a Jamaican-Canadian with a deep interest in a diversity of issues—women's ministries, single ministries, and minority issues. Glenda-Mae enjoys travel, working on tapestries, walking by the beach, words, and, above all, "the Word." **Jan. 6, Feb. 7, Sept. 30.**

Meibel Mello Guedes writes from Brazil, where she is the director of Women's Ministries for the Central Brazil Union of Seventh-day Adventists. Meibel coordinates ministries and programs for women in seven conferences centered in São Paulo. She has two children. **Apr. 7, June 25.**

Alberta Hack is a wife, mother, piano teacher, music committee member, church pianist, school board member, and editor of her church's publication for women. Her interests are flowers, music, and decorating their home. She worked in the primary Sabbath school for 21 years. **Nov. 13.**

Dessa Weisz Hardin traveled solo to the Ukraine by train from Romania and through Moldova in 1993, losing her passport along the way. She is a freelance writer living in Massachusetts. Throughout the school year she does volunteer work for children, periodically telling them Russian stories. **Jan. 2, Oct. 1.**

Lea Hardy, a former English and religion teacher, now finds her greatest satisfaction serving as a local church elder, speaking, and conducting spiritual gifts seminars. She is a published author who enjoys reading and spending time with her family. **Dec. 20.**

Peggy Harris is an elder and musician in her local church and chair of WASH (Women and Men Against Sexual Harassment and Other Abuses). Her writing includes prose and poetry for various religious magazines. She presents biblical hospitality seminars and has her own business as an insurance agent. She and her husband have two children and two grandchildren. **Mar. 23, Dec. 18.**

Lucile Hassenpflug, retired after teaching 20 years in public and private schools, is an honorary lifetime member of the PTA. She assists her evangelist husband, Ben, both in the U.S. and abroad. **Feb. 29.**

Ann VanArsdell Hayward has retired to North Carolina after 30 years in the health-care industry. She is an active worker in her church and likes reading and sight-seeing. **Apr. 21.**

Heartsong is a pseudonym. **Nov. 15.**

Alice Heath is a clinical nurse specialist in obstetrics living in northern California with her husband and three children. Working toward a postgraduate degree in ethics/theology, she treasures having 10 minutes all to herself. **Apr. 20.**

Helen Heavirland spends her time in homemaking, Bible study, bookkeeping, gardening, bird-watching, reading, writing, songwriting, and singing. Her writings have been published in a variety of magazines, and she has contributed to several books. She lives with her husband in Oregon. **Jan. 30, Feb. 17, Aug. 26.**

Ursula M. Hedges is a secondary school teacher/administrator. Born to missionary parents in India, she and her Australian principal-husband have given 10 years in mission service in the Pacific. She has written books, stories, and articles. Other hobbies include interior design, sewing, cooking, and producing dramas. **June 14, July 20.**

Lorabel Hersch is community pastor of the Southern College church in Tennessee. A former librarian and English teacher, she writes for religious magazines. Traveling and being hospitable are two of her chief delights. She and her husband have six children and seven grandchildren. **Feb. 20, May 16, June 7.**

Myrtle Hicks spends her spare time gardening, bird-watching, and making crafts. After 48 years of marriage, a nursing diploma, two daughters, and a sporadic nursing career, she is now enjoying country living with the activities and challenges of a small church and community. Three great-granddaughters add to her joy. **Apr. 19, July 1.**

Kyna Hinson, a journalist and assistant college professor, is involved in Women's Ministries through her local church and conference. She is a published writer and enjoys working with teenagers, embroidery, reading, and baking. **Dec. 3.**

Elizabeth "Betty" Woodmansee Hoehn is a retired medical technologist who has worked in hospitals in the U.S., Canada, and Jamaica. She collects poetry, seashells, and sunrise/sunset pictures. After age 50 she received her master's degree in management/supervision and public health. JULY 19.

Roxy Hoehn writes from Kansas, the geographical center of the United States. A teacher, she has done quite a bit of writing for children, including several teen Bible school quarterlies. She is the director of Women's Ministries for the Kansas-Nebraska Conference. MAY 18.

Karen Holford writes from England, where she is a pastor's wife and mother of three young children. She enjoys traditional American crafts, interior design, family ministry, and times of creative praise and worship. Karen is the author of *The Loneliest Grief,* a book about miscarriage recovery. FEB. 1, MAR. 4, MAY 11.

Carol June Hutchins Hooker is a community health nurse working with homeless people in Maryland and is a church deaconess. Married to a math teacher, she has a teenage daughter and son, and enjoys nature and its patterns. JULY 15.

Lorraine Hudgins, a retired administrative secretary, has worked for Faith for Today, the Voice of Prophecy, and the General Conference of Seventh-day Adventists. Her poems and articles have appeared in various publications. A book of poems, *Almost Home,* was published in 1994. FEB. 8, MAR. 3, APR. 5, MAY 3, MAY 20, AUG. 2, OCT. 16.

Barbara Huff writes from Mound, Minnesota. The wife of a church administrator, she is a mother of two adult children, and a grandmother. She is a freelance writer, as well the Communication and Women's Ministries director for the Minnesota Conference. JAN. 8.

Faith Hunter is a recently married teacher with the Washington, D.C., public schools and resides in Maryland. A regular contributor to *Cornerstone Connections* youth quarterly, she also enjoys travel, meeting people, phoning friends, and eating multicultural foods. FEB. 11, MAR. 10, APR. 4.

Lois E. Johannes is retired from mission service in Pakistan, India, Singapore, Okinawa, and the Caribbean, as well as several institutions in the United States. Now living in Loma Linda, California, she serves as a treasurer and telephone ministry member at her church. JULY 14, AUG. 18, OCT. 15.

Anna Johansen fortunately likes to travel and meet people, for the Lord's work has taken her and her husband from Iceland to West Africa, and from Scandinavia to the Middle East. Other interests include music, crossword puzzles, and cross-stitch. Her three grown children live in Denmark. She now lives and writes from Cyprus. SEPT. 11.

Grace Johanson works for AT&T and lives in New Jersey with her daughter, Tedi, and Tedi's 7-year-old son, Ryan. A mother of five, she likes gardening, all kinds of sewing, camping, flowers, and bird- and butterfly-watching. JULY 13, AUG. 17.

Marianette Johnston is now retired after more than 40 years of serving with her husband in pastoring, college teaching, and church administration. She now hopes for more time to spend with family, friends, quilting, and cross-stitching. MAY 17.

Jeanne Jordan is a retired teacher living in Michigan with her husband. They have been married for 44 years, served as missionaries for 12 years, and have two grown children. The author of three books and countless articles in church magazines, Jeanne also enjoys reading, traveling, and words. APR. 29.

Nyla Juhl is a nurse educator at the University of North Dakota. Her articles have appeared in several nursing and health-related journals. Camping, hiking, jogging, gardening, and assisting in health/lifestyle seminars are some of her favorite activities. APR. 17.

Beate Karbstein is a secretary and professional massage therapist from Australia. She has been the leader in the primary/junior Bible class at her church for the past 10 years. Her achievements include being a mother for more than 11 years and developing a love for Jesus in her son, writing several skits that have been performed, and selling some of her paintings. FEB. 12, MAR. 2.

Lucile Freeman-Kime is a freelance writer from the state of Washington who has had articles published in the North Pacific Union *Gleaner* and the *Adventist Review.* She currently serves in the Walla Walla College church as an elder and a member of the communication committee. MAY 13, JULY 25, DEC. 19.

Marguerite V. Knauft is a minister's wife of 55 years and a retired registered nurse of 27 years. A Bible worker and Sabbath school teacher of all ages, she enjoys sewing, art, nature study, and nutrition. She has worked in many cancer drives and community service centers. SEPT. 25.

RosaLynda "Gina" Kosini is a business correspondence specialist, creative writer, church communication secretary, and part-time health major from Texas. She likes reading for pleasure and spiritual/personal growth, health issues, experimental cuisine, and getting her hands dirty in potting soil. SEPT. 18.

Karen Kotoske, a dental hygienist, is founder and director of the Amistad Foundation, which provides medical and humanitarian services to remote Indian tribes in Mexico. Her nonprofessional interests are her flower garden, making photographic greeting cards, church, and her town's program for the homeless. AUG. 21.

Criss Kramer is a wife, stepmother, grandmother, and an insurance agent. She is the vice president of her local American Business Women's Association and editor of the church newsletter. She loves her work, writing, decorating her home, and doing things for others. MAR. 11, JULY 12.

Kay Kuzma is a wife, mother of three, and the president of Family Matters, a media ministry providing services to families. A teacher for 25 years, she now has a syndicated daily radio feature, a weekly television broadcast, and a free quarterly newspaper, Family Times. Dr. Kuzma has written more than a dozen books, including A Hug and a Kiss and a Kick in the Pants, Building Your Child's Character From the Inside Out, and When You're Serious About Love: Straight Talk to Single Adults. NOV. 6.

Eileen E. Lantry is from north Idaho. A librarian, teacher, homemaker, minister's wife, and Bible instructor, she spent 14 years as a missionary in eastern Asia. Eileen has authored 13 books and loves nature, gardening, hiking, and cross-country skiing. JAN. 7, AUG. 13, SEPT. 7, NOV. 26.

Lorna Lawrence holds a doctorate in marriage, family, and crisis counseling. Residing in northern California, she teaches school, composes music, writes, conducts seminars, and offers individual counseling. She is also the director of the Lorna Lawrence Women's Ensemble, now in its seventh season. OCT. 25.

Gina Lee is a freelance writer with more than 350 stories published in various magazines. Her work has been included in five books. She and her four cats live in a trailer surrounded by shoulder-high geraniums. JAN. 9, MAR. 24, APR. 16, JUNE 13, JULY 11, AUG. 16, OCT. 13.

Irma Lee, a mother of an adult son, enjoys photography, poetry, and listening to the sea. She is a human services major in college and a student of the violin. SEPT. 17.

Karen Lindensmith is a pastor's wife and a mother of two young children, John and Emily, both "made in Japan." She and her husband worked in that country for six years, teaching in language schools before pastoring Japanese churches. The family currently lives in North Dakota. Writing has been a hobby of Karen's since childhood. JULY 10, AUG. 30.

Bessie Lobsien is a retired librarian who has served in Pakistan, Hong Kong, and Mexico, as well as in the United States. Since the age of 16 she has had her poems and articles published in several church papers and poetry collections. MAY 19.

Merri Long has done much of the preliminary typing for this devotional. A pastor's wife and mother of two young girls, she loves to collect recipes and study sign language. If she had any spare time, she would like to spend it reading, crocheting, walking, or eating chocolate. AUG. 27.

Gina Youngberg Lonser is the mother of two and a nurse whose many hobbies, including knitting, quilting, dress designing, camping, and bird-watching, have been suspended until completion of a M.S.N. program. APR. 15, SEPT. 26.

June Loor loves singing in the choir, writing letters, camping at the ocean, and building houses. She is a retired nurse living on top of a mountain in North Carolina with her minister husband. They have two children and five grandchildren. AUG. 22.

Aileen Ludington and her husband are both physicians and have a medical practice in Loma Linda, California. She has been a regular contributor to Signs of the Times for the past seven years and has had two books published. The mother of six children and grandmother of 11, she enjoys writing, reading, hiking, and walking. NOV. 3.

Pat Madsen does extensive traveling but calls California her home. She is a superintendant in her local church and is involved in a Bible study group. She is a published writer of poems, stories, and songs. SEPT. 16, OCT. 26, DEC. 8.

Eunice Mason, originally from the United Kingdom, is an accountant for Adventist Community Services, with 16 years of mission service. She is also a qualified Bible instructor and is currently one of the teachers of the baptismal class at her church in Pinetown, South Africa. Eunice prepares the quarterly conference newsletter on a voluntary basis. A grandmother, she enjoys knitting, sewing, and gardening. DEC. 29.

Peggy Mason, living in Wales with her husband and one of her two adult sons, is an English teacher and writer whose hobbies include dried flower growing and arranging, cooking, sewing, and gardening. She is a pianist/composer and enjoys working for her church and community. Aug. 28.

Linda McCabe is a pastor's wife and mother of two boys. She leads two women's fellowship and study groups, edits a newsletter for abuse victims, and speaks at retreats. Also she writes, arranges, and produces music in her home studio for Thy Word Creations—a company that publishes children's Scripture music materials. She and her husband are working on their second tape. Apr. 14, June 23, July 9.

Wilma McClarty is an English and speech professor at Southern College of Seventh-day Adventists, a wife, and a mother of two. She is a public speaker and writer who has received many honors and awards, one of the most recent being the Sears-Roebuck Teaching Excellence and Campus Leadership Award for 1991. Jan. 10, Mar. 7, Dec. 15.

Gloria McLaren is the mother of five children (three are young adults, two are deceased). She is the chaplain for the Hospice of the Florida Suncoast in Largo, Florida. Her hobbies include writing, sewing, cooking, knitting, crocheting, and gardening. Mar. 25.

Marge Lyberg McNeilus is the bookkeeper for her husband's business, McNeilus Auto & Truck Parts. She is also a homemaker, mother of four children, and has four grandchildren. Her hobbies include photography, crafts, writing, music, and traveling. Aug. 24.

Retta Michaelis is a part-time medical technologist living in California with her husband and two daughters. She works with the Women's Ministries and the children at her church. Her interests include reading, writing, Bible study, and spending time with her family. Jan. 20, Feb. 16.

Barbara Smith Morris is executive director of a nonprofit retirement center and a former Tennessee delegate representing housing and services needs of the low-income elderly. The mother of four grown children and grandmother of six grandsons, she writes a daily devotional for the retirement center and loves to be surrounded by people of all ages. Apr. 3, July 8, Aug. 15.

Teresa Musson is a registered nurse and vice president of Living, Inc., a health education corporation. She also cohosts the radio program Living and the cable television program Living Today. The Women's Ministries coordinator at her church, Teresa lives in Michigan with her doctor husband and two young children. Mar. 26.

Beatrice S. Neall recently retired after 16 years of teaching Bible at Union College. Previously she was a missionary in Cambodia, Vietnam, and Singapore, and has written several books and numerous articles for church publications. She has raised African violets, vegetable gardens, and two special hybrids, Randy and Cherie. June 2, June 21.

Joan Minchin Neall was born in Australia, lived in England, and now makes her home in Tennessee, where she is a registered nurse. She and her pastor husband have four grown children. The Women's Ministries coordinator for her church, she enjoys nature, sewing, journalism, and her grandchildren. Jan. 11, Feb. 10.

Bienvisa Ladion Nebres comes from the Philippines but writes from Zaire where she is serving as a missionary. She enjoys teaching, church work, music, poetry, and collecting stamps. Aug. 14, Dec. 12.

Joyce Neergaard lives in Cyprus and works with her husband for the Adventist Development and Relief Agency as assistant for project development. She is a nurse and enjoys working with her local church in community health promotion programs and teen Bible classes. Singing, reading, writing, snorkeling, and skiing are some of her leisure pleasures. Apr. 30, June 12.

Turkeah Nimri writes from Jordan, where she worked as a security guard in the king's palace for 18 years. Now retired, this mother of five and grandmother of 13 enjoys homemaking and reading. Turkeah is a deaconess in her church and actively seeks situations in which she can help people less fortunate than she. July 6.

Mabel Rollins Norman graduated with her eldest son in 1973 from Oakwood College, where she taught for eight years in the Elementary Education Department. The senior staff writer for Speakin' Out News, a weekly newspaper circulated in 27 states and throughout Alabama, she has also authored several hundred articles and a manual entitled Women: Organizing for Ministry. As a certified prison fellowship volunteer, she gives her time twice monthly as pianist/facilitator for Bible classes and seminars. July 18, Oct. 31.

Connie Nowlan has been an English teacher, a girls' dean in academies, a preschool teacher and director, a wife, a biological mother, an adoptive mother, and always a writer. Her devotionals are the results of her experiences in her varying professions. Apr. 12, May 12, July 17, Dec. 14.

Sheree Parris Nudd is the founder of NonProfit Forum (TM), a comprehensive online information resource for nonprofit organizations on CompuServe. An accomplished speaker and published author, Sheree is a consultant in philanthropy with a notable background in health-care administration, development, and public relations. She and her husband, Evan, have two daughters. JULY 16.

Erika Olfert was born in Yugoslavia and migrated to Canada as a teenager. She and her minister husband have been missionaries in India, but now live in Washington State. A nurse working as a consultant for nursing homes, she also teaches a nursing assistant program that she developed. The youth leader and Women's Ministries coordinator for her church, she is the mother of two grown boys. When time permits, she enjoys oil painting, sewing, knitting, swimming, bicycling, singing, and housecleaning. JAN. 14.

Gail M. Ormsby, an Australian who worked several years in the South Pacific region as a teacher and health educator, now works as the senior manager for the Adventist Development and Relief Agency's international office in Maryland. She has worked in Indonesia and the West Indies and spent many years in public health and nutrition education. A former editor of *Alert* magazine, her hobbies include photography, art, design, and music. JUNE 22, AUG. 6.

Rose Otis is the director of Women's Ministries for the General Conference of Seventh-day Adventists. Since the office was established in 1990, she has helped to develop programs that benefit women in countries around the world. Her work includes training leaders and speaking to women's groups. She enjoys her grandchildren, writing, and being home. FEB. 14.

Ofelia Pangan is a secretary and former teacher living in central California with her husband, who pastors two churches. They were former missionaries in the Philippines, Thailand, and Canada. Their two daughters are nurses, and their son is an optometrist. Together they have provided four grandchildren. Some of Ofelia's hobbies are reading, walking, gardening, sewing, and crocheting. JAN. 17.

Revel N. Papaioannou is English, born in India, and married to a Greek pastor. She writes from the biblical town of Berea, Greece, and has four adult sons and two grandchildren. Her many roles include being a part-time English teacher, youth Bible class teacher, preacher, translator, and stamp and coin collector. OCT. 8.

Norma Jean Parchment is a pioneer for Women's Ministries in Canada. She currently serves as director for Women's Ministries, family life, and Sabbath school for the Ontario Conference and as Women's Ministries director for the Canadian Union of Seventh-day Adventists. A mother of two sons, she and her pastor/administrator husband reside in Oshawa, Ontario. NOV. 18, DEC. 5.

Gwen Pascoe is trained in horticulture, but is currently majoring in history at the University of Melbourne in Australia. She greatly enjoys playing around with words. Most of her writing has been for children, with 15 titles published so far. JUNE 6, JULY 23.

Julia L. Pearce is a nursing instructor and consultant in women's health services. She has been involved in Women's Ministries activities at her church and enjoys making presentations about women and health-care history. AUG. 29.

Ivy Petersen writes from South Africa, where she has recently retired after 34 years of being a teacher, lecturer, and principal from first grade to college level. She and her husband have both served as local elders and lay preachers. They have five grown children. AUG. 23, OCT. 23.

Ivadel Peterson is a retired teacher living with her cat in Washington State. She is the mother of three and grandmother of 13 grandchildren. Her hobbies include music and children. Besides working actively in her own church, she regularly plays piano and organ in two other churches, as well as directing the choir in one of them. Her husband, who died on July 14, 1994, had Alzheimer's disease and Parkinson's disease, and she would like to share her story. NOV. 11.

Kathleen Stearman Pflugrad and her husband serve at a one-room school in Grayling, Michigan. They enjoy taking extended wilderness canoe trips. She has been a missionary in Indonesia, Thailand, and Guam, and has written for *Adventist Review* and *Insight* magazines. MAY 4, JUNE 24.

Felicia Phillips is the wife of an Adventist Development and Relief Agency director and the mother of three college-student sons. Felicia has a M.A. in theology and is a chaplain at Manila Sanitarium and Hospital in the Philippines. She serves as an elder in her church and enjoys preaching, teaching, giving Bible studies, and homemaking. APR. 28, JUNE 1, JULY 3.

Lorrine Phillips is entering her golden years and expects them to be just that. She will spend winters in the Florida sun and summers in Michigan, where she lives with her husband and near her two grown children and four grandchildren. Although Women's Ministries has been her main focus lately, she also enjoys travel, reading, collecting pictures, genealogy, and calligraphy. SEPT. 2.

Barbara H. Phipps is a retired reference librarian who taught library science at Andrews University and Pacific Union College, and continues to volunteer at the PUC library. Her articles have been published in *Adventist Review, Youth's Instructor, Insight,* and professional journals. She wrote *Test Tubes and Chalkdust,* a biography of her father, B. H. Phipps. JULY 30.

Alyce Pickett fulfilled her cherished dream for decades when she went back to college and, at age 52, became a nurse. Now retired, this mother of two sons and grandmother of two is a contributing author for Rainbow Books' puzzle books series and Standard Publishing Company's children's program books. Her articles, poems, and children's stories have appeared in *Celebration! Adventist Review, Light & Life, Mature Living, Sunday Digest, Clubhouse, Primary Treasure,* and others. APR. 27, JUNE 11.

Julianne Pickle has enough "dreams" to fill up more than a lifetime. She is a young homemaker living in Iowa who loves flowers. She authored the cookbook *100 Percent Vegetarian: Eating Naturally From Your Grocery Store.* Currently she is working on writing Christian Bible poetry books for young children. AUG. 31, SEPT. 15.

Birdie Poddar is from northeastern India. The wife of a retired division Communication Director, she is the mother of three grown children and grandmother to three grandsons. She worked as an elementary teacher, cashier, cashier accountant, and statistician before retiring in 1991. Sewing, gardening, and composing poems are some of her hobbies. OCT. 4.

Myrtle A. Pohle spent seven years in mission service with her husband in Guatemala and Mexico before settling in Tempe, Arizona, where they started a hospital and helped build a church. She has three children and many foster children and has served as a chaplain's assistant and Bible instructor for 20 years. An author of numerous articles and poems, as well as a book entitled *The Truth Seekers,* she was cited by Tempe as one of the outstanding women of the year and honored by Loma Linda University as Woman of the Year. JULY 29.

Irene Powell and her husband live in Australia and have two grown children. A former church school teacher, she is an active layperson who has served in most areas of her church. She loves gardening, reading, art, and music. Her biggest thrill was being chosen to represent the South Australian Conference at the General Conference session in New Orleans. JULY 28.

Vivian Prewitt is a teacher, wife, and mother of two sons. She enjoys being active in local church affairs, occasionally giving the sermon. Adventurous activities such as hiking, skiing, sailing, and snorkeling are her favorites, along with wildlife photography. She has had two books published, along with several magazine articles. DEC. 2.

Trudy Rankin has had many articles published in America, Australia, and in New Zealand, where she lives with her husband and works as a part-time lab tutor at the University of Auckland. When she is not studying for her Bachelor of Commerce degree, she likes reading, outdoor activities, and music. She plays the French horn in her little church orchestra. MAR. 12, JULY 27.

Jeanne d'Harimalala Rasoanindrainy writes from Madagascar, where she is a teacher and pastor's wife who moves abroad a lot. She has written a book on vegetarianism and a children's book. Jeanne is currently working on an educational book, the theme of which has been inspired by the experiences her family went through in Rwanda. MAY 15, AUG. 5.

Julie Reynolds is a registered nurse and currently a full-time homemaker and mother living in North Carolina. She is the Women's Ministries coordinator in her church. Her favorite activities include gardening, hiking in the mountains, walking on the seashore, and playing with her children. MAR. 5.

Mary Margaret Richards is a writer and teacher living in southern California. She is married to H.M.S. Richards, Jr., speaker emeritus of the *Voice of Prophecy* radiobroadcast. JULY 5.

Kay D. Rizzo, the mother of two daughters, is a freelance writer living in central California with her husband. She is the author of 18 books, the most recent being *She Said 'No'* and *More Than Mountains.* Kay is a public speaker and is active in Women's Ministries in her local church. JAN. 18, MAR. 8, OCT. 2.

Barbara Roberts is a stay-home grandma, caring for her grandchildren while their mothers work. Previously, she has worked at a Christian bookstore and at her church's conference office in Washington. She enjoys growing orchids, sewing, writing, and serving her church as head elder. OCT. 29.

Sharyn Robichaux writes from Louisiana where she is a secretary. She is the mother of three adult daughters. APR. 26.

Adelle Rochford, although born in Australia, spent 20 years living in Cape Town, South Africa. A single parent of two and a high school English, music, and speech and drama teacher, she enjoys writing—

particularly poetry—and has performed with many music groups. She loves people. **MAR. 29, NOV. 14.**

Mindy Rodenburg is a nursing student who has lived in Indiana, Washington, Virginia, Maryland, British Columbia, and Alberta. Her hobbies include writing, sewing, cross-stitch, swimming, water-skiing, and traveling. Like a magnet, her dorm room draws friends in for foot, back, neck, and shoulder massages, haircuts, or just a good chat. **JULY 4.**

Jean Reiffenstein Rothgeb has been a church school teacher but currently works as the medical secretary for an orthopedic surgeon. She also serves as the school board chair, and as organist at her church. She and her husband have two surviving daughters, four grandchildren, and one great-granddaughter. She loves all of the homemaker, mother, and grandmother responsibilities, as well as sewing and handiwork. **APR. 24, DEC. 17.**

Terrie Ruff is an assistant professor in the Behavioral Science Department at Southern College. An active member of various professional and volunteer organizations, she enjoys public speaking, singing, and interacting with people. She is a member of the Big Brothers/Big Sisters of Chattanooga. **APR. 23.**

Ella Rydzewski is an editorial assistant who enjoys reading, especially in the fields of science and religion. She and her husband lived many years in southern California but returned to her old homestead in Clarksville, Maryland, 10 years ago. Ella is a member of The Writing Academy, an interdenominational writing school. **SEPT. 24.**

Deborah Sanders is a mother, housewife, community service worker, and writer. She and her husband and two children make their home in Canada. Author of a collection of poetry, she goes by the pen name "Sonny's Mommy." **NOV. 27.**

Shelia Sanders, a speech therapist, is a transitional counselor for retarded adults in California. A widowed mother of two and stepmother of four children, she teaches a Bible class in her church. She has contributed to the *Collegiate Quarterly* and enjoys photography, travel, reading, sewing, and singing. **OCT. 5.**

Bonita Dudley-Scott is a risk control/quality assurance technician for one of the country's largest healthcare corporations. She and her husband, Joseph, live in Nashville, Tennessee. Having birthed no children of her own, she claims Joseph's two grown children and two grandchildren. Her interests include sewing, designing, graphics, computers, singing, piano, and sincerely loving people. **JUNE 18.**

Marie H. Seard is retired but remains active in Women's Ministries and is the newsletter editor at her church. She enjoys writing, reading biographies, photography, collecting quotations, sending cards, shopping, coordinating weddings, and traveling with her husband, an employee with the General Conference. They have one adult son in California. **NOV. 25.**

Roberta Sharley is an active member in her church, serving as family coordinator and elder. A retired R.N., she and her husband have four adult children. One is a minister, two are builders, and one an archaeologist. Roberta's privilege has been to spend six months in Israel—her favorite place in the world besides home. **DEC. 10.**

Donna Lee Sharp is a retired social director and administrator of retirement facilities. She enjoys the piano and organ, photography, hiking, traveling, bird-watching, and gardening. Donna has four sons, one daughter, one stepdaughter, and five grandchildren. **NOV. 23.**

Penny Shell has been an English teacher for 14 years and hospital chaplain for 10 years. Currently she is a chaplain at Shady Grove Adventist Hospital in Maryland. Penny enjoys writing, and many of her articles have been published in magazines. She also enjoys puttering around her home. **SEPT. 1.**

Carrol Johnson Shewmake is a retired academy librarian living with her retired minister husband in southern California. They have four children and seven grandchildren. Carrol has enjoyed writing since childhood and has written four books: *Practical Pointers to Personal Prayer, Sanctuary Secrets to Personal Prayer, New Words for Witnessing,* and *Sensing His Presence, Hearing His Voice.* She has given numerous seminars on how to maintain an intimate family relationship with God. **JAN. 19, DEC. 21.**

Juanita Slack is a retired secretary who has also served as a judge on election boards. She has written many articles and two books, entitled *The Importance of Touch* and *The Gentle Art of Saying Thank You.* Other interests are stamp collecting, reading, and helping others. **NOV. 24.**

Ann E. Slaughter is a married legal secretary living in Ohio. She enjoys writing devotionals, poetry, articles, and stories. Playing the piano, singing, reading, listening to books on tape, and entertaining in her home are some of her other hobbies. **DEC. 13.**

Cherie Smith is currently adjusting to an "empty nest" and is trying to reorganize her priority list. She likes to walk, read, and cross-stitch. Much of her time is consumed with her job as administrative assistant at Southern College in Tennessee. She and her husband have two daughters and a son-in-law. Aug. 20, Nov. 29.

Reva I. Smith, a retired church school teacher, says her middle name should be "Kids." Her life has revolved around her 11 grandkids, 9 great-grandkids, and the hundreds of youngsters she has taught in church school, Pathfinders, and junior camp. She has published two books and dozens of stories, plays, and articles for and about children. Other interests include oil and acrylic painting, quilting, sewing, and music. Apr. 13, Nov. 30.

Elva E. Springer is a retired medical assistant and X-ray technician whose hobbies are camping, boating, flying, writing, and church activities. She has three children, eight grandchildren, and six great-grandchildren. Elva and her husband of 53 years still take their annual 5,000-mile motorcycle trip. Oct. 10, Oct. 28.

Dorothy A. Starks writes from Maryland where she and her husband of 53 years have retired. A minister's wife, mother of seven, and grandmother of 10, Dorothy taught church school for 34 years. She has a special love for all children, and enjoys spending time with her family, sewing, crocheting, and helping others. May 31.

Kathleen Staubach, a native of California, graduated from Loma Linda University and has taught junior high math and Bible for the past seven years in that state, where she lives with her husband and three sons. Kathy is known for the stories she regularly uses to illustrate her points. Oct. 27.

Ardis Stenbakken was an active Army chaplain's wife for 23 years until her husband "retired" to work at the General Conference of Seventh-day Adventists. They have one adult son and a daughter. Ardis has been a high school teacher and principal, is concerned about women's issues, and enjoys church work, crafts, reading, travel, and public speaking. She is also the coordinator for "The Year of the Adventist Woman" for the General Conference Women's Ministries Department. Jan. 31, Oct. 17.

Beulah Fern Stevens writes from Portland, Oregon, where she is the director of pastoral care at Portland Adventist Medical Center. A chaplain and nurse, she has written and taught internationally about spiritual care in nursing. Mar. 9, Sept. 3, Nov. 4.

Helen Stiles was a missionary to India from 1960 to 1975. For the past nine years she has been the editorial secretary of *Signs of the Times* magazine at the Pacific Press Publishing Association in Idaho. She enjoys globe-trotting. Dec. 31.

Iris L. Stovall has had several articles published in *Celebration!* magazine. She is personal ministries leader, superintendent, and audiovisual assistant at her church. Writing for children is her primary interest. May 30.

Cindy Sumarauw came far from her home in Indonesia to study at Pacific Union College. She graduated in June of 1994 with degrees in psychology and predentistry. Sept. 4.

Loraine Sweetland, a recently retired library director, writes book reviews for *Library Journal* and has taught church school for 14 years. She enjoys reading, antiques, gardening, and computer work. She has served as personal ministries director for her church, as well as holding many other church offices. Feb. 19, Dec. 28.

Arlene Taylor is risk manager at St. Helena Hospital in Northern California as well as the founder and president of her own non-profit educational foundation. An internationally known speaker and brain-function consultant, she is the creator of and presentor for BRAINWORKS UNLIMITED, a new four-day live-in program at the Health Center at St. Helena Hospital. She is also the radio host for *Living Profiles,* a "Year of the Adventist Woman" project. Jan. 1, June 17, Nov. 1, Nov. 28, Dec. 7, Dec. 25.

Margaret E. Taylor is a retired widow living in Florida, where she stays busy taking care of her 95-year-old mother. She is the communication director and a choir member at her church. Many of her poems have been published in several magazines, including *The Quiet Hour* and *Poetry Press.* Several of her articles have been accepted for publication in *Guideposts* and *The People's Digest.* Jan. 21.

Monica Stocker Taylor is a homemaker in Tennessee who enjoys cooking, baking, sewing, writing, animals, and meeting people. She is active in her local church. Jan. 15.

Marguerite Thygeson, a native of Washington, D.C., lives in Maryland and works as an analyst programmer for the General Conference Information Systems Services. During the school year she spends two evenings a week tutoring for the Prepare Our Youth program. Her hobbies include vocal and instrumental music, knitting, brainteasers, and getting near the ocean and mountains whenever possible. Oct. 18.

Joy Totenhofer lives in a suburb of Melbourne, Australia. Previously she worked in public relations and as a news editor. She and her minister husband retired in 1992 and have since served as volunteers in pastoral ministry in Nizhniy Novgorod, Russia, and Launceston, Tasmania. **Feb. 21.**

Dotti Tremont is a single parent and works as a secretary for the purchasing and contracting office at the Department of Veterans Affairs in Anchorage, Alaska. She teaches in the primary division at her church and has had several short stories published in *Primary Treasure*. **Jan. 22.**

Nancy Van Pelt, a family life educator, certified home economist, author, and internationally known speaker, has written 18 books on family life. Her newest releases are *My Prayer Notebook,* a prayer notebook for an organized prayer life, and *Creative Hospitality.* She and her husband make their home in California and are the parents of three grown children. Her hobby is quilting. **Jan. 23, Mar. 1, May 29, July 24, Oct. 19.**

Janis Vance is a registered nurse and licensed counselor with a master's degree in educational psychology. She and her husband, Norman, are the parents of three grown children. Also she directs the Home Health Agency and is the founder of Take Heart retreats, a spiritual ministry devoted to helping adults who were sexually abused as children. **Sept. 22.**

Evelyn VandeVere is the director of Women's Ministries for the Southern Union Conference. She has had articles published in *Our Little Friend, These Times,* and *Adventist Review.* Her hobbies and special interests include putting together family albums of pictures and mementos, reading books, and writing articles. **Sept. 5.**

Nancy Cachero Vasquez is an administrative secretary in the North American Division (NAD) office at the General Conference of Seventh-day Adventists. She is the wife of a vice president of the NAD and mother of three young adult children. Nancy enjoys reading, writing, crafts, shopping, and baking. **May 2.**

Tammy Vice writes from Alabama, where she is a wife and mother of two very active daughters. She has learned many spiritual lessons from her girls and would like to share one experience with the readers. **May 5.**

Carolyn Voss, Ph.D., is presently teaching in an associate degree nursing program and writing a book on her experience as a young nurse in the hills of Kentucky. An active church member since the age of 15, she also enjoys walking, traveling, nature, quilting, and flower gardening. She and her husband, Calvin, have been married for 15 years. **May 14.**

Nancy Jean Vyhmeister is the editor of *Andrews University Seminary Studies.* She also teaches research methods at the Theological Seminary and writes regularly for church periodicals. Nancy enjoys homemaking, traveling, and her family, which includes two married children and two grandsons. **Oct. 24.**

Lilya Wagner is vice president for development and corporate membership at the National Association for Community Leadership based in Indianapolis. Previously, she worked in health care and taught at private high schools. She is the author of six books and numerous articles, as well as a musician. **May 1, June 9, Aug. 3.**

Cindy Walikonis is a registered dietitian and pastor's wife in Canada who works as a part-time nutrition consultant while raising her two daughters. She has been published in *Primary Treasure* and *Insight* and enjoys crafts, creative vegetarian cookery, the great outdoors, and Women's Ministries. Most recently, Cindy has been involved with a support group for women with eating disorders and presented a workshop at a women's retreat on this topic. **May 6.**

Celeste perrino Walker is a professional freelance writer living in Rutland, Vermont, with her husband, Rob, and 2-year-old son, Joshua. She has authored hundreds of articles and stories, a quarterly, and several books. In her spare time she enjoys hanging out on CompuServe SDA forum, trying to play the violin, painting in watercolor, backpacking, and cross-training. **Feb. 22.**

Ruth Wall is semiretired, working part-time at Portland Adventist Hospital in the Dietary Department. She collects cups and saucers from different countries. Ruth also enjoys bird-watching, cross-stitch, and especially her 7-year-old grandson. **Nov. 19.**

Gwendolyn Ward is married to the current pastor of the Oakwood College church in Huntsvillle, Alabama. She is a retired schoolteacher whose hobbies are playing the piano, cooking, and gardening. Gwendolyn serves on the music committee at the church and has been the personal secretary to her pastor husband for the past 21 years. **Mar. 13.**

Elizabeth Watson, mother of three, is an associate professor of social work and the director of a single-parent program at Andrews University. She serves as a local church elder, enjoys child evangelism, and tells and writes children's stories. A frequent contributor to the Message Junior section of *Message* magazine, she is one of the authors of a new members' book, *Stepping Stones*. **SEPT. 14.**

Dorothy Eaton Watts is a freelance writer, editor, speaker, and conference president's wife in Canada. She was a missionary in India for 16 years, founded an orphanage, taught elementary school, and has written 12 books, including a 1996 devotional for juniors, *Friends for Keeps* and *PALS, Prayer and Love Saves*, a series of 11 lessons for small group study. Her hobbies include birding, gardening, and hiking. **NOV. 2, DEC. 1.**

Lois May Watts is a retired teacher. She and her husband, Carl, were missionaries in Japan for 18 years. They now live in Berkeley Springs, West Virginia. **MAY 7.**

Shelly Curtis Weaver lives in Tulsa, Oklahoma, with her husband, who is finishing his surgical residency, and their three young children. She previously taught English at Loma Linda Academy, where she especially enjoyed teaching creative writing. Her other interests include reading, quilting, gardening, art, and photography. **OCT. 20.**

Veryl Dawn Were writes from South Australia, where she is a homemaker and mother of one son. She has written for various religious publications and is currently involved in the church's community service with her husband. Hobbies include gardening, bird-watching, cooking, and knitting. A nurse by profession, she served as a missionary to Kenya for eight years. **SEPT. 12.**

Penny Estes Wheeler is the editor of the new women's magazine, *Women of Spirit*. The mother of four adult children, she lives in Hagerstown, Maryland, with her husband. She has written eight books and numerous articles for religious publications. Penny enjoys storytelling, flower gardening, and spending time with her family. **OCT. 21.**

Connie White is a teacher, musician, and, as a senior software engineer, was a designer of databases for Norad. She is active in the church and enjoys reading, composing music, caring for animals, and most of all, working for the Lord to mend broken people. **MAY 8.**

Verna White was employed in the Book Department at the Review and Herald Publishing Association for 30 years, then worked in the Treasury Department of the General Conference of Seventh-day Adventists for 10 years. After retiring, she taught conversational English for International Teachers Service in Chongqing University in Chongqing, China. **NOV. 10.**

Carlene R. Will teaches seminars on home organization and personal devotions. She is the Women's Ministries leader for her local church and the mother of four boys. Carlene also works in her ophthalmologist husband's medical office. **NOV. 12.**

Mildred Williams is a semiretired physical therapist, the mother of two grown daughters, and grandmother of one. She teaches a Bible study class at her church. Her hobbies include writing, sewing, cooking, and gardening. She has been published in several religious magazines and has written a book. **APR. 8, MAY 10.**

Rhoda Wills is an English teacher at Andrews Academy near Lake Michigan. She is the mother of three grown children and enjoys gardening, reading, and music in her spare time. **SEPT. 6.**

Debby Gray Wilmot, a registered nurse, homemaker, pastor/chaplain's wife, and mother of two, lives in California. She enjoys acrylic painting, flowers, and landscaping. Debby also is an accomplished accompanist and composes music for voice, keyboard, and guitar. **NOV. 5.**

Kathy Jo Duterrow Yergen is currently working with her pastor-husband as administrative assistant. Other interests include watercolor, poetry, and the arts; collecting tea cups, dolls, and other memorabilia; and parenting her two energetic children, Amy, 10, and Georgemichael, 7. **OCT. 22.**

Sandy Zaugg teaches English as a second language at Walla Walla College. She is active in the family church at the college and is a member of the board of directors of the local Goodwill Industries. A widow with one married daughter, she likes to read, write, and travel—or even talk about travel! **MAR. 14.**

Inas Ziegler is a widow writing from Mt. Vernon, Washington. Her typewriter keeps her busy typing bulletins for two churches as well as poems and stories for special people. **MAR. 15.**

Now Is the Day

Behold, now is the accepted time; behold, now is the day of salvation. 2 Cor. 6:2, NKJV.

alking through the grocery store one day, I heard a child's
voice asking insistently, "But what does procrastination really mean?" Obviously trying to explain it in words the
child could understand, the adult answered, "Well, it means putting
off doing something until some future time."

We are not usually surprised to hear of people postponing tasks
that they do not enjoy, but sometimes we hear of individuals who
put off doing something that is in their own best interest.

The Bible talks about King Agrippa, for example, who was a victim of procrastination. You recall the story told in Acts 26:24-28.
When Paul urged the king to make Jesus first in his life, Agrippa
replied that he was almost persuaded. But almost is not *now*. Almost
is not good enough. Almost is procrastination.

Many people procrastinate because of faulty thought patterns.
Thoughts are not just psychological in nature—they have physiological aspects, too. Thinking involves electrical and chemical trig-
gers. Our thoughts create pathways in our brains—cut grooves, as it
were—that influence us to make specific choices or to act in a certain way. Because of that fact, we can, if we really want to, change
the way in which we think. We can create new brain pathways that,
in turn, will affect our choices and behaviors.

Many of us have thought patterns that weigh us down and keep
us from taking full advantage of all life's opportunities. These self-
defeating thought patterns can stop us from taking that course in
school that would move us a step closer to our educational goals. Or
they might prompt us to put off saying "I'm sorry" when it might
help solve a communication problem. Sometimes they even prevent
us from putting Christ first in our lives.

This brand-new year offers a fresh opportunity to spring free
from the trap of procrastination. It will allow us to throw off the
weights that hinder our life journey. In order to do that, we need to
change some of our thinking patterns. Proverbs 23:7 reminds us
that as we think in our hearts, so we are. So stop putting off that
something you should do now. Above all, make Jesus first in your
life throughout this new year—because now is the day of salvation.

ARLENE TAYLOR

I Love Life

This is the day which the Lord hath made; we will rejoice and be glad in it. Ps. 118:24.

One evening I read to my husband a story from a book by June Strong. She described a little boy named Thad who was at a picnic dinner on a hot August day. The little boy had just made new friends, and life was going well for him. His mother filled his dish with his favorite Mott's applesauce. He took his first spoonful of the chilled sauce, savored it lovingly, and said, "I just love life."

After my husband had fallen asleep, I picked up another book, *Journey Into the Whirlwind*, by Eugenia Ginzburg. She described her arrests and imprisonments during the Stalinist purges in Russia. Just days before her final arrest, the authorities summoned her to return to Moscow by train. As the train sped through the night, Eugenia walked to the last car garbed only in her light dressing gown. "I opened the carriage door slightly. The cold air rushed in my face. I looked down into the noisy blackness, my mind finally invaded by a torturing vision. One step . . . one instant . . . It would be so easy to commit suicide." And then she felt the strong grip of Markarova, a woman doctor also traveling on the train. The doctor led Eugenia back to her compartment and sat with her, saying only, "All this will be over one day, and you've got only one life."

And of that life, Eugenia spent 18 years of it in prisons and labor camps. She recounted what had happened to her during those terrible years. But the day did finally come when the authorities finally freed her and allowed her to return to a normal life—her one and only life.

Each day of our life is important. Yesterday is forever gone and only a memory, and tomorrow has not yet arrived. The precious moments of today are for you. You can make what you will of them. We can wake up joyful and say, like Thad, "I love life," and go forth doing our duties cheerfully. And we must cherish even the days of trials and tribulations like Eugenia went through. The sun will shine again.

DESSA WEISZ HARDIN

Practicing the Presence of God

For I the Lord thy God will hold thy right hand, saying unto thee, Fear not; I will help thee. Isa. 41:13.

I was in my teens when I first read about Brother Lawrence, a pious monk of the Middle Ages. Brother Lawrence lived in a monastery in which, in addition to spending time in prayer, study, and meditation, every monk had to work. He seldom had time for anything else except work. It was his task to clean the huge pots and pans used to prepare and cook the monks' meals.

In those days people cooked over an open fire. Having been on campouts, I've experienced the "joy" of washing smoke-blackened pots and pans, and I sympathized with the poor monk. But Brother Lawrence didn't need my sympathy. He was known throughout the monastery and the surrounding districts for his holy character and calm acceptance of his humble lot.

Fellow monks noticed that Brother Lawrence had little time for personal or corporate devotions, and they asked him how he maintained his Christian experience when he labored such long hours scouring pots alone. He replied that he wasn't alone. His life was a joyful round of devotion and adoration because Jesus was always with him in the scullery.

Brother Lawrence's story greatly impressed me. From my childhood my parents had taught me that angels guide and guard us. One of the first texts I ever memorized was "Lo, I am with you alway, even unto the end of the world" (Matt. 28:20). But I thought that promise was only for emergencies. Now Brother Lawrence's concept of God being a constant companion, friend, counselor, and guide appealed to my heart.

I've heard of others who "practice the presence of God." Some set an extra place at the table and pull up a chair at mealtimes for their Unseen Guest. Others reserve a place in the car for Him to accompany them on their journeys. In the years since then I too have tried to practice the presence of God. He has become such a part of my life that He laughs when I laugh and weeps when I do. He soothes me when I hurt, and He reproves when I make mistakes.

Sometimes, our relationship is spoiled. In the rush of daily life I forget that He is there, and I do or say things that I shouldn't. He does not leave me, but I know that my behavior saddens Him. When I cool down, I ask Him to forgive me. He does, and I resume my walk with Him, daily trying to become more like my heavenly Companion. His promise is certain: "Lo, I am with you alway."

GOLDIE DOWN

Dream . . . but "Continue to the Goal"

Brothers, I do not consider myself yet to have taken hold of it. But one thing I do: Forgetting what is behind and straining toward what is ahead, I press on toward the goal to win the prize for which God has called me heavenward in Christ Jesus. Phil. 3:13, 14, NIV.

I recently returned from a vacation in California and Mexico. What a marvelous experience it is to be near loved ones! Thus it shall be when we arrive in our celestial home on the sea of glass. Rejoicing will fill the heart when we see Jesus.

As soon as I arrived home, I wrote my son, thanking him for taking me sightseeing to various places and for the hours he had spent reminiscing with me about the past and planning for the future. It is good to remember our accomplishments, and from the bad experiences of life, learn lessons that will help us advance toward our goals.

Every Christian woman needs to have clear goals and objectives with an unshakable desire to reach them. Doubtless, as 1996 begins, you have made many plans. Some will be completed and others won't, but in spite of that, do not give up. Continue praying to achieve your goals, assisted by Christ.

It was fascinating to be in Mexico City with its music, foods, and rich artistry. I will never forget it. I dream of traveling to Acapulco and Cancún with my husband someday. However, I must not forget that my most important dream must be to meet Christ.

What is your dream for this year? Let us pray that the Lord will grant us His grace as the prize for our perseverance in having "continued to the goal" of our faith. That goal is to see Christ.

LIYDA E. DE JUSTINIANO

Loving Yourself

He answered, "Love the Lord your God with all your heart and with all your soul and with all your strength and with all your mind; and, love your neighbor as yourself." Luke 10:27, NIV.

*W*e have heard many sermons and discussions on the above text, and most of the time their emphasis rests on loving God and loving your neighbor, in that order. However, we usually miss the portion of the text that tells us to also love ourselves.

If we read this text closely, we will see that Jesus is actually saying that we cannot love our neighbor unless we first love ourselves. As Christians we sometimes find that the hardest thing to talk about and to practice is self-love. This fact causes the breakup of many marriages, families, and other relationships.

When I was a teen someone taught me a little acrostic based on the word JOY: Jesus first, others next, and yourself last. The concept behind it was supposed to bring us much happiness. However, it can be a source of great sorrow. If we continually put ourselves and our needs in last place, we can never be truly happy.

When we look at our text again, we will see that Jesus first says to love the Lord and then our neighbor as ourselves, thus implying that we already love ourselves. The order, therefore, is to love God and ourselves, and then this love will spread to others.

Those of us who are parents should instill the concept of self-love, which we must not confuse with selfishness, in our children, so that the next generation can be more loving toward each other.

Let us start today trying to love and accept ourselves, and we will experience how much easier it will be to love others.

KAREN BIRKETT

I Know the End of the Story

I know that my Redeemer lives, and that in the end he will stand upon the earth. Job 19:25, NIV.

*J*remember telling my 3-year-old niece the amazing story of Abraham's painful journey to sacrifice his beloved son, Isaac. As I described the father's breaking heart and the son's carefree enjoyment of the trip, her big brown eyes grew round with wonder. When I recalled the part where Abraham revealed the true purpose of that trek up Mount Moriah, she held her breath. Then I eagerly recounted the reprise. A ram would take Isaac's place. To my surprise I saw her lips quiver and two huge tears roll down those chubby cheeks. "Poor little ram," she sobbed.

I hadn't expected her to understand the story from that perspective. But the timing was perfect. Hastily I sought to explain the symbolism. Jesus was that little ram. He had to be killed so that we could live. Cuddling her on my lap, I waited for fresh tears. Instead, her eyes brightened, and she slid off my knee—happy.

Bewildered, I asked her, "Why didn't you cry when I told you that Jesus had died on the cross?"

"Because," she called from the other end of the room, "I know the end of that story. He's alive!"

Her 3-year-old mind had grasped a concept my 40-something brain often ignores. We've already won! No matter how treacherous the journey, how laborious the task of daily living, ultimate victory is ours!

She reminded me that I have nothing to fear for the present except as I forget that God has already deeded me a glorious future. Because of Him, we shall live. Because we know the end of the story.

GLENDA-MAE GREENE

JANUARY 7

Lost in the Jungle

For the Son of Man has come to save that which was lost. Matt. 18:11, NKJV.

*W*e left the city of Singapore for a few days of camping in the jungles of Malaysia. A logging road led to a jungle river where we set up camp. Our son, Kevin, said, "See that trail that goes into the jungle? Let's go exploring."

"Sounds great. We need some exercise," my husband answered. In a short time we came to a small stream. As soon as we crossed it, the trail started up a high ridge. We wondered if it would circle back to our camp. An hour later we reached the top. There it veered to the right. "Shall we turn back now or hope this will lead us toward camp?" he asked.

"Let's follow it for 15 minutes," I suggested. Soon we came to a fork. We stopped to pray for guidance.

"I'll take the left fork and come back soon," Kevin said. A few minutes later he returned, shaking his head. "It goes in the wrong direction."

The right fork seemed to lead toward camp. "This trail seems overgrown with vines and bushes. I fear it was made by animals, not man," my husband said. Shortly it disappeared into thick jungle.

Blazing a trail through virgin jungle, we found every shrub armed with thorns. Thick vines tripped us. The stream plummeted down a cliff. Slipping much of the way, we slid down the steep, muddy banks, grasping on to tree trunks. Fallen trees and thick vegetation impeded our progress. We were lost! Often we stopped to pray for guidance.

Crossing and recrossing the stream, we picked our way over slippery, wobbly rocks. Two more hours went by. Leeches clung to our ankles and legs, now oozing blood from their bites. Though scratched, dirty, tired, and hungry, we thanked God for the occasional refreshing drink from the stream.

By late afternoon we pushed ourselves faster, fearing we'd spend the night in the darkness. We prayed as we hiked. Our son had gone ahead. As we rounded a bend in the stream, we saw him waving from the far side. Again splashing across the stream, we found the trail we had left at noon.

What a relief after being lost for hours! As we had pushed blindly on, our constant contact with God gave us courage. He knew where we were, safe in His care. Now, standing together on the trail, we thanked Him for saving not only the lost jungle hikers, but a whole world lost in sin. — EILEEN E. LANTRY

JANUARY 8

I Know His Voice

My sheep listen to my voice; I know them, and they follow me. I give them eternal life, and they shall never perish; no one can snatch them out of my hand. John 10:27, 28, NIV.

*H*as your husband ever embarrassed you? My preacher husband has a nice, clear, distinct voice. Elderly people hard of hearing linger as they shake his hand after church and will tell him how well they heard the sermon. They beam as they say, "I could hear every word!"

One time when my husband was a guest speaker at a church, I heard a little boy in the pew behind me ask his mother, "Why is the preacher shouting?" I cringed, but my husband laughed when I later told him about the little fellow's comment.

Yes, my husband's voice is not only clear and distinct, it's loud—even when he's talking on the telephone. It is his habit to call in to the office every day when we are traveling or when we're away from home. His phoning often becomes quite involved, so he tries to stop and make his calls at a roadside rest area or at a shopping center so I can make use of my time by exercising or shopping while he's taking care of his business.

But that loud, clear, distinct voice that is a boon to elderly listeners will then often embarrass me to death! When he is talking on the phone, I can hear every word he says even when I'm some distance away.

I plead with him, "Don't talk so loud." He turns down the volume for a short time, but then, before long, I am again hearing him above the noise of the highway and/or the shoppers. Sometimes I could just die because I picture every passerby stopping and listening to his animated conversations. I don't want him to make a spectacle of himself. Sometimes he gets annoyed with my protests and tells me that no one else pays any attention to what he is saying.

And you know what? He's probably right. It's just that I know his voice so well that I can hear it above most noises, and I can certainly detect it above any conversation.

When we fall in love with Jesus Christ and really get to know Him, we will always hear and recognize His voice too. But you don't get to know Him just by accident. It takes a commitment every single day. First, request that He come into your heart. Then open your Bible and ask Him to send the Holy Spirit to show you what He wants you to learn about Him today. You will soon know His voice as well as I know my husband's! BARBARA HUFF

JANUARY 9

The Prisoner

To open the blind eyes, to bring out the prisoners from the prison,
and them that sit in darkness out of the prison house. Isa. 42:7.

*T*he 7-year-old boy left in my care at the church nursery was
autistic and blind. While the other children played all
around him he sat in the middle of the floor, rocking himself. He couldn't speak or communicate in any meaningful way with
other people. His silence and the nonstop chatter of the other children made a startling contrast. Usually the noise level of the nursery
frustrated me, but on that day I welcomed it.

I couldn't help thinking that he was in the worst kind of
prison—a prison of the mind. Blind children could still laugh and
talk. Deaf children could learn sign language. But this boy couldn't
do either. I wondered if a real boy hid behind those blind eyes,
locked up in that silent mind.

We usually think of prisons as rooms with barred windows and
locked doors, but there are many other kinds of prisons. In a sense,
we are all prisoners. Some of us are prisoners within our own bodies, locked behind a dependency on drugs, alcohol, or tobacco.
Others of us are emotional prisoners, trapped in unhealthy relationships, the excitement of gambling, or even self-pity. And still others
are locked behind prisons that are not of our own making—poverty,
disease, mental illness.

Once criminals have served their time, the authorities will allow
them to leave their cells and resume living outside the walls, but
there is no easy escape from our invisible prisons. All our human efforts to escape may prove futile. Only through Jesus can we loosen
our bonds and become free. By accepting His sacrifice, through
God's grace, no prison can hold us.   GINA LEE

JANUARY 10

Words of Restoration

And, behold, they brought to him a man sick of the palsy, lying
on a bed: and Jesus seeing their faith said unto the sick of the

palsy; Son, be of good cheer; thy sins be forgiven thee. Matt. 9:2.

*A*lthough the diseases of the mind are numerous, as any college psychology textbook will demonstrate, I still couldn't help wondering if most cases didn't share some common characteristic. I decided to ask Dr. Blackwell, a psychiatrist who saw hundreds of patients every year, what he had observed. Since he practiced in a large state hospital, he dealt with every known mental disorder.

"Could you make any generalization about all these people you see every day?" I asked. "Is there any one problem, behavior, or trait they all share?"

"Guilt," Dr. Blackwell replied.

With a shortage of hospital beds for mental disorders, is there no remedy for these diseased minds, these distraught souls in their anguish?

Those who recognize the guilt inherent in so much illness recommend one of two basic ways to relieve the stress. Counselors can recommend either changing the patient's concept of what sin is, *or* they can recommend changing the behavior that caused the guilt in the first place.

Christian and non-Christian psychiatrists alike wrestle with these alternatives. Although Christian counselors often suggest behavior changes, they too realize that disturbed minds can distort a perfectly moral behavior by thinking it is sin.

Psychiatrists need great wisdom to heal the troubled and restore them to mental wholeness. Physicians also must know how to minister to diseased minds. But who will help them know what to do? Doctors who make God their trust can have a powerful influence for good.

Never using a wrong approach, never recommending a worthless remedy, never trying a futile strategy—the genius of the Great Psychiatrist never once failed to heal.

When Jesus saw the suffering paralytic, He understood his condition perfectly. The story tells us that this wretched man had a sickness that was more than just physical. Jesus instantly comprehended that the sick man's illness stemmed from his burden of guilt. So Jesus immediately did what needed to be done: He forgave him his sins.

The Master Diagnostician, He still knows the prescription for mental and physical health—no guilt. And He still exercises His powers of restoration. To anyone who suffers today, He can still say the most comforting of all words: "Be of good cheer; thy sins be forgiven thee." WILMA MCCLARTY

A New Heart

I will give you a new heart and put a new spirit in you. Eze. 36:26, NIV.

A friend handed me a newspaper clipping entitled "New Cardiac Treatment Available." It immediately caught my interest.

For 29 years I had lived with episodes of fast heartbeat caused by abnormal pacemaker tissue in the heart. I had been born with the condition, and it had no cure. Doctors would say, "Take this medication to control it. It is something you will have to live with."

Now, a doctor qualified to do a newly developed procedure to correct the problem had moved to our area. I felt like the paralytic who, lame from birth with no hope of healing, had suddenly heard of a Saviour who could heal him.

I made an appointment with the doctor, and he set a date for the procedure. The doctor told me the risks of the operation and the possible complications, so it was with a certain amount of apprehension, along with expectation, that I entered the surgery. Family and friends were praying for me, and the women of our church set up a prayer chain. The doctor told us the average length of time for the procedure was three and one-half hours. Time dragged on without success. Eight hours passed, and the doctor continued to work to eradicate the offending tissue. He persevered and tried every instrument available. Family and friends poured out the matter before God. Then in the ninth hour it happened. God heard and answered.

I felt overwhelmed with gratitude—to the doctor who painstakingly worked those long, tedious hours to correct the heart condition and to the heavenly Physician who intervened. Now I want to tell the world "I am healed." I want to shout it from the mountaintops and tell everyone about my doctor who restored me.

Then I think of my spiritual heart. I am born with aberrant tissue woven into its very fibers. It is called *SIN*. Powerless to eradicate the tissue myself, I can medicate it, but never remove it. It is only when I submit myself to my heavenly Physician that He will work constantly, just as my earthly doctor did, to extract this tissue. As long as I continue to submit, He will not give up until the work is complete. In deep gratitude, I will proclaim from the mountaintops that He is the one who can remove my sin and give me a "new" heart.

JOAN MINCHIN NEALL

He Will Not Let You Fall

Though [she] stumble, [she] will not fall, for the Lord upholds [her] with his hand. Ps. 37:24, NIV.

*W*ebster defines a parasite as an organism that grows, feeds, and is sheltered on or in a different organism and contributes nothing to its host. In April of 1991, two months after my mother's death, I found myself in the hospital hosting such an organism. Tests had verified that I had picked up a parasite.

Upon release from the hospital, I was 15 pounds lighter and very weak. Not only did I feel bad, I also looked it. I couldn't seem to eat the correct combinations of food for some time, and I continued to lose weight.

A friend who lives nearby came to visit. When she saw me, being the honest person that she is, she said, "Your eyes are really sunken in!" I knew she was just voicing her concern, but her reaction only confirmed how near death I looked. Another friend paid a visit, and upon leaving, she leaned over, hugged me, and said, "We will pray for you." Now I was more upset because I could feel in her hug what she was feeling: I was very ill, and she was worried about my recovery. It seemed that I would never regain my strength, and I wondered if my life would be spared.

Early one morning, as I lay in bed feeling alone and frightened, I tuned my radio to a Christian station. As I listened, I started to cry. Even though I knew it is Satan—not God—who causes pain and sickness, I still questioned the Lord. What had I done, or not done, to deserve this? As I finished my prayer and lay there quietly, suddenly a song on the radio caught my attention. It was a repetitious song, and the words began to register: *He will not let you fall.* Over and over the phrase kept ringing in my ear until I opened my eyes and sat up in bed. "That's right!" I shouted. "He will not let you fall." God was speaking to me then. He was with me, and He would not let me fall.

From that point on I began to recover and have hope. I learned from this that we must trust God. We must have complete confidence in His ability to save. "Therefore, my brothers, be all the more eager to make your calling and election sure. For if you do these things, you will never fall" (2 Peter 1:10, NIV).   JESSIE BEARD

JANUARY 13

Lost Treasure

Or suppose a woman has ten silver coins and loses one. Does she not light a lamp, sweep the house and search carefully until she finds it? Luke 15:8, NIV.

*W*hen I arrived at the student union at college, I searched through, and thoroughly emptied, my school bag. To my chagrin, I noticed my key chain/purse was missing! It had my driver's license, student identification card, library cards, credit cards, and money.

Quickly I retraced all my steps that afternoon. The campus was so huge that it took a full hour. I questioned students, faculty, and others, but found no sign of my most prized possession.

Calling my husband at work, I asked him to pray that I would find the key chain/purse. When I hung up the phone, I retraced my steps again. Earlier that morning I had used the computer lab, and now I felt impressed to return there.

As soon as I entered the lab someone asked, "Excuse me, don't I know you? And aren't you missing something?" After carefully describing the contents of the wallet, I was greatly relieved to recover my valuables without going through the expense of replacing everything. However, I do remember that I had been tempted to give up my search because I doubted that there would be any students honest enough to turn in someone else's personal belongings.

I'm glad that my perseverance paid off. Based on this experience, I feel the woman in today's text and I have something in common. We both know what it's like to lose something very valuable and very special to us. On a more spiritual level, I can now better understand why Jesus never gives up until He finds His lost children.

CAROL ANN FRASER

JANUARY 14

Blake Island

I am the vine; you are the branches. If a man remains in me and I in him, he will bear much fruit; apart from me you can do nothing.

If anyone does not remain in me, he is like a branch that is thrown away and withers; such branches are picked, up thrown into the fire and burned. John 15:5, 6, NIV.

*F*inally the long-awaited Sunday "surprise" boat trip to Blake Island arrived—a trip arranged as a gift to our church school children for their cooperation in a well-performed Christmas program.

The trip was fantastic. The children and the adults learned more about boats and navigation methods. Once on the island, and their hunger satisfied, everyone engaged in different outdoor activities. Some played ball, while others decided to walk on the beach.

My husband and I opted for a walk on the beach with some newly made friends. As we admired the magnificent beauty around us, I had a strong desire to especially watch for something that God would teach and show me that day. As we proceeded along the rocky beach, I kept looking about me. Then I spotted it! A beautiful straight, symmetrical, healthy, 15- to 20-foot-tall evergreen tree growing upright from a very large, old, uprooted, weather-beaten, bark-free, and fallen tree. Stopping, I examined it. The tree rested on two other dry fallen trees—their roots exposed, torn, tide-washed clean, and barkless. I stood there and marveled—how could a tree so beautiful grow from an old dead and fallen one? There had to be a reason, so I began to examine the tree more closely. Sure enough, a small root, almost undetectable, penetrated securely into the ocean bank.

A passage of Scripture instantly came to mind: "I am the vine; you are the branches." Here before me was a single branch that had turned into a vibrant evergreen tree because it had the life-giving line well rooted in its source. As tears filled my eyes, God gently reminded me through it that just as that tree received life from its "vine," I too need to be well grounded in Him, the source of my strength and life. Thank You, Lord, for teaching me and loving me that day, and every day. — ERIKA OLFERT

Seasons

To every thing there is a season, and a time to every purpose under the heaven. Eccl. 3:1.

inter is my favorite time of the year. Everything that was once green now appears dead, but there's a certain beauty in seeing the barrenness of the land. Spending time outdoors is invigorating. It's a wonderful feeling to have my cheeks stung with the cold, turning them a rosy pink. The air seems cleaner, fresher. What I like best about winter is the snow. It brings cleansing to the earth, covering all that is dead. "Though your sins be as scarlet, they shall be as white as snow; though they be red like crimson, they shall be as wool" (Isa. 1:18).

Spring is the season for renewal. Streams of water once locked in the clutches of winter now flow freely. Birds who wintered elsewhere return, singing their carols of praise. On every hand we see trees, flowers, and new life in every species. It's a time to forget the past. A time for putting into action some of the plans made for cleaning, gardening, and dieting. It's name says it all—*spring* forth into new life. "Old things are passed away; behold, all things are become new" (2 Cor. 5:17).

Summer. Its heat urges on the growth of plant life. Those who do any gardening know that the conditions must be just right. We don't want it to be too dry, and we want the rainfall to be gentle and steady, ending when we've had enough. Rapid changes occur in all of nature in anticipation of the harvest. "But grow in grace, and in the knowledge of our Lord and Saviour Jesus Christ" (2 Peter 3:18).

Autumn. Time of ripe pumpkins and corn. Beautifully colored leaves and Indian summer days get us ready for the climax of the harvest. Those who have worked hard will reap the benefits of their labors. "But when the fruit is brought forth, immediately he putteth in the sickle, because the harvest is come" (Mark 4:29).

Perhaps we will have just one more winter in our lives, one more spring, one more summer, one more autumn. Let's all be ready for that final seasonal harvest when Jesus puts in His sickle.

MONICA STOCKER TAYLOR

JANUARY 16

The Friendship Quilt

See, I have engraved you on the palms of my hands. Isa. 49:16, NIV.

*H*aving never yearned to be a career girl, I was delighted when we moved to Lincoln, Nebraska, and my husband said I really didn't need to work if I didn't want to.

I thoroughly enjoyed my year and a half of "temporary retirement." With my children grown, I had time to enjoy unhurried devotions, try out new recipes, create unusual window treatments, travel with my husband, take creative writing classes, and indulge my passion for quilting. I joined the Lincoln Quilters' Guild and a small quilting group that met every week.

After growing up and living almost my entire life in communities composed mainly of other members of my own church, I found it a novel and mind-stretching experience to develop friendships with many people who had backgrounds different from my own.

I grew especially fond of the other nine girls in my quilt group as we sat around a table at the back of the quilt shop every Tuesday morning. Martha, Jean, Sara, Cathy, Donna—each one of them became a special and unique friend over the months.

When I learned we would be moving back to Maryland, I knew I would greatly miss my friends in Lincoln. We had had such good times together, and I wondered if we would lose track of each other when we were far apart. Would they eventually forget me?

Three months after I left Lincoln, the only other girl in the group who was a member of my church came to Maryland and stopped by my office. She opened her large handbag and pulled out a beautiful wall quilt made up of nine star blocks. In the center of each star was the name of one of my quilting friends in Lincoln, written in her own handwriting and embellished with flowers and other ornamentation. As I looked at those names I could see each of them again: Roxanne, Joan, Kathy, Jaynee . . . They had used my favorite colors in the quilt, and along with it they had sent pictures and notes. None of them had forgotten me! And every time I look at my friendship quilt, I remember them.

Jesus will never forget us either. Like my quilting friends who wrote their names on their quilt blocks so I would remember them, Jesus says that our names are written on the palms of His hands as an everlasting reminder of His love for us.   CARROL GRADY

"Before They Call, I Will Answer"

And it shall come to pass, that before they call, I will answer; and while they are yet speaking, I will hear. Isa. 65:24.

*I*t was a bitterly cold morning, and thick snow still covered the ground that day in 1982 when I started for the church school in northern Ontario, Canada. I was feeling sorry for myself because I had to take public transportation instead of being driven to work by my husband as usual. He was sick with a bad case of the flu, and the doctor ordered him to stay in bed to avoid contracting pneumonia. Since I didn't know how to drive then, I had to catch a bus.

With a big bag of schoolbooks and a handbag with my lunch, I wanted to be sure that I was on time at the bus stop. Since I was the teacher-principal of the newly opened church school, I didn't want to be late, because the kids would be cold waiting outside.

Halfway to school, I searched frantically in my bag and purse for my school keys. They were nowhere to be found. Then I remembered that I had left them on top of the dresser. How could I be so foolish as to forget that bunch of keys? Right there on the bus I bowed my head in prayer, asking God to let my husband see those keys on the dresser and bring them to me in spite of his sickness.

My mind was in turmoil as to what I should do when I got to the premises. As soon as I arrived, I breathed a most sincere and agonizing prayer. Again I searched in the bag of books, but still no keys. Although I wiggled the doorknob, it would not budge. A second time I searched my purse. With trembling fingers, I miraculously withdrew the set of keys.

Isn't that just like God? In spite of my foolishness, He knew my predicament, and He knew what to do. Many times we are so careless and forgetful that we reach the end of our ropes. Perhaps God allows these incidents in our lives so that we may focus our attention on Him, as Peter did on the Sea of Galilee. Our extremity becomes God's opportunity.   OFELIA PANGAN

JANUARY 18

Have You Hugged Your Teacher Today?

Let the little children come to me, and do not hinder them, for
the kingdom of God belongs to such as these. I tell you the truth,
anyone who will not receive the kingdom of God like a little
child will never enter it. Mark 10:14, 15, NIV.

*I*f heaven will be filled with little children, Lena Hutchins will
feel right at home. For Mrs. Hutchins is a special woman.
She's one of the faithful ones who shepherd children
through the cradle roll and kindergarten departments, generation
after generation. Long after her only child had grown up and married, Mrs. Hutchins still devoted many hours to cutting out felt
hearts and gluing messy glitter on star-studded crowns. And every
week for decades she guided little fingers as they made the rain
come down with a pitter-pitter-pat, and taught lisping lips to praise
the name of Jesus.

I clearly remember those mornings in the cradle roll/kinder-
garten room behind the pipe organ in our church in Troy, New York,
gluing bluebirds on my attendance card, telling her my latest secrets.
She always took the time to listen patiently and showed genuine interest in me and my childish trivia. Her interest in me didn't lessen
when I graduated into the next class and beyond. Later, when I came
home from school, her interest continued. When I brought my own
babies to her class, it was like they were her own grandchildren.

Others I met along the way made an impression on me, too—
the Bucks, the Grimeses, and the Taylors who opened their homes
to rowdy teenagers for Saturday night parties, harvest corn roasts,
moonlight skates on the pond, and weekend campouts. I had favorite teachers such as Marie Johnson, who recognized more potential in me than I ever could see in myself. Busy church pastors
encouraged instead of quenched my overexuberant spirit. At times
each of these hardworking saints must have felt lonely, bored, exhausted, and unappreciated. However, their reward is sure.

As Mrs. Hutchins sat at her kitchen table gluing stars on five-
pointed cardboard crowns, and when Mrs. Grimes vacuumed the
spilled popcorn from her living room carpet, or when Mr. Buck
filled bushel baskets with ears of corn for the Saturday night corn
roast, they might not have realized it, but they were gathering
stars—stars for their crowns. I can only imagine the number of stars
their crowns will have to hold. I do know, however, by the grace of

my Saviour, that one star in each of them will have my name on it. In the meantime, my heartfelt thank-you will have to suffice.

Do you have a Mrs. Hutchins, a Mr. Buck, or a Mrs. Johnson in your past? In your local church, are there teachers and leaders who, year after year, spend their own time and money, who open their homes on Saturday night, and more important, who open their hearts to the Saviour's "little ones" today? If your answer is yes, take the time today to tell them so. A phone call, a note, a batch of cookies, can be just the right medicine for sagging spirits.

Jesus said, "Do not hinder them." By supplying a safe place for the little ones to grow in Jesus, the Mrs. Hutchinses fulfill the Saviour's command. By providing a safe place for the children to learn, the Mrs. Johnsons of our classrooms fulfill the Lord's commission. And by offering a safe place for the youth to "test their wings," the Pastor Hartmans fill the Master's table—for of such is the kingdom of heaven. KAY D. RIZZO

Daughters of God

How great is the love the Father has lavished on us, that we should be called children of God! 1 John. 3:1, NIV.

The other afternoon I was scrubbing the tile counter in my kitchen vigorously, meanwhile musing on some areas in my life that just seemed impossible for me to keep right with God—the plague spots in my character. I say I was musing. Well, I was really *crying* on the inside, weeping at how I so often dishonored God by my thoughts and feelings—and sometimes actions. Scrubbing the dirt from the grout between the tiles aptly portrayed what I wanted done in my life.

"O God," I cried as I scrubbed away. "Will I ever learn? Whatever do You think of me?"

I don't believe that I really expected God to answer, for I was astonished when my spiritual ears caught His response. "Carrol," He said, "you are My beloved daughter, in whom I am well pleased."

I was amazed! In spite of my struggles—and numerous failings—God still called me His beloved daughter, and He was pleased with me. How could that be? He surely couldn't have been pleased with my failures! I tried to think what in the world He could possibly be pleased with about me. Finally I decided that it was my turning to Him for help, my dependence upon Him, my willingness to try again. I remembered that "he knows how we are formed, he remembers that we are dust" (Ps. 103:14, NIV).

It is only within the framework of our acceptance as God's dearly beloved sons and daughters, in whom He is well pleased, that we are free to minister to others: as intercessors, teachers, comforters. When we fully comprehend this basic truth—that we are daughters of God, blood sisters of Jesus Christ, with all the privileges and duties this entails—then we are free to exercise authority over Satan and the strident gods of this world, and to work in joyful anticipation of the final restoration.   CARROL JOHNSON SHEWMAKE

JANUARY 20

A Matter of Perspective

One thing I do know. I was blind but now I see! John 9:25, NIV.

That morning, as most mornings, my two preschool daughters and I waved goodbye to my husband as he headed for work. As we stood in the driveway, I noticed a strange blue cloud of smoke coming from somewhere under his 18-year-old car.

That little blue cloud seemed to hover over me for the remainder of the day, reminding me of all our financial needs. The girls needed new shoes and winter pajamas, the house needed paint, and now, it looked as though the car needed work. It should be expected—after all, the car was 18 years old! Throughout the day I reminded the Lord of our problems and asked Him to provide for them.

That evening, as I flipped through the channels on the television, I found myself drawn to a documentary about famine. The camera zoomed in on a mother and child. The sight of the child brought tears to my eyes. I guessed he was a boy. His belly was distended and the veins on his head stuck out. Each rib was clearly visible, and his eyes were fixed in a hollow stare. I felt sick.

But more terrible than the sight of the child was what I saw in the eyes of his mother. Suddenly I stood in her place. The realization that my precious child was dying and I could not help him, nor could I even alleviate his pain, hit me full force. It made me nauseous. I wanted to scream.

After I turned the TV off, the image of that mother's eyes remained with me. I could not escape it. I began to wonder about this woman I hardly knew. How old was she? Had she ever known happiness? What about the father of her child? Had they ever been in love? Had she ever heard her baby laugh? Was there ever a time she had not known hunger?

I tiptoed down the hall to the room where my baby slept. As I watched her even breathing, I ran my finger over her fat cheeks. Realizing that she was warm and comfortable, I began to cry. The needs of the day suddenly seemed small and insignificant.

My prayers that evening overflowed with thankfulness for the blessings in my life. I confessed that I had been blind to them, that my selfish heart had kept me from seeing that I was rich. I also prayed for a fellow mother I had never met, and yet would never be able to forget. A mother whose eyes I would never stop seeing.

RETTA MICHAELIS

JANUARY 21

Behind the Curtain

Let your light so shine before men, that they may see your good works, and glorify your Father which is in heaven. Matt. 5:16.

*M*y husband had been an invalid for nine years and totally dependent on me for everything. In 1990, when this incident occurred, he had been a Christian only a short time. In spite of this, he was a strong prayer partner and a real spiritual rock.

It was about this time that I fractured my back. I had to have him admitted to a nursing home until I was well enough to care for him again. As soon as I was able, I spent as much time with him as possible. Each evening around 6:30 I would draw the curtain for privacy so we could read the Bible and have prayer together before I left. The room had two other patients, and we didn't want to disturb them. After about the first week the wife of one of the patients came to me.

"Excuse me," she apologized. "I didn't mean to eavesdrop, but I've been interested in your evening ritual. It's so sweet. Would you mind including me some evening?" I had no idea anyone was listening, and I eagerly agreed to include them the very next night.

It wasn't long until our new friend was going to church with me. A short time later she enrolled in a Bible study course and soon after was baptized. My husband and I rejoiced that the seeds we had unknowingly sown behind that curtain were bearing fruit.

Since then I have thought, *How many times do we pull the curtain around our lives and shut out those who may be hungry for the bread of life?* Let's not exclude others on the presumption that they may not be interested. We may hold the key that will unlock the door to their eternal life. MARGARET E. TAYLOR

JANUARY 22

The Carpenter

The Lord is not slow about his promise as some count slowness, but is forbearing toward you, not wishing that any should perish, but that all should reach repentance. 2 Peter 3:9, RSV.

*M*y father was a laborer, a mill worker with rough calloused hands and fingers that wouldn't straighten out. He used to say he spent so much time carrying lumber that he had almost forgotten how to let go. I remember watching spellbound as those same hands turned rough lumber into beautiful and useful objects. Dad was a craftsman. None of the furniture he made was ornate, but it all had a quiet elegance that would have looked good anywhere. While visiting my brother one day, I again examined a coffee table and two end tables Dad had made.

I still remember the day Dad brought the lumber home. The wood had been cut wrong and was going to be turned into sawdust. He asked his foreman if he could have it. Dad was always salvaging lumber. Now he attacked this pile of wood with a zeal I had never seen before. My older brother, Bobby, was getting out of the Navy in two months and would be bringing back his bride. Dad wanted to have their wedding present done before they arrived home.

The tables swiftly took shape. Even at a time when I would have considered them perfect, Dad continued to sand the wood. It shocked me when he took one of the end tables apart and remade it. When I asked why, he pointed out a small flaw that would have marred the finished piece of furniture.

Once he had the tables shaped to his satisfaction, he spent hours rubbing mahogany stain into the wood, making sure every spot was the right color. Next he varnished them and cut glass exactly the right shape to cover the top of each one.

The iridescent mahogany stain and glasslike smoothness of the tables invited touch. The structure of the tables was so timeless and sturdy that I realized they would one day be priceless heirlooms. Several days later, when my sister-in-law turned to Dad with tears in her eyes and said that no one had ever made her anything so beautiful, he was finally satisfied.

I miss Dad's quiet, homey wisdom. I am thankful for the patient love I saw in everything he did. Through him I saw a heavenly Father willing to prepare His children for eternity. As Dad saved the lumber from destruction and turned it into an object showing his love, God labors over each one of us. He is shaping, smoothing, and staining our lives with His love so that none of us need perish. DOTTI TREMONT

JANUARY 23

Childlike Faith

Therefore I tell you, whatever you ask for in prayer, believe that you have received it, and it will be yours. Mark 11:24, NIV.

My daughter, Carlene, is a very busy mother of four boys. In order to juggle the many hats she wears as wife, mother, homemaker, church worker, and part-time office manager of her husband's medical practice, she finds it necessary to employ a nanny to assist her with caring for the children. All her nannies must be creative in involving the boys in arts, crafts, and educational activities. Even though it is not an easy task to find a suitable individual, Casey was one such find.

This young woman was attempting to pull her life together after having a baby out of wedlock. Although Carlene said nothing to her directly about spiritual matters, Casey began to ask questions about this God who was a part of everyday life in Carlene's household.

One day Casey was caring only for 4-year-old Nicholas, the youngest member of the tribe. She decided to take him to the science center in downtown Seattle. While they were traveling along the freeway, her own 18-month-old child began to fuss and cry. Casey stopped the car along the freeway to settle him down. When she attempted to continue on her way, the car wouldn't start. Repeated tries produced little more than frustration. The engine turned over, groaned, and died. With two children on a busy freeway in a stalled car, Casey naturally became upset. She laid her head down on the steering wheel and muttered, "What a mess."

From the back seat, Nicholas asked, "Why don't you pray about it?"

41

Prayer was not yet a regular part of Casey's life. "Why don't *you* pray?" she countered.

Nicholas did what he was used to doing even at 4 years of age. He folded his hands, bowed his head, and prayed simply, "Jesus, please get us out of this mess. Amen."

Casey turned the keys again. The car started immediately!

Are you struggling with a problem? Then pray! You don't need to beat your head on the steering wheel or moan over your dilemma. Tell Jesus about it. He's always there to listen. Whatever personal "mess" you are dealing with today, do as Nicholas did. Pray a simple prayer: "Jesus, please get me out of this mess." Let's exercise that simple, childlike faith beginning now.   NANCY VAN PELT

JANUARY 24

Dangerous Items in Your Baggage

Wherefore lay apart all filthiness and superfluity of naughtiness, and receive with meekness the engrafted word, which is able to save your souls. James 1:21.

*A*ll of you need to get off this plane. Please take all your hand luggage and get off immediately." The order sounded urgent, and we passengers shuddered with concern.

"What's happened? What's the problem?" people whispered.

We were traveling from Sri Lanka to Karachi, and it should have been only a stopover in Bombay. Several passengers had already disembarked, and some joined us. But what had happened to create such a commotion?

Officer after officer came in to check the plane. Counting the number of passengers, they looked this way and that. They checked one list and another. Yet they continued to wear the same puzzled expressions. At last they announced, "Everyone please get off the plane with your hand luggage!"

Stepping over to one of the officers standing nearby, I inquired what the real problem was. He nervously replied, "Someone is missing, but his luggage is still here with us. This passenger may have purposely done this. He may have dangerous items in his baggage, and we need to find out! We cannot take a chance." Someone nearby shrieked about the possibility of explosives.

The ground crew removed all the luggage from the plane, and the airport officials requested each passenger to identify his or her baggage. Each item was sorted out as an officer investigated the contents with a grave sense of responsibility. At last everyone seemed satisfied. The extra baggage was identified and removed to safe quarters. Finally we boarded the plane again. How wonderful it was to feel safe!

We are all on a trip, too—a very important one! Each of us is headed for heaven. Are we carrying dangerous baggage with us? Baggage that can ruin our Christian experience, baggage that can explode and mar our travel to the land the Lord is preparing for us? Have we identified it? Maybe you need to look through your own baggage today and find them: jealousy, envy, hatred, faultfinding, distrust in God, dishonesty, etc. Then dispose of whatever it is! Our journey is too important to be ruined by any explosives in our baggage. May the Lord help each one of us to sort out these dangerous items and rid ourselves of them.   INDRANI J. ARIYARATNAM

JANUARY 25

Fingernails

May the words of my mouth and the meditation of my heart be pleasing in your sight, O Lord, my Rock and my Redeemer. Ps. 19:14, NIV.

As I stepped through our big metal gate to climb into the Suburban, I found strangers already in the car. "We have company," Ed, my missionary husband, commented.

"*Buenas tardes. ¿Cómo están?*" I greeted the three in their own language. They responded in the same and then fell silent. Living and working in the area of the church's national headquarters and university exposed me to many more people than my mind could keep track of. Because I was one of very few foreigners working at the mission, everyone knew who I was. Experience has taught me that they assumed I also knew them. Any exchange of what they deemed unnecessary introductions would cause them discomfort, so that day I did not pursue the topic.

Lima's summer air steamed around us so we kept the windows open as we drove, but wind and street noise discouraged conversation between front and back seats. Seeing that there would be no spontaneous chatter from that quarter, I took up a rambling, mostly one-sided, English conversation with Ed.

We discussed our new servant, the children's schooling, difficulties in our telephone system, and much more. Then, as we approached town 30 minutes later, Ed spoke over his shoulder. "And where shall we drop you off, LeRoy?" he asked.

I felt instant pain in my palms, fingernails digging in—my own. *English!* He'd spoken English! Someone in the back understood English, and I hadn't known.

What had I said? What had we talked about the past half hour? I raced through a review of our conversation. Had I criticized anyone? Said anything that sounded intolerant? Anything private to family life? Anything I'd rather not have rushing through the church grapevine? Finally I felt satisfied that our conversation had not been offensive. A verse came to mind, though: "Now all has been heard. . . . God will bring every deed into judgment, including every hidden thing, whether it is good or evil" (Eccl. 12:13, 14, NIV).

"O Father," I prayed, "I don't want to feel fingernails digging into my palms on the Second Coming day! 'Set a guard over my mouth, O Lord; keep watch over the door of my lips' [Ps. 141:3, NIV]."

PAMELA BAUMGARTNER

JANUARY 26

In His Hands . . . Always

They shall bear thee up in their hands, lest thou dash thy foot against a stone. Ps. 91:12.

My memory travels back 20 years. It was then, and still is now, my constant prayer that God will not forsake my children.

My daughter was a very active 3-year-old who would not simmer down unless asleep. Her eyes always sparkled with cleverness and alertness. It necessitated that I answer all her never-ending questions and watch her every minute of the day, lest she hurt herself somehow. Yet, despite all my efforts, following a moment of absentmindedness, I saw her standing on a small table in front of a window. She was so happy that she had been able to climb up by herself and stand there alone. As she was trying to attract my attention, one of the table legs slipped, and it tipped over, causing my daughter to fall. She hit her head against the window, shattering the glass into lethal fragments, and came to rest against the window among the broken shards.

Normally she should have fallen through the window to the

ground below, and normally she should have been badly lacerated from the broken glass surrounding her. But when God intervenes, surprising things happen. And that is exactly what happened. Not a single scratch on her head, her face, or anywhere! My search for injuries turned up nothing. Spontaneously I quoted many Bible verses, thanking God for His presence, and I felt assured that His angels would indeed "bear her up in their hands."

My experience with Jesus constantly increases because of my trust in His promises. He is with us, though we do not see Him. We may go astray a little, but He will definitely carry and help us as we walk life's pathway. Just ask me about my daughter.   DALAL AZIZ

JANUARY 27

Our Father's Care

Take no thought for your life, what ye shall eat, or what ye shall drink. . . . Your heavenly Father knoweth that ye have need of all these things. Matt. 6:25-32.

*D*uring the dry season in 1983 the authorities declared Ghana a disaster area. Brush fires had swept throughout the country, destroying farms, personal property, and forest. International organizations rushed food and medicine into the country in order to save lives.

One week we had little food at home. When we got to church, we were surprised to see a singing group from our former mission station. They had come to Accra to do some recording of their songs. Telling us that they would come to our house to see us, they actually followed us to our home, bringing their lunches.

When we had finished eating, they asked if they could stay overnight. Even though we did not have extra rooms, my primary concern was how to feed all the young people. "Well, the Lord will provide," I assured myself, hoping they would leave the next day. However, owing to problems they were having with the studio, they extended their visit by three more days.

On Monday night our prayer was an appeal to the Lord to provide food. We did not even have five small loaves for Him to multiply, yet we were certain in our hearts that His promise that we should not worry about what we would eat tomorrow because He will care for us would be fulfilled.

My husband drove to the nearby village in search of something to buy. He returned empty-handed. Around lunchtime my husband came home from work. Normally our meal would have been ready at this time, but we were not sure we could provide even a sandwich for these people. We went to our room and again petitioned our Lord. After our short prayer we saw a minivan driving into our yard and heard the voice of one of our fellow pastors from another district. Speechless, my husband and I looked at each other. Our immediate reaction was "Oh, no!" Rushing to the door to meet the man, I fought the temptation to let him know about our food situation right at the door, since culturally I would be committing an unpardonable sin.

After shaking hands with me, he went back to the van and talked to the driver. Then I saw the driver unloading large sacks of food. When the pastor returned to the house, he informed us that when his church members heard about the food shortage in Accra, they sent him with the food for us. They could not eat while another pastor had no food. We were dumbfounded!

We all knelt to thank God and pray for these wonderful church members. Yes, we serve a God who still works miracles on behalf of His people. His promises are sure. ELIZABETH BEDIAKO

JANUARY 28

For You I Am Praying

We give thanks to God and the Father of our Lord Jesus Christ, praying always for you. Col. 1:3.

The line was moving slowly, but the friendly chatter of those around me made the wait short. It is always a thrilling experience to gather with hundreds of Christian women at a retreat. At last I reached the head of the registration line and gave my name to the receptionist. As I did, the woman standing behind me nearly shouted, "Praise the Lord! Who would have thought?" Then, grasping my arms, she looked at me, a smile lighting her face. "Is that really your name?" I assured her it was. But who was this excited, unfamiliar woman? I asked her where we had met.

"Last year at a women's retreat I pulled your name from the prayer basket," she replied. Still standing in line, we hugged and thanked God for each other. She promised she would continue to pray for me, and I said I'd do the same for her.

The retreat was Spirit-filled and informative, but somehow meeting and greeting my new friend was the high point of the weekend. What a blessing to know that someone—not even a friend, but a stranger—was praying for me. Not once, but *twice* a day! A stranger was praying for my safety on the streets of New York, praying that I would have wisdom as I did my job, praying for my success, and above all, praying for my spiritual growth. What a joyous yet sobering thought!

Now I understand how the Colossians must have felt when they read Paul's words: "praying always for you." The power of intercessory prayer cannot be measured. It blesses the one praying and brings joy to the one being prayed for. Each day prayers are answered and lives saved because someone, somewhere, is interceding on another's behalf. What a simple but important responsibility we have!

The busy schedule at the retreat did not permit me to meet my new friend again, but each day I pray for her and am more confident and encouraged knowing that someone hundreds of miles away is praying for me.

Today someone somewhere is praying for you. Why not do the same for someone else?　　　　　　　　　　　　MAUREEN BURKE

JANUARY 29

Abiding and Trusting

But when Jesus heard it, he answered him, saying, Fear not: believe only, and she shall be made whole. Luke 8:50.

*O*ur youngest lay on a white hospital bed, both legs suspended from ropes in traction. A pair of brown eyes looked up imploringly and filled with tears every day when it came time for us to leave. At home it was almost impossible for me to do everyday tasks. My mind was continually reverting back to that little cubicle in the hospital. Then my memory played back a promise that my mother had sung long ago:

"Under His wings I am safely abiding,
　Though the night deepens and tempests are wild,
　Still I can trust Him; I know He will keep me;
　He has redeemed me, and I am His child."

A whisper of hope that the angels would keep my little one in the hospital "under His wings" and that God would bring healing to him escaped my lips. God answered that whisper.

After what seemed an endless age the little legs came down and were put in a cast. Eventually that was removed, and he became the fastest runner in the neighborhood.

Then came the letters from my missionary sister, spelling out the news of her small daughter. Unless the physicians performed a very delicate operation, the child would die. Facilities in India were far from the best. In the letters that flew back and forth the suggestion arose that perhaps Jeanne should be flown home and taken care of in the hospital here. Back over the miles came the message: "The same God who watches over you in America watches over us in India. We will stay!"

"Under His wings I am safely abiding." We had grown up and left home, but the words of that song remained etched indelibly in our memories. "Still I can trust Him; I know He will keep me." Though separated by miles, the song of faith that Mother sang anchored our hope in Jesus' power to heal.

When furlough time came, a team of experts examined Jeanne and checked her with the latest medical equipment. They reviewed her medical records from India with a fine-toothed comb, but no sign of her condition remained, nor were there any abnormalities. The doctors said, "We can't believe it." We said, "Our God is still the same today. He will not fail us, come what may."

ELLIE LUKENS CALKINS

JANUARY 30

The Main Ingredient

They profess that they know God; but in works they deny him.
Titus 1:16.

I'd never before noticed the similarity between pasta salad and a Christian life.

I keep pasta spirals stocked in the pantry. Pasta salads make a great one-dish meal. One day I set out to make my famous concoction. Having purchased all the vegetables, I sliced broccoli and cauliflower florets, carrots, zucchini, olives, and celery. I chopped sweet onions and wedged a ripe tomato. Next I stirred the vegetables, admiring the color, and added a little Italian dressing. Then I shook the salad bowl to distribute the dressing and set it in the refrigerator to marinate.

My husband worked late that evening. Dishing up a plate of salad, I settled into a comfortable chair to enjoy one of my favorite meals. But something just didn't seem right. It was edible, but it

48

seemed as if *something* were missing. Mentally, I listed the vegetables. Sometimes I added others, but the main ones I always used were there. It looked beautiful with all the color. I puzzled over what was wrong through the entire meal.

The next day a friend described her family's unpredictable schedule and bemoaned the difficulty of preparing meals for them. I launched into praise over the prepare-ahead, ready-when-you-are meals my husband and I enjoyed.

"What is it?" she inquired.

"Pasta salad," I answered. Suddenly the light dawned. "Pasta," I blurted. "I left it out." My friend's eyes knitted into question marks. "I made pasta salad yesterday," I explained, "and it just wasn't right. I couldn't figure out what was wrong until just now when I said the name." Shaking my head in disbelief, I said, "I left the *pasta* out of the pasta salad."

We laughed. But the next morning when life's commitments and surprises threatened to steal my quiet time with Christ, I thought of pasta salad without pasta. *Whether it's pasta salad or a Christian life,* I mused, *the name includes the main ingredient.* I thought of other mornings when I'd rushed into the day on my own and considered the times I'd failed my Saviour because I'd forgotten Him, or because I'd not asked Him to lead me, or taken time to listen to Him. I knew the emptiness of feeling "something missing" in life.

An unopened Bible is like uncooked pasta in the pantry. If you don't use either one, it's neither pasta salad nor a Christian life. You'll still be missing the main ingredient.   HELEN HEAVIRLAND

JANUARY 31

He Knows My Name

But now, this is what the Lord says . . . : "Fear not, for I have redeemed you; I have summoned you by name; you are mine. When you pass through the waters, I will be with you; and when you pass through the rivers, they will not sweep over you. When you walk through the fire, you will not be burned; the flames will not set you ablaze. For I am the Lord, your God, the Holy One of Israel, your Savior." Isa. 43:1-3, NIV.

The night was hot, and it seemed like the sirens blared on and on, closer and closer. Finally I got up to look out the hotel window down over Alexander Platz. And then I could see the Berlin medical emergency people working on someone in the middle of the broad avenue. With my binoculars I could make out someone holding an intravenous bottle. Another ambulance arrived, and several people rushed over with a stretcher.

Soon people were packing up equipment and moving away, leaving the shrouded form on the stretcher in the street. Cars passed by slowly, and the few onlookers faded away into the now still darkness.

I felt strangely unemotional and uninvolved. It was no one I knew, here in this large but strange city. My loved ones were all safely in the room with me or at home in another country.

But I remembered the rush of adrenaline and panic I have felt when a call has come in the middle of the night, or the cold fear when someone was too late getting home. Or the churning stomach and dread when an accident held up traffic and I knew my husband had gone on ahead of me a short time before.

What made the difference? It was knowing, or even thinking I knew, the people involved. It was that personal, meaningful relationship. More even than just knowing the name.

God sent His only Son to this world that He may identify with us personally—we were not to be someone unknown somewhere off on an alien planet. He died for us individually, by name, because He had created and known us individually since before we were born. And He knows my name—even how many hairs are on my head— He knows me even better than I can know myself.

God knows my wants, desires, and emotions. He remembers what we talked about in our last conversation even after I have gone off to sleep or forgotten. He cares about what happens to me and those I love. Jesus has died for me. I know He cannot watch unemotionally from the vast unknown when something happens to me. We have a relationship. God knows my name.   ARDIS STENBAKKEN

FEBRUARY 1

Angel in His Heart

See that you do not look down on one of these little ones. For I tell you that their angels in heaven always see the face of my Father in heaven. Matt. 18:10, NIV.

I always intended to make sure that I looked nice and attractive for my family, but with three small children and a hectic ministry schedule, it was hard to find the time to brush my hair, let alone curl it or do anything else. If I did decide to curl it, I'd usually find myself sitting on the floor of the bedroom playing with a toddler, or reading a story at the same time. A couple pregnancies still hadn't completely shed themselves from my body, and the practicalities of nursing babies meant I'd usually be wearing sweatshirts and pants, not my favorite Laura Ashley dresses.

So I usually felt saggy and baggy, frumpy and drab, before the day had barely begun. And by the evening I was also adorned with gluey fingerprints, globs of dried-on cereal, and grass stains from a frolic in the garden. Oh yes, the baby had also spit up in my hair, and every now and then the fragrance of a cheese factory wafted past my face, reminding me to change a diaper. Bathing the children, I dried them, one at a time, as they sat on my lap. The inevitable happened, and while I caught most of the puddle in the towel, I could feel a warm wet area spreading down the leg of my pants. *Oh well*, I thought, *I'll change and have a shower once they're all in bed.*

Rebathing the wet child, I powdered and dressed them all for bed. We had a story and a prayer, and I was gratefully tucking them in for the night when a happy, cozy, drowsy little boy turned to me, and said, "Oh Mommy, you look just like an angel!" Unfortunately, I didn't feel like an angel, and I knew that I looked more like the prodigal son in the pigsty than anything celestial. But I smiled and stored those words away in a special corner of my heart.

One day, I hope and pray, Nathan will see a real angel in perfect beauty and loveliness. Here, he knows he has a guardian angel that is with him every minute of the day and night. It must be wonderful to look like an angel—so perfect, so beautiful, so spotless—but it's not looks that count when you are an angel. The important thing is being there for the one you care for, providing, protecting, loving.

I'm no angel, but I have also been with Nathan every minute of the day, meeting his needs, protecting him, and loving him in everything he's done, and it shows. It shows in my hair, it shows on my clothes, it shows in the tired lines and smiles on my face. But most of all, I hope it shows in his heart. KAREN HOLFORD

FEBRUARY 2

Talking With the Father

Be joyful always; pray continually; give thanks in all circumstances, for this is God's will for you in Christ Jesus. 1 Thess. 5:16, NIV.

*T*wo tasks that many women usually hate I actually enjoy. I love to hang wet clothes on the clothesline, and I love to iron clothes when they are dry. The reason I delight in these tasks is they give me an opportunity to talk to God.

In the Bible God tells us that He likes us to talk with Him as much as possible. His request challenges us to find creative ways of doing just that. As I hang out the laundry, each garment reminds me either to talk with God or thank Him for something special in my life. For example, when pinning Jonathan's hiking trousers to the line, I thank God for the fun weekend we spent in the Yorkshire Dales. The girls' school clothes urge me to ask God to protect them while they are at school and to help them in their studies. Socks beckon me to ask God to guide our feet wherever we go and whatever we do. Washcloths invite me to ask God to cleanse and wash away the dirt in me. Church clothes encourage me to thank God for His presence in our lives and to direct us to share Him in a practical way with others.

Ironing the clothes also encourages me to talk to God. As I iron my dress, I implore the Lord to erase out the creases in my life. Or as I move the iron over my husband's work shirt, I ask God to make his ministry as smooth as possible. Bed sheets or pillowcases that a visitor may have used beckon me to pray for their individual needs.

It is always good to combine prayer and praise together. So often we are experts at asking God for something but novices when it comes to thanking Him.

Keeping an eye on the clock also encourages times of conversation with God. Sometimes I carry a small key ring with names of people to pray for. When I can, each hour I present a name to God with a Bible verse to support my plea. I passionately believe in intercessory prayer and marvel at the way God frees people to make a decision for Him.

Family worships, too, are a great time to pray to God in a different way. At present, we pray by using a letter of the alphabet. One morning the girls thanked God for everything they could using the letter "E." Jonathan and I wearily asked God for energy.

God is rich in His creativity, and I believe He has sprinkled fragments of that upon each of us. Why don't you use some of that to enhance your friendship with Him?   MARY BARRETT

52

Possibility Thinking

Jesus looked at them and said, "With man this is impossible, but not with God; all things are possible with God." Mark 10:27, NIV.

I want to be a possibility thinker. Some people always expect the best from a situation. Even when faced with problems, they feel confident that there's a ready solution. Me? I always tend toward logic. Assessing the situation, I come up with the logical conclusion. If the odds are against me, I hesitate. Why move forward and expend energy or emotions when the probability of success is only marginal?

Good thing my husband is a possibility thinker. Over time it should rub off—either that or I'll keep eating my words. That was the scenario one evening when my husband wanted to check out a certain tool at a hardware store. I looked at my watch and logically concluded that our chances of getting across town through heavy traffic before they closed were slim to none. He thought we could just slide in.

On the way over, you would expect me to be the model wife—sweet and encouraging. But no, I told him the whole time, "We're not going to make it" and "Look at all the time we're wasting." We made it in time, and I apologized for my negative spirit.

Recently, while reading the story of the Resurrection, I felt prompted to be a possibility thinker. The women who came early Sunday morning to anoint Jesus' body had one immediate question on their minds: "Who will roll the stone away from the entrance of the tomb?" (Mark 16:3, NIV). A major obstacle. The disciples were hiding. The guards were under orders not to disturb anything. And the Pharisees obviously wouldn't lend a hand. But the women were possibility thinkers. Why else would they buy spices, rise early, and head for the tomb? With a government seal on the stone, it was not logical. But through deep love and hopeful expectation these women moved forward, and the obstacle vanished.

Jochebed was another possibility thinker. Chasing depression away, she did the impossible and muffled her baby's cries for three months. Using even greater imagination, she made a floating cradle for Moses. How long did she think she could hide him in the Nile reeds? What about crocodiles or soldiers? The probability of him surviving to adulthood was also slim to none. Yet faith and a mother's love spurred her to dream the impossible. Who would ever have imagined that the princess would find her baby and then even pay her to take care of him? Totally illogical, but God delights in doing the impossible.

I still use logic, but pray that it's mixed generously with faith and possibility thinking.   HEIDE FORD

I'm Ter-rific!

This is the day that the Lord has made; let us rejoice and be glad in it. Ps. 118:24, NIV.

To say that he was enthusiastic would be a gross understatement. Tom made a habit of replying to "How are you?" with a resounding "I'm ter-rific!" His positive attitude affected our whole office. Even on days when I didn't feel like going to work, after hearing Tom's "I'm ter-rific!" I felt better. I'm not sure it made me feel "ter-rific," but I'm not sure Tom always felt that way, either.

A positive attitude has a profound effect on how we feel, both physically and emotionally. Likewise, our attitude, be it positive or negative, also affects those about us. Tom handled everything in the office with a positive attitude. He taught us by example that we had "challenges"—not "problems." The word *challenge* is positive, upbeat, and motivating, while *problem* is negative and defeating.

I had an aunt who faced the challenge of debilitating physical pain in her final illness. Many who knew her had no idea how she suffered, because she never complained of her discomfort. Her reply to "How are you feeling?" was always positive and hopeful, always cheerful. I even heard her say she was feeling terrific. In retrospect, I realize now she was probably saying, "I'm better than yesterday, and yesterday was terrible!"

I learned a lot from my aunt and Tom. They truly exemplified that a merry heart is good medicine (Prov. 17:22).

I may respond to "How are you?" with either "I'm fine" or "I'm ter-rific." Both responses mean I'm doing fine, and I'm not sick. But "I'm ter-rific" goes a step further and suggests, "It's a wonderful, exciting day to be alive. I can hardly wait to see what things God has in store for me today!"

Christians should be the most expectant, excited, happy people in the world. Jesus is in control of our lives. What could be more "ter-rific" than that?   MARLENE ANDERSON

Fervent Prayers Avail Much

And he spake a parable unto them to this end, that men ought always to pray, and not to faint. Luke 18:1.

*A*s I look at the above scripture, I cannot help thinking of my mother. Six years ago I could not have said that she waited for Jesus' return, but—praise the Lord—she gave her life to Him before she died. She was able to experience the joy of serving Him. I had given my life to the Lord in 1976, and immediately began to share the wonderful message of God's redeeming love with my mother and the rest of my family. Mom had been brought up in a Christian home, so it was not a new concept for her. Yet she refused to surrender to the Lord. I continued to pray and share the love of God with her. As the years passed, she developed a love-hate attitude toward church. One day she would want to join it, and the next day she'd say she would never be a member. Like so many, she was torn between the desire to serve God and the desire to enjoy the world. Yet I kept praying.

She often persecuted me because I "spent too much time in church." Being very active in the church, I did not spend the amount of time at home that my mother wanted me to, and she became jealous of my church life. Yet in her heart she know the Lord was calling her. Years passed, and her rebellion continued, until one day she found out that she had cancer.

In the quietness of home, after surgery and chemotherapy, Mom had time to think about eternal things, and finally surrendered her life to the Lord. She was baptized on my birthday in September of 1987. As we worshiped the Lord together, I praised God for once again answering my prayers.

My mother died three months after her baptism, yet she received the greatest healing I could ever ask for: the healing of her heart. I encourage you not to faint in prayer. The greatest rewards are still ahead. What wonderful joy awaits us as the Lord reveals to us the results in the lives of those for whom we have been patiently praying!

CARMEN O. GONZALEZ

Choices

Do not press me to leave you or to turn back from following you!
Where you go, I will go; where you lodge, I will lodge; your people shall be my people, and your God my God. Ruth 1:16, NRSV.

The story of Ruth is one of the oldest, most touching love stories in the Bible and the world. Why is the story so moving,
so powerful? What does it have to do with women today?

Because of famine in the land, Ruth's in-laws, Naomi and
Elimelech, moved to Moab, nearly 40 miles from Bethlehem. While
they were living there, Naomi's husband died. In time her two sons,
married to Ruth and Orpah, also died. It was a crushing blow! Now
three women were facing losses and uncertain futures. Naomi
longed to return to the land of her birth. Orpah turned back to her
own mother's house. And Ruth—what would she do with her life?

Ruth made a choice on a dusty road between Moab and
Bethlehem. She chose to stay with Naomi's people and her God.
And she decided in the spirit of love.

The story has a beautiful ending. Ruth, the lovely stranger in
Judah, became the wife of the rich landowner, Boaz. By the grace of
God she had achieved the seemingly impossible—being lifted out of
obscurity and poverty to influence and wealth.

You might say life was easier for Ruth. Today life is more complex, relationships more strained, and people are more difficult,
more fast-paced. Did Ruth have obstacles? Yes—the death of her fa-
ther-in-law and husband, no children, a foreign country, and a
strange people. Nonetheless, she was calm and courageous in the
face of adversity.

Ruth faced still another obstacle: she had to support herself and
her elderly mother-in-law in a time and culture when it was almost
impossible for a single or unmarried person to survive alone. When
they arrived in Bethlehem she found work as a gleaner following the
reapers and gathering up the fallen grain left behind for the poor—
a lowly, hard job.

I remember well, as a child of poverty, my family gleaning the
walnut grove. It was a humble task indeed, yet we were happy to
have something to eat, for often we had little food. As children who
longed to identify with our schoolmates, gleaning the fields was em-
barrassing to us. Ruth, however, expressed no self-pity or dread of
the difficult task. After gleaning all day in the hot sun, she returned

to Naomi joyfully with her small harvest.

How did Ruth do it? How do women today in the same circumstances cope? Only by the strength of God. Ruth had chosen the God of Israel, and that made the difference.   RAMONA PEREZ GREEK

I Am Somebody!

"Then neither do I condemn you," Jesus declared. "Go now and leave your life of sin." John 8:11, NIV.

Occasionally I work with young women who are ashamed of their past. As they begin their healing process, we often turn to the Scriptures for help. One of our favorite passages is one that almost didn't get included in the Gospel manuscript. Apparently some scribes had neglected to copy it in several of the early documents. It took three centuries before it achieved its place in the eighth chapter of John. Three centuries of oral tradition and a few faithful scribes kept alive this beautiful story, which didn't start out that way. The account records both the most dehumanizing act of violation and the most uplifting act of love.

The manipulative Pharisees rudely interrupted Jesus as He was teaching in the Temple courts. They dragged behind them a woman they themselves had plotted to lead into a life of sinfulness. She was a mere pawn. Mistreated, overlooked, spat upon, and talked about—a nothing in their eyes.

I can imagine the Pharisees eagerly waiting to see if Jesus could get out of the corner they had forced Him into. When He stooped down, they moved in to harass Him. But then a hush fell over the crowd as He wrote with His finger on the dust, straightening up only to ask if anyone had the right to cast the first stone. I picture Him looking up just in time to see the Pharisees slinking out of the presence of infinite purity, caught in a trap of their own making.

I have often wondered why the woman did not leave as well. Perhaps she stayed behind because Jesus' attitude gave her that first glimmer of the hope she had so long forgotten. She stood there because she sensed a restoration of her dream. When He said "Go, and sin no more" (KJV), it was as if He had said, "Go out and be somebody!" In that brief moment He had blotted out her pain and sin and given her reason for hope and redemption—the motivation for heart reformation.

Her fear turned to faith. She realized that she had not lost her future. Jesus had changed her life destination from one of destruction into one of distinction. He didn't change the robe of the woman. Instead, He changed the woman to fit the robe. Although she had been dragged into a nightmare, He now sent her forth with a vision: "Go, and sin no more."

Those words released the psychological baggage of self-deprecation, despair, and disgust. Relieved of that awesome weight, she could shape a dream. All because He said, "You are somebody!"

GLENDA-MAE GREENE

FEBRUARY 8

Coupons and Christians

Fear not, for I have redeemed you; I have summoned you by name; you are mine. Isa. 43:1, NIV.

Coupons! You see them everywhere. They come in as many shapes, sizes, and colors as people. Without them, both the producer and the consumer would suffer a certain amount of loss. The next time you cash in your grocery coupons, you may wish to consider the following observations:

I have a coupon that I clipped from a magazine.

It had no voice in how it was designed or into whose hands it was placed.

Of minimal worth in itself, its value is determined solely by its producer.

Its value is not measured by its color, shape, size, or style.

It was created specifically to benefit others.

It bears a saving message to those who observe it.

The redemption plan is written clearly on its face.

Its value is in its surrender and purchase of the manufacturer's product.

It is void where prohibited or restricted by law.

It must be clipped from all attractions that surround it if it is to be redeemed.

If, through abuse or neglect, it fails in its mission, its redemption is in jeopardy.

It points the viewer, not to its own merits, but to the reward offered.

It will witness until it expires or is finally taken to its producer.

It will not be reclaimed after the redemption date has expired.

It never tires of sharing its saving opportunity.
A Christian is like that, too.   LORRAINE HUDGINS

FEBRUARY 9

The Good News

As a mother comforts her child, so will I comfort you. Isa. 66:13, NIV.

The question asked by the teacher of our Bible class arrested my thoughts: What do you see as the greatest good news in the gospel? As discussion continued to flow around me, my mind remained intrigued by the question.

Is it the great love God demonstrated for us by sending His Son to our fallen planet? Is it Jesus' identification with the human race, or His willingness to suffer unbelievable humiliation and agonizing pain to save us from the result of our sin?

Could it be Jesus' promise that He is preparing homes for us in heaven? The hope of a world free of sickness, pain, sorrow, and death, where Jesus Himself will wipe all tears from our eyes? Or anticipation of spending eternity with Jesus, where we shall learn to know Him, even as He knows us?

Perhaps it is God's offer of His power to free us even now from the slavery of sinful habits, His offer of a new heart.

All of these are indeed great good news. But as I considered all the possibilities, I finally decided that the good news of the gospel that I could relate to most personally is God's comparison of His love for us to that of mothers and fathers for their children.

Yes, I have had a taste of God's love through the strong, deep love of my human parents for me. But my understanding of this love was not complete until I became a parent myself.

None of my three boys is perfect. At times each of them has disappointed and hurt me. But my love for them is fierce and strong and protective. When they hurt, I hurt. And when they are happy, I am happy. I cannot bear the thought that any one of them might be lost.

If God loves me the way I love my sons, I know I am safe. He will not let me be lost, will never give me up. Yes, He may have to discipline and correct me, but it is because he *loves* me! I am His dearly beloved child! And I am so glad God put that illustration in the Bible to give me comfort and security. To me, that is the best news of the gospel.   CARROL GRADY

FEBRUARY 10

It Is Not Supposed to Be This Way

Yet man is born to trouble as surely as sparks fly upward.
Job 5:7, NIV.

*M*ama, it is not supposed to be this way." The troubled voice of my daughter came to me over the phone. "It is not what the book says."

Shelly, my younger daughter and a young pastor's wife of four years, was struggling with the challenges of her newborn baby—her first. She had a normal pregnancy, punctuated in the midst by the stress of the move to their first district. When the time came for the delivery, God blessed her with a healthy baby girl.

But now the challenge of nurturing a newborn, the day and night feedings, the loss of sleep, the baby's low weight gain, and the feelings of failure all were taking their toll. "Church members wonder why I'm not out, and I can't even cope here at home," she added amid her tears. "It is not the way it is supposed to be."

No, life here is not the way it is supposed to be. God made us for a better world, a better life. We were not supposed to be overwhelmed with trials, problems, and struggles. Our heavenly Father's heart must ache as He sees His struggling, hurting children depressed over trials that are "not supposed to be." As He witnesses the effects of sin carried down through generations, He longs to gather us to Himself and give us the life that *was* "supposed to be."

Soon He will be coming to do that very thing.

The memories of the struggles in caring for a newborn, though weighty at the time, fade as the babe grows and time passes. Likewise, we will scarcely remember the trials that seem to overwhelm us now when we see the paradise prepared for us in our heavenly home. JOAN MINCHIN NEALL

FEBRUARY 11

See Reverse for Care

A wise son heeds his father's instruction, but a mocker does not listen to rebuke. Prov. 13:1, NIV.

I was browsing in the store when I saw it and knew I had to have it. It was the perfect sweater—long, white, beautiful. A necessary addition to my wardrobe. Eventually, through the wonderful procedure of layaway, the coveted sweater was mine.

I wore it the first day with pride and beamed with the compliments I received. Quite quickly, as is the way of white clothes, it came time for me to wash it. Carefully I checked the label on the inside to find out how to clean my treasured possession. The front label said, "See reverse for care." Instructions filled the entire other side: "Turn garment inside out, hand-wash, cold water, mild soap, dry flat, do not bleach, do not dry-clean, no direct sunlight, no direct heat on beads." Dutifully I followed the instructions.

The next time the sweater needed to be washed, I was not so enthusiastic about the lengthy laundry process. So I used regular laundry detergent instead. By the next laundry date I was rather tired of the inconvenience that washing it caused me and the length of time it took to dry in the bathroom. Rationalizing that machine washing and drying could not hurt it just this once, I tossed it in with all the other white clothes.

Later that day while I put away the laundry, I retrieved my sweater from the laundry basket. Then I saw it—a large hole in the back of my sweater where the threads just seemed to be eaten away. It devastated me. All the plans that I had made for the sweater for that weekend suddenly evaporated. My defiance against directions had ruined my lovely sweater.

God has also given us directions to take care of our most treasured possession—our relationship with Him: "Pray earnestly and often, read the Bible daily, share your faith, show My love to all."

When we first accept Christ we start out enthusiastically doing the things we are supposed to do. But by and by, taking care of our relationship becomes inconvenient, so we toss it in with all the other responsibilities of life. Sometimes it even gets the least attention of all. Eventually we end up with a gaping hole where the threads of our relationship to Christ have disintegrated.

After months of wistfully looking at my sweater in the closet I decided to mend it the best way I could. I didn't do too badly. It has a slight imperfection, but I can still wear it. Fortunately, God can do better than mend our torn lives. He can re-create and make us anew. However, we can save ourselves a lot of pain and be more consistent witnesses if we follow the care instructions in the first place.

FAITH HUNTER

Trust in the Lord—No Matter What

The Lord is good, a strong hold in the day of trouble; and he knoweth them that trust in him. Nahum 1:7.

For two years my husband and I had lived in a caravan (as a travel trailer is called in Australia). After that, we moved into our first house. I remained at home as mother and housewife. Our financial situation at that time was such that we were just able to make the down payment for our house, and most of our furniture was borrowed.

As soon as we had moved into the house we tried to sell our caravan, since we were still paying it off. One mortgage was more than enough for us. For about seven months my husband tried everything possible to sell the house trailer, but to no avail. He became quite anxious about it. One day I told him to trust God. If God wanted us to sell the caravan, we would sell it. But if not, then He would help us to cope. My husband could not understand my faith. Yet he must have pondered about my "simplicity" because the next day he was calm and at peace. Within a week we had sold the caravan—with a profit and *after* the main holiday season when no one needed a trailer nor had money to buy one.

About two years later we had saved just enough money for a trip to Germany to visit our parents. Three months prior to our departure there was an international fund-raising campaign for Cambodia. I felt convicted that we ought to donate quite a substantial amount of money. When I suggested it to my husband, he thought I was crazy. First of all, we didn't have much money ourselves, and second, the amount I suggested would have been the better part of our pocket money for the trip. After discussing it further and realizing that people in Cambodia were far worse off than us, he agreed to donate the amount under the condition that he would pay half of it before our trip and the other half after we came back and had financially recuperated.

When we reached Germany, my husband was able to sell his stamp collection for quite a large sum, and both our parents gave us money as a present. When we got back to Australia we had about 12 times the amount of money that we had pledged for Cambodia, so it wasn't hard at all to donate the other half of our pledge.

Sometimes situations may overwhelm us, but if we trust the Lord and completely hand over our worries to Him, then He will keep His promise either to provide for us or to help us cope. Praise the Lord for His goodness! BEATE KARBSTEIN

Mosquitoes!

If you keep on biting and devouring each other, watch out or you will be destroyed by each other. Gal. 5:15, NIV.

More rain has fallen than we really need, leaving many little wet areas where mosquitoes are hatching by the millions. The dogs, cattle, and wild animals swish their tails and twitch their skin as they try to drive the biting insects away. Going to the garden to work and harvest the produce is a major source of discomfort as they descend upon every exposed area of our skin to bite and draw blood. The resulting welts itch and are uncomfortable. One wishes they would feed upon each other!

Mosquitoes are not like humans. They draw blood from species other than themselves. We humans at times seem to take delight in biting and devouring one another. The resulting welts are very uncomfortable, and we wish that by scratching and rubbing, the discomfort would go away. Sadly, it doesn't. So we need to seek other ways to find comfort.

We try to understand why someone feels it necessary to "bite" us. Hurting, we cry to God for relief. Our sense of self-worth reaches an all-time low. Sometimes we strike back, thinking it will make us feel better, but it doesn't. Our sense of pride tells us to develop "thicker skin" and ignore the jabs. Poisoned stingers hurt so much.

Mary felt the sting of Martha's words as she chided her for not helping with the work. The woman at the well had often heard the whispered, biting words that criticized her lifestyle. How the woman taken in adultery hurt as she heard her accusers! Yet in all these situations, Jesus did not respond as others would have. He said that Mary had chosen the good part by desiring to listen to His words. He used the testimony of the woman at the well to bring people to listen to His message and to turn their hearts to Him. To the woman taken in adultery, He said, "Neither do I condemn thee: go, and sin no more" (John 8:11).

Jesus gave us the perfect example of how we should speak to one another and about one another. Mosquitoes need to feed upon the blood of others in order to procreate. But people don't. Words that come from our lips can bring cheer, comfort, and peace. Our work is to build and encourage. Biting and devouring one another will only leave us empty.

"Dear Jesus, give me a heart and thoughts that are like Yours. May my words be words that will have a positive influence for You. Make me an instrument of peace in this world of pain."   EVELYN GLASS

FEBRUARY 14

Forever Yours

Give thanks to the Lord, for he is good; his love endures forever.
Ps. 118:1, NIV.

*J*f I close my eyes, I can still see the box. It was a big red box, and it sat next to the teacher's desk in the one-room Michigan schoolhouse where I attended kindergarten. I watched closely as most of the 18 other students took turns slipping their valentines through a slot in the top of the paper-doily decorated box. I was 5 years old, and it was my first Valentine's Day at school.

The teacher announced that we would skip reading class and spend the last hour of the school day exchanging valentines and enjoying heart-shaped sugar cookies and punch. Even today I can still remember having a hard time keeping my mind on my schoolwork that day. I was the youngest one in the classroom, and I wondered if anyone had remembered to bring me a valentine.

The clock seemed to move slowly, but when the long-awaited hour finally came, the teacher asked me to help pass out the valentines. The girls giggled, and I heard an occasional spontaneous yelp when one of the older boys read a sentimental verse coming from someone he disliked. And yes, I did get some valentines. I opened the small white envelopes with extreme care and read each verse as if it were the gospel. I was "loved," and it felt good!

Since that day I've grown to know what real love is. I have loved and have been loved in return by my parents, my husband, my children, grandchildren, and friends. Since I was 15 years old my husband has expressed his love by sending me roses on Valentine's Day. Through snowstorms, from long distance, and even while working in Russia, he hasn't missed a year! Some have suggested that we should have taken a picture each year. I guess that would have made an interesting scrapbook for our children and grandchildren, but I never could have imagined that this loving practice would continue for so many years. Do I get tired of receiving roses? Do we ever get tired of being loved? Never!

The Lord sends us love messages, too. But His messages are in the form of promises filled with agape love. We search for these expressions of His love. They cheer us along the way and remind us that we are cherished children of the King. And we never need to wonder if we'll be forgotten—because He loves us all with an unwavering love. —ROSE OTIS

FEBRUARY 15

A Gospel Sermon on a Tennis Shoe

The Lord says, "Now, let's settle the matter. You are stained red with sin, but I will wash you as clean as snow. Although your stains are deep red, you will be as wool." Isa. 1:18, TEV.

One night I stayed late on campus, and it was so dark that I could hardly see. The weather had been bad all week with heavy rains, so it was not unusual to find swamplike areas of mud all over the place.

In one particular area the mud was so thick that people might literally sink into it if they did not watch their step. I took one look at this spot and thought to myself, *I'll never allow myself to get caught in the mud!*

Wrong! Somehow I became distracted by the cares of this life: bills, relationships with my coworkers, and my career. More important, even though I knew my feet would sink into it if I walked across the mud, I thought I could handle it. In fact, the idea that I could walk on mud like Peter walked on water challenged me!

I was bold. Not only did I walk on the mud, I ran so fast that my right tennis shoe came off. When I finally recovered it, I thought I would need to bleach the shoe in order to make it white again. In fact, my shoe was so dirty that I even considered buying another pair. Luckily, hot water and a little detergent took care of the stains.

The incident reminded me of the cleansing agent Jesus uses to remove the dirty, hard-to-clean sins in our lives. I am glad to know there is a special cleanser that is able to remove any stains in my heart no matter how deep or ugly they may be. —CAROL ANN FRASER

Forgiven!

I will forgive their iniquity, and I will remember their sin no more. Jer. 31:34.

It is a wonderful truth that God forgives us. Even more wonderful is the *way* He forgives. When He forgives, our sins are gone forever. At times we find this hard to comprehend because we are so unlike Him.

Human nature seeks to keep score, to harbor wrongs done, and to remember the sins of others in an attempt to look better ourselves. Our heavenly Father, on the other hand, tells us that He will remove our sins from us as far as the east is from the west (Ps. 103:12). God picked two extremes that can never be brought together to remind us of the distance He will place between us and our sins!

Scripture also tells us that God casts all our sins behind His back (Isa. 38:17). Have you ever tried to look at something directly behind your back, only to discover that you cannot do it? Here the Lord is lovingly telling us that our sins, once pardoned, cannot be seen—they are in a blind spot.

Isaiah 44:22 declares that God blots our sins out like a thick cloud. This brings to mind the scene at the Red Sea when the pillar of cloud intervened between God's people and their pursuers. It was such a thick cloud that the Egyptians could not see God's people.

God will throw our sins into the depths of the sea (Micah 7:19). It is a place no one can go. The water pressure is too great. But just in case we might still doubt whether God will really forgive our sins, we can turn to Revelation 21:1 and learn that in the earth made new the sea is no more! Even the place where He disposes of our sins will vanish forever. He cannot go back and retrieve them.

Our loving Father assures us in so many different ways that when He forgives, our sins exist no more. Knowing this makes me want to throw myself at His feet and worship Him. It also causes me to seek to know Him better because I cannot forgive others the way He forgives me unless *He* does so *through* me. And the only way for that to happen is to spend time with Him.   RETTA MICHAELIS

Sacrament of Lunch

He that is faithful in that which is least is faithful also in much.
Luke 16:10.

*W*hether it involves one lunch or a half dozen to prepare, I don't know a single person who looks forward with a thrill to sandwich-making, thermos-filling, carrot-cleaning, or planning for variety and nutrition in lunches. I wonder if lunch-making got the same "Oh no! What do I put in the bag?" groans in Bible times.

However she felt about lunch-making, one unnamed New Testament mother sent a lunch with her son. A simple lunch. Just five barley loaves and two fish. Her son went to hear Jesus. His teaching must have fascinated the boy, since he forgot all about his lunch. Finally, evening arrived.

Jesus suggested to the disciples that they feed the crowd of perhaps 10,000 to 15,000 hungry people. The disciples had already taken stock of what was available: one lad had a lunch of five barley loaves and two fish. After Jesus blessed the loaves and fish, He broke them. And broke them. And broke them. His disciples passed out baskets and baskets full of barley loaves and fish. And all the people ate until they were full.

Why was Jesus able to feed this mass of people? For two reasons. First, an unnamed woman had faithfully cared for her son's needs and made him a lunch. Second, God blessed what was available.

The mother had no inkling that the lunch she made for her son would feed a multitude. She had no idea that the story of that lunch would be told for an eternity, blessing untold millions. She just faithfully did the routine duty that needed to be done. And the ripples of her faithfulness still broaden across the sea of humanity.

"And whatsoever ye do, do it heartily, as to the Lord, and not unto men" (Col. 3:23). As you faithfully make lunches, go to work, scrub floors, arrange a bouquet, visit a friend, run errands, or do any of a thousand other routine duties, do it for God. God will turn your faithfulness into a blessing. You may never know on this earth how God blesses your faithfulness. And even if others realize the blessing, they may not recognize the human source. You may remain anonymous, like the anonymous mother of the anonymous boy who shared his lunch with Jesus, yet the blessing will ripple on.

Through your faithfulness, God will bless the world in ways He could not bless otherwise. Won't you offer the sacrament of lunch, the sacrament of your routine duties?   HELEN HEAVIRLAND

FEBRUARY 18

I'll Be Somewhere Listening

But whoso hearkeneth unto me shall dwell safely, and shall be quiet from fear of evil. Prov. 1:33.

*A*s I left the store snow was falling, coming down in thick, soft flakes. When I reached the car I gave myself a few vigorous brushes, slid in the car, and started the engine. Then it happened. Inaudible, but unmistakably distinct, the message clearly came: "Go see Sylvia!"

I glanced at my watch. *This is silly,* I thought. *It's 11:30 a.m., almost lunchtime. No one goes visiting at this hour of the day.* Then another thought, unbidden: *Ask her to come with you.* Should I? I had not visited Sylvia all winter.

As I pulled away from the curb, little doubts nagged at me as to the wisdom of what I was doing. But pushing them away, I drove on. When I finally arrived, the house looked quiet, almost deserted. I rang the bell and waited. No answer.

As I turned to leave, suddenly the door opened. Relieved that my trip had not been in vain, I burst out, "How would you like to get your coat on and come home with me for lunch?"

If I had stopped to think a moment, I would have noticed the tired look around her eyes. "Oh, I'm sorry," I said. "You were lying down, weren't you?"

"Yes," she replied. "I'm not feeling well today. But come in."

Thinking that I had made a mistake, I went in, took off my coat, and made myself comfortable while Sylvia stretched out on the sofa.

For a while we talked of inconsequentials, but as we warmed to each other, she began to speak of things that had been bothering her, making her feel discouraged. Yes, she had prayed about them, but it just seemed as if . . .

The time slipped by. I could see that her face had brightened during our conversation.

"I really ought to be getting home," I said. "I hadn't intended to stay this long."

"No, no," Sylvia said, sitting up. "I feel ever so much better now. I haven't had anything to eat all day. Let's go to the kitchen, and I'll fix us both some lunch."

We shared a little prayer and a deliciously simple lunch. When I finally rose to go, she put her arm around me and said, "Thank you for being my sister," and I hugged her back.

The warm sun had melted most of the snow. As I drove into the street, my heart was singing, "Thank You, God, for teaching me to listen!"   ALICE COVEY

A Refuge in God

The Lord also will be a refuge for the oppressed, a refuge in times of trouble. Ps. 9:9, NKJV.

*I*t was early June in North Carolina, and I had been watching a mallard duck and its 10 tiny fluffs of down swimming along the edge of the pond. The mother left the water and waddled up the bank, followed obediently by nine of her babies. One little duckling continued to paddle alone in the water. When it realized that it was alone, it screamed for its mother. Its mother calmly quacked a reply, and following her voice, the tiny duck, after stumbling up the hill, finally reunited with its mother and the other ducklings.

As I watched this scene unfold, I thought how like the ducklings we are. Although we start out with God, often we become separated, unaware, like the duckling, that we *are* separated. Then we go on our merry way, doing our own things, giving lip service to spiritual things in our lives. We are still reading our Bible, and from all outward appearances appear to be a child of God. But suddenly one day we become aware of our condition and start frantically fighting our way back to God. As we struggle and scream in our frustration, God calmly leads us back to Him. He's been there all along, just as the mother duck was, waiting for us to realize our separation from Him so He can welcome us home with open arms. God is with us always, our refuge, waiting for us to return.   LORAINE SWEETLAND

Lesson From Lane

Commit thy way unto the Lord; trust also in him; and he shall bring it to pass. Ps. 37:5.

My sister-in-law, Chris, has a fascinating hobby—training Seeing Eye dogs. She takes them one at a time and keeps them for one full year. Then they go to a special school that trains each dog with the sightless person it will serve.

The current dog Chris is training is named Lane, a handsome, smooth-haired collie with a sleek body, a long, sensitive nose, and eyes that would melt a heart of stone. I was interested in how my sister would train this beauty.

The main characteristic she has to cultivate in each guide dog is concentration. It means the animal will focus so intently on its duties that it will not do the things dogs otherwise do naturally. In essence, the dog will not be allowed to be itself, to follow its natural instinct and enjoy the happy, free life of a well-behaved dog.

Lane is not in training 24 hours a day. It does begin, however, as soon as my sister puts his training coat on. This signals to him that he is no longer an ordinary dog, but rather a "canine on a mission." During this time he may not show any interest in food or water. He may not sniff it or even approach it. Nor is he to leave the side of his trainer for any reason. He must be constantly aware of the trainer's face. Also, he must always be alert to the ground surface, stopping when he encounters a large crack or other obstruction in the path or any low-hanging interference overhead.

Furthermore, the trainee dog is not permitted to make noise. The animal cannot follow such natural behavior as barking, whining, or woofing. It may not relieve itself until the designated time. During training it may never romp with children or chase squirrels. Indeed, all the things a dog does so naturally are suddenly forbidden. It has to concentrate so intently that it becomes a different creature while it functions as a guide dog.

I learned quite a spiritual lesson the first day I visited Chris! Here was a mere dog who was willing to completely reverse its natural behavior in order to serve someone in need. That calls for commitment and requires dedication. It's natural for Lane to chase squirrels and whine for attention. And it's just as natural for us to sin. Lane was born a dog—we were born sinners.

Only by using the keenest powers of concentration and commitment can we escape our natural estate. Lane was performing beautifully in his training to be a guide dog, but first he had to be willing to let his trainer restructure his canine nature.

We, like Lane, must let God place on us His coat of submission and allow Him to rework our carnal nature. If we concentrate on His real goal for us, perhaps He could lead us to help some spiritually sightless person. ⟶ LORABEL HERSCH

The Wonder Cloth

I am not ashamed of the gospel, because it is the power of God for the salvation of everyone who believes: first for the Jew, then for the Gentile. Rom. 1:16, NIV.

After years of feeling dissatisfied with the results of my kitchen bench wiping, I've discovered a new "wonder cloth." It has quite revolutionized my cleaning tasks. Now, with just one wipe of the surfaces, they come up dry and without smears.

I was so elated at my discovery that I told my neighbor about it. She was just as pleased with the results as I was. So I telephoned my sister with the news. After purchasing one, she soon called me back to say how delighted she was. Nothing she had used in the past had proved so efficient as this cleaning cloth.

My sister gave one to her daughter-in-law, who was soon enthusiastic also. And so was her husband, who had borrowed the cloth when he couldn't find a chamois to wipe down his newly washed car.

I sent each of my sisters-in-law a "wonder cloth." They told me that they had tried the cloth and were thrilled with the results. "I've never known anything to absorb so much moisture and wipe so dry . . . I'm buying some more to give to my daughters," one of them wrote me.

I have provided each area of my home that needs a wiping cloth with a "wonder cloth." No matter what needs to be mopped, only one cloth is adequate for the task: the "wonder cloth." I considered writing to the manufacturer to express my appreciation for such a product and suggest they might like to take me on as a salesperson!

Friends and extended family members are also rejoicing in transformed cleaning operations. Not only are the kitchen bench and tabletops smear-free and shiny when dry, but the bathtub comes clean so easily. The "wonder cloth" quickly takes care of floor and table spills.

As I completed my kitchen tasks with this superabsorbent wiper, I reflected on how it had changed my outlook on this daily chore and how much pleasure it had given me to share a knowledge of it with others.

Then it occurred to me: why had I not been just as enthusiastic to tell others of my Christian faith? Surely nothing had changed my life more than accepting Christ as my Saviour! He is the center of my life, and I talk to Him constantly, committing my family to His care, asking for His guidance and blessing. But why was I reticent to share the good news of His salvation with all whom I met?

Are there things you are excited to tell others about? Make it your practice to share the good news of God's salvation with the same enthusiasm. Let us search daily for opportunities to tell others about our "Wonder God." JOY TOTENHOFER

FEBRUARY 22

Because He Said So

The ravens brought him bread and meat in the morning and bread and meat in the evening, and he drank from the brook. 1 Kings 17:6, NIV.

I'd had a little experience relying on God to provide for my family, but it had been a long time, and I was rusty. The lesson that I had learned so painstakingly I thought was etched on my heart forever, but it had deserted me sometime during the easy years that cushioned me from the lean ones. As my career blossomed and we had money again for all the little "extras," I slowly had forgotten how to rely on God.

During the long winter months my husband's business slowed down to a protesting halt. The money that had gone to pay for having a baby without insurance instead of padding our savings account might have helped us now, but it was no use thinking about it. We hadn't any choice. The months I had taken off for maternity leave couldn't be recaptured and made productive.

So we faced the unknown. A yawning expanse into which we had to fling ourselves, completely confident that the Lord would catch us. That's where the trust comes in—the trust I had lost.

I found it the other day when I was retelling my 10-month-old son his Bible lesson. The story was about Elijah and how he walked and walked until he came to a little stream. He was very tired, thirsty, and hungry. Although he knelt down to have a drink, he didn't have anything to eat. But soon ravens came, carrying bread in their beaks. Every day Jesus took care of Elijah, I told my son, sending him water in the little river and ravens carrying bread. And every day Jesus takes care of us.

Elijah thanked Jesus for taking care of him. I thank Him too for caring for us every day. We may not have money for all the little extras, but we have food every day, a house to live in, and money to pay our bills. He takes care of us today. And He will take care of us tomorrow. Because He said so. — CELESTE PERRINO WALKER

FEBRUARY 23

He Sees the Look in Your Eyes

The eyes of the Lord are on the righteous and his ears are attentive to their cry. Ps. 34:15, NIV.

*A*unt Jeanie's three young nephews could hardly wait for school to end and summer vacation to begin. They looked forward to a visit with their aunt in the big city and attending Vacation Bible School. After all, they lived in a small rural town in which were only two other children their age in their church.

The excitement mounted as they headed for their first day at Vacation Bible School in the big city. Aunt Jeanie had included it in their summer activities because she believed that such an experience would give them an advantage in building a strong faith in Christ.

The strange place with unfamiliar faces was a bit overwhelming for little Willie, who was only 2. Aunt Jeanie felt his tug, and seeing the look in his eyes, she sensed his need for reassurance that all was well. She gave him a hug and a kiss. Little Willie giggled and flashed a broad smile, then ran off to join the other children.

Later, a friend that Willie had found approached Aunt Jeanie with a yearning look in his eyes. He lifted up his arms as if reaching for affection. She embraced him, kissed him repeatedly, and let him go. He giggled and skipped away to catch Willie and join the other youngsters. Aunt Jeanie mused, *That's just like grown-ups.*

We also need to have our moments of reassurance that all is well with us and that somebody bigger than ourselves and our circumstances is in control of the situations in our lives. Jesus is always

73

there to comfort and cheer at times when we need a special touch. We can hasten to our heavenly Father, for He sees the look in our eyes and knows just how to fix the situation, whatever it may be. Indeed, His eyes are upon us and His ears open to our cry.

ELLEN ANDERSON

FEBRUARY 24

Answer

Before they call I will answer; while they are still speaking I will hear. Isa. 65:24, NIV.

*T*he setting sun took all semblance of warmth from my makeshift kitchen. I pulled on another sweater and instructed myself, "Be thankful for what we have. Don't complain over what we lack." After all, we had a gas hot plate, two dishes, and the pressure cooker essential to cooking at an altitude of 13,000 feet. Moreover, we possessed a luxury in this frigid land—a warm water bed in which to snuggle down at night in our unheated rooms.

"Sure," I argued with myself, "and the bed lies on the floor, supported by used form boards from the mission's construction site." My mind, like a magnet, was drawn to negative thoughts.

My husband and I were new volunteer missionaries in the high Andes. We found the adjustment difficult, and at the moment it seemed more than I could handle. As I shivered, I griped at God. "Lord, here we are sharing an apartment with older missionaries. My few 'possessions' are borrowed. My independence, my identity, is gone—no car, no income-producing job. I am counseled and advised at every turn. I feel like a 13-year-old again! Even when our monthly 'spending money' arrives, some translator must accompany us to market to help us spend it."

My mind raced faster as I recalled scanning Indian faces, longing for a familiar smile from home. Our daily dependence on others overwhelmed me. Homesick, I wished for something that would feel like home.

"O Jesus, stop me!" I cried as I recognized the whirlpool into which my thoughts pulled me. "Please give me some happy ideas."

But I received no response, felt no comfort. Was my line to heaven cut?

"Where are You, Jesus?" My question echoed in my mind as I moved into our other sparsely furnished room.

Out of the silence came a knock. At the door stood another missionary wife. In her hand Kathy held a loaf of oven-fresh banana bread.

"Here, Pam." Kathy's casual smile showed her unawareness of the depth of her ministry. I reached out to accept the blessings, bread and friendship, as if they came from the hand of Christ Himself. How did Kathy know I badly needed that touch of home, that tangible sign of love?

She visited briefly, sitting in one of the homemade canvas chairs at one end of our room while her children rolled on the water bed at the other end. Her conversation encouraged me, although she didn't seem conscious of that.

Later, as I closed the door behind them, I smiled. "Thank You, Jesus. You really did hear." PAMELA BAUMGARTNER

God of the Hills

I will lift up mine eyes unto the hills, from whence cometh my help. My help cometh from the Lord, which made heaven and earth. Ps. 121:1, 2.

Sitting at my desk in the study loft of our Rocky Mountain home, I often gaze at the beautiful hills in the distance. My husband even took out several tall trees so I can now see majestic, snowcapped Byers Peak.

I find a certain security and stability in those hills. They never move, are always there morning, noon, or night. They remind me of God's dependability and perpetual presence in my life.

At times, however, the hills become obscured by winter snowstorms or fog rising from the valley. I know the hills haven't moved, but I feel separated and shut away and long for a clear view again.

And at times in my life I feel something has come between me and my Lord. He's still there, but something seems to make Him less visible. Satan attacks me with health problems or relationships that seem difficult. Life's storms sometimes strike briefly, but at other times they seem to stretch on endlessly. I am tempted to question whether God is still really there.

It is at such times that I need to remember the God of the hills. Like my Rocky Mountains, He has not moved. My faith and trust in Him must remind me that my trials are only temporary, that although I cannot see it clearly at the moment, "all things work together for good to them that love God" (Rom. 8:28).

If I can just hold on, the clouds will lift and it will be easy to see again that God was there all the time. He is dependable, caring, and patiently waiting for me to learn the lessons He shows me through my beautiful hills.   ELLEN BRESEE

What's in a Name?

Give thanks to the Lord, call on his name; . . . and proclaim that his name is exalted. Isa. 12:4, NIV.

We've all heard the folklore that Eskimos have dozens of different words for snow, but have you ever wondered why they might have so many? If it were true, I believe it would be because snow is so important to them. The type and duration of a snowstorm can mean life or death.

I began to ride this train of thought during a Bible study that mentioned some names for Jesus with which I was unfamiliar: "the messenger of the covenant" (Mal. 3:1), "a Star out of Jacob" and "a Sceptre . . . out of Israel" (Num. 24:17). They intrigued me, so I began to keep a list. I started by looking up those most familiar: "Wonderful Counselor," "Prince of Peace" (Isa. 9:6, NIV); "the way," "the truth," and "the life" (John 14:6); and "Alpha and Omega" (Rev. 22:13).

Then I discovered that Job called Him "my witness," "my advocate," and "my friend" (Job 16:19, 20, NIV). The psalmist referred to Him as "my light" (Ps. 27:1), "the rock of our salvation" (Ps. 95:1), and "the capstone" (Ps. 118:22, NIV).

Most interesting are the names Jesus used for Himself. He is not just "the Lamb" (John 1:29) and "the good shepherd" (John 10:11), but also "the gate for the sheep" (verse 7, NIV). He is "the living bread which came down from heaven" (John 6:51), which is all the more fascinating when you know that Bethlehem, where He was born, means "house of bread." Jesus referred to Himself as "Lord of the harvest" (Luke 10:2) and "the Amen," "the faithful and true witness," and "the ruler of God's creation" (Rev. 3:14, NIV).

He is the "Overseer of your souls" (1 Peter 2:25, NIV), "the great prince" (Dan. 12:1), and the "perfecter of our faith" (Heb. 12:2, NIV). His name means "The Lord saves" (see Matt. 1:21) and "God With Us" (see Isa. 8:8).

I now have 128 names on my list, and it is an indescribable

thrill when I find a new one. I love to ponder my list, as each name reveals a different facet to God's character. Most of us have nicknames and "pet" names for those we love most. Shouldn't Jesus, our beloved Saviour, have more? — JACQUELYN COCHRAN

You Must Be Dreaming!

I alone know the plans I have for you, plans to bring you prosperity and not disaster, plans to bring about the future you hope for. Then you will call to me. You will come and pray to me, and I will answer you. Jer. 29:11, 12, TEV.

Leah? Try out for the cheerleading squad? She's deaf! Are you *dreaming*?

Ben? A neurosurgeon? He's not even passing his subjects! You *must* be dreaming!

What? Create a theme park in the Florida swamplands where people would travel from all over the world? You *are* dreaming!

Yes, and all these dreams became realities.

Throughout the years I have been fascinated with visionaries and how they accomplished their goals. As a child I was sure that only "exceptional people" would get positive results. I thought they had something magical about them, or that it was their circumstances that caused their dreams to come true.

Much to my surprise, I discovered there *is* something magical about dreamers—they *are* unique. They have the ability to believe in the unthinkable, in things that they cannot see, touch, taste, or feel. With childlike faith, persistence, and prayers, dreamers often watch their hopes come to fruition.

I am suggesting that life without dreaming is like a sandwich without a middle. I call it a "disaster sandwich." Ironically, Webster's dictionary illustrates the sandwich metaphor quite well. Notice that it sandwiches dream between dread and dreary.

Dread—to feel extreme reluctance to meet or face

Dream—to conceive as possible, fitting, or proper

Dreary—causing feelings of cheerlessness; gloomy

When you reflect on this sandwich metaphor, can you recall times when you worked toward a dream and were unable to accomplish it because of reluctance that led to feelings of gloom? Haven't we all shared our hopes with someone only to hear an unenthusiastic response that implied, "No way!"

The next time you encounter what appears to be an insurmountable obstacle, face it head on. Remember God's plans to bring you "prosperity and not disaster, plans to bring about the future you hope for." And when someone says "You must be dreaming!" simply acknowledge the fact and reply, "I am!" LYNN MARIE DAVIS

FEBRUARY 28

We're Moving . . . Again!

Knowing in yourselves that ye have in heaven a better and an enduring substance. Heb. 10:34.

We just joined the other 242,000 people in North America who moved this year. Only we moved twice! Leaving one's family, friends, and church behind is hard enough without all the other work that goes with transferring. I'm so tired of sorting and cleaning and packing boxes, yet not knowing where anything is. Or not being able to find what I'm looking for because it's in storage. It is exciting (and relieving) now to be finally settled in a home of our own where we have enough room and a safe place for our little girl to play—and where we hope to stay for many years!

As I decorate the house and plant flowers in the yard, I recall the lives of women in the Bible who had to move. Think of Abraham's wife, Sarah, and how she was asked to leave everything behind and go with her husband, who had no idea of where they were heading! Rachel and Leah left family and friends to travel long distances, as did Naomi and Ruth. I pray that none of us will be like Lot's wife, who couldn't bear to abandon her home and possessions when the angels instructed her family to flee.

There is, however, one "move" that I'm looking forward to. When Jesus comes to take us to our heavenly home, we will not have to sort or clean or pack. That work will have been done already. And when we reach our home in heaven, we'll be surrounded by family and by friends that we've known over the years. Best of all, we'll be continually in the presence of Jesus, and we'll never have to move again! Now, *that's* good news! BRENDA FORBES DICKERSON

He's Prepared

I will answer them before they even call to me. While they are still talking to me about their needs, I will go ahead and answer their prayers. Isa. 65:24, TLB.

*I*t had been a long and tiring day. My husband, Ben, and I were nearing the small college town where we lived. Night was fast approaching, and we were anxious to get home. Our small motor home had been working well until a loud noise and steam rising from the engine suddenly alarmed us. Pulling to the side of the road, Ben got out to investigate. One of the several fan belts had broken, entangling the others in a hot, unworkable mass. We couldn't go on. The 20 miles to home never seemed so far away.

After talking it over with God and ourselves, Ben decided to walk to a small office about a half mile away to use the phone for help. Just as he started across the small country road, a pickup pulled up in front of us. A man stopped, stepped out, and inquired if we needed help. Who was this man? An angel smoking a cigarette? We don't know the answer to everything and everyone that God sends into our lives, but this one thing we do know: God cares about us.

The stranger was a mechanic from the city nearby and had suddenly found himself taking a roundabout way home. In less than 10 minutes we were homeward-bound. Refusing to accept any payment for his services, he drove away saying, "Now I know why I came this way." A friendly, helpful stranger was on his way to help us long before we asked. And we were both blessed.

Another time I remember so vividly the heavy rainstorm that God sent when we were traveling by train into a Socialist country. Our suitcase contained Bibles and religious books—forbidden at that time—for one of the national ministers. When we arrived at the station, rain fell in such torrents that it flooded the floor, and the tourist authorities rushed us onto a bus. None of us had to open our suitcases for inspection. The books were safe and were delivered to a gracious receiver.

Once again, I remember when my husband's work took him away from home for extended periods of time. Those bitterly cold winters and icy roads often presented quite a challenge for me to drive the nine miles to my teaching position. I never missed a day getting to work in all those years. Heavenly helpers were always at my side, and I had the delightful experience one time of a sand truck arriving at just the right time.

We can face each new day with assurance! Our heavenly Father recognizes our needs before we ask. With confidence we can know He's with us on each winding path we tread. Let us trust Him. He is prepared.

LUCILE HASSENPFLUG

Repressed Anger

"In your anger do not sin": Do not let the sun go down while you are still angry. Eph. 4:26, NIV.

*J*onna grew up in a family that had misconceptions about anger. Anger was often present, yet never expressed outwardly. She clearly remembered the red flush, followed by a hasty exit, that signaled her father's wrath. At the same time she received reprimands whenever she displayed any degree of temper. If she slammed a door, she had to open and close it quietly a hundred times.

"It's a sin to be angry" her home, her church, and the conservative religious elementary school she attended drilled into her. These lessons, learned in early childhood, followed her the rest of her life. She knew she wasn't happy, but she didn't know she was angry. Jonna suffered from repressed anger.

Pretending you are not angry solves nothing, but it does pave the way for an eruption later on. Repressing anger is a destructive and immature method of handling anger, yet Jonna knew no other way.

The refusal to deal with the presence of anger constructively can create some major health problems: ulcers, headaches, anxiety attacks, and depression, just to name a few. When a person denies or mishandles anger, it will come out indirectly. And remember, when you cut off one feeling, you cut off all feelings. If you repress anger, you will also turn off love, happiness, and joy. Anger is a Creator-given emotion. He planted all of our emotions in us. Scripture instructs us not to repress, suppress, or express anger, but rather to process it. Paul describes processed anger when he says, "In your anger do not sin." According to this verse, you will be aware that you are angry, but you will be in control of your temper and not allow it to get out of hand.

God approves justifiable anger when we keep it under control and direct it toward eradicating sin. Healthy anger fires us up to fight for truth rather than allowing us to remain indifferent. When others are hurt or victimized unfairly, taken advantage of, or are suffering needlessly, we become angry over the conditions that permitted it. Aroused angry feelings can motivate us to change or correct injustices.

Are you dealing with an anger problem? When and if you do, commit yourself to a method of venting your feelings in a constructive manner. If you become upset emotionally, it is difficult to be rational or objective. Reduce the anger, and you can deal with the issue more effectively. Admit to God that you are angry. Then give Him your anger, asking Him to work effectively in you for its resolution.

NANCY VAN PELT

MARCH 2

Miracles Do Happen

Honour the Lord with thy substance, and with the firstfruits of all thine increase: so shall thy barns be filled with plenty, and thy presses shall burst out with new wine. Prov. 3:9, 10.

*B*ack in 1981 my husband was the only breadwinner in our family, since I stayed home looking after our 3-year-old son and our home. My weekly shopping allowance was $60. I was just able to manage on it by making needs a priority over wants. I had to plan very carefully because there simply wasn't more money available.

During that time, however, we got to know a couple with two small children, who even had less money than we. Not being able to give them any money, I started to buy groceries for them. Approximately half of everything that I purchased for myself I bought for them. I still don't know how it happened, but I did not spend more than $60 per week, even though I bought one-and-a-half times the previous quantity. I did that for several months. As soon as I stopped buying for them and went back to the normal quantity, I still spent $60 per week.

Two years later my husband was unemployed for eight months, and I was still a housewife and mother. As you would expect, our financial situation became desperate. During that time, however, we never had to go hungry. One church member, who had a small farm, regularly gave us boxes of fruit and vegetables. The Dorcas leader arranged for us to receive rejects from the sanitarium. In fact, we had so much that we were able to share some of it with those less fortunate.

However, we became so destitute that my husband—for the first time—considered not paying tithe in order to make the house mortgage payments. I didn't agree with that idea, since tithe is the Lord's money. Toward the end of the eighth month our church organized a fly-and-build team to go to Vanuatu. One church member who wanted to go but didn't have the time paid the fare for my husband. I told him that while he was in Vanuatu I would continue to pay tithe, and when he came back, we would discuss it further. He argued that we would lose our house, but my trust paid off. On that trip my husband met his future employer, who was frantically searching for someone at that time.

My prayer today is that you too may find help in the Lord to remain strong and faithful and trusting. He is good, and He cares.

BEATE KARBSTEIN

MARCH 3

What Happened to Your Hand?

But Jesus called for the children and said, "Let the little ones come to me; do not try to stop them; for the kingdom of God belongs to such as these." Luke 18:16, NEB.

What happened to Your hand, dear Jesus? Was somebody there
To help You when it happened? Didn't anybody care?

Did the doctor try to fix it? Did it bleed so very much?
Did he put a bandage on it? Does it still hurt to the touch?

Do You think it was on purpose, or a terrible mistake?
Why would someone hurt You? Did it cause Your heart to break?

Did the people try to stop them? Were they too afraid to try?
Were You all alone, dear Jesus? Did it make You want to cry?

Was it late at night or raining? Did You stumble down and fall?
Would You share Your story with me? I would like to know it all!

Did You try to rescue someone? Did You save a child
    like me?
Could that be just how it happened, Jesus? Did Your
    Father see?

It must have hurt most dreadfully, because it goes
    clear through!
I'll bet that You were awfully frightened. I would have
    been too!

God must have cried to see You hurting. Do You
    think He heard You pray?
Was it because You loved us? Will it ever go away?

I wish I could have helped You, 'cause I love You.
    Can't You tell?
If I kiss it for You, Jesus, would that help to make
    it well?

LORRAINE HUDGINS

The Best Job in the World

But thanks be to God that, though you used to be slaves to sin,
you wholeheartedly obeyed the form of teaching to which you
were entrusted. You have been set free from sin and have become slaves to righteousness. Rom. 6:17, 18, NIV.

I've found a wonderful job! The best job in the whole world:
working for a multinational corporation.

I used to work for my Boss's main competitor. It was hell
on earth, and I ended up hopelessly in debt to this evil tyrant. I discovered that he rewarded all his employees with a hot, sticky, and
very short retirement scheme. No career prospects. No job satisfaction. Only guilt and meaningless activity.

Then I heard about a Boss who took on anyone who wanted to
work for Him. Immediate acceptance into the workforce. Equal opportunities for everyone. Exciting and enjoyable. Each person offered a tailor-made position, designed around his or her own
individual skills, gifts, and potential. It all sounded so marvelous!

Initially I was worried about the old boss's response when I
handed in my resignation. He isn't exactly renowned for tolerance

and caring, and I was concerned about my massive debts. But I discovered my new Boss had paid off my debts years ago—before He'd even employed me. I had been worrying about them for ages, and suddenly I didn't owe a penny!

The new Boss gave me in-service counseling and treatment to help me recover from my previous traumatic work experience. I received a comprehensive study manual, with daily on-the-job training.

I love my new career, and I can even work in partnership with my husband. Together we train and recruit new workers, manage personnel, and provide catering services, public relations, and plant maintenance. We have multitudes of invisible helpers working for us all the time.

Although the immediate pay may not match the salaries of executives of other companies, our Boss makes sure that all our needs get perfectly met.

We also have the best pension plan available. Every loyal worker is entitled to a luxury home in the most beautiful retirement complex of the universe—Club Paradise, complete with an exciting, all-expense-paid space voyage!

Sometimes the work seems hard, lonely, and unappreciated. But we never forget who we are working for, and how much He loves us. Nothing could be better than working for Him. And one thing I know for sure: I never want to work for anyone else. Do you?

KAREN HOLFORD

MARCH 5

Rainbow

I have set my rainbow in the clouds. . . . Whenever I bring clouds over the earth and the rainbow appears in the clouds, I will remember my covenant between me and you. Gen. 9:13-15, NIV.

It was one of those days when everything seems to go wrong. After a sleepless night with a colicky infant I finally collapsed into a deep sleep. In what seemed to be a very short time I was suddenly awakened. Christine, our 3-year-old, came bounding onto our bed, exclaiming cheerfully, "Mommy, I'm awake!"

I prayed, "Lord, give me strength."

Wearily I placed both feet on the floor as I glanced sideways into the mirror. Hair flat and dark circles under my eyes, I was certainly the picture of glamour.

As I descended the stairs at a snail's pace, Christine erupted into loud protests. "Come on, Mommy! I'm hungry!" The noise jolted infant Jennifer into action. Now she also loudly exclaimed that she too was hungry. As I sat down to nurse Jennifer, big sister proceeded to poke her nose and eyes. Soon baby was crying, then Christine in the time-out chair, and finally me.

It rained all day. The day unfolded from bad to worse. My written goal for the day was to make granola. It burned. Even the squirrels wouldn't touch it. I prepared lunch in anticipation of some adult conversation. My husband called to cancel. The hope of a nap spurred me on. Neither child napped at the same time.

As I peeled potatoes over the kitchen sink I prayed, "Lord, where are You this day? Have You forgotten me?" Feeling sorry for myself, I looked out the kitchen window. My eyes rested on the largest rainbow I had ever seen. It seemed to blanket the whole sky with vivid colors as it curved to the ground. Awestruck, I realized that God chose this rainbow to communicate His love to me. I was renewed.

JULIE REYNOLDS

MARCH 6

Search

Receive my words. . . . If thou seekest her as silver, and searchest for her as for hid treasures; then shalt thou understand the fear of the Lord, and find the knowledge of God. Prov. 2:1-5.

Let's go panning for gold today," my husband, Carl, invited. He had just built a sluice box, a device for washing river sand in search of gold. Naturally he was eager to try it out. He took his rusty old gold pans from a box in the garage, and we headed for the Mother Lode area in central California.

I tried my hand at panning for gold, but it takes a lot of patience and know-how, and I'm a little short on both commodities. Every shiny or gold-colored grain of sand appeared to me as a fleck of gold or a nugget. But Carl knew what to look for, and he dumped out my "treasures" by the panful.

Carl has been interested in rocks since he was a little boy. We have gone on many family expeditions to the desert and to the mountains in search of crystals, Lake County diamonds, gold, and a variety of rocks whose names I find hard to pronounce.

He learned early on that I didn't know much about rocks and minerals, and he identified most of the rocks I picked up as "leaverite." Translated, that means "leave 'er right where you found it." Needless to say, I never did find any nuggets or gems!

The Bible is filled with gems more valuable than any gold nuggets, diamonds, or crystals. In His parables, Christ encourages us to diligently dig for its treasures as we would for a treasure hidden in the ground. He further assures us that by deep searching, we will find the treasures He has placed there for us.

The casual reader of the Bible has only a limited knowledge of its contents and, therefore, doesn't recognize its valuable gems. The expert, however, is the person who studies God's Word carefully and prayerfully and probes deeply to find its gems. With a little practice, we can all become expert "gold diggers." MARLENE ANDERSON

MARCH 7

The Words of the Prideful Pharisee

The Pharisee stood and prayed thus with himself, God, I thank thee, that I am not as other men are, extortioners, unjust, adulterers, or even as this publican. Luke 18:11.

Joyce sat in the room of losers, she herself professional, collected, in control. On assignment she was visiting a therapy session for substance abusers, observing with detachment the group dynamics and processes. At her next staff meeting she would share her report with other mental health nurses.

With a frankness born of despair, the participants one by one introduced themselves, sharing briefly their backgrounds and current problems—stories of broken homes, severed relationships, and shattered lives. Intrigued by their tragic tales, Joyce was not prepared when they asked her to introduce herself. Startled, she wondered, *Me? . . . I'm no misfit. I've no problem with alcohol.*

"Yes, me? Sure. I'd be glad to," she said aloud, moving her chair to be part of the circle. "My name is Joyce Lavin. I'm a mental health nurse from nearby Concord. And, well, I've never had anything stronger to drink than a Diet Coke." The group laughed politely.

"Our home, though, has had its share of tension lately." Joyce's voice lost its patronizing tone. "I've just discovered that my son is suicidal." Her voice broke, then she lost control completely, sobbing, embarrassed, yet for the first time aware of her own vulnerability.

Have you had a similar experience in which you went about in almost haughty detachment, having classified yourself as noticeably superior to the rest of humanity, only to have your own vulnerability somehow exposed?

Have you prayed the Pharisee's prayer: "Lord, I thank Thee I am not like other people—drug addicts, child abusers, or check bouncers"? Then has some experience heightened your awareness of your own humanity, making you humbly acknowledge your kinship with sinners, all of whom desperately need a Saviour? You and the drug addict; you and the child abuser; you and the check bouncer?

We must all—everyone who is rich and increased with goods and in need of nothing—we must all learn from the Pharisee's prideful prayer. Maybe we should pray instead the un-Pharisee prayer: "Lord, I thank Thee that I am like other men, and please be merciful to me, a sinner, a member of the sinful human race."

The un-Pharisee prayer—just the prayer for those who think they don't need it! WILMA McCLARTY

MARCH 8

Truth of the Ages

For God so loved the world, that he gave his only begotten Son, that whosoever believeth in him should not perish, but have everlasting life. John 3:16.

*T*he guest theologian completed his exegesis on John the revelator and his apocalyptic warnings. A thunderous applause echoed off the century-old chapel walls. The graduate students of Harvard's School of Theology rose to their feet to honor the aging scholar. The man's profound understanding of the cryptic passages had bedazzled even the most jaded of the religious scholars present.

When the host professor asked the guest speaker if he'd entertain a question-and-answer period, the man agreed. Students from all over the auditorium bounced their most difficult questions of Scripture off the scholar. Flawlessly, he answered each inquiry with the same depth and perception that he had demonstrated during his lecture.

Finally the host professor called a halt to the question-and-answer period. But before he could dismiss the students, a young man, his eyes glassy with cynicism, raised his hand and said, "I'd like to ask the learned doctor one last question." The host granted his request.

"Doctor, you obviously know your scriptures. You have a comprehensive grasp of Greek and Hebrew and the customs of Bible times. Please, in all your years of study, what would you say is the most important truth you've discovered?"

The lecturer didn't answer the young man immediately. Instead he walked over to a grand piano at one side of the platform and played a chord. In a broken, raspy voice, the holder of doctorates in biblical history, Latin, Greek, Hebrew, and Sanskrit sang, "Jesus loves me, this I know, for the Bible tells me so . . ."

When the old man finished the familiar children's hymn, he spoke directly to the questioning student. "All the Ph.D.s in Greek, Latin, or Hebrew; all the advanced studies in homiletics, biblical history, or prophecy are a waste of time if you have not grasped this one simple truth. 'Jesus loves me, this I know.' A truth so simple a child can understand. A truth so profound that it will take you eternity to explore."

Sometimes when I find myself hung up on the meanings of this scripture or that passage, or when I allow myself to get caught up in biblical numbers, dates, and word definitions, I pause to remember the cynical young man's question: "What is the greatest truth?"

And the wise old scholar's answer: "Jesus loves me, this I know . . ." And I am a child again—my peace is restored and my perspective realigned. — KAY D. RIZZO

MARCH 9

Quilt Blocks—The Beginner

Warn those who are idle, encourage the timid, help the weak, be patient with everyone. . . . Try to be kind to each other and to everyone else. 1 Thess. 5:14, 15, NIV.

I heard you're a quilter!"

The enthusiastic voice at my office door startled me. I looked up from the column of budget figures and lists of goals and objectives. Balancing available resources with projects that need them is, at times, intense work. Quilting was far removed from my mind at that moment. Yet there stood one of the hospital volunteers, beaming with anticipation of having found a fellow quilter.

Now, to call me a quilter really stretches the title. I modestly explained that I had made one crib quilt for my great-nephew and a lap cover for my mother in the nursing home. Both creations had been extremely simple by quilters' standards. I hadn't even considered quilting by hand. For the baby quilt, I'd used stitch-in-the-ditch on the sewing machine. Mother's throw I had stitched around the pattern on a printed design.

I can hardly be called a quilter, but I was being greeted as one. I've discovered that a bond exists between quilters, and I was accepted—even at my beginning level. Since then, I've found myself excitedly viewing someone else's projects, studying patterns, and even venturing into a larger project of my own.

Today as I stitch strips together to make my second full-sized strip quilt, I think of these enthusiastic quilting friends. No one criticizes my work. They don't seem to mind that I am a beginner. Rather, they rejoice with me in choices of colors, fabric, patterns, special effects, and the joy of creating. But a thought disturbs me. Is it as easy for a beginning Christian to be accepted and integrated into a community of believers?

No one has scolded me because some of my strips varied a fraction of a fraction of an inch. Instead, they've beamed over the details that were noteworthy. They've also shared their own projects, inspiring me to keep going. I really felt accepted when an accomplished quilter asked to borrow one of my patterns. Isn't this how a new Christian is best encouraged: through sharing and acceptance?

Perhaps my quilting friends have taught me lessons that far surpass the fellowship of quilting. I shall give more attention to love, enthusiasm, and nurture of the beginners I meet along life's spiritual journey. After all, isn't that how God treats me?

BEULAH FERN STEVENS

MARCH 10

Think About Such Things

Finally, brothers, whatever is true, whatever is noble, whatever is right, whatever is pure, whatever is lovely, whatever is admirable—if anything is excellent or praiseworthy—think about such things. Phil. 4:8, NIV.

About 10 days ago my husband and I moved into our first apartment. Once we had carried all the boxes in, I went over to the bedroom window and looked out. They were still there.

When we had come to view the apartment, I was concerned

about the view. I had not been impressed. Our apartment was in the back of the building. The view from our window off to the right was that of beautiful trees beside the walkway that led to the tennis courts and the pool. To the left was the road leading to the loading dock area of the building and the left wing. Between the road and the trees was a sloping, well-kept grassy area. The view would have been fine except for what was below the grass: a concrete area with about four or five large garbage dumpsters. If the garbage truck crew was less than accurate, there might be an occasional spattering of refuse here and there. Not pretty.

I would have preferred a front apartment that looked out onto the parking lot and beyond that onto the busy street that ran beside the plaza. Since I had to settle for a back apartment, then trees or the nicely kept lawn minus the dumpsters would have been fine. But we were locked into a 12-month lease—and stuck with the dumpsters.

So on moving day, here I was at my window hoping for a miracle, but the dumpsters didn't magically disappear. Instead, I realized that I could choose not to look at them. If I looked up and out, I would see only the beautiful trees swaying in the wind or glistening with rain or radiating with sun rays. A few days later I discovered that from a certain position on the patio the dumpsters remained completely hidden from view.

Life is the same way. We can choose to look down and dwell on the negatives, or we can lift our vision to the positive and beautiful. Paul knew of the choices that each of us face day after day, and so the advice he gave to the Philippians rings resoundingly true for us today. "Whatever is lovely . . . think about such things." As you go through today, ask God to help you not to see the dumpsters because you choose the lovely view of the trees.   FAITH HUNTER

MARCH 11

Willow or Evergreen?

Happy is the man who doesn't take advice from the ungodly, who doesn't participate in the ways of wicked men and who doesn't criticize others, but who delights in the law of the Lord and meditates every day on God's word. He will be like a tree planted by a stream which always bears fruit and which will not die in times of drought. Whatever good he does will last forever. Ps. 1:1-3, Clear Word.

I'm most fortunate to live in the "Great Northwest," as we often proudly refer to our area. We are blessed with an abundance of varieties of trees and rain. They don't call Washington the Evergreen State for nothing!

The day after a new rain I like to just sit and look at the trees and inhale the fresh scent of the cedar and pine that grace our street. As I was contemplating this one day, it occurred to me that trees and people are very much alike in some ways.

I've noticed that the willow, while its roots spread deep and wide, seems to often turn its branches in different directions. The branches seem to be reaching for something just beyond its grasp.

The cypress tree, on the other hand, stretches right to the heavens with its branches and keeps its leaves all year long.

Sometimes in my walk with the Lord I'm sure I must appear like the willow, reaching for something just beyond my grasp, turning in all different directions, not always sure of what it is I'm searching for. Peace, perhaps. Reassurance, maybe. Comfort, definitely.

However, I long to be like the evergreen tree—stately, majestic, confident in my journey and where it will take me, always stretching straight up to the heavens, and yet deeply rooted in the strength I receive from Him.

As He prunes my branches through the whisperings of His Holy Spirit and nurtures my heart with His loving kindness, I know there is hope for new growth. And I long to be a living testimony to the fact that the possibility for growth exists within each of us simply because He exists.

CRISS KRAMER

MARCH 12

Starting Over

I have swept away your offenses like a cloud, your sins like the morning mist. Return to me, for I have redeemed you. Isa. 44:22, NIV.

*I*n the beginning there were three of us—God, my husband, and me. We were very much in love. Nothing could keep us apart. Little things and big things and everything in between—we shared it all. But life has a nasty habit of getting in the way of lovers, and life happened to us.

Two children joined our family. They depended on us. It was

natural that their needs got first priority. Where we had once spent long evenings just being with each other, we now fell into bed exhausted.

Then *the* job came along, the sort of job everybody dreams about. It was challenging and rewarding. Lots of career prospects loomed on the horizon, and it paid heaps.

Well, yes, the hours were a bit long. In fact, the job was so demanding that even the children got pushed to one side. And the three-way relationship between God, my husband, and me quietly slipped away and was gone before we noticed.

It was a real jolt to wake up one day and suddenly realize that I was talking to a perfect stranger. I didn't have a clue what my husband thought or believed or wanted. I didn't even know what God wanted anymore. It was a sad time, a difficult time. Because out there, outside the now dead relationship, were other very interesting possibilities . . . for both of us.

Was it possible to rekindle a flame from cold ashes? Did I want to? What would life be like without him anyway? What would life be like without God?

Finally, I reached one simple conclusion. I needed God. Without Him, life wasn't worth living. Then I made a decision. Somehow I had to get that old feeling for my husband back, that sense of rightness and belonging.

I couldn't do it. The old relationship was dead. I won't bore you with all the hard cold details, but we had both changed too much. In the end we had to go back to the beginning and get to know each other all over again.

We're still extremely busy, and life being life, that's never going to change. But things are different now. Instead of spending the evening together, we get up a bit earlier in the morning and talk. Or we'll have lunch with each other. Sometimes we'll get a baby-sitter and go somewhere by ourselves, just the two of us. And God is a part of our lives again.

I was very fortunate. My husband was willing to try again. And God had been there all the time, waiting. And you know something? It's pretty exciting getting to know someone again, especially if that someone used to be your first love. TRUDY RANKIN

Love for One Another

And as ye would that men should do to you, do ye also to them likewise. Luke 6:31.

*I*t has been said that "those who deserve love the least need it the most." We talk a lot about such things as human relations, getting along with one another, inner peace, and joyful living. But it can all really be wrapped up in one word. Undoubtedly, the most difficult and beautiful word in all human language: love. People have sung more songs about it, written more poems about it, and preached more sermons about it than any other topic throughout the ages. Yet few seem to recognize it as the most powerful force in the universe.

I recently heard of a sergeant who ran up against the power of love and has never been the same since. It happened in Egypt. His company had traveled from Malta to Egypt and turned in for the night. Wet and muddy from rain, the men went to bed exhausted.

One private knelt quietly beside his bed to pray. His sergeant took offense to the unusual display of devotion and reached for one of his boots. He struck the man on the side of the head with the rain-soaked, muddy boot. Then he took his other boot and smashed the private on the other side of the face with it. The soldier's face stung. But perhaps worse was the pain of humiliation. Despite such harsh treatment, however, the private continued praying.

It wasn't until after the sergeant went to sleep that the young soldier paid him back. When the officer awoke the next morning, he found his boots beautifully polished and standing neatly beside his bed. As that crusty sergeant told the story, he said, "That was his reply to me, and it just broke my heart."

That was the day the sergeant ran up against love. He received an unexpected and powerful reply, and things have been different for him since then. He's given his life to the cause of love and God, and he has become a radiant example of the power of love.

Let's pray that we will always demonstrate the love of God to everyone with whom we come in contact. GWENDOLYN WARD

MARCH 14

Thank You, Lord

I have never stopped thanking God for you. I pray for you constantly. Eph. 1:16, TLB.

Yes, I know that Paul was talking about his Christian friends at Ephesus, but ever since I met Ira and Janine I've been thinking about this text. Let me introduce them to you. "We've been married for 45 years," Janine said proudly as she patted Ira's knee and smiled. I had met the couple only a few hours earlier, but it was easy to see their affection and consideration for each other.

The next morning they asked me to join them in their worship. They explained that after they read from the devotional book they both prayed, and they invited me to pray first. I was glad I did, because when they finished praying, I had a small lump in my throat. One brief sentence in both prayers caused it.

"And, Lord, thank You for Ira; I love him so much," Janine said.

"Thank You, Lord, for my precious Janine," murmured Ira.

I had never heard that kind of thing in a prayer before. My mind went back to when my husband was alive. We prayed together every day and studied the Bible together. I had thanked the Lord silently for him many times, but to say it aloud where my husband could hear me? But why not?

What is it about human beings that makes us reluctant to praise or be publicly thankful for those who are nearest and dearest to us? Many wives I've met talk only about the weaknesses of their mates, turning these real or imagined faults into entertainment for their friends.

I'm sure that Ira and Janine have had differences of opinion and even arguments over the years, but always there was the underlying note of "I love you." Now, 45 years later, the commitment and joy in marriage was still there.

What about saying "Thank You, Lord," for your spouse, your sister, your mother? Invite the Lord to remind you of their endearing qualities—even if they've just forgotten your birthday!

SANDY ZAUGG

Lord, Make Me a Blessing!

You shall be a blessing. Zech 8:13, NKJV.

Lord, make me a blessing today." My idle prayer sounded memorized, meaningless, methodical. Newly retired, freshly widowed, no experience in solo living, and near tears, I felt more like complaining to my Lord. Three small words would summarize my heartfelt distress: "Nobody needs me!"

Often during my long life I had felt my responsibilities far exceeded my capabilities. But after my pastor-evangelist husband succumbed to a heart attack, our children flew to ports of their own choosing, and young leaders took over the church responsibilities, I felt I had no further reason to live. Nobody needed me.

About 1,500 years before the birth of Jesus in Bethlehem, the 80-year-old shepherd, Moses, faced an opposite situation. From a burning bush, God spoke to him and gave him an assignment. He pleaded inadequacy. And God asked him, "What is that in thine hand?"

"A rod" (Ex. 4:1, 2). A simple shepherd's stick—yet in the hands of faith, God used it to crumble Pharaoh's kingdom and deliver His people from cruel Egyptian bondage.

Now a question plagued me: What did I have that God could use? My limited assets consisted of a modest home, adequate clothing, and food. In addition, I housed similar aches and pains as do others who, by God's grace, have exceeded their allotted lifespan of threescore and 10 years.

I glanced at the typewriter on my desk. As my husband's secretary I had used it extensively. Perhaps God could use it. I prayed, "Lord, make my typewriter a blessing to someone." And that He has. I became bulletin secretary for two churches, joined a local creative writing class, and typed poems, memoirs, and manuscripts for others. Always plenty of typing to keep my fingers busy.

But one morning I turned on my electric typewriter and it refused to purr. I called a repair shop. The expense involved in replacing the broken part would far exceed its worth—and my ability to pay.

Crushed, I took my problem to the Lord in prayer. "You know I have these weekly bulletins to type, plus these manuscripts. Just speak the word, and my typewriter will come alive again. I just know it will." In full faith, I added, "You can do it!"

But He didn't. Instead, when a young businessman heard there would be no more church bulletins, he (I think prompted by heaven) appeared at my doorstep carrying a new IBM Wheelwriter 6 typewriter with memory and fantastic capabilities far exceeding my old one. At no cost to me. A gift.

Truly our God has a thousand ways to answer our prayers. And as I sit here caressing its keys, I'm humbly praying, "Lord, make me and Your typewriter a blessing today."

INAS ZIEGLER

MARCH 16

Before I Called

And it shall come to pass, that before they call, I will answer; and while they are yet speaking, I will hear. Isa. 65:24.

e had received a phone call one morning requesting that we appear at my husband's head office. Quickly we canceled appointments and hastily rearranged schedules. Two hours later we both sat in stunned silence as John's supervisor told him that my husband's pastoral duties would be terminated in two months. Leadership would also have to lay 15 others off because of lack of funds.

All the way home I argued with God.

"Why did You allow me to leave my job as a college teacher to come all the way across the country, only to get sick and then have John lose his job?" I demanded of Him.

"Why did You let him take four long years of training for *this?*

"Why, Lord? You know there are no jobs available in this recession, even for someone who is bilingual."

Our beautiful rental home on the lake would have to go. "Why, God? This was such a peaceful setting for my healing.

"Why? Why? Why?"

Finally I prayed: "Lord, if Your hand is in this mess anywhere, please give me a sign—find us a cheaper rental home." That would be impossible, I was certain. But I didn't care. I was hurt and angry.

We set out for town the following morning. John bought a paper and rummaged through the ads. After placing a few telephone calls, I heard him say, "We need it right away." "We have a kitty." "We do have a lot of furniture." "We can't tell you how long we'll be there." "Great."

Fifteen minutes later we drove down the little country lane. On the hillside a long, cedar-sided home stood guard over a romantic, tree-shrouded lake. Humiliation and awe flooded simultaneously across my consciousness.

The landlords were friendly. Even though they were particular about their tenants, they had accepted our request without hesitation. Three weeks later willing church members helped us pack and relocate. By the next morning I was pounding nails and hanging pictures.

"How long will we be here, Lord?" I mused. "What does our future hold? At least John's unemployment insurance will pay this rent." A ringing phone interrupted my thoughts. John's boss just wanted to let us know that the layoff had been canceled. The employees had agreed to take a pay cut. I wasn't sure whether to laugh or cry.

That spring we planted a large garden and explored the surrounding territory. We enjoyed the morning mists and evening sunsets on the tranquil water. And we saved enough money to take a coveted vacation to the Gaspé Peninsula.

I will never forget how God answered my prayer before I even called.

DAWNA BEAUSOLEIL

MARCH 17

Little Words of Wisdom

But the Comforter, which is the Holy Ghost, whom the Father will send in my name, he shall teach you all things, and bring all things to your remembrance, whatsoever I have said unto you. John 14:26.

One morning when I was so discouraged that I could barely face the day, I read Psalm 116:1: "I love the Lord, because he hath heard my voice." As I was reading, I heard it! A small child's voice repeated the verse over and over, emphasizing the words strongly. "I LOVE da LORD, because he hat HEARD MY VOICE!" I realized that I was remembering the voice of our daughter, Sandy, when she was only 2. She had always enjoyed saying that verse. "He heard me!" she would say, as if there was no mistake about it. Sandy is now 37, but it amazed me that the incident came back to me so clearly that morning—like a blanket of comfort from the past.

God has promised that when we memorize Scripture, it will come back to us when we need it. He'll write it in our hearts and minds.

The same thing happened to my sister one day when she was in the depths of despair. To take her mind off things, she went to a local sale, and on the bargain table she spotted a bright green greeting card, her son's favorite color. On the card was this verse: "For he shall give his angels charge over thee" (Ps. 91:11). Then she heard it too! Her son Michael's voice at the age of 3 repeating the passage. "He shall give his angels CHARGE over thee." "CHARGE!" he had exclaimed, as if a whole army of angels stood poised, ready to attack the enemy. Tears came, and she bought the card, reflecting on how that verse had returned in her hour of greatest need. Michael, now 20, chuckled when she reminded him of his memory verse. At Christmas she gave him the card and asked him to keep it someplace where he would always be able to find it.

How wonderful that Bible texts make such strong impressions on children. They quote their verses with such gladness, placing emphasis upon certain words. God brings those verses back to both parent and child with forceful remembrance at a time when they are most needed. How good it would be if we would read Scripture with a child's enthusiasm every day. — DARLENE BURGESON

MARCH 18

"No Wheelchairs, Mom!"

Then wolves will live in peace with lambs. And leopards will lie down to rest with goats. Calves, lions and young bulls will eat together. And a little child will lead them. Isa. 11:6, EB.

Her name was Melody, and she stole our hearts immediately. She came to live with us the day before her seventh birthday, and her cooperative manner and quick smile was a joy from the beginning. Being licensed foster parents had proven to be interesting to say the least. After a hyperactive 9-year-old, two fighting brothers, and a stream of teenagers, I watched Melody with anticipation that first night to get a clue as to what our new "foster family" might be like.

As I observed her voraciously gobbling her brussels sprouts, I knew I had it made. She wasn't a picky eater! "Thank You, Lord," I breathed as my mind danced with memories of children who refused to eat anything that remotely resembled a vegetable.

The caseworker said that Melody had an IQ of 51. Educable mentally disabled, they called her. Unsure as to whether her disability was physiological or from years of neglect, we set out to nurture this new little one that God had sent to our home. Melody had never had the opportunity to learn the social graces, so we began teaching her the basics: using the commode, brushing her teeth, dressing properly, and not eating with her hands.

A few weeks later my husband sat in the waiting room of the dentist office while she went in to have many teeth extracted. Anxiety built as he imagined the trauma of her first dentist visit. But all concern vanished as Melody emerged, toy in one hand, new toothbrush in the other, mouth full of gauze, and her usual big smile on her face. She spent weeks showing everyone the holes in her mouth.

Melody enjoyed learning. It was a delight to watch her develop and thrive. The wheelchair that I use fascinated her, and she was always showing me off. But my favorite time was when we talked to her about God. She loved to hear about heaven, and I would have her repeat what I told her so I could make sure she understood what I was saying. As she would tell her part of the story, she would describe lions that don't bite, gold streets, and people who never cry.

One night after telling her a heaven story, I asked, "Melody, what else is heaven going to be like?" Jumping up with face aglow, she pointed her finger at me and cried, "No wheelchairs, Mom! No wheelchairs!" She flung herself into my arms as if it were her own personal victory. I held her close as we made a pact to meet in heaven someday and run a race together.

Three and a half years later with an IQ testing out at 69, Melody left our home and foster care forever. She began a new life with an adoptive family who had committed to help her and her three brothers.

O my Father, help me to trust You faithfully. I have a promised race to run.   JOAN BOVA

MARCH 19

A Strong Tree Planted by a River

Happy is the person who doesn't listen to the wicked. . . . [She] loves the Lord's teachings. [She] thinks about those teachings day and night. [She] is strong, like a tree planted by a river. Ps. 1:1-3, EB.

Grandma Laura derived her source of happiness from a trusting relationship with her God. She took comfort in Christ as her shepherd so beautifully portrayed in Psalm 23. Life was not always easy for her. She lost an infant son, had a home and all her possessions destroyed by fire, had to adjust to a debilitating illness, and put four children through college during the Depression years. But such things just sent her running to her source of security and strength, to her divine, benevolent Shepherd. Every trial was a call for her to remind us of her constant faith in God's promise that "all things work together for good to those that love God" (Rom. 8:28).

Last January I preached the funeral sermon for Grandma Laura. She was 92 when she died. Her life had greatly inspired her friends and family. It has been said that "the true measure of a person is not known until the tree is felled." And so it seemed to us.

I thought about how my grandmother's deep trust in God nourished the roots of my own spirituality. Glimpses of "God with skin on" such as my grandmother provided bring a knot in my throat and a feeling of awe in my heart. Roots! May mine and yours grow deeply, watered from the same source from which Grandma Laura's roots drew their strength. SHARI CHAMBERLAIN

MARCH 20

Looking Out My Window

Now learn a parable of the fig tree; When his branch is yet tender, and putteth forth leaves, ye know that summer is nigh: So likewise ye, when ye shall see all these things, know that it is near, even at the doors. Matt. 24:32, 33.

Looking out my window, I thanked God for allowing me to awaken to behold the beginning of another spring, my favorite season. I noticed the little crocuses planted a few years ago. Some peonies were in bloom. Double strawberry bushes with their lovely saucer-shaped white flowers had burst forth into bloom. They would sprout red berries for the birds to feed on. Soon the privet hedge will blossom with delicate lacy clusters of sweet-smelling flowers. I'll make a healthful tea for my husband with some tree leaves.

Although it has been a hard winter, God has been marvelous in His natural world. Through my window I have viewed cardinals, blue jays, doves in pairs, small flocks of chickadees, purple finches and the titmouse, the noisy crows and woodpeckers usually heard before seen, and the sparrow that the eye of God is always upon.

As spring approaches, I especially watch the coral bells plant.

Each year its panicles shoot up from heart-shaped leaves, and when the flowers open, the hummingbird appears. It is always a joyous occasion that I find myself comparing to the return of our Lord.

The scene has been set. It has been a long and hard winter in this world. But the signs appearing, like the blossoms outside my window, foretell that He will soon come. Oh, I must be ready! My life must be as fragrant as the lily of the valley, for His coming will far, far eclipse that of the hummingbird. What a grand and glorious appearing that will be!

Be sure you are ready too, for "spring" is drawing near!

ARLENE BRATHWAITE

MARCH 21

The Visit

Behold, I stand at the door and knock; if anyone hears My voice and opens the door, I will come in to him, and dine with him, and he with Me. Rev. 3:20, NASB.

I raised my fist to knock on the door. Anxiety overwhelmed me. For six years I had worked in familiar territory—the hospital had been my home ground. I knew well where to find things, those people I could contact and rely on, what type of patients to expect, and what I could do to assist them. But here I was embarking on a new mission in an unknown land. With one knock I would face my first home health care patient. I would be expected to enter the patient's own turf. Somehow I felt like an intruder. No longer would the familiar equipment and surroundings of the hospital aid me in my work. I would go it alone.

As I knocked I held my breath. A small man in his 70s answered the door. His smile could light up any dark night. "Come in," he said, opening the door wide. "We are so happy you're here." He ushered me back to the bedroom where his wife waited for her dressing change and blood pressure check. "Can I get you a drink?" the man asked. He showed me where they kept the supplies, assisting and directing me as to what should happen next throughout the procedure. His wife had been ill for quite some time, and he knew every move needed to care for her. The entire visit continued in the same vein as the couple made me feel like an honored guest instead of an intruder. I left their home feeling secure in my new role. I had been received with open arms and hearts.

Life brings many opportunities knocking on our door. It is up to us to choose which of them we deem as important. But most important of all, Jesus stands knocking and waiting for an invitation into our lives and hearts. We must each decide how we will receive Him. Will we make Him feel like an intruder or an honored guest?

Luke 12:36 tells us: "And be like men who are waiting for their master when he returns from the wedding feast, so that they may immediately open the door to him when he comes and knocks" (NASB).

CAREL CLAY

MARCH 22

Loneliness

I have learned the secret of being content in any and every situation. Phil. 4:12, NIV.

*L*onely. We've all been there. For me, the clouds gathered when we moved into the "real world" after enjoying the bustle and friendships of four years of college and two of graduate school. Though I was part of a pastoral ministry to a warm church, some days the soggy showers of loneliness engulfed me. No longer were close friends down the hall or across the street. To reach out and touch was definitely long distance. And day-to-day sharing found itself reduced to monthly reports of how things had been.

As humans we were created with a need to belong, to be loved, and to be cared for on a personal level. A move uproots us from all that is familiar. Not only must we find a new grocery store, another bank, and the closest mall, but new friends as well. Church members and coworkers may be friendly, but it takes time to develop those close friendships in which you can take off your mask and be open and vulnerable.

During those lonely showers after our move, I finally discovered what would part the clouds and let sunshine in. I learned, like Paul, "the secret of being content in any and every situation." Each of us has an emotional cup within us that longs to be filled with love. But who fills your cup? If we depend on friends to fill it, we may have times when our tears drop into the bottom of an empty cup. Friends are not always available when we need them. They may be busy, tired, or inattentive. No person can meet our needs 100 percent of the time. Then how can we keep our "love cup" filled?

"The Lord is my shepherd, I shall not be in want. . . . My cup overflows" (Ps. 23:1-5, NIV). The Lord is the only one who can keep our cup full. If we let Him, He will even fill it to overflowing. Although this insight wasn't entirely new to me, it penetrated deeper this time. I realized that to be content at all times in any situation, Jesus must fill my love cup to the brim. Then I am never empty, and the friends the Lord blesses me with are the delightful froth topping my cup.

When Jesus was here on earth He also knew this secret of contentment. He had moved far away from His familiar surroundings. And though He had a few friends among the thousands of wonder-seekers that followed Him, they failed Him in His time of greatest need. That is why it had always been His habit to rise early and seek a solitary place to have the only One who is always available, ever attentive, and able to do so, to fill His love cup. And He will do the same for us.

What a burst of sunshine it was in my lonely, soggy night!

HEIDE FORD

MARCH 23

You Know!

As I have loved you, so you must love one another. John 13:34, NIV.

*Y*ou know?" That irritating little phrase bombards me in so many conversations. It seems that some feel they must remind me in every sentence that "you know." Maybe what they really mean to say is "you don't know, so I will tell you." It's like a grain of sand in my shoe. Pretty soon all I can feel is the rock in my shoe, and I must get rid of it somehow, anyway possible. So the words "you know" grate on my nerves until all I hear the person saying is "you know." This phrase drowns out everything he or she is trying to tell me.

I like much better the way God says "you know." He reminds me in 66 books that—"you know"—He loves me over and over in many different ways, in many stories. Again and again He lets me know just how much He really cares, as if I were the only one that really matters. Yet the message also comes through loud and clear that we all are very special to Him, and we should treat each other that way too.

Besides the 66 books, He encapsulates His love for us into 10 glorious "you know"s, explaining 10 different ways that He cares for me. Ten guides to be my help. Ten standards to live by. Ten ways for me to know Him better. Ten ways for me to have good relations with others I like and even those I don't like. Then He is even gracious enough to condense these into just two "you know"s that say everything we need to know about how to live.

But amazingly, He doesn't stop with just the two! He continues to boil those down into just one! Very simple, so anyone can get it. No big words. No excuses. "As much as I have loved you, so you must love one another."

God reminds me that He loves and knows all about me and wants me to love and know much, much more about Him.   PEGGY HARRIS

MARCH 24

Welcome Home!

In my Father's house are many rooms; if it were not so, would I have told you that I go to prepare a place for you? John 14:2, RSV.

When I was a young teen, my mother had to stay in the hospital for several days. I stayed with my grandmother and left my father to fend for himself, something he had not done since his bachelor days. Knowing how fussy Mother was about things being tidy, I imagined she would be rather upset at the state of the house when she returned.

I got home an hour before she did, and I found the entire household a beehive of activity. Everywhere I looked a girl was cleaning. All my friends from the neighborhood showed up to help in the effort. The dishes were washed, linen was changed, and floors were mopped. Other neighbors brought casseroles and cakes. Fresh flowers decorated every room. Instead of the messy house she had expected, Mother came home to a house that was "company clean."

It's always more fun to prepare our home for friends and loved ones than it is for company that we don't know. We know our friends' favorite dishes and other things that make them happy.

Although we may wonder what sort of place our heavenly home will be, we needn't worry about the accommodations. A Friend is preparing for our homecoming. Jesus knows what will make us happiest, and we know that He will have everything "company clean" for us. He eagerly waits to welcome us to our new home. I can't wait!

GINA LEE

A Dying Man's Smile

And ye shall be sorrowful, but your sorrow shall be turned into joy. John 16:20.

While doing a residency as a hospital chaplain, I ministered to a dying man and his family. His wife, daughter, and son stood at his bedside. I talked about the unconditional love of Jesus, His presence and personal involvement in the life of the patient and other members of his family. Then I suggested that each one talk about the special moments they had experienced with the patient, and they did so with deep emotion.

The love of Jesus and the thought of eternal life with Him when He comes again were meaningful to them. We repeated the shepherd's psalm, and I spoke of the glory of the resurrection and the reality of being united with loved ones again, never to part.

What happened next amazed me. Until this point the patient had been unresponsive. His vital signs were falling, and the nurses expected him to die that evening. But as I lifted up the name of Jesus, this dying man turned his head and gave us a big smile. Can you imagine the joy that filled his wife and the rest of the family?

We all returned his smile, which turned into a joyful laugh. Then we hugged, and cried together. Although the patient closed his eyes and was unresponsive again, he gradually gained consciousness, and finally died peacefully after seven days. The family's faith was strengthened, and they gave thanks to God.

A dying man smiled, and how I pray that this smile will be contagious through me as I continue to minister in the name of Jesus to the sick. There will be many smiles when Jesus bursts through that eastern horizon. And we will see the glory of His smile, too.

GLORIA MCLAREN

Roll Out With Your Right Clothes On

Be strong in the Lord, and in the power of his might. Put on the whole armor of God, that ye may be able to stand against the wiles of the devil. Eph. 6:10, 11.

*I*n my youth, when I picked cotton or blackberries in the sunbaked fields of Alabama, or worked the corn and pea fields, somehow I couldn't imagine myself doing it in my finest formal attire of evening wear!

One of my father's favorite "get the kids out of bed" bugle calls was "Roll out with your right clothes on!" All of us knew exactly what he meant.

We still need to put the "right clothes" on. Have you ever experienced a situation in which you found yourself either overdressed or underdressed for an occasion, on which you felt that you weren't wearing the "right clothes"? Depending on the situation, you may not have been able to carry out the duties required of you, or at the very least, you felt embarrassed and out of place, especially since all eyes were on you and all jokes were directed at you.

Whether we realize it or not, most of us have been taught how to clothe ourselves with the correct apparel for various occasions or events. The "right clothes" are for our own good. Can you imagine a scuba diver jumping into the ocean in a policeman's uniform, or an astronaut gearing up in a baker's attire and blasting off into space?

As Christians our task is to be active and victorious participants in a spiritual warfare. Ephesians 6:10-18 admonishes us to "put on the whole armor of God" because God's armor makes up the "right clothes" for our spiritual fight. It prepares us both inwardly and outwardly to subdue and conquer the enemy.

Jesus is gently calling each of us, saying, "It is high time to awake out of sleep" (Rom. 13:11). He wants us to "roll out" with our loins girded with the gospel of truth, our breast plated with righteousness, our feet shod with the preparation of the gospel of peace, the shield of faith ever before us, the helmet of salvation crowning our heads, the sword of the Spirit as our weapon, and finally, that we always wear a spiritual attitude of unceasing prayer and perseverance.

So when it comes to the most important task of our lives, that of seeking the kingdom of God and His righteousness (Matt. 6:33), it behooves us to "roll out with our right clothes on"!

TERESA MUSSON

The Sky Above

Unto thee lift I up mine eyes, O thou that dwellest in the heavens. Ps. 123:1.

*H*urricane Andrew had struck Miami, Florida, with full force. My church asked me, as a trained disaster worker, to fly to Miami to help in the aftermath of the terrible storm. The plane took off from the Connecticut airport on a deeply overcast day. Everything was gray and drab, and as we prepared to take off, it began to rain heavily. Settling back in my seat, I thought of the victims of this hurricane and became depressed.

In a short time after takeoff we climbed to more than 20,000 feet. As we rose above the earth, it vanished under the deep blanket of gray fog below us. Suddenly I saw the sky over us—clear and incredibly blue. The sun was shining brilliantly, and below us, what had been an impenetrable gray was now fleecy, billowy white, like giant snowdrifts.

My spirits soared, and I thought about how often we become so enveloped in earthly cares and duties that we cannot see God. All seems dark and dreary. We feel hopeless. But it is at those times we must climb higher spiritually above the surrounding gloom, and then we, too, can bask in the sunlight of His glorious love, wrapped in the soft clouds of His care.   PAM CARUSO

Star Light! Star Bright!

Do all things without murmuring and arguing so that you may be blameless and innocent, children of God without blemish in the midst of a crooked and perverse generation, in which you shine like stars in the world. Phil. 2:14, 15, NRSV.

*I*ncreased age leaves only a few childhood wonders untarnished. The night sky is an elite member of these few wonders. Who of us no longer gazes with awe into the twinkling face of darkness? Even knowing that there are 200 billion stars and that the fastest jet would take a million years to fly to the nearest star other than the sun cannot dampen our amazement when a crystalline night beckons our eyes upward.

Did the apostle Paul feel the same way so many of us do? Is that why he compared Christians "in the midst of a . . . perverse generation" to stars shining in the night? Exactly how are Christians like stars?

First of all, stars help pilots and sailors find their way. For example, the North Star guides a traveler northward because this star always appears to be in the same place over the North Pole. Likewise, Christians "in the midst of a crooked generation" can direct people Christward. Their loving attitudes and generous deeds reflect Christ, who is always there for us.

We can also compare a star's energy source to the Christian's energy source. A star's energy source lies deep within itself. Hydrogen nuclei change into helium nuclei through a process called nuclear fusion. During this process, the helium produced does not equal the hydrogen used. Some of the material that makes up the original hydrogen changes into energy rather than helium. The Christian's energy source is the Holy Spirit deeply rooted in the heart and mind. As a result of our invitation for Him to live in our lives, the Holy Spirit changes us through a process called the new birth (Titus 3:4-6; John 3:1-21. Thus we become "blameless and innocent" of sin and receive the energy, so to speak, to "do what is true" (John 3:21). We are enabled to live "without murmuring and arguing."

Finally, Christians are like stars in that even though stars seem small, they are actually huge. The sun is only a medium-sized star, but its diameter is more than 100 times the earth's diameter. Likewise, to the unconverted, Christians appear small and frail. Yet in reality, our Energy Source endows us with superhuman strength to be "children of God without blemish," shining against the gloom of sin like stars against the velvet night.

Christ has commissioned us to shine like the stars. "Ye are the light of the world. . . . Let your light so shine before men, that they may see our good works, and glorify your Father which is in heaven" (Matt. 5:14-16). In the night of spiritual darkness God's glory is to shine forth through His children by encouraging the discouraged and comforting those that mourn.   LYNDELLE CHIOMENTI

Walking in the Shadows

Yea, though I walk through the valley of the shadow of death, I
will fear no evil: for thou art with me. Ps. 23:4.

*W*hen I was a little girl, I suffered from chronic earaches, and
can still feel the pain and fear. Usually the attacks came in
the early hours of the morning. I can remember my father
picking me up in his arms and gently rocking me. With his not-
quite-in-tune voice he would sing the chorus of "Standing
Somewhere in the Shadows, You'll Find Jesus."

The words of that song have stuck with me and, strangely, I
don't associate them with pain or fear. Instead, they fill me with incredible love and security. Once again I find myself being held in
the arms of a caring father until the pain subsides and I can sleep
again, at peace in the shadowy time before the dawn.

I have often wondered about life's shadows, and usually I have
been afraid. Afraid of the pain of an almost breaking heart. Afraid of
failure as a parent. Afraid of failure as a daughter of God. I have been
afraid of tomorrow and have ached for comfort.

David, in the twenty-third psalm, refers to the shadowy times
and places when he says, "Yea, though I walk through the valley of
the shadow of death, I will fear no evil." He obviously knew the
same kinds of fears and pain and the need for comfort that I have
experienced, because he described just what I feel—just what I fear.

And then, in that shadowy time when I walk through the valley,
I call out to my heavenly Father. I ask Him for peace and the
strength to bear the ache. Now I ask for remembrance so I will not
forget the words of the songs I learned as a child. The One they are
about is there in the stillness.

Then He speaks to me and reminds me that although the walk
is through the valley of the shadow, it doesn't end there. Beyond the
valley, He lifts me in His arms so that I can gaze upon the hills. He
promises that I can soar like the eagle and be with Him.

ADELLE ROCHFORD

Whom Shall I Fear?

Behold, all they that were incensed against thee shall be ashamed and confounded: they shall be as nothing; and they that strive with thee shall perish. Isa. 41:11.

I pushed the iron back and forth on my son's playsuit, but I didn't see the bright design or cheery colors. Instead, I saw the contorted face and wagging finger of the man confronting my young husband. I heard his angry voice, "Pastor, you won't get by with this. Your conference president will hear from me before another day is done!"

A situation had arisen in my husband's church. He had tried his best to give counsel in a way that would not take sides, but both sides misunderstood and misrepresented him. Now he was being threatened and hammered by criticism.

A hard lump pressed against my throat, and tears welled up in my eyes. I swallowed hard and blinked. Then at that moment I saw something in memory: my mother, her hair pinned up behind her ears, mop in hand, singing. I heard the words again: "The Lord is my light, my strength and my salvation; whom, then, shall I fear? Whom, then, shall I fear?"

The songs Mother sang were songs of experience. She had been raised in Australia and pampered by a showman father. Life in Canada was vastly different from her easy life in Melbourne. In place of balmy sea breezes, she endured winds fresh from the north pole, whistling and whining around our house. My father was frequently gone on business, leaving her alone much of the time to raise four small children.

Her clear, mezzo-soprano voice had chased away many childish fears while I was struggling to grow up. Now memory brought it back again, and it filled my mind with a childlike trust in my heavenly Father. "Even though a host of men rose up against us," the words came soft and clear, "yet shall not my heart be afraid." Peace flooded my heart. I finished the ironing and had just put the clothes away when my husband came in the door with good news. The situation had been resolved.

Songs my mother sang have often come to soothe my fears and help me regain faith in God's goodness and love. God had blessed her with a beautiful voice. She had won awards on the stage in Edmonton and Calgary and was in constant demand for solos in both community and church events. But she did not reserve her voice just for those special occasions. She sang during the daily problems and humdrum tasks at home. While she thought she was singing to herself, she was impressing and molding small minds to trust in God and not be afraid. Those songs came straight from her heart. They remain in my heart even today.   ELLIE LUKENS CALKINS

MARCH 31

Pressed Pajamas and Ironed Sheets

Making the very most of the time—buying up each opportunity—because the days are evil. Eph. 5:16, Amplified.

My friend Carol irons her pajamas, pillowcases, and sheets. She explained to me that the items look neater when pressed, and they fit nicely in her drawers. Her closets are immaculate, and she can tell where every item is. I don't know whether to smile to myself or envy her, although I wish that my drawers and shelves looked as neat as hers. She is a detail-oriented person. Obviously I am not.

Through the years, as a working mother and wife of a pastor/evangelist, I struggled with this thing called time and how to use it wisely. But I've come to the conclusion that I can't keep everything at home in tip-top shape and work full-time in public ministry with my husband. I do good to *wash* my linens, let alone *iron* them.

Rushing isn't the answer, either. I can't imagine Jesus frantically running from one person to another, healing them, preaching to them, and then dashing off to another appointment. He took time with people and was never hurried in spite of the fact that He had little more than three years of public ministry.

So I searched the Bible and other books by Christian writers on the topic of time. What is important and what is not? I found this quote by one of my favorite authors, Ellen G. White. "If every moment were valued and rightly employed, we should have time for everything that we need to do for ourselves or for the world" (*Messages to Young People*, p. 322).

The key word here is "need." While I'm not condemning Carol, my pajamas don't *need* to be ironed. I don't lie awake at night worrying over the neatness of my drawers, though my husband may wish that I did, and Carol's husband may wish that she didn't! Our personalities and backgrounds are different. I am a people person. Carol is a quiet, working-behind-the-scenes type of woman.

Yes, I need to be better organized because organization saves time. But we all should avoid extremes. Even neatness should be kept in proper perspective. All activities must be balanced. Sometimes it's more important for me to order my own life so that I may be a better influence on a neighbor.

Certain things are essential. I do need to spend time with Jesus, to do my part in telling others about His love and mercy. I need to use my talents wisely and improve them. And I need to be all that I can be as a daughter of the King. I now pray daily that God will direct my activities every moment of every day.   CRYSTAL EARNHARDT

APRIL 1

The Nettle and the Dock Weed

And now just as you trusted Christ to save you, trust him, too, for each day's problems; live in vital union with him. Let your roots grow down into him and draw up nourishment from him. Col. 2:6, 7, TLB.

My husband and I had just begun a week's walking tour in Yorkshire, England, along with a dozen other hikers. Following the ancient stone walls across folded green velvet hills, clamoring over wooden stiles, and breathing in the early spring air made us feel invincible. This was living!

Our leader, Malcolm, stopped abruptly by an innocent-looking clump of weeds as we entered another farmer's field. "Watch out for these nettles," he warned. "They look deceptively mild, but their capacity for prolonged stinging and itching is no joke. You folks with shorts need to be especially careful." We all eyed the culprit warily and stepped widely around it.

As we continued our hike, the sight of newborn lambs wobbling around on matchstick legs entertained us city dwellers. Suddenly my husband, Bryan, gave a yelp and slapped his calf. He was the first victim of the stinging nettle. Malcolm came over quickly and looked sharply around the area of the nettle clump. Smiling, he plucked a nondescript plant and called the group over.

"Please observe nature's antidote for nettle poisoning," he instructed us cheerily. "This is called 'dock weed,' and it grows around nettles. If you pick it quickly and rub the saplike substance on the nettle wound, your discomfort vanishes."

We all watched as Malcolm rubbed the sticky plant on Bryan's fiery leg welt. Sure enough, within 30 seconds the swelling had subsided as well as the pain and itching. My husband continued the walk with no ill effect. We all marveled at how these two bits of weed grew in close proximity—the hurtful and the healer.

That evening in our room, Bryan and I mused on the parallel between this dichotomy in nature and a similar one in our daily lives. We are constantly beset with the stings of Satan's temptations and the pain of human sorrow. But close by, never more than a prayer away, awaits an antidote to the human condition—peace and comfort from a loving God. Our job is to avail ourselves of the pain reliever quickly, rather than waiting for the hurt to fester and swell.

As a favorite Christian author put it: "In every trial, if we seek Him, Christ will give us help. Our eyes will be open to discern the healing promises recorded in His Word. The Holy Spirit will teach us how to appropriate every blessing that will be an antidote to grief. For every bitter draft that is placed to our lips, we shall find a branch of healing" (*The Ministry of Healing*, p. 248). CAROLE BRECKENRIDGE

APRIL 2

Remember the Barnacle Geese

Be self-controlled and alert. Your enemy the devil prowls around like a roaring lion looking for someone to devour. Resist him, standing firm in the faith, because you know that your brothers throughout the world are undergoing the same kind of sufferings. 1 Peter 5:8, 9, NIV.

*B*arnacle geese migrate each summer from the waters of Ireland and Scotland to the arctic regions of Greenland. Summers are short in the Arctic, so the birds waste no time finding a spot on the high rocky cliffs overlooking the sea. Here, each pair of geese begin their family, usually with four healthy goslings. However, their fortress nest soon becomes a dangerous place for the newly hatched young.

Adult geese cannot bring food to their young, as most birds do. Goslings have to feed themselves. But there is nothing to eat in a nesting area several hundred feet up, clinging to the side of a rock. So within the first day or two, these babies must make a life-or-death journey, beginning with a literal leap of faith.

Following their parents' lead, the day-old goslings step off into the air and attempt to navigate a 300-foot free fall, relying on their big feet and fluffy down to slow their descent and cushion the impact as they crash-land among the big rocks below. Only about half survive this fall, but if they don't take the leap, they have no chance at all.

Those who live through this incredible "flight" must immediately begin running the half-mile gauntlet to the sea over a rock-strewn, crevice-hidden beach, avoiding arctic foxes, gulls, and other predators who would have tender young goose for a meal. It seems a miracle that any at all survive. But many make it to the water and life. The parent-geese hover and encourage, group them together, and guide their steps, all the while watching for danger and fiercely protecting them when necessary.

Satan, like a hungry arctic fox, is just waiting for us to crash-land on the rocks. He is a devouring, gorging predator who would have us for lunch. You may be a bit bruised and hurting, but don't give up. Listen to the heavenly Father's encouragement. Stay with the group. Let your steps be guided by the One who knows the dangers and the shortest route to safety. He will fiercely protect you whenever necessary.

So when it seems you are surrounded by spiritual enemies on every side and destruction is certain, remember the barnacle geese.

DELILAH BRIGGS

APRIL 3

Goodbyes

He will wipe every tear from their eyes. There will be no more death or mourning or crying or pain, for the old order of things has passed away. Rev. 21:4, NIV.

J have always felt that goodbye has to be the saddest word in the vocabulary. Whether parting from someone for a brief moment or forever in death, it means separation. I have always been a sentimental person. My greatest desire was to have every one of my children, family, and friends clustered close around me. But, as for almost everyone else, this has not been so.

I remember one time several years ago leading a youth discussion group in church. Everyone was asked to give an impromptu answer to what would be special about heaven. It had to be something other than the experience of meeting Jesus. Without hesitation, I responded, "I will never have to tell anyone goodbye again."

Not long before, I had had to make a move across country, far away from family and friends. I had also left a child in school in Arkansas and another in California. Now I lived for the times we could have them back home for brief weekends. Their visits were short, and it seemed I'd spend the rest of my life looking forward to the family being together again, only to have to quickly say goodbye again.

Also, I marked time until the once-a-year vacation would arrive so that we could go back to see our parents. But then would come the tearful goodbyes. Each time I knew that with God's grace and protection, I would see them again. But love does not tolerate separation.

Jesus' disciples felt this loneliness when before His ascension He blessed them. He gave them the assurance that though He was leaving them, He would return and take them, and each of us also, to be with Himself (John 14:1-3). And in heaven, we are assured there will be no more goodbyes, for separation from loved ones will never happen again. BARBARA SMITH MORRIS

APRIL 4

Making the Switch

Taste and see that the Lord is good; blessed is the man who takes refuge in him. Ps. 34:8, NIV.

few days ago when I phoned my mother, she mentioned that she had been planning to call me. Then she said, "I don't know if I can dial '1' anyway." In the United States, dialing "1" before a telephone number is the access that many long-distance companies use to allow customers to make a long-distance call.

"Why?" I inquired curiously. "Is your long-distance service cut off?"

"No," she replied matter-of-factly. "I'm switching back to AT&T."

I laughed as I considered my mother's history with the long-distance phone companies. Just a few months before, she had changed long-distance companies because one company had written to her and offered her a free month of weekend long-distance calling if she would join them. So she made the switch.

Now after a few months her original company had written, offering her a $50 check toward her next bill if she would transfer back. So she was making the switch. "After all," she told me, "am I bound to any of them? Whichever one has the best offer, that's the one I'm going with."

While I applaud my mother's business savvy, it occurred to me that unfortunately many of us treat our spiritual lives the way my mother treats long-distance companies. When we first accept Christ, He is everything to us, but by and by the devil comes along with a seemingly more attractive offer. He promises fame, riches, total satisfaction in relationships, and more if we would make the switch. Many of us do, and after months, maybe years, of broken dreams, Jesus' offer again seems attractive to us. So we transfer back.

Unlike switching long-distance companies, switching Lords in our lives can be fatal. Jesus invites us to taste and see that He is good and to take refuge in Him. Once we really get to know Him, we'll lose our desire to make the change. FAITH HUNTER

APRIL 5

With Christ in Gethsemane

Then all the disciples forsook him, and fled. Matt. 26:56.

*D*ear Saviour, if I'd been with You in old Gethsemane,
I would have stayed awake that night and shared Your agony.
I would have prayed while You poured out your soul in grief to God,
And knelt right there beside You, as Your blood-sweat washed the sod.

I would have tucked my cloak around You—with my tears, consoled;
That cup that trembled in Your hand, I'd beg to help You hold.
The burden of this sinful world lay crushing on Your heart;
How eagerly I would have asked to bear a measured part!

The tempter urged You to refuse the potion You must drink.
He knew how much the Father's separation made You shrink!

The watching angels longed to intervene with heavenly
    power;
But friends You loved lay sleeping. Sleeping in that trying
    hour!

Mob footsteps boldly tramped into that garden place of
    prayer,
Then rushed You through the streets! But no disciple
    paused to share
Your agony; in haste they all forsook, and fled in fright.
And You—the Saviour of the world—were left alone
    that night!

John found a corner near You in Caiaphas' palace hall,
And Peter soon gained entrance, but he seemed not to
    recall
That he had ever known You—till the cock crowed
    once, then twice;
And Judas—in remorse—burst in with his betrayal price.

I wish I could have been there! Oh, I know I would have
    stayed
Beside You when that piercing crown of thorns Your
    head arrayed.
I would have sponged the gashes on Your brow and
    smoothed the strands
Of bloodstained hair, not left You as You suffered at
    their hands.

But now, in silent horror—in remorseful disbelief
I realize my guilt, and weep in overwhelming grief!
How oft' I sleep when You would bid me rise and kneel
    to pray.
Like Peter, I deny You—turn and go my stubborn way.

For less than 30 pieces I've betrayed You! Now I see
I, too, forsake You—like they did in dark Gethsemane.
But now Your loving presence cloaks me—warms my
    heart of pain;
Relieves my anguished soul and takes away the guilty
    stain.
I pray that You will no more find me sleeping at my post,
Or with life's nonessential duties ever be engrossed.
I pray the cock will never crow because I have denied

Your name, dear Saviour. Keep me near! I must stay by
    Your side.

May Your sweet Spirit each new day ignite my love again;
Change me, like those disciples who became converted
    men.
This one desire consumes my heart—to share with all I
    see,
The beauty of Your sacrifice—and what it's done for me!

Lorraine Hudgins

APRIL 6

The Precious Blood of Jesus

For you know that it was not with perishable things such as silver
or gold that you were redeemed from the empty way of life handed
down to you from your forefathers, but with the precious blood of
Christ, a lamb without blemish or defect. 1 Peter 1:18, 19, NIV.

*W*e need your type," said the voice on the phone. "Can you
come in soon to donate?" Thus late one afternoon I went to
the blood center where preliminary checks cleared me to
give a pint of blood. After a busy day I was glad to relax in the contour chair. With my neck supported and my feet and legs elevated,
I let the pleasant view take my mind off the needle in my arm.

The arrival of another woman in the donor area caught my attention. A friend, holding a wad of cotton against her finger, followed. "You get to save a life today; I don't," the second person said.

"You'll get your iron back up by next time," the first woman reassured her.

That brief exchange started me thinking about the lifesaving
blood of Jesus. My pint of blood, if separated into its components,
might help several people at most—but Jesus' donation was sufficient for all humanity.

What did giving blood cost me? Approximately an hour of my
time, a pricked finger for the hemoglobin test, an interrogation
about my lifestyle and health, a moment of discomfort as the needle
went into my arm. Giving blood certainly did not take my life. After
juice and cookies, I was on my way with no more mark than a bandage on my arm for a few hours.

But what did giving blood cost Jesus? More than I can fully comprehend. The price of His final commitment to be the sacrifice was agony so intense that "his sweat was like drops of blood falling to the ground" (Luke 22:44, NIV). He was subjected not to just a few questions, but to a grueling trial. His blood flowed not from a mere needle prick, but from a scourging and thorn punctures. Having no comfortable contour chair or soothing scenery, He made His donation while hanging in pain and shame on a cross. Giving blood cost His life and left everlasting nail prints in His hands and feet and a scar in His side.

Why did I give blood? Because my type could help someone recover from disease or injury. Why did Jesus give blood? Because only His type could save me and you from the disease and injury of sin, and because He loved us enough to give His precious blood.

Rita Eisenhower Duncan

April 7

Beautiful Hands

And when he had so said, he shewed unto them his hands. John 20:20.

*I*t is possible to identify someone just from observing his or her hands. A farmer's hands are rough, but those of a typist are smooth. A pianist's hands must be strong with fingers long enough to reach the keys. Many times the hands of a mother or housekeeper involved in chores like cleaning, washing, ironing, and cooking become wrinkled, but they are beautiful even so.

I love to think about Jesus' hands when I read the story about that Sunday evening on the Emmaus road. There walked two of His followers. They were returning home, feeling sad and depressed because their Master had been crucified and was dead. Peacefully, Jesus joined them, but they didn't recognize Him. When they entered the village, they asked the Stranger to stay with them. At dinnertime they asked the Guest to pray. When He raised His hands, they saw the marks of the nails and immediately recognized their Lord. Then He disappeared.

The same night the disciples met together in the upper room to talk about the day's events. Suddenly Jesus stood before them. At first they were afraid, but the Bible says He showed them His hands. Nothing more was necessary. Those marks proved His story, and the disciples became convinced that He was really Jesus.

Your hands and mine don't have nail marks, but they can have signs of work, selflessness, and love for others. When we put our hands in Jesus', they can do many good things, for they will become stronger and more powerful. They'll change tears into smiles. Or they'll bring comfort and joy to the distressed and hopeless, and virtue to those feeling lost.

Let's pray that the Lord will take our weak and empty hands and put them into His own that they might become strong, powerful, and full of love and kindness by His divine touch.

MEIBEL MELLO GUEDES

APRIL 8

The Stranger

For I was hungry and you gave me something to eat, I was thirsty and you gave me something to drink. Matt. 25:35, NIV.

He was sitting on the curb in front of the supermarket. However, it is not unusual to see people near this particular store. Most of them have signs such as "Help Rehabilitate an Addict," "Send a Poor Child to Camp," or "Save the Black Bears." Occasionally a cute little boy or girl will stand near the door, clutching an overpriced candy bar in one hand and a small box bearing a school logo in the other.

But this man was different. He simply sat there, head hanging down. His dirty, worn-out clothes sagged on his tired body. Long, grimy hair framed his unshaven face. He had no sign, held no items for sale, asked for nothing.

The man stayed on my mind while I collected canned goods, frozen food, fresh fruits, and vegetables. Finally I was ready to go to the checkout line. But the man's pathetic image remained with me. Pushing my cart to a safe place, I went outside to look for him. He was surveying the dry, crusty skin on the bottom of his weary, soiled feet when I approached.

"Are you hungry?" I asked.

He barely raised his head, hesitated a moment, then softly answered, "Yes, I am."

"Would you like a sandwich?"

"Yes, I would," he replied in the same soft voice.

Then I offered him a choice. "Or would you rather have a salad?"

He raised his head enough to look up at me. "Either one will be

120

all right," he replied. But when I started back toward the store, he gathered a bit of courage and called after me, "Could I have both?" I added his sandwich and potato salad to my basket and went to the checkout line.

He looked up once more when I handed him the see-through containers that held his meal. "Thank you, ma'am," he said, eagerly opening the tops.

Some days I sit on the curb of life, broken in spirit and tired of trying. Everything has gone wrong, and I am desperate for help, yet I do not dare express my need to the successful men and women who pass me by.

Then a Stranger stands before me. "Is your soul hungry?" He asks.

I hesitate to answer. Could this Man be interested in my case? "Yes, it is," I softly say.

"Would you like relief?"

"Yes, I would."

"Do you want hope or peace?" He queries.

"Either is all right," I reply, fearful I should give the wrong answer. Then gaining a bit of courage, I look up at Him, and seeing love in His face, I change my answer. "Could I have both?"

He smiles, and with His own blood, He buys me peace and hope and faith and eternal life.

"Thank You, Jesus," I respond, eagerly receiving the wonderful gifts He offers to me. MILDRED WILLIAMS

APRIL 9

He Does Care

But my God shall supply all your need according to his riches in glory by Christ Jesus. Phil. 4:19.

I wondered why I was even bothering to attend the retreat that summer. The mother of two tiny boys and wife of a too-busy pastor, I was worn out and discouraged, my faith at an all-time low. God seemed far away, and I doubted His care and concern for me personally.

Urged by a friend to attend the evening youth meetings, I reluctantly bundled my sleeper-clad babies into the stroller and made my way to the chapel.

The theme of the meetings was the ABCs of prayer. The two speakers led us through the steps of "Asking, Believing, and

Claiming" Bible promises for prayer needs. Would God actually fulfill His promises to me just by my claiming them? I was eager to put Him to the test.

My opportunity came the following morning. It was my habit to rise and take a shower about 5:00 a.m. while the rest of my family still slept.

Now the showers on that particular campground operated on a meter to conserve water. A quarter would buy five minutes worth of water. One quickly learns to take an adequate shower, complete with hair-washing, in that amount of time.

On this particular morning a thorough search of my purse and my husband's pants' pockets failed to produce a quarter. Frustrated, I wondered what to do. Then the thought came: *Claim a Bible promise.* Here was God's chance to prove He really would answer prayer. The only one I could think of was Philippians 4:19: "My God shall supply all your need."

Having asked God to fulfill this promise to me and thanking Him for it, I confidently gathered my towels, shampoo, and soap, and headed for the shower house. Along the way I scrutinized the ground, expecting to find a quarter, but saw nothing. Not to be deterred, I repeated again, "My God shall supply all your need."

A sign on the shower-house door that read "No Water" startled me. This was really getting interesting! How would God handle this one? As I entered the building, a friend advised, "You can't get a shower; there's no water." Amazement registered on her face at my report, "I am taking a shower."

I stepped into the stall, and with no quarter to put in the slot, turned the switch on the meter. Immediately the water poured out, and I luxuriated in its warmth far longer than the usual allotted five minutes. My heart sang, "Thank You, Lord, for caring enough to supply my need!"

Later, I learned that the campground did not have a drop of water anywhere else until noon that day. I was awed and jubilant that God had worked a miracle just for me to bolster my struggling faith. He understood my heart-longing behind that seemingly presumptuous prayer and proved that He did indeed care about me and the circumstances of my daily life.   SYLVIA ATKINS

Twenty Dollars

The Lord your God is with you, he is mighty to save. He will take great delight in you, he will quiet you with his love, he will rejoice over you with singing. Zeph. 3:17, NIV.

*M*oney was tight. Extra car expenses hadn't helped. I was having a hard time keeping our minimum $100 in the checking account. That was our emergency money, and as long as we kept that minimum in our checking account, we wouldn't have to pay any service charge. It was an extra incentive to keep us from spending our last dollar.

Even though money was tight, we still needed groceries, so I went to the store and started putting things into my cart. I'm pretty good at keeping an approximate account in my head of what my groceries will cost, and I was watching quite closely that evening. I went to the checkout stand with the idea that I'd still have about $3 to $5 left in our checking account, besides the $100, after writing a check to pay for the groceries.

Oh no! Somehow I must have made a mistake. The charge was $20 more than I had estimated. Now what?

Because of other things, I was already discouraged. This was the proverbial "last straw." Oh, I know it may not seem like a very big problem to most people. After all, I still had plenty of money in the account to cover the check, but it still bothered me, however unreasonable it might be.

I couldn't imagine where my family would receive money until payday, at least a week away, but I decided we had to get that $20 back in that account right away. As I drove home that night, I told God we needed that $20 in time for me to deposit it the next day. Yes, my attitude was bad!

When I got home, I started putting the groceries away. As I did so, I compared them with the sales receipt, as was my custom. Wait! There in front of me was a mistake. The clerk had obviously hit the "two" twice, charging me for 22 of an item when I had bought only two.

Hurrying out to the car, I headed back to the store and showed my receipt to the clerk. She agreed there had been a mistake and handed me a $20 bill. On that $20 bill someone had written "I love you."

CHERYL BRATTON

Don't Be a Cucumber

Always be joyful. 1 Thess. 5:16, TLB.

I used to naively think that when others asked "How are you?" that they really wanted to know. Unfortunately few people really want to hear about the most recent argument with your mother/spouse/friend, or how the weather makes your back ache, or how poorly you slept last night.

A friend once bluntly told me (and yes, she was a true friend), "I was only saying 'Hi.' This isn't a signal to spill yourself!"

Suddenly I felt myself taken back to a Ghanaian beach as a little girl, investigating rock pools with my daddy. Among the seaweed, shell creatures, and starfish, I discovered a strange-looking creature. It resembled a shaggy cucumber with a flower at one end. I watched it for some time, but apart from occasionally waving its flowerlike arms, it did nothing. I decided to put it in my pail and take it to Dad for identification.

Very gently, I scooped it up. Suddenly the little creature convulsed and started oozing from the flowerlike end. I dropped it immediately and watched in horror as its internal organs spewed out of its mouth and lay around it in a smelly unattractive pile. The little sea cucumber had spilled its guts on me. It had the desired effect. I withdrew.

I later learned that sea cucumbers (a relative of the starfish and sea urchin) expel their intestinal organs for protection when they are afraid or feel attacked. Later they grow a new batch or reabsorb the old ones for future use.

Unfortunately people often respond the same way to a spontaneous spilling. While there is a time and place for sharing our difficulties and sorrows in life, we shouldn't share them frequently and with just anyone.

"All have trials; griefs hard to bear, temptations hard to resist. Do not tell your troubles to your fellow mortals, but carry everything to God in prayer. Make it a rule never to utter one word of doubt or discouragement. You can do much to brighten the life of others and strengthen their efforts, by words of hope and holy cheer" (*Steps to Christ*, p. 119).

Lord, make me a blessing to my friends and acquaintances, and not a sea cucumber. SALLY DILLON

APRIL 12

Doing Nothing for the Lord

He considereth all their works. Ps. 33:15.

*B*eing a mother to my three small children was my full-time job. All the outreach activities others did made me feel I was doing nothing for the Lord. Pangs of guilt swept over me. I didn't even attend a Bible study group, visit nursing homes to help cheer lonely inhabitants, or conduct cooking classes. The only positive thing I was doing was reading my Bible through in the few minutes between interruptions. Did God understand why I did nothing, or should I become a better organizer of my daily 24 hours?

Six days came and went. Grimly I sat in church again. A grandmother and her granddaughter reported going to a nursing home each Wednesday afternoon. I was still doing nothing.

In desperation, I called the pastor on Monday. "What bothers me, Pastor," I began, "is that I'm doing nothing."

"Doing nothing?"

"Yes. Other Christians are involved with others. I'm reading my Bible, but those other things—Bible study group, cooking classes, visiting nursing homes—I just don't have time for them."

I didn't understand his laugh. "You mean you aren't doing all those things? Maybe God's records aren't the same as yours. Did you study the Bible lesson with your three children this week?"

"Yes. Each evening."

"Let's see. I'd say you conducted 18 Bible studies with your children. Not bad. And you prepared three meals a day for your family?"

"Well, yes," I admitted slowly.

"I'd say you conducted 21 cooking classes for your children. And you prayed before meals with them, right?"

"We always do."

"And you prayed with them before they went to sleep, right? Let's see, you have three children, and you prayed before three meals a day and before they went to bed—that's four prayers for each child times seven days—I'd say you had prayer with 84 people this week. And Connie, you'd rather take your children to heaven with you than any other three people?"

"Oh, yes!" His words were true.

"Each person has a different place to work. A mother's place for outreach is in her home. Because of your life and training, your children will follow your example. Your reward will come when your children choose to be in heaven with you."

"Thank you, Pastor." I blinked away the tears of gratefulness I felt at his words—I who was doing nothing. God recognizes that we mothers have an important work and will reward our faithfulness.

CONNIE NOWLAN

APRIL 13

As Little Children

Forgive as the Lord forgave you. Col. 3:13, NIV.

While I was teaching grades 1 through 4 in a small parochial school, the Lord blessed me with many opportunities to observe the work of His Holy Spirit on the hearts of young children. One of the most memorable occurred one day at recess time. Two second-grade boys got into a fistfight. It seemed Jimmy had teased and pushed Gregory beyond his small measure of endurance. My first thought was to isolate them, but something stopped me. I moved between them to stop the battle and put an arm around each little fellow's neck. Panting and fuming, they boiled with anger. I simply held them still for a few moments, and then, drawing them together in front of me, I said, "Boys, we're Christians, aren't we? We don't want Satan in our school."

Jimmy, the older yet smaller of the two, had been baptized that year, and had recently had the joy of seeing his father baptized in answer to his prayers. "Jimmy," I said as he looked up at me with both fear and hope in his brown eyes, "I know you don't really want to let Satan get you to do things like this, do you?"

"No," he murmured.

"Would you like to tell Gregory you're sorry?"

Without an instant's hesitation he said, "I'm sorry, Gregory."

At this Gregory's heart melted, and he put his hand out to Jimmy and said, "I like you, Jimmy." (It was simply beneath his little-boy dignity to say "love"!)

We had a short prayer asking God's forgiveness and help, and the two went back to their game the best of friends, and with no guilty feelings to cast an adverse influence on their future behavior.

A short time later I found on my desk a note in red crayon from Jimmy. It read, "I really am sorry I was mean to Greg."

The very real sense of the Holy Spirit's presence that day has been a wonderful help in my efforts to forgive as little children do, as well as to accept God's forgiveness with the simplicity of a child.

REVA I. SMITH

APRIL 14

Hunger—A Parable

Blessed are those who hunger and thirst for righteousness, for they will be filled. Matt. 5:6, NIV.

Come with me to an imaginary land where hunger is nonexistent. In this land, although food is abundant, no one *feels* hunger, even though many are in fact starving. As we visit one of the homes in this country, we notice that it has two cars in the driveway and an immaculately landscaped lawn. But as we enter the house, we are shocked at the condition of the occupants. They are clean and wear expensive clothes, but they are so painfully thin! Their condition puzzles us.

Our hosts, we learn, belong to a local organization that teaches people the necessity of eating. They describe in glowing terms their involvement in its weekly meetings. Proudly they show us framed certificates from food preparation courses and emergency famine readiness seminars. Their shelves bulge with cans and sacks of food, but we notice that dust and cobwebs cover most of it.

Finally we can stand it no longer, and ask, "How often do you eat?"

Mr. Eater rolls his eyes to the ceiling and counts, "Two, three . . . maybe four times a week." Mrs. Eater smiles approvingly, and says, "I know that we should eat more often, but we can't work it into our schedule, with our jobs and the house and all. But we eat more than many in our eaters group!"

"But don't you get hungry?"

"I used to," Mr. Eater responds. "When I first joined the group, I was hungry all the time! I had never seen food like that before. I ate and ate. And the energy I had . . ." He trails off wistfully.

"We see that often in new eaters," Mrs. Eater adds brightly. "It wears off, though. You can't expect to go through life that way— somebody has to get the work done!"

Later, at the weekly eaters meeting, members mingle around a tableful of food and discuss the various dishes. They shun one dish as being "too hard to digest." Another gets denounced because it is "different than the usual." Some are even dissatisfied with the way food is arranged on the table. In spite of their obvious malnutrition, and the fact that for some it is the only meal of the week, many do not consume more than just a few bites. One eater leads a lively discussion on how to find time to eat, while another presents a talk on how to convince noneaters of the value of eating. There is even a group teaching eaters how to manage their fatigue and to get more done with the little energy they have. As we walk out, shaking our heads at the absurdity of the situation, our eye catches sight of a verse over the door. "He has filled the hungry with good things but has sent the rich away empty" (Luke 1:53, NIV).

And we wonder—could it ever happen to us?   LINDA McCABE

APRIL 15

First Flight

He protected them and cared for them, as he would protect himself. Like an eagle teaching its young to fly, catching them safely on its spreading wings, the Lord kept Israel from falling. Deut. 32:10, 11, TEV.

After years of piano lessons, our daughter, Naomi, agreed to play the piano for the kindergarten group at our church. She confided this commitment to me late the night before. Of course, I drove her over to pick up the music. Although I encouraged her through her early-morning practice, she resisted my assistance. As my frustration level escalated, I withdrew to the breakfast nook to eat a leisurely meal, pondered my behavior, diagnosed myself as displaying symptoms of pianist-mom-hoveritis, and meditated with the delightful sounds of recognizable songs played slowly in the background.

Jesus also caught my ear. Yes, He hears more than a few of my own "sour notes." He lets me "do it myself" when I insist on having my own way. Jesus waits patiently while I slowly work up speed, lacking confidence in tasks He knows I could do with His expert help. And He sustains me as I let go of a beloved teenager so she can stretch her wings, aided by the protective wings of a heavenly Parent.

Who needs to remain anxious with those same strong wings under my own?   GINY YOUNGBERG LONSER

Follow Me

And he saith unto them, Follow me, and I will make you fishers of men. Matt. 4:19.

I was sitting in my college dorm room reading when Jeanne burst in like a small tornado.

"Gina!" she yelled. "Drop what you're doing and follow me!"

"What is it? Is something wrong? Wait until I get my sweater."

"No, there's no time. He might have already left. Come on!"

She grabbed my hand, and we ran down two flights of stairs to get to the yard. Then she stopped suddenly and pointed to a tree.

There sat an owl, blinking in the sunlight and looking as if it were wondering what all the fuss was about. As we cautiously drew closer, we saw that it wasn't a wild owl at all, but was enclosed in a wire-mesh cage under the shade of the tree. Although I enjoyed seeing the bird up close, all the rushing was completely unnecessary. The owl wasn't going anywhere.

It's not always easy to drop what you're doing when a friend calls—especially for women who have been brought up to notice dirty pots and pans, unmade beds, and dusty shelves, and who feel they have a personal responsibility to make the world a cleaner place. But when we refuse to tear ourselves away from the kitchen, we cheat ourselves of the ability to see and appreciate the world outside.

The other morning a hummingbird hovered so close to my face that I could hear its wings and feel the rush of air on my cheeks. Another day a butterfly came and landed on my shoulder. These things happened because I was willing to drop what I was doing.

Sometimes the benefit of dropping what you're doing is even greater. I'm thinking of the time when Jesus called some poor fishermen to follow Him. They had to leave their work in order to accompany Him. Probably they had no idea where He would lead them, but they followed Him anyway. What would have happened if Peter and the others had said, "Sorry, Jesus, not right now. I'll see you after I've finished my chores"? Only by listening to our Friend's voice and being always ready will we reap the rewards of following Him!

GINA LEE

A Morning Prayer

A word in season, how good it is! Prov. 15:23, RSV.

*T*oday I lay my plans at Your feet. Lead my feet on the pathway I should travel. You know the appointments already scheduled. And You know the phone calls that will come; the knock on my door; the hesitation in the hallway of someone who needs a listening ear; or the student who pauses after class to rejoice in a success.

Today, may I reflect You. Grant me the wisdom to know when to be silent, when to speak, and how to share words of comfort, encouragement, praise, and joy. May my actions cause others to desire a closer walk with You.

Words of advice may hurt. Instead, help me to share patiently the pain and soothe the wound through a gentle touch, to care rather than advise and fix, to listen and understand. Lord, I know You care for people through people. Help me to be one of those caring people, reflecting Your character, Your joy, Your love for people. May I celebrate my love for You by being "quick to hear" and "slow to speak" (James 1:19, RSV). May others catch a glimpse of heaven today.

Thank You, Jesus, my very best of friends! Amen.   NYLA JUHL

The Mysterious Rake

Remember the words of our Lord Jesus who said, "Happiness comes from giving, not from receiving." Acts 20:35, Clear Word.

*M*ysterious flowers with notes reading "Have a nice day," "Hang in there, vacation is coming," or "Hope you feel better" were appearing all over the campus in Cedar Lake, Michigan. Girls, guys, and faculty were all among the recipients. Each day-brightening surprise was simply signed "RAK."

"Who's initials are those?" "Who is sending the flowers?" and "What does RAK stand for?" were three often asked questions. Thank you's to RAK appeared on signs in windows and as classified ads in the school newspaper. RAK fever spread everywhere.

As a sponsor for the Student Association, I was always on the lookout for innovative and creative ideas. Earlier in the summer I had read a magazine article on random acts of kindness, and I felt impressed with the thought of doing something nice for someone else "just because."

Random acts of kindness. The phrase kept coming back to me all summer. How could we put that concept into practice on our campus? Anonymous notes with a small gift of some sort? Yes! It could work! After sharing the article and my ideas with the other Student Association sponsors, we decided to bounce it off our officers.

Excitement permeated the air as the Student Association officers and sponsors for the 1993-1994 school year gathered to regroup and finalize plans after the summer vacation. They discussed the challenge of making the year fun, yet meaningful, and of involving a large number of students.

As plans for the upcoming school year started to jell, I pitched the idea of random acts of kindness to the officers. Their faces brightened as they absorbed the potential of the proposal. They took a vote and decided to go ahead.

Although the students and faculty on the receiving end of those random acts of kindness benefited, the impact on those behind the scenes was much greater. By cultivating the spirit of giving, a chain reaction started whose end we will know only when we reach heaven.

Students and faculty suspected many organizations on the Great Lakes Adventist Academy campus of being the mysterious RAK, but the secret remains safe with the 1993-1994 Student Association officers and sponsors.   JUDY GLASS

APRIL 19

Loving-kindness and Tender Mercies

Give all your worries to Him, because He cares for you. 1 Peter 5:7, EB.

*W*hatever version I looked at, it said the same thing: Give Jesus Christ your problems. I needed to remember that promise, but memory isn't always reliable.

Some time after reading Dorothy Eaton Watts' *Prayer Country,* I found myself fighting discouragement. Usually such thoughts don't last long, as I believe discouragement is sin, and I know what to do about that. But this time the depressed feelings refused to leave.

After my pastor friend prayed with me, things were a little better, but I really did not know what was causing the problem.

With slightly renewed courage, I decided to write down everything I could think of that might be "bugging" me: "I long for . . ."; "I got out of the habit of . . ."; "Maybe I haven't had enough challenges . . ."; "I would like to be . . ." By the time I had finished writing, I had 14 complaints of perceived desires or wishes that might be triggering emotional stress.

Next I thought over everything I had written down. Finally, following one of Dorothy Watts' suggested patterns, I sat down, closed my eyes, and, concentrating on God's promises, named each one of the 14 statements, wondering if they were important to Him. My prayer continued like this: "Lord, I give You all these frustrations. Take them please." In a little while I felt both His presence and the relief of casting them all His care.

Soon the story of the seven spirits of Matthew 12 came to mind. Because the house was clean but empty, they all moved in. That frightened me, so on another sheet I devised 14 requests from my Lord that would fill the place of each of the 14 frustrations that I had turned over to Him (never before had I asked God for that many things all at once).

Perhaps a little skeptically, I waited, like Jonah, to see what the Lord would do. In just a day or two, positive answers started coming. My discouragement was vanishing, my worries lessening, and courage prospered. Day by day answers continued coming even beyond what I had asked.

Today as I write this, I look over that list of requests again. Entered by 13 of them I have scribbled "ans." The fourteenth frustration and request is progressively being resolved. God indeed has crowned me with loving-kindness and tender mercies.

MYRTLE HICKS

APRIL 20

No Matter What

This is love: not that we loved God, but that he loved us. 1 John 4:10, NIV.

While my 12-year-old daughter and I were driving one day, she asked why I had started to go to church. I had never gone before during her entire life. In fact, our home hadn't discussed or mentioned God, and she wanted to understand the change that had taken place in me.

We talked, but she wasn't really satisfied with my answers. I wasn't surprised, though, since no single specific occurrence had happened to cause this change in my life, at least not consciously. So I tried an example, reminding her of our beautiful and independent fluffy gray kitty. I love Bailey. So does she. I explained how I love Bailey no matter what. I love her when she deigns to allow me to scratch her head, and I love her when she walks away as I reach down to touch her. I love Bailey when she's loving and friendly and cute, and I love her when she's naughty or shows her claws. In fact, I even love Bailey who, as I stoop to pat her, snootily lifts her nose and, refusing my affection, turns away. I love Bailey no matter what.

My daughter's response was: "Well, Mom, so what. When she does that, you just run after her and pick her up anyway." Yes, my love, I do. And that's what God did to me. Even when I was impossible, when I resisted His offer of affection, when I turned away instead of responding, God loved me no matter what. Finally, one day, He just reached down and picked me up anyway. And I won't ever be the same again. ALICE HEATH

APRIL 21

Our Father

Our Father which art in heaven, . . . Matt. 6:9.

*D*ee was alone now. The children were all grown, so she was able to do the work she loved: traveling as a Bible worker with an evangelist. Regrettably, only a short time passed until Dee's young, recently widowed daughter with a small child drifted into a lifestyle that prohibited her from being able to care for her child.

Soon Dee gave up the work she loved to establish a home for her little granddaughter. It was in the 1930s, and times were hard. The only employment she was able to secure was a job mending clothes in a hot, sweaty laundry. The little girl did not know that times were hard or what her grandmother had given up for her. She only knew that Mama Dee loved and cared for her. I know this because I was that little girl—a little girl who learned to pray at her grandmother's knee.

Many years have passed, but every day I see how my childhood shaped my life. Prayer is still an important part of my life, and I follow the example of Jesus, who taught us to say when we pray, "Our Father . . ." But maybe you, like me, grew up in a fatherless home, and it is hard to grasp the real significance of the word *father*. We may have to bring to mind another loved one. I find that when I pray, I am thinking:

Our Father—You are as loving and accessible to me as was my dear grandmother. Father, You are my caregiver, my gentle shepherd, my strength, my protector. You carry me in Your bosom.

Which art in heaven—Even though we may have abandoned You, You have not abandoned us, as have some earthly parents. You have made sure that we know where home is. Help us to long for that home. You are the light. Thank You for keeping the lamp burning to guide us home.

Hallowed be thy name (as is her name)—Your name is holy, Lord, because You are our Creator, our beloved Originator—as my grandmother is my beloved ancestor. Your name is dear to me, as is her name. Father, I am proud to bear Your name. May I never bring disgrace to the family name.

As I finish my prayer, I praise Him, and I can do so with all confidence because I know what it means to have benefited from earthly love and sacrifice. ANN VANARSDELL HAYWARD

APRIL 22

Daddy Will Come

Behold, I come quickly. Rev. 3:11.

The sun was low over the horizon. It was time for our 4-year-old son, Scott, to go to bed.

"Please, Mama," he said. "Let me stay up till Daddy comes. He said he would be home before I go to bed. I know he'll come." His voice had such conviction and his big green eyes reflected such belief that I didn't have the heart to argue. Nor did I want to discuss possible reasons for my husband's delay—such as an accident—with a 4-year-old.

"OK," I said. "Let's sit on the porch and read while we wait for Daddy." I began reading his favorite stories, certain that sleep would overtake him. Once he was asleep, I planned to carry him to his bed without any protest from him.

The sun slowly disappeared over the horizon. The stars began to twinkle in the night sky. It became too dark to see the pages of the storybook, and still his daddy had not come.

"Scott," I said, "I think it's time to go 'nighty-night.'"

"No, Mama, please," he begged, his eyes suddenly bright with tears. "My daddy said he would come, and he will. Just wait a little longer, please." It was a warm summer evening, and we were cozy together. I agreed to wait a few minutes longer, thinking Scott would fall asleep.

The boy still was wide awake about 30 minutes later when his beloved daddy turned into our driveway.

"See, Mommy?" Scott squealed triumphantly as he jumped off my lap and headed toward the driveway, waving wildly. "I told you he would come!"

I received a lesson in faith and patience that evening from my son. Yesterday I vividly recalled this incident as my son again gave me the same lesson—only this time it was about my heavenly Father's return!

Years have passed, and Scott is now an attorney. This week he served as executor of the estate of my father and his grandfather. For several days he rushed to perform the tasks associated with closing the earthly history of a loved one. We then attended the memorial service for Dad. As we drove home from the service, Scott and I began talking about the beliefs of our family members, death, and the second coming of Jesus.

"It seems that Jesus will never come," I lamented.

Scott turned to me with the identical facial expression and look in his eyes that I had witnessed 24 years ago on that warm summer evening with stars twinkling overhead. With absolute conviction in his voice and belief reflected in his adult green eyes, he said, "Mama, He *said* He will come, and He *will*."   ELLIE GREEN

APRIL 23

Single Is a Family, Too

For you did not receive a spirit that makes you a slave again to fear, but you received the Spirit of [daughter]ship. And by him we cry, "Abba, Father." The Spirit himself testifies with our spirit that we are God's children. Now if we are children, then we are heirs—heirs of God and co-heirs with Christ, if indeed we share in his sufferings in order that we may also share in his glory. Rom. 8:15-17, NIV.

ebster defines *family* as "the unit consisting of parents and their children; descendants of a common progenitor; a class of things sharing certain characteristics and functions." On the surface one might conclude that single is not a family. As a single woman I am happy to be independent. But God's "Book" adds new meaning for me. I am a family. God is my "Abba" (Father), and I am His child. Now even Webster would have to see this as a family affair.

I am therefore an heir, that is, I have rights to my Father's stuff. His belongings are mine! My family has even made provision for the orphaned. Ephesians 1:5, Romans 8:23, and Romans 9:4 assure me that although I have lost my earthly parents, I have been adopted into the divine family of God. "A father of the fatherless, a defender of the widows, is God in His holy habitation" (Ps. 68:5, NKJV). So when people see me, they shouldn't *just* see me, they should see the spirit of my Father's love shining in my life.

I am a part of a royal priesthood. God specifically chose and created me for a purpose that no one else can fulfill on this earth but me. My Father wants me—that's why He created me. I was planned! I am a family, and I was lovingly created in my Father's image—I am His descendant. We share commonalties because He became a part of me by becoming human. "And yet, O Lord, you are our Father. We are the clay and you are the Potter. We are all formed by your hand" (Isa. 64:8, TLB).

So the next time you feel tempted to exclude or look with pity on a single person or feel his or her life could not possibly be complete, think again! The Father supplies all the needs of His children. He has filled my life with friends and family. Whole and happy, I await my Father's return. What a family reunion that will be (see John 14:1-4)! Open your hearts and your minds. Be sensitive and supportive to all the members of the Father's family. We are all brothers and sisters in Christ and need each other. So realize and remember that single is a family, too!   TERRIE RUFF

APRIL 24

Someone to Bear My Burdens

Give your burdens to the Lord. He will carry them. He will not permit the godly to slip or fall. Ps. 55:22, TLB.

*W*hen our three children approached their teens, our family often discussed going backpacking. It had the potential of being the ultimate "togetherness" experience. Our friends, who had backpacked several times, spoke enthusiastically about the beautiful scenery that we could enjoy "off the beaten path." They carefully tutored us on the different types and brand names of equipment and cautioned us about the importance of carrying plenty of water and of traveling light.

As the time approached for our first outing, we felt we were as knowledgeable as seasoned travelers, fearless and confident. We considered several options, but finally decided to pack into an area known as "Little Yosemite." The planning and the packing took almost more time than the actual trip.

As we loaded our packs in the comfort of our living room, I began to feel apprehensive. A chronic back condition had plagued me for years, and as everyone began weighing their packs, I began to wonder how I was going to carry 35 pounds up the trail that followed the falls. I confided my fears to my husband, who quickly concluded that maybe I should not go, since anyone else carrying my 35 pounds would be out of the question.

Our 16-year-old son, without a moment's hesitation, offered to carry all of my load if I would just go along to cook. (At that period in his life, food was the most important item to have along.) Finally I agreed that I would do fine by carrying only my change of clothing. He carried the heavier items for me. In fact, in all of the many subsequent backpack trips we took, that bargain held. And since his legs were much longer than mine, he always hiked on ahead, dropped his pack at the destination, and came back to carry my little load for me. Sometimes he would even take on his sisters' loads.

I have often compared this incident with the agreement we can make with our Elder Brother. He has offered to carry all of the loads we face in life. It is such a simple arrangement. All we have to do is ask Him to take on our burdens, and without a moment of hesitation He accepts them. We do not need to bargain or trade off, only make a simple request. Nor do we have to plan ahead or wait for His convenience. He is there always, waiting for us to ask.

Today, if you are carrying burdens, however light they may be, turn them over to the divine Burden Bearer. You will find that life is so much easier when you are not struggling to do it all in your own strength. And then thank Him.   Jean Reiffenstein Rothgeb

His Never-failing Promises

Thou wilt keep him in perfect peace, whose mind is stayed on thee: because he trusteth in thee. Isa. 26:3.

I sat by myself in the very nose of an almost empty jetliner as its crew made preparations for takeoff. I had never been in this section of an aircraft before, and the position felt rather strange. This, added to physical exhaustion and the sadness of leaving so many loved ones behind, cast a pall over my homeward trip. The captain's announcement of mechanical problems that delayed us a full hour, and the giant aircraft's creaking and groaning on takeoff, intensified the feeling of fear and apprehension that swept over me as we ascended through the clouds.

I gripped the arm of my seat and prayed earnestly, "Lord, take this fear from me. I know You are in charge, I know You are able, and I'm committed to You, Lord."

Then the thought hit me that it would be good therapy to write my prayer in poetry, so I got out my pen and pad. The inspiration that God gave me was so comforting and reassuring that I want to share it with you today.

Lord, thank You for the way You take
The fear away from me,
And put Your peace within my heart;
The way You set me free.

Because You are my only hope,
My Guide and Friend so sure,
And only as You keep me, Lord,
Is life at all secure.

But You are able, and I know
That You so deeply care
That You regard the tiniest bird
That flies up in the air.

Yet, nothing is too hard for You,
No problem is too great;
For You can yet destroy, dear Lord,
And You can yet create.

And in Your hands You have my life,
My future and my past;
You've washed away each load of care
That at Your feet I cast.

And You have given me so much—
Such love, such hope, such joy—
That nothing You will now allow
To hurt or to destroy.

Your purpose You will so fulfill
Within this feeble frame,
To be a light, to honor You
And glorify Your name.

DAPHNIE M. CORRODUS

APRIL 26

My Brother

A man that hath friends must shew himself friendly: and there is
a friend that sticketh closer than a brother. Prov. 18:24.

I grew up in a large family. The middle child of seven children, I have three sisters and three brothers. Brothers have always intrigued me. They could be your best friend one minute, sharing the treasures of their pockets, and other times, they'd pull hair, fight, and tease unmercifully.

My brothers and I have shared touch football, baseball card toss, and marble games in the backyard. Once when I needed a dollar for school I remember Butch, my oldest brother and quite grown-up at the time, graciously writing out a check for me to cash at the corner grocery for the sum of one whole dollar!

Kenny, my middle brother, and I shared many walks, talks, and adventures in the cow pasture together. We had our share of battles, too.

One of my favorite memories is watching our dog, Tammy, having her puppies in my brothers' bedroom under their bed. We all sat there, in awe, and watched the miracle of birth, canine-style.

My youngest brother, Kevin, was born when I was already 13 years old. The little "king" of the family, spoiled by everyone, he would amaze us at an unusually early age with his intelligence. He loved to be read to. At age 1 he could tell you the names of all his "Little Golden

Books." We almost lost Kevin to spinal meningitis when he was a baby. When he recovered, we hovered over him even more.

As wonderful as my brothers and my memories of them are, they can't compare with my other Brother. I share many memories with Him, too. Not always pleasant ones—like the time I was despondent, lonely, hurting, and all I could do was scream my pain at Him. He took it, as He always did, not yelling back or walking away from or deserting me. He loves me and will never forsake me. I have learned to love Him through every trial and trouble. Not only is He my favorite brother; He is my friend. I want to tell Him how much I love Him—in person.

"Even so, come, Lord Jesus" (Rev. 22:20).   SHARYN ROBICHAUX

In Time of Need

Do not be anxious about anything, but in everything, by prayer and petition, with thanksgiving, present your requests to God. Phil. 4:6, NIV.

Several years ago I was the sole support of a son in medical school, committed to helping him realize his dream of becoming a doctor.

One day a letter came from him telling me he could no longer depend on his present transportation and would need to buy a used car. He had worked during the summer, but still needed $1,000 more. As it happened, my bank statement arrived in the same mail. It showed a balance of $6.85.

Our resources were low because I too had been attending school. Just two weeks before I had received the degree in nursing that I'd wanted for decades. Now I was happily doing the work I loved, but I didn't have $1,000.

Some moonlighting is in order, I thought, glad that I had opportunity to relieve a friend who did private duty at the hospital where I worked. I could work extra and repay a loan. First I must borrow the money. That night I mentally explored the fund-raising avenues open to me and debated the merits of each one. A bank loan seemed to be the answer.

Early next morning a friend stopped to see me and asked my plans for the day. "I'm going to the bank to see about getting some money," I told her. She didn't ask how much money I needed, but surprised me by saying, "I can let you have $1,000 if that will help."

For a moment I stood staring at her . . . speechless. "I can't believe this," I said. "That's the exact amount I need."

She took her checkbook from her purse, wrote the check for me, then said quietly, "I wondered why I felt impressed to leave more in my checking account this time. Although I never leave large amounts, I did yesterday. I think God must have known you'd be needing it today."

She was right. God knew I'd be needing it and made provision even before I stayed awake wondering what I could, or should, do. Then He sent my friend to my door early to save me the trouble of going out to borrow.

Since that time I've never worried about finances. Why should I when I have Someone who takes care of things like that for me? Instead, I repeat Isaiah 65:24: "And it shall come to pass, that before they call, I will answer; and while they are yet speaking, I will hear." God has shown me it's *my* promise, and I claim it.   ALYCE PICKETT

APRIL 28

All She Had

Truly I say to you that this poor widow has put in more than all. Luke 21:3, NKJV.

Somehow I believe I know a little bit how Jesus felt when He saw the poor widow drop her two mites in the offering box. I'm sure it deeply moved Him and He loved her for it. He knew that she had made the supreme sacrifice of giving all she had.

Lamar and I had gone starry-eyed and newly wedded to Panama as missionaries. We spent three intense years there serving a school in the interior of the country. That was nearly 30 years ago now, but some memories remain vivid yet. One is the mirth we felt when a rooster crowed lustily just outside the open window of the church on our first visit.

We had the normal adjustments of the newly married to make and a new language and culture to learn. Our first anniversary passed without a peso in our pockets and without so much as a light bulb or a roll of toilet tissue to grace our new home. But quickly our hearts became intertwined with the lives of the students of three races.

All too soon furlough time arrived, and we had a request to work in Costa Rica. We felt that our hearts would break. We had

struggled so hard to provide Christian education for the young people of Panama, and had grown to love them as if they were our children, though some of them were nearly as old as we were.

I had bought a boxful of lovely hankies to take home as gifts,
but alas, I had to use every one to wipe my tears as so many students, faculty, and parents came to bid us farewell. They came
bringing gifts and keepsakes.

The only gift I really remember was one from an elderly widow
who lived in a little shack on a side street of town. I don't know if I
had ever known her name, but the last evening she also came with a
parting token. Her gift—two eggs. "It's all I have," she said with a
snaggletoothed grin, holding them out to me. Then she shyly hugged
me and was gone. How we relished those two eggs as we ate our last
breakfast in Panama. Her gift will linger in my heart as a rare treasure.

FELICIA PHILLIPS

APRIL 29

A Full Circle Offering

He who is not against us is for us. Luke 9:50, NKJV.

*D*uring my teaching days in a public high school in Michigan, I
was the sponsor of the Cercle Français, the French Club. The
group's consuming passion was their plan for a trip to the city
of Quebec, where they could attempt to communicate in French.

To achieve it, they successfully pulled off countless moneymak-
ing projects over a two-year period, including the usual bake sales
and car washes. As the money in their savings account mounted,
their enthusiasm waxed proportionately. It would soon be time to
set a date. Then, from out of the blue, it came: a request for my husband and me to return to mission service in Africa.

Anticipating the disappointment on the part of my class, I post-
poned telling them. Finally, in one of the last classes of the school
year, they discussed the time for the trip and settled on a date the
following October when the Canadian *couleurs d'automne* would be
at their height.

"But I won't be here," I reluctantly told them. "We are leaving
for Africa in August."

A stunned silence followed. Then, as if on cue, they all burst
into tears, boys and girls alike. I had taught French to this group

since their seventh grade, and to many of them, English as well. We were bonded in two languages.

Their emotional upset lasted only a few moments, though, as they struggled to regain the full dignity of being juniors in high school. The boys were the first to restore their composure. As the girls smothered their sniffles and tissued the last tear away, the club treasurer arose.

"I move we contribute all the money in our account to the mission school where madame is going to teach."

The vote in favor of the motion was unanimous. Now it was my turn to cry. "*Merci, merci beaucoup*" was all I could murmur between sobs.

At the tearful end of that school year, the Cercle Français handed over to me its precious treasury, destined not to fund a trip north to Quebec for a carefree band of teenagers, but for a waiting circle of African students.

Separation of church and state notwithstanding, these public school students of mine representing a cross section of America—including Christians and non-Christians—served the cause of missions as truly as if they had been in my church Bible study group. For the love of their teacher? No, prompted by the Lord, the source of every good motive in human beings.

Nor is this the end of the story. One of them wrote to me overseas to inquire about how I became a Christian, and she received a full account of that story. Will I see her, and perhaps others of the group, someday in the kingdom? Let it be so, Lord.   JEANNE JORDAN

APRIL 30

A Vision of Jesus

And the King will answer and say to them, "Assuredly, I say to you, inasmuch as you did it to one of the least of these My brethren, you did it to Me." Matt. 25:40, NKJV.

She was lying on the side of the road. A crowd had gathered around her. Someone held an umbrella, shielding her from the hot morning sun. As I came to her, I saw dust, sand, and blood covering her face. I bent to take her pulse. Some thoughtful person had brought a bottle of water, so I moistened tissues from my purse and bathed her face.

"What happened to her?" I asked the onlookers in English. No one offered an explanation. I could see she was very old and dressed in black. An elderly widow no doubt. Had she fallen and broken a hip? Had she been hit by a car?

"Is anyone here her relative?" I tried again, wishing my Greek were adequate for the situation. Someone told me she lived alone, and another pointed vaguely in the direction of her house.

"Has the hospital been called?" They assured me it had been done. I kept bathing her face. Her pulse was still steady and strong, and she was conscious and trying to speak.

"Who is she asking for?" My limited Greek told me she was calling out for someone. In Greek, they explained, "O Theos"—God. Ah, yes, now I remembered—she was calling for the virgin Mary.

I continued stroking her cheeks with soft, damp tissues, cleaning her face little by little. She tried to look up at me and kept calling for Mary. I wondered if she had children. Perhaps they lived in another city or even another country. How alone she seemed. My heart went out to her. Somehow I no longer saw her as an old woman in black but as my own grandmother, and I wanted to help her all I could.

I stayed by her side until the ambulance came. It whisked her away to the hospital, and I went on about my business, but I couldn't forget her. I wondered how she was doing and thought I might go see her. However, an article in the newspaper the next day crushed my plans. She had died. I felt sad. The old woman had been in need, and somehow my heart had seen my grandmother in her.

Looking through spiritual eyes, we can see someone even more special in a needy person. We can see Jesus. No matter how hurt or old or ragged or dirty or drunk, we can look through the outside shell and see Jesus inside. With this new vision, what a privilege it will be to lift a cool drink to thirsty lips, to feed a hungry indigent, to clothe a naked refugee, to visit a convicted criminal in prison.

Dear Jesus, give us the vision to see You in each person we meet.

JOYCE NEERGAARD

Little Things Do Mean a Lot

The master answered, "You did well. You are a good servant who can be trusted. You did well with small things. So I will let you care for much greater things. Come and share my happiness with me." Matt. 25:23, EB.

*I*n January of 1986 I sat at the organ during a chapel service at Union College in Lincoln, Nebraska, ready to begin playing the closing hymn when a faculty member unexpectedly came to the pulpit and announced, "The *Challenger* just blew up in space." We sat in stunned silence, hardly able to grasp the enormity of a tragedy that shocked and saddened the entire nation.

Investigators who examined the retrieved evidence concluded that the fatal explosion occurred when the right solid rocket booster (SRB) broke free at its base and pivoted into the fuel tank. What caused the SRB to fail? Suspicion centered on the small, synthetic rubber O-rings that sealed the joint between the lower two rocket motor segments, each weighing about 300,000 pounds.

Then, and often since then, I've pondered how sometimes it's those parts of life we think may be insignificant that have the greatest impact. Little things, minor details, acts that seem inconsequential, may add up to a major disaster. When considering the power, size, and magnitude of the space shuttle, it's mind-boggling to realize that what caused the explosion was truly a minor item. It's like someone once said, "It's not the lions and tigers that'll get you. It's the mosquitoes!"

Jesus understood the importance of little things. He told of a rich man leaving on a business trip. Just before he departed he called three of his servants and gave them some money to work with while he was gone. They may have shown some promise or unusual traits of character, and perhaps the master wanted to test their potential.

He gave one five pieces of money, another two, and the final person one. The one who received the most quickly put it to use, as did the one with the lesser amount, and they reaped their monetary rewards. However, the servant with the smallest amount buried his and enjoyed sunning himself in his hammock.

The master returned and asked for business reports. After the one with the five pieces of money told about his work and results, the master said, "You have been faithful in handling this small amount. Now I'll give you more responsibilities. Begin the joyous tasks I've assigned to you."

The second man received the same commendation, but what happened to the third? The wrath of the master came down on him, and he was kicked out.

I've learned that while we notice and applaud major achievements, flashy accomplishments, bigger-than-life times, it's still the little things in life that count—and perhaps count the most. The little things we say, those parts of our daily activities that appear in-

significant, may have the greatest impact for good, both for ourselves and others.   LILYA WAGNER

Remember

Then Samuel took a stone, and set it between Mizpeh and Shen,
and called the name of it Ebenezer, saying, Hitherto hath the
Lord helped us. 1 Sam. 7:12.

Call me melancholy, but I like to keep souvenirs and remember special events. I still have all the letters my husband wrote while he was courting me, the engagement
watch he gave me, and the bench on which he proposed to me
(but that's another story). This year we celebrated our thirtieth
wedding anniversary. August 16 will forever be a date etched in
our minds. But that's not the only anniversary we celebrate each
year. We have an anniversary for our first date, the day we became
engaged, and our first kiss. It's nice to remember those special
times. They bring back warm memories and nice feelings. And it
helps keep the spark in the relationship. Once in a while I'll get
out those old love letters and read through them, and something
happens to me. The same feelings I felt then now come back, and
I fall in love all over again.

I think that's what God wants us to do with Him—He wants us
to remember Him and all He has done for us. God longs for us to
read and reread His love letters to us that He has put in the Bible.
He desires for us again to feel that love we had for Him when we
first came to know Him.

The Old Testament records a unique way of remembering special events and blessings from the Lord. His people chose stones and
set them up as memorials of certain events. Then whenever the people saw the stones, they would remember how God had led and
blessed them in the past.

I know of a family who practices that unique custom. They
mark smooth stones with the date and special event or blessings in
their lives. Then they carefully place the stones right at the front entrance to their house. What a wonderful way to remember!

It would be good for us to remember the specific ways and times
that God has led in our lives. Doing so can help put a spark in our
spiritual relationship with Him. So why not write those special

blessings down on paper—or on stones? But above all, don't forget
to "remember."
NANCY CACHERO VASQUEZ

Unsung Heroes

And whosoever shall give to drink . . . a cup of cold water. . . ,
he shall in no wise lose his reward. Matt. 10:42.

I marvel when I read accounts of heroes in God's Word.
How they were used so mightily, and how their hearts
were stirred;
But somewhere in those pages are recorded stories rare
Of steadfast unsung heroes—precious jewels sparkling
there.

Grave Martha in her apron oft' provided for the crowd.
You'd find her in the kitchen over pots and kettles
bowed.
And Andrew the disciple, constant, humble, and re-
served,
Led many to his Master, witnessing quite unobserved.

The little captive maiden served the leper Naaman's
spouse,
And witnessing, brought hope and healing to her master's house.
Though Leah longed for Jacob's love to be his cherished
wife,
The names of all her sons are etched on gates of pearl
for life.

A little boy sat spellbound at the stories Jesus told;
He gave his loaves and fish, and watched a miracle unfold.
And grateful Hannah gave to God her precious little
child
To serve Him in the Temple. How the angels must have
smiled!

A host of others in the Bible we could long discuss.

147

There's Simon of Cyrene, Cornelius, and Onesimus;
The two restored demoniacs, and lame Mephibosheth.
Imperfect they, but trusting God, they loved Him unto
   death.

How oft' in life we feel like unsung heroes after all,
And goals that we have tried to reach seem trivial and
   small.
But there are folks somewhat like us recorded in God's
   Book,
Tucked in between the pages, that we cannot overlook.

I'm sure when God's redeemed are safe within those
   gates sublime,
The stalwarts will be honored all through heaven's unending time.
Their lives will kindle gladness; holy joys they will impart,
But the quiet unsung heroes will be nearest to God's
   heart!
                                          LORRAINE HUDGINS

MAY 4

Mud Puddle

And we, who with unveiled faces all reflect the Lord's glory, are being transformed into his likeness with ever-increasing glory, which comes from the Lord, who is the Spirit. 2 Cor. 3:18, NIV.

Father, this morning I saw something that reminded me of my life. It wasn't pretty, or even useful. And it certainly wasn't noteworthy, unless You count a mention of its inconvenience there. It was at ground level, to be trodden around and avoided. I'm thinking of that lowly, muddy puddle in the center of the walk.

I knew You didn't want me to view myself that way. But it seems I never measure up. I'm not graceful, or charming, or even energetic. My muddied failures don't reflect the high hopes I've had. Yes, Lord, I know You love me, but I don't understand what You see in me.

You must have known my thoughts, Lord, because as I retraced my steps a half hour later, the puddle had been transformed. It was still a puddle, and still at ground level. But walking into the sunrise,

I saw the once-ugly puddle as a gem in my path. Now it reflected the brilliance of the sun's heavenly glory. And that once-ugly, once-useless puddle had become not only beautiful but useful. It served now as a pool of refreshment for the waking birds.

Thank You, Father, for letting me see myself in a new light. Thank You for reminding me that Your Son can make all the difference. Thank You for showing me that He can transform mud to molten gold. And thank You for illustrating His power to make me attractive and useful. Please help me to remember to face the Sonrise as I appraise the value of a puddle.

Today, Lord, please give me contentment with my humble lot in life. Help me to reflect Your brilliance faithfully. And remind me that even a puddle has choices to make. I can seep into the dirt in self-pity and shame. Or I can wait patiently until the warmth of the sun transforms a lowly puddle into a soaring cloud.

KATHLEEN STEARMAN PFLUGRAD

MAY 5

Cooperation: Not Being a Sore Toe

For as we have many members in one body, but all the members do not have the same function, so we, being many, are one body in Christ, and individually members of one another. Rom. 12:4, 5, NKJV.

Children are not able to appreciate the art of sleep fully. It takes total cooperation of all the body parts. The brain tells the whole body to relax, and then it must itself let go and wait for sleep to come.

If you watch a baby before naptime, you will see the lack of co-operation. The eyes are trying to shut, but the hands continue to play. Finally the mouth will let out a desperate yawn, and the body will shut down in midplay with hand still clutched around the toy.

Adults, however, have learned to cooperate with sleep. Watch dad in his easy chair. He says he's just going to "rest his eyes." Soon all the other body parts join in. Finally the mouth will drop open, and he will snore happily. Total cooperation makes sleep so pleasant.

One night while I was diligently practicing the art of sleep, the familiar word "Mommy!" suddenly awakened me. My eyes flew open; then my brain, which was still asleep, told my ears they were only dreaming. The eyes shut momentarily; then again I heard

"Mommy!" Now my brain was awake, and my eyes flew wide open. My feet, which were still asleep, hit the floor and dashed to her room. Unfortunately my little toe did not see the fireplace hearth in its path. The moment they made contact, my toe awakened in excruciating pain. I hobbled the rest of the way to my child to see what was wrong.

"Is it morning yet?" she asked.

"No, dear. Go back to sleep," I answered patiently, then limped back to bed. My child was fine, so my brain told my body to relax and go back to sleep. Unfortunately, my little toe now felt the size of a basketball and was demanding my body's full attention.

That night while I lay there unable to return to sleep, I learned a valuable lesson from that sore toe. It's amazing how such a tiny part of the body can affect the whole. The Bible says we are all part of the body of Christ. When we injure another person in word or deed, we are hurting a part of that body. Furthermore, we become that sore toe, demanding all the attention. But when we cooperate with others and live in harmony, we are healing that body. Each one of us, no matter how small we are, can make a difference.

TAMMY VICE

MAY 6

Memo to Mothers From Jesus

And alas for those who are with child and for those who give suck in those days! Matt. 24:19, RSV.

It was Sunday morning, and I was exhausted. I had just spent three days alone with my 3-week-old and 3-year-old daughters while my husband went backpacking with a group of young people from our church.

How do single moms ever survive this? I wondered as I reflected on my lack of rest during the last few weeks of a difficult pregnancy and the demanding schedule of breast-feeding every two or three hours.

Glancing at the clock, I wearily calculated the hours until my husband would arrive so I could take a much-needed nap. I looked down at the coffee table and noticed my Bible still open to the Gospel of Matthew. I had been too busy and tired to spend time in His Word. Suddenly I longed for spiritual refreshment to compensate for my physical exhaustion.

The baby was asleep and my toddler was momentarily occupied

with her toys, so I grabbed my Bible and hungrily dug into Matthew 24 where I had left off. Soon my eyes started to get heavy. Maybe I really was too tired to benefit from reading. Somehow the destruction of Jerusalem and the end of the world seemed unrelated to surviving motherhood for another day. I was just about ready to close my Bible and succumb to a little shut-eye when verse 19 jumped right out at me. "And alas for those who are with child and for those who give suck in those days!" Why in the world did Jesus pop this seemingly unrelated sentence into His discussion of prophecy?

Suddenly tears of understanding filled my tired eyes. Yes, He would know what it was like to raise small children, as He watched the mothers in His village. Perhaps He even helped them care for their children. My job was important to Him. After all, He stopped right in the middle of a deep theological discourse on eschatology and added a line to let all the tired, pregnant, and nursing mothers know He cared deeply about them. I was still physically exhausted, but I had renewed inner strength to make it through my day.

CINDY WALIKONIS

MAY 7

Our Stove From God

Ask, and it shall be given you; seek, and ye shall find. Luke 11:9.

The *Pennysaver* was the only paper delivered to our door, and I was busy searching the ads under "home appliances" and praying that the Lord would help us find a stove. Our baby boy was sleeping in his basket, and our 2-year-old daughter was quietly playing on the floor nearby.

We had returned to college with lots of faith but few finances. The only place we could find to rent that we could afford had only an electric hot plate in the kitchen. It wasn't adequate. We *really* needed a stove—at the right price!

The ads listed very few stoves, but one caught my eye. It was the *right price* and was located at a home in our area. That was important, because we did not own a car. I silently offered a prayer of gratefulness for this encouragement and awaited my husband's return from classes.

"Honey! Look!" I cried as he entered the door. "Here's an ad for a stove, and I think we can afford it, and it's located not too far away."

All four of us bundled into a borrowed car and searched out the address. It was now getting dark. We finally located the house, but it had no lights on. All four of us trekked up on the porch and rang the bell—and waited.

No answer. We rang again. The porch light came on. The front door opened, but not the screen.

"Yeah?" grunted an unfriendly voice from the darkness.

"We are wondering about the stove . . ."

"We've got no stove and never did have!" Slam went the door. I didn't cry, but I certainly felt like it.

A sad little family returned to the car. We checked the paper again. Yes, we were at the correct address, but they had no stove. Never did have! What had happened? I had been so sure it was the answer to our prayer.

We started to drive home. Then the Lord planted a thought in my mind: could there have been a mistake in the address? Obviously the people at the place we'd just visited had not placed the ad—but someone had.

I suggested that the address should have been for *North* 52nd Street instead of *South*. We decided to check, so off we drove across the city to an unfamiliar area. It was quite dark, and house numbers were hard to read. Then we saw a porch light shining. Yes, the house had the right number.

Again we piled out of the car and rang the doorbell and waited. This time smiles and a warm greeting met us. Yes, they had a stove for sale. Frankly, they wondered why no one had come to see it. Out spilled our story. And there stood our stove—spotless, with a wonderful oven, and the right price. It was the stove the Lord had saved for us.

LOIS MAY WATTS

MAY 8

Don't You Trust Me?

Trust ye in the Lord for ever, for in the Lord Jehovah is everlasting strength. Isa. 26:4.

*A*s I was lying there in the hospital bed that night, I realized that I possibly was not going to live. It had been days since I had been able to eat or drink anything, including water. IVs were keeping me alive. The anxious expressions on the doctor's and nurses' faces told me that things were rather serious.

I was a fighter and determined that it would not get the best of me. My husband had already gone home for some much-needed rest, and the stark reality of my condition filled my mind as I lay in the darkness of the hospital room. I just couldn't (or didn't want to) believe God was finished with me here on this earth.

"Lord, You know that my husband would not do well without me. He needs me so much. How would he deal with his sorrow?"

"I'll take care of him, Connie."

"But Lord, You know he needs me, and then there are my parents. Who will take care of them during their golden years?"

"Connie, I'll take care of them."

"And then there are the new rottweiler puppies and their mother, Yodi Lin. My husband really doesn't know much about dogs. They need me."

"I'll take care of them, too."

His sweet, melodious voice was calming, yet I kept wrestling with Him. Finally I reached the point where I said, "Lord, You can't let me die. I'm needed, don't You understand?"

And then He spoke the sweetest words, which cut straight to my heart. "What's the matter, Connie? Don't you trust Me?"

At that moment I realized my lack of trust in my Saviour, and my helplessness. Here I was trusting in self instead of relying on Christ. I was making myself responsible for the total care of others. Broken, I replied, "Oh yes, Lord, You would take care of them much better than I could." As I gave Him my entire will and being, a sweet peace flooded my soul. I knew no matter what happened, everything would be well taken care of.

It has been more than four years since our talk in that hospital room, and He has never failed to let me know of His love and presence. What a joy it is to be His child and to trust in His goodness.

Where are you today? Do you trust Him? Study with Him, pray with Him, give yourself to Him daily, moment by moment. Put your life in His hands and feel His peace and assurance flood your soul.

CONNIE WHITE

MAY 9

The Fragrance of the Rose

For we are a fragrance of Christ to God among those who are being saved and among those who are perishing. 2 Cor. 2:15, NASB.

*A*s a child I loved to wander over the prairie roads and fields of our uncle's farm. During one of my walks an acrid smell filled the hot summer air. Smoke from a distant fire rushing through a forest or sweeping across the grasslands obliterated the sun. A blue haze had settled like a pall over the vast prairie of southern Alberta.

As I walked with the smell of smoke about me, I suddenly became aware of a sweet fragrance. Then I saw them. Growing in profusion along a barbed-wire fence were masses of bushes, heavy with wild roses.

Those lovely wild roses bloom wherever nature plants them. Each flower has five deep-pink petals surrounding a heart of gold. The perfume is the closest to a heavenly scent I have ever known.

Many of these wild roses bloom far from the eyes of humanity. Yet they do not withhold their beauty or their sweet fragrance. I am sure they have never heard the motto "Bloom where you are planted," for they blossom just as sweetly in some waste corner as in a royal enclosure. The perfume liberated for the queen's delight is no more special than the fragrance caught by a schoolchild passing by. Perhaps my childhood eyes were the only ones that ever saw those cascading roses on that hot summer day long ago.

I think of many people blooming alone in some faraway place—or perhaps close by. As the roses make the world brighter and sweeter by their existence, so those who bloom alone may shed love and kindness to those about them. Thomas Gray's famous elegy reminds us:

> "Full many a flower is born to blush unseen,
> And waste its sweetness on the desert air."

We all exude fragrance in our lives. No one lives to themself. The influence we exert bears testimony to what is in our heart—be it good or bad.

I want my influence to be like those wild roses, giving off the sweet scent of love and beauty. The fragrance of those roses I found long ago still lingers in my memory. And may the memory of my life be as Thomas Moore depicts:

> "Long, long be my heart with memories filled,
> Like the vase in which roses have once been distilled—
> You may break, you may shatter the vase, if you will,
> But the scent of the roses will hang round it still."

MARGARET I. CAMPBELL

God's Time

Wait on the Lord; be of good courage, and He shall strengthen your heart: wait, I say, on the Lord! Ps. 27:14, NKJV.

*W*e taxied out to the end of the runway in the large 747 jetliner. "Ladies and gentlemen," the pilot said over the intercom system, "we are going to have a 20-minute wait here before we can take off."

My daughter and I looked at each other and sighed. We had been planning this four-day vacation for a long time, and we hated having to spend part of it waiting on the ground at the airport when we should be in the air.

After sighing again, we then laughed. "Might as well enjoy it," my daughter chuckled.

After what seemed like much longer than 20 minutes, we heard the pilot's voice once more. "Ladies and gentlemen, prepare for takeoff."

We rechecked our seat belts as the plane taxied to another section of the runway and stopped again. But before we could let out another of our impatient sighs, we heard the engines revving up. Louder and louder the noise boomed, until we could hear nothing but the earsplitting roar. Then suddenly we took off down the runway at breakneck speed and shot into the air, reaching our altitude with no difficulty and in record time.

I sat quietly for a few moments of contemplation. Sometimes I seem to be sitting on the runway of life wondering why God doesn't answer my prayers in my time schedule. Doesn't He realize I am in a hurry?

But in His time He prepares me for takeoff, filling my soul with Holy Spirit power. Then together we zoom into action such as would not be possible had I not been forced to wait for the Spirit's infilling.

Lord, teach us to be patient and to wait for You.

MILDRED WILLIAMS

The Mother on the Mountain

The prayer of a righteous [wo]man is powerful and effective.
James 5:16, NIV.

Nothing moves me like the story of a mother. My heart aches for mothers whose children die in tragic circumstances. Mothers whose children are missing or murdered. My vivid imagination imagines how it would be for me in their situation.

One evening, several years ago, long lines of weary, broken people walked across my television screen, carrying a few belongings tied in a sheet or old sack. The Kurdish refugees were fleeing Iraq. Pregnant women were giving birth by the side of the road, then forced to get up and continue walking. In the refugee camps, people were already dying because of inadequate food, warmth, water, and sanitation. Mothers rocked their tiny, starving, sick children, giving the only comfort they had to offer. The situation was desperate. It was breaking my heart that mothers and children were suffering like this, and I could do nothing about it.

The news report ended. I sat alone in the quiet of the evening and just felt. I experienced all kinds of strange feelings as I put myself in the situation of those Kurdish mothers, trying to do their best for their children. Soon I tasted a little of their salty tears, imagined their breaking hearts as they watched their little ones suffer and even die.

"Dear Father, what can I do for them? I feel so helpless here. Nothing I can do can make a difference to their lives right now when they need so much help. How can I show I care?"

As I sat in the stillness, I seemed to hear a voice say, "You can pray. I want you to pray for one particular mother out there on that hillside. Her little child is very sick, and she doesn't know what to do. Just pray for her. And I will hear your prayers."

And so I prayed, and prayed, and felt a sense of peace. I was doing the only thing I could do, and it was much more than a few pennies in a charity box, or a piece of wornout clothing, or a tin of beans. It was being part of a channel of love from heaven to earth—tapping the greatest resource in the universe.

Out there on the hillside . . . what happened? I may never know. Maybe a mother felt strengthened and comforted. Maybe a little child received some medicine and food from an aid worker. Maybe the child fell asleep and woke with the fever gone. I don't know, and it doesn't matter. It was enough to reach out through the night, with a prayer and God's love, and share the burden of a suffering mother.

Today, as you listen to the news, focus in on a mother whose life has been directly affected by the world's events, and make her the subject of your prayers.

KAREN HOLFORD

Christ—A Mother's Role Model

Neither do I condemn thee: go, and sin no more. John 8:11.

The only difference was the eyes. Twenty years earlier they had been blue-green. Last week the eyes were brown. Both sets of eyes were fearful.

In our living room stood an arrowleaf plant. I especially loved the plant when all outside was white and blustery.

One January day when I came into the room, I saw the arrowleaf's green leaves on the floor. Shawn, our 2-year-old son, knelt next to them, his blue-green eyes fearful.

"Shawn, you pulled off all the leaves on my plant!" My tone was harsh.

His voice trembled, "Yes, Mommy." I marched to the kitchen to get my "spanking spoon." Crying, he ran toward my sister. "Aunt Beth, save me, save me!" I took my son, a bit brusquely, and used the spanking spoon. Sobbing, he grabbed me around the neck and kissed me. I was forgiven. But I will never forget those fear-stricken eyes as he ran from me.

Last week Sam, a 3-year-old at my preschool, pulled all the leaves from a plant. Standing beside the pile of green leaves, the boy looked up at me with brown eyes. I looked down and again saw the fear of a guilty child. Kneeling down to his level, I put my arm around him. "Sam, you really didn't want to hurt my plant, did you?"

"Oh no!"

"Without leaves, plants can't grow. You want the plant to grow, don't you?" He nodded, tearful. "Let's pick up the leaves." As we picked them up and threw them in the wastebasket, his fear disappeared.

Since then, neither boy has pulled leaves from plants. Both know it is wrong.

In the Bible I have studied how Jesus dealt with wrongdoers. I have read and reread the story of the adulterous woman the religious leaders brought to Jesus. Instead of the just punishment according to the law the men clamored for, Jesus knelt and started writing in the dust where the wind could erase the message. When pressed further, He replied, "He who is without guilt, let him cast the first stone."

Jesus' words, "Neither do I condemn thee: go, and sin no more," sink deep into my mind. They are balanced words, neither excusing sin nor castigating the sinner.

In 20 years He has taught me how better to deal with little boys who pull leaves off my prize plants. No condemnation, no grabbing for the spanking spoon, only a warm hand on their shoulder, joining them in correcting their mistake, repeating to them His words, "My child, go and sin no more."

I give to them what I have received from Jesus. I need no harsh reminder of how delinquent my own promises have been. Instead, I, a guilty sinner, look to Him, and my own fear also disappears.

CONNIE NOWLAND

MAY 13

A Secure Anchor

We have this hope as an anchor for the soul, firm and secure. Heb. 6:19, NIV.

*D*uring spring break my two college-aged brothers decided to introduce the rest of the family to the thrill of their newly learned sport of rappelling down cliffs, harnessed to a rope. They gathered the necessary equipment, then we all packed a picnic lunch and headed to Joshua Tree National Monument in the California high desert.

There they selected a 20-foot cliff for a practice site and secured two ropes to metal pitons on a wide ledge where we would have plenty of room to maneuver. I had severe rheumatoid arthritis in virtually every joint, so I elected to sit on a rock and watch. Also being afraid of heights, I didn't feel like I was missing out on the fun.

One by one the family members took turns putting on the harness, clipping it to the rope, and descending beside one of the "experienced" brothers. Another family member would be at the bottom holding on to the loose end of the rope. If a climber lost control, pulling on the end of the rope would stop his/her descent.

As I watched the technique used, it gradually dawned on me that if I could get up to the staging area, I could do it too. It didn't require muscle and joint strength. The most important requirement was to lean on the rope and let it do the work. Suddenly I felt a strong desire to try it. When Mom finished her turn and came to sit beside me to watch, I casually mentioned that it looked like something I could do. Mom lost no time in yelling, "Lucy wants to do it too!" Now I was committed.

It took some doing to adjust the harness to fit my small frame. Then they wrapped the rope an extra turn around the clip so that I had to push the rope through in order to make any progress instead of gripping the rope to slow me down. I didn't stop to worry about what I was doing. I just leaned on the rope, started pushing it through the clip, and backed up.

At one point on the way down my foot found only air instead of solid rock, and I slammed into the side of the cliff. Although I received scrapes and bruises, the rope held secure and I arrived at the bottom exhausted, but exhilarated. My disability had worked in my favor, and I had learned a lesson that still helps me today.

As long as my soul is firmly anchored to the Rock, I am safe, and I can do what I could never accomplish on my own. All I have to do is lean on the rope of God's promises and start moving, keeping my eyes on the Lord instead of my circumstances and refusing to worry about seeing too far into the future. LUCILE FREEMAN-KIME

MAY 14

God's Flower Garden

Consider the lilies, how they grow; they neither toil nor spin; yet I tell you, even Solomon in all his glory was not arrayed like one of these. But if God so clothes the grass which is alive in the field today and tomorrow is thrown into the oven, how much more will he clothe you, O men of little faith! Luke 12:27, 28, RSV.

This morning as I look out my big picture window I see the rain gently falling to nourish nature. The spring flowers bowing their heads in approval. The lovely carpet of green grass soaking up the gentle drops. The many birds singing their songs of rain and melody. The beauty of God's nature overshadows the blemishes of weeds and dead leaves from last summer.

God gently reminds me of all the blemishes of sin in my life—jealousy, greed, low self-esteem, laziness, fear, and many more. He assures me that He has showers of blessings just waiting for me to enjoy as I surrender and let the rain of His love fall on my heart to produce new growth. He will care for me abundantly if I allow Him to.

I thank Him today for the softness of His world. For the gentle rain followed by the sunshine. For the rosy sunrise at early dawn. I thank Him for the robin that sings its cheery musical song.

I thank Him for the blessings of His Son, who died on Calvary to wipe away my tears of sadness and sin. For healing my pain. For the softness of His love and care for both the lilies and the burdens and cares of my heart.   CAROLYN VOSS

MAY 15

Our Father Is Almighty

For I know the thoughts that I think toward you, saith the Lord, thoughts of peace, and not of evil, to give you an expected end. Jer. 29:11.

*I*s anything too hard for Me?" That was God's question to Jeremiah, and it is still His question to us. And we chorus, "Surely, no!" But do we really believe and mean it? Don't we doubt from time to time? The two following experiences our family lived through in Rwanda in April 1994 have revived our faith.

The war and its horror had just begun, and everyone on the college campus was frightened and tired. We heartily longed for a quiet Sabbath, but was it possible? However, that night we slept deeply, and the next day went by without disturbance because the villagers and soldiers had fled. We later discovered why. They had heard gunshots and grenade explosions from the mountains and even the noise of troops coming! But we heard nothing and were able to rest peacefully on the Lord's day. How mighty is our Father!

The second event happened the following Sunday. We were supposed to have left two days earlier, but were still waiting for an escort, who hadn't arrived because of blocked roads. Humanly speaking, we were trapped. Our anxiety mounted when the pregnant wife of one of our deans felt some labor pains.

But nothing is too hard for our Father!

Two foreign military officials drove up in a small car with six nationals to convoy the pregnant woman to safety. Almost all the university families seized the opportunity to follow in their personal cars. We were evacuated from the hot furnace of the war thanks to our loving Father who used the birth of a new baby to deliver us.

"He alone is my rock and my salvation; he is my fortress, I will not be shaken. . . . He is my mighty rock, my refuge. Trust in him at all times, O people; pour out your hearts to him, for God is our refuge" (Ps. 62:6-8, NIV). May we always remember that our God is the Almighty One.   JEANNE D'HARIMALALA RASOANINDRAINY

MAY 16

Color-blind

There is neither Jew nor Greek, slave nor free, male nor female, for you are all one in Christ Jesus. Gal. 3:28, NIV.

*M*y favorite doll was a rag doll named Topsy. She went everywhere I went, did almost everything I did, and was my closest friend and confidant. The doll never chided me, never disagreed with me. I loved her passionately and could not fathom heaven without her. I don't know who made her, but most likely it was my grandmother.

If I had that doll today, she would be called a freak. She had two heads and two bodies—two trunks with two sets of arms. And no feet. But she was soft and cuddly and a forever kind of friend.

The Topsy end of my doll had a black face, curly black hair, shoe button eyes, and a long red calico dress with yellow ribbons around the neck and sleeves. When I turned the doll upside down, she became Mopsy with a white face, blond ringlets, shoe button eyes, and a long blue calico dress with pink ribbons around the neck and sleeves. Two friends in one. Sometimes I'd sleep with Topsy, sometimes with Mopsy. Each looked different, but both were precious, one no less loved than the other. In retrospect, I can see that it was a good educational toy.

I wonder if Paul had a toy like mine to help him with his unbiased vision toward people of other cultures. He lived in a time when hatred ran rampant. The Greeks hated the barbarians, the Jews hated the Romans. Since that time many wars between different cultures have raged for generations. "Cold wars" we call them, but they are deadly—just as deadly as war on an open battlefield. Wounding a person's self-worth is one of the cruelest kinds of fighting. It has no place in Christian warfare.

Sometimes when I see an insult heaped on someone of a different background, my righteous indignation rises. Defaming a person of another race or culture actually insults everyone. Clearly, it is one of Satan's devices to wound a child of God, a product of His divine design.

I long for heaven and all the surprises God has in store. While I don't know what color we'll be, I hope everyone is not the same. But until that happy day comes, I am particularly thankful for the diversity of colors and backgrounds we have here in this world. Our lives are richer for the mixture.   LORABEL HERSCH

MAY 17

He Cares

And why worry about your clothes? Look at the field lilies! They don't worry about theirs. Yet King Solomon in all his glory was not clothed as beautifully as they. And if God cares so wonderfully for flowers that are here today and gone tomorrow, won't he more surely care for you? Matt. 6:28-30, TLB.

When we moved from Singapore to Sarawak on the island of Borneo, we inherited an ugly cactus plant from the former occupants of the mission house. It looked almost dead, with only one long-angled branch protruding from a large clay pot. Setting about to put our house and yard in order, I kept shoving the unsightly plant from place to place, hoping to hide it among the more attractive plants and flowers. In a land whose humid climate was so conducive to lush growth, I thought that even my "brown thumb" might produce green and lovely things. After all, didn't the Lord provide a natural watering system with an afternoon shower almost every day?

Some months passed before I saw any change in the ungainly plant, but one day a bump appeared on its only branch. On closer examination, it appeared to be a bud, and sure enough, it grew larger and fatter. One evening we saw two or three petals appearing. It was then someone speculated that this plant just might be a night-blooming cereus. The dictionary provided more details—"*Selenicereus grandiflorus*—a cereus with climbing angled branches and large fragrant white flowers opening about midnight." Our ugly plant had a very dignified name.

We continued to watch the unfolding flower and also enjoyed its unusual fragrance. It was truly breathtaking. The night-blooming cereus lasts only one night. By morning the blossom had faded and was gone. After its delightful exhibition, the ungainly plant took an honored place where I could explain to our visitors the surprise it held.

Months later, when I was alone at home, I happened to see not just one blossom opening, but six creamy white flowers in full display! It was already 11:00 p.m., too late to call in my neighbors or to phone friends in town to come share the joy of this grand production. I could only praise the Lord for His love and care that seemed to be enfolding me as I treasured those moments of pure pleasure that my Creator had planned just for me on a night alone.

Reminded of our text, I asked myself, "Why am I so prone to worry?" It is actually impertinent to worry when I claim to trust the Lord to supply my every need. Our heavenly Father knows our circumstances, and if we keep centered in Him, we will grow spiritually as the lilies—or maybe even a night-blooming cereus! He wants to surprise us with His joy.   MARIANETTE JOHNSTON

MAY 18

The Gift of Words

Do not let any unwholesome talk come out of your mouths, but only what is helpful for building others up according to their needs, that it may benefit those who listen. Eph. 4:29, NIV.

*M*y father was a minister, and although I don't remember many sermons from my childhood, I readily recall his using this little couplet:

Boys flying kites haul in their white-winged birds,
But you can't do that when you're flying words!

Have you ever realized that it's the words we let fly without thinking that we often regret and wish we had never said? Usually the conversations we're most pleased about later are the ones in which we took time to think out a tactful way to approach someone, to brighten a friend's day with a compliment, or to give a warm fuzzy to a family member. The words said in haste often reflect anger or sarcasm and come from an uncontrolled tongue.

Solomon painted a beautiful picture when he said that "a word aptly spoken is like apples of gold in settings of silver" (Prov.

25:11, NIV). Apt words, appropriate words, are those we think about in advance.

I recently attended a women's dinner that used the theme of Florence Littauer's "Silver Boxes" story. The stage was decorated with large boxes wrapped in silver paper. Each place setting at the table had a small silver box with a beautiful silver bow. The woman giving the devotional told Mrs. Littauer's story about the little girl who tried to describe the way words make us feel. "They're like a little silver box with a bow on top," the child proclaimed.

After the dinner I took my small silver box and put it on the desk at my office. It has been such a gentle reminder of an inexpensive gift I can give. I love to give gifts, and the little box helps me remember to plan "word gifts" of encouragement and appreciation to brighten someone else's day. Such gifts don't even hurt my budget!

In the verse for today, Paul referred to "flying words" as "unwholesome talk." I'm sure he would consider the silver box gift as the words that build others up and benefit those who listen. Whose day could you brighten with a little silver box with a bow on top?

ROXY HOEHN

MAY 19

Joy Cometh in the Morning

Trust in the Lord with all thine heart; and lean not unto thine own understanding. Prov. 3:5.

The year of my divorce was a very difficult time for me. It seems so long ago now, but the memory of God's guidance is still clear and sharp. I had no one else to turn to—but there really isn't anyone better to turn to, right? God taught me to trust fully in Him, and when I did, He led me to the still waters of peace and safety.

After an updated education, I had the skills to do God's work in many parts of the world, and my eyes opened to a wider perspective. A friend sent me this poem, which did a lot for me, and I hope it will help you, too.

> There must be thorns amid life's flowers, you know,
> And you and I wherever we may go
> Can find no bliss that is not mixed with pain,
> No path without a cloud; it would be vain

For me to wish that not a single tear
Might dim the gladness that you hold so dear.
I am not wise enough to understand.

All that is best for you; the Master's hand
Must sometimes touch life's saddest chords to reach
Its sweetest music and His child to teach.
To trust His love till the long weeping night
Is all forgotten in the morning light.
Trust, trust Him then and thus shall good or ill
Your trustful soul with present blessing fill.
Each loss is truest gain if, day by day,
He fills the place of all He takes away.

— *Author Unknown*

Bessie Lobsien

May 20

I Prayed for You

Always in every prayer of mine for you . . . making request with joy. Phil. 1:4.

In quietness I sought the heavenly
Father in my room,
And thanked Him for His loving care,
Mid rays of morn's first bloom.

And then I told Him all about you,
And of your needs today;
He was expecting me, because
I told you I would pray.

I prayed for you this morn.

I prayed He'd give you special help,
And extra angels send
To lift the burdens that you bear,
Because you are my friend.
I asked Him to be with you
Every hour the whole day long
To comfort you in sorrow and

In weakness make you strong.

I prayed for you today.

My heart is filled with gratitude.
Words fail me to express
My deep appreciation for
Your love and thoughtfulness.

I cannot recompense you for
The trust you have in me,
But I can share with you our Friend
In silence on my knee.

I prayed for you tonight.   LORRAINE HUDGINS

MAY 21

From Mourning to Morning

He who loves father or mother more than Me is not worthy of
Me; and he who loves son or daughter more than Me is not wor-
thy of Me. And he who does not take his cross and follow after
Me is not worthy of Me. Matt. 10:37, 38, NASB.

*H*er heartbeat seemed to rock her little body as my mother
scurried to the mourner's bench. She was 7 years old.
The pastor in the family's Baptist church had invited
those who wanted to be baptized to come forward—to the
mourner's bench. This signified not only a mourning for sin but a
willingness to surrender to the Lord's will. Ethel Marie Jackson joyfully said yes to both.

But her path to the Lord didn't end at the river baptism. The
path wound on and dipped into the baptismal pool of the Tenth
Street Seventh-day Adventist Church in Erie, Pennsylvania, some 40
years later.

It was a glad/sad day when Ethel Marie Jackson walked into that
pool. Glad because she had grown closer to the Lord—learned
more, accepted more. Sad because she was ending her Baptist heritage. Her name would be removed from the membership role that
contained the names of parents and grandparents and great-grand-
parents on back to just this side of slavery. When she stepped into

the second baptismal pool, she stepped outside of the comfort of the social and familial closeness that had nurtured her. That circle now closed behind her.

Jesus said in Matthew 10:37, 38 that those who put family before Him are not worthy of Him. But humanity's need for human acceptance is strong, and many chose to stay within their comfort zone. Not Mamma. She got about her Father's business, wooing her former church members, bringing to her newer relationship with Christ some of her sons and daughters and neighbors. "God is good and greatly to be praised," she told them.

Her friends and family mourned their loss in Mama's eighty-eighth year. Yet they celebrated a life lived gloriously in Christ. The funeral program echoed her heart's rejoicing that had so long ago resounded from the mourner's bench and pointed to that "Great Gettin' Up Mornin.'" "God is good and greatly to be praised."

FAITH JOHNSON CRUMBLY

MAY 22

God Stays With Us

And my God will meet all your needs according to his glorious riches in Christ Jesus. Phil. 4:19, NIV.

Last night my two children and I went through the evening routine of baths, family worship, teethbrushing, drinks of water, and then to bed.

Then I lay down beside my 5-year-old son for a few minutes as he slipped easily into sleep. Next I went into my daughter's room and snuggled with her for a little while. Becky is my night owl and lay wide-eyed, listening to a Christian tape on her cassette player. She seemed engrossed in a story about the writing of "The Star-Spangled Banner." I paused the tape a moment, kissed her nose, and recited "The Lord bless you and keep you; the Lord make His face shine upon you, . . . and give you peace" (Num. 6:24-26, NKJV). Then I patted her shoulder and turned the cassette player back on, thinking I'd slip out into the backyard and water our parched little garden. "I'll be back in a little while," I promised.

Out in the yard I enjoyed the slight breeze as I watered trees and garden. Heading closer to the house to turn the water down to an all-night slow drip, I heard unmistakable screams and cries coming from the house. I ran in to find Becky and Benjy sobbing together in

Becky's room, their faces soaked with tears. They were overjoyed to see me and explained between subsiding sobs that they had thought I'd been "kidnapped by a robber." Quickly I explained to them I had just been outside for 10 minutes giving some thirsty plants and trees a drink. Becky told me that she had gotten up to ask me why the British had come over here with soldiers to fight us after the U.S. declared independence, only to find me gone from the house. She had then awakened Benjy, and they had searched the house for me in growing panic, concluding I must have been stolen away from them. "We both prayed, Mommy," Benjy told me solemnly.

With more hugs and kisses I reassured my little ones that God is always with them. Mother may fail, or be too far away to hear the child's cry (much to her regret!), but God is always with us, always available.

As my children slipped off into sleep again, I thought about how dependent on me they are and how important it is that I be there for them. It also forcefully reminded me of my limitations. I can't always hear or always be there. But I can point my children to God-With-Us, our eternal hope and source of strength.　　　JUDY BROECKEL

A Woman Who Fears the Lord

Who can find a virtuous woman? . . . Give her of the fruit of her hands; and let her own works praise her in the gates. Prov. 31:10-31.

This very familiar chapter of Proverbs on the qualities of a "virtuous woman" mentions some form of needlework five times. Verse 13 tells us that she looks for the wool and flax to work with her hands, and verse 19 says that she takes those materials and spins them into thread. She makes warm clothing for her family, and her own clothing is a tapestry of silk and purple (verses 21 and 22). The woman sells the extra linen and belts (verse 24).

As this paragon of virtue takes care of her family, oversees a household of servants, and goes into business for herself, she also manages to do volunteer work for the poor and needy (verse 20), plant and tend a field and vineyard (verse 16), and work long hours, even after everyone has gone to bed (verse 18).

I wonder how this "superwoman" does all that she does? Don't her dishes ever break? What happens when the power goes out and she oversleeps because the alarm didn't go off? Has drought ever killed her garden? Or an overabundance of rainfall flooded her basement? Has she ever forgotten her checkbook with a long line behind her at the grocery store? Have her children ever gotten into trouble at school or her husband lost his job? Maybe. Maybe not. But these verses never tell us that she loses her temper. How does she do it? We may not all be able to do everything she does. Some of us have a business. Some of us have gardens. Some of us raise children. Some of us do more than one of these things. But I've read a little further and discovered her secret. Verse 30 says that she is a "woman that feareth the Lord."

DEBORAH BILBY

MAY 24

Friendship Gardening

Greater love has no one than this, that he lay down his life for his friends. John 15:13, NIV.

*B*eryl and I—you couldn't pick two closer friends. She was so much more mature than I—at least three or four years. Thin, with flaming red hair, she was better educated than I. And she was my best friend from the time I was about 5 years old until I was 8. I considered her better educated, since I hadn't even started school yet. She gave me my first reader—the "see Spot run" variety. I wasn't sure then what it was about her that made me feel good about myself, but I kept going down the street to visit her.

Friendships take time. Often we miss out on friendships because we allow life to get too cluttered with living.

As I became aware of how cluttered my own life is, I realized how much I needed to grow and cultivate my relationship with Jesus. Helping our friendship to grow takes a concentrated effort from me. It means I have to see myself as I really am. I need to take time to read, study, and, most of all, to pray.

The wonderful thing about Jesus is that He is always there. I may move away or get distracted, but He's always waiting for me to talk with Him, read His love letter to me in the Bible, and enter into communion with Him.

Many friendships have come and gone in my life. I don't know whatever happened to Beryl, though Jesus does. But He is ever ready to be all any of us ever need in a best friend.

Take time to retill the soil in the garden of your heart and allow the Master Gardener to cultivate His love in you. You will soon grow the most beautiful friendship you have ever seen in your life.

MOIRA BARTHLE

MAY 25

Healing for Hurt

My grace is sufficient for thee: for my strength is made perfect in weakness. 2 Cor. 12:9.

*D*uring the past three years our family has lost five close relatives and friends, and I had a bout of serious illness that lasted for nearly a year. One might imagine that they have been very depressing years, weighed down by grief and sorrow, and indeed, in many ways they have been. However, it has also been a time of great happiness, personal fulfillment, and joy.

At the beginning of our "time of trouble" our faith struggled. We could not understand how a loving God could let such things happen, and we found it hard to pray. Two bereavements and an illness. The next year had to be better. It brought two more deaths, and this year, another.

Initially we were weak and broken, but the prayers and support of loving friends helped us cope. Their prayers carried us when we couldn't pray for ourselves, and God reminded us: "I am still here. I do care. I suffer with you." He taught us that the way out of darkness and despair is to rely on Him, to think of others, and to work for them. We learned that we can laugh through our tears, and that we can experience real joy in our lives.

Most of all, we discovered that being a Christian does not guarantee that we will escape being touched by the evil in the world. Being a Christian, rather, means knowing that God can make good come out of evil. Being a Christian involves relying on God's strength, and not our own. And being a Christian compels us to go to God when we hurt.

They say that time heals. I have found that time only grows a scab over the wound. Sometimes the scab gets knocked off, leaving the wound raw and bare and sore again. Only the healing balm of Jesus' love can make it well again.

If you hurt or are sad or lonely, if you are feeling weak and depressed, go to Him. He will make you strong again and will put laughter and love back into your life.

AUDREY BALDERSTONE

MAY 26

Salvation Is Only by His Grace

For by grace are ye saved through faith; and that not of yourselves: it is the gift of God: not of works, lest any man should
boast. Eph. 2:8, 9.

"The fire-walking ceremony is on at Kataragama, and it will be
interesting to see it," Daddy announced, eager to attend this
very outstanding event among the Hindus.

Soon we reached Kataragama and found much excitement in
the area. People crowded the area where the fire-walking ceremony
would take place. We looked closely at those who were preparing
for their walk. More than 25 fire walkers stood in line. The bed of
embers glowed brightly in the dark night.

"Why are they doing this?" our daughter, Virginia, questioned.
"Why do they have to go through this terrifying experience?"

"For merit," volunteered someone who had overheard her question. "If they walk on these embers, their sins will all be burned out,
and they will become very holy people. Not only that, their diseases
will be healed, too. And some are doing it to fulfill vows."

"How sad," Lavona, our younger daughter, whispered. "Don't
they know that Jesus died for them? That we are not saved by our
own merits, but by the blood of Jesus Christ, who gave His life for
each one of us?"

"I am glad we don't have to walk on those hot embers to go to
heaven," another in our group sighed with relief.

"The path that God has prepared for us is really strewn with
flowers and not embers," Aunty joined in. "His love is different from
anything that these people have known."

You and I have a Saviour who cares for us, who does not require
us to earn our salvation by our own merits. Let us daily draw closer
to Him and accept that free salvation.   INDRANI J. ARIYARATNAM

MAY 27

I Will Get Up

This is the day which the Lord has made; we will rejoice and be
glad in it. Ps. 118:24, NKJV.

To get out of bed on a cold morning, whether in Massachusetts or Missouri, in Idaho or Iowa, is one of the really hard decisions we have to make. Along with the warmth of the flannel sheets, the pleasure of half dreaming, and, for many of us, the nearness of a beloved spouse, is the subtle pressure that Satan puts on us to get a little rest instead of beginning the day in communion with Christ. Sleep at the moment seems so much more important than prayer or study.

All of us know that the whole of our Christian life hinges on spending some time alone in God's presence. When the preacher read "'Now in the morning, having risen a long while before daylight, He [Jesus] went out and departed to a solitary place; and there He prayed'" (Mark 1:35, NKJV), we silently said "Amen," and vowed that we too would rise early to pray and to study our Bibles.

But now it is morning, and things suddenly seem different.

Last night we may have retired at a reasonable hour, having put aside the magazine, bundled up the work from the job, or called it quits with the never-ending housework. But that was last night, and now it is morning.

A litany runs through our minds. "It's time to get up." "I ought to get up." "I should get up." "I must get up." We begin to feel miserable and guilty. But when we say "I will get up," the will becomes involved, and we leave our beds and soon know the joy of growing closer to God.

I once heard a seminar presented by Christian author June Strong. She suggested, "Begin your morning prayer with this verse from Psalm 118:24: 'This is the day which the Lord has made; we will rejoice and be glad in it'" (NKJV).

It works. I find that this verse is a good one to recite to myself before I throw back the covers. Since God has made this day, He will be in control of all its circumstances, its worries, and its struggles. My instructions are to be glad, to rejoice, to bring those struggles and worries to my Maker. Peter reminds us to cast "all your care upon Him, for He cares for you" (1 Peter 5:7, NKJV). But that can happen only if we begin each day with Him.

Pray with me this morning, "I will get up." Amen.   RUTH ANNEKE

Our Ticket to the Future

Some trust in chariots, and some in horses; but we will remember the name of the Lord our God. Ps. 20:7, NKJV.

I collect tickets to events I've attended over the years and keep them in a beautiful crystal bowl on my dining-room table. On the tickets I've written the names of the people I've gone to the event with, the outcome of the game, the conductor or soloist of the concert, actors in the play, etc. Whenever I get lonely or feel that my life is boring, that nothing good ever happens, I go to that crystal bowl and pull out a ticket stub. Immediately memory takes me back to the event, reminding me of all those people in my life with whom I have experienced joy. Many of those people are still there for me. All I have to do is get in touch with them.

Memory is a wonderful thing—perhaps because it is selective. We tend to forget the more unhappy times of our lives and remember only those worth holding on to. The trouble comes when we forget to remember. We can get discouraged quite easily about our lives, especially if we look too closely at what's going on around us. Treachery and tragedy abound everywhere, sometimes in our own lives. We might ask ourselves where God is in all this. At times we might even conclude that He's abandoned us. Sometimes we forget God altogether, or worse, think He's forgotten us.

But that's where memory comes into play. And where better to go to jog our memory than the Bible, that wonderful collection of ticket stubs for events featuring God and His love? Where better to go to see how God cares deeply about us and how He is there to give us all the strength and support we could possibly ever need to get through our trials and challenges? Where better to go to understand His purpose for us in our present as well as our future? Or where best to learn of His plan for our lives?

If we feel lonely and neglected, if our hearts ache and our minds struggle with doubts, perhaps it is because we have forgotten how life can be when Christ is a part of it. It is important then—even essential—to look back and remind ourselves of the events of the past. Reminded of how He has led others to victory, we can rest assured that He will guide our lives as well. Strengthened and encouraged by memory, we can then invite Him into our own lives.

RONDI AASTRUP

Practice Hospitality

Share with God's people who are in need. Practice hospitality.
Rom. 12:13, NIV.

*T*he Living Bible throws a little more light on this verse: "When God's children are in need, you be the one to help them out. And get into the habit of inviting guests home for dinner." During my travels over the past 20-plus years I've been a guest in many homes. The vast majority of these homes have been beautifully decorated.

God has obviously blessed such women with superior talents. Some have table settings that are second to none, with beautifully served food. The talents and abilities that God has given them in turning their homes into places of beauty are outstanding. And they love to do it! To such women this is not work, but as natural as breathing.

To all such talented homemakers, I send a message: God has given you such talents to use for Him. The ability to make your home beautiful, to decorate, coordinate colors, blend furniture styles, and put it all together in a harmonious manner is not frivolous or wasted energy. To make a home comfortable for everyday family living as well as to say "welcome" to guests is truly a talent and gift from God.

Many women have these gifts but have never thought of themselves as having done anything significant for the Lord. It has not occurred to them that through creating a centerpiece, setting a beautiful table, or cooking a meal for guests, they were making a significant contribution to the work of God.

To all of you who open your home to others, cooking, cleaning, and preparing for guests, you are fulfilling the commission to "practice hospitality." You are making a significant and meaningful contribution to your friends and your church.

All the time, effort, and money you put into making your home comfortable and beautiful is not wasted or lost. Nor has all the cooking, vacuuming, dusting, cleaning, decorating, and money spent gone in vain.

Every time you feel exhausted from the effort, thank God you had the strength to clean and prepare. Every time you plan a menu for guests and do the grocery shopping, thank God He has provided you with the resources that allow you to entertain. And every time you entertain, be thankful you have someone to encourage through your friendship. Many have no friends.

Hospitality is so much more than what appears on the surface. Through the gift of hospitality, we can make friends, and thus keep ourselves emotionally and socially healthy. We can also become a vital link in witnessing and proclaiming the gospel. But we also, by extending hospitality to others, can make the world a better, warmer, friendlier, and infinitely more interesting place. Take your talents and carry on! NANCY VAN PELT

MAY 30

A Sample Lesson on Perfection

Be ye therefore perfect, even as your Father which is in heaven is perfect. Matt. 5:48.

*B*ut Teacher," the rosy-cheeked, blond-haired 5-year-old child stated emphatically, "it's not like yours!"

"Yes, it is, Kristen," I assured her hastily. "See, it's got the green planter, the pretty pink flowers, and the cute little colored fuzzy balls. You did a great job. Really."

There. I'd praised the child. Surely she was happy with her newly created craft now. Swiftly I moved toward some other children. Younger and less verbal, they, too, were busily attempting to finish their craft.

"No, Teacher," Kristen said impatiently as her tiny fingers tried unsuccessfully to finish shaping her work. "It doesn't look like yours. It doesn't." She banged on the table to show her irritation.

"Oh boy," I muttered quietly, "what is her problem?" I had no idea that being a first-time crafts leader for Vacation Bible School would be so exasperating. My desire to discover a new Picasso or two slowly dwindled. During the planning sessions beforehand, experienced leaders had instructed me several times, "Let the children work on their own projects by themselves. Let them create their own masterpieces . . . and don't correct their work. Praise it no matter what it looks like."

"Kristen," I said curtly, trying hard to regain my composure, "what's wrong with yours?" I stooped down beside her. Why did she insist on having hers look exactly like mine?

"Look," Kristen remarked smartly, "yours curves. Mine doesn't. It's not like yours!" Pouting, she shoved them both toward me.

Dumbfounded, I glanced at hers, then mine. Suddenly I felt embarrassed. Hers was perfectly straight in every corner, while mine did curve. Because of lack of time I had made my samples in record time. I recalled that I had told the children to follow my instructions, but to remember that theirs wouldn't curl at the edges like mine did. Somehow I hadn't realized that these eager artists would look at my sample as being "perfect."

"Forgive me, Lord," I whispered. Tears welled up in my eyes. I squeezed them back, struggling to find the words to tell Kristen how sorry I was. Kristen grumbled on, trying to perfect her craft. I worked on mine too, trying to straighten it up as best I could.

Suddenly I became mindful of how wonderful God, our Creator, is. He sent His Son to earth—not a warped, carelessly contrived misrepresentation of Himself, but perfect in every way. A true example of what we should strive to be. The innocent questionings of a young girl striving to be perfect had indeed taught me a valuable lesson.

IRIS L. STOVALL

MAY 31

Brand-new Clothing

Joshua's clothing was filthy as he stood before the Angel of the Lord. Then the Angel said to the others standing there, "Remove his filthy clothing." And turning to Joshua he said, "See, I have taken away your sins, and now I am giving you these fine new clothes." Zech. 3:3, 4, TLB.

Now so many years later, I cannot remember whether it was the shrill voices or the stifling odor that jarred my senses first. A line of children began shouting, "Greg fell in the pond! Greg fell in the pond!" I rushed to the stairs. Only his brother, David, and his best friend, Darryl, were touching him. The others walked at a discreet distance.

We had recently moved to a home on campus. The children had vast stretches of play areas. Somehow the groundskeepers had overlooked a small stagnate pond. On this particular day the children had been playing "Ring Around the Edges" by the forbidden pond. Five-year-old Gregory lost his balance and toppled in. It wasn't deep enough to drown in, but deep enough to soak him from cap to boots.

"Greg!" I screamed as I reached for him. Quickly I unbuckled his cap, struggled with the buttons on his coat, fought with his boots and socks, and peeled off his other clothing. The stench was overwhelming. The cliché came to mind: "Don't throw the baby out with the bathwater." But this was my child—no odor could drive me from him.

Several baths later I wrapped his small body in a towel, and we both smiled. The expensive woolen coat, leggings, cap, boots, and other clothing had to be thrown away. But Greg was clean. "Be more obedient, Sugar Pie," I whispered into his ear.

We come to God all soiled from blundering around and falling into the stagnate pond of sin. But God in His infinite love, as our Father, has a special preparation of cleansing for us. This preparation was made at Calvary. Then He clothes us in His robe of righteousness. He whispers to us, "Lean on Me, child, and I will guide you so you won't keep falling into sin. Lean on Me."

DOROTHY A. STARKS

JUNE 1

Burst Balloons

"For I know the thoughts that I think toward you," says the Lord, "thoughts of peace and not of evil, to give you a future and a hope." Jer. 29:11, NKJV.

As a little girl I was entranced by balloons—bright red, blue, and yellow. I loved them in all sizes and shapes. They glamorized parties or a trip to the county fair. Though it was beautiful to see a balloon sailing high in the wind, I would feel regret that it had been lost.

When a naughty boy steps on a balloon, popping it intentionally, I'm offended. As a child I cried when my balloons would burst. I still jump and wince when a balloon explodes. It's such a waste and disappointment.

Life is so much like a children's party with burst balloons. Dreams and goals go up in the air with a bang. What seemed so glamorous or important can shatter in an instant. We try to hang on to what used to be or what we wanted it to be—only to have it blow away.

My husband and I have tried to hold on to our own personal dreams as we have worked for God in different places and several countries. As we have received requests to work in new positions, it seems like we just can't turn loose of our dreams for the work where we already find ourselves. We feel like we are needed right there. It's difficult to let go and take up a new challenge.

Yet it never fails that after the move we distinctly see the hand of the Lord in it. Sometimes we have been spared heartaches in the former location, and the challenge is often greater in the new place. Every move has brought us blessings. Isn't hindsight marvelous?

How thankful I am that God has foresight, seeing the end from the beginning, and leads us in the paths we would have chosen for ourselves if we had had His wisdom. It is infinitely reassuring to know that He is planning for us in love to give us "a future and a hope"! How comforting to know that as we follow His leading we will always find happiness.

I wonder why we hang on to our own hopes and dreams, afraid that they will get popped, when God already has a glorious plan for every detail of our lives. In fact, many of my burst "balloons" have become my richest blessings.

FELICIA PHILLIPS

JUNE 2

Pushy-Cat

Let us therefore come boldly unto the throne of grace, that we may obtain mercy, and find grace to help in time of need. Heb. 4:16.

One morning after we had just moved into a new neighborhood and I was curled up with a book on the sofa, I was startled to see a cat come walking through the open deck door. It inspected the dining and living rooms (things didn't look quite familiar) and made a dignified exit. Not long afterward when we returned from a walk, it ran up to us and rubbed its body against our legs. It enjoyed being picked up and loved. I was captivated by its blue eyes, long beige fur, and the white smile on its dark face. Its owner, the woman next door, told me its name was Zeus—"king of the gods." He was king, all right!

One bitter January night as Ralph and I returned from a meeting, Zeus pushed his way between our legs and through the door. Since it was too late to send him home, I decided to let him spend the night on our sofa. We had no sooner snuggled under the warm blankets when he pounded and scratched at our bedroom door. *Now, that's being pushy,* I thought. *He wants to come right into our inner sanctum.* But he wanted more than that—he was determined to get in bed with us! Not only that, he marched right up to my pillow, draped his head and paws over my face, and purred wildly as he massaged my forehead. Then he proceeded to give Ralph the same treatment.

Some nights later he stayed too late again. This time I tried to settle him down in a comfortable chair in our basement study. I petted him, put a pillow over him, and swiveled the chair around so he couldn't see when I left. Then, crouching out of his sight, I inched my way to the stairwell and made a beeline up the stairs. But before I could close the door on him, he shot past me and skidded clear across the kitchen floor on his way toward our bedroom. Doubled up with laughter, I couldn't resist him after that. I was putty in his hands.

Zeus's yowl is not exactly beautiful. He uses it when he wants to enter or exit or be fed. When he keeps on yowling I have found out that he wants love. I think that's kind of nice. He likes me for myself and not just for what I give him.

And God doesn't mind either when we yowl to Him about our needs and scratch on His door for admittance. He even invites us to enter His inner sanctum—to jump on His lap, even His pillow. But what He likes best is when we purr out our ecstatic love for Him.

BEATRICE S. NEALL

JUNE 3

Light the Darkness

I am the light of the world; he who follows Me shall not walk in the darkness, but shall have the light of life. John 8:12, NASB.

The hammering on the front door of our home at 1:00 a.m. awakened me, and I was terrified.

"Open up," the stern voice called.

It was a cold, snowy night in 1941. The United States was involved in World War II. America's East Coast cities, fearful of being bombed, staged blackouts every night. Blackouts meant that one had to cover all windows with black shades that obliterated all inside light. Automobiles could not drive at night with their headlights on. Men were instructed not to smoke a cigarette outside in the darkness. It was said that a lighted match could be seen for miles and could guide a bomber pilot to your city.

The pounding continued on the front door. My father sleepily hurried to open it.

"I'm the block warden, and you must put out the fire in your fireplace. I'm afraid the enemy will spot the light from your chimney and bomb us. One small light could change everything!"

My mother got out more blankets as Dad put out the fire in the fireplace. Even though it was the only heat available in our home that cold December night, we had to extinguish it until morning. I remember mother hugging us children with reassurance that morning would come soon.

Last week, while flying from Baltimore to San Francisco, I stared from the window of the airplane at the vast blackness 33,000 feet below. Suddenly I spotted a small flicker of light. Instantly my stomach clenched in fear. Then I smiled at the power of childhood memories. After all those years I can still hear the block warden's voice saying, "One small light could change everything."

Fascinated, I watched the tiny light disappear as the plane continued onward, wondering who had lit the darkness. Did they realize that a stranger six miles above them had noticed their light? From how many miles away would that light be visible?

A thought occurred to me: Light is always more powerful than darkness. When one small light is set aglow, there is no earthly way to measure its effect in the universe. And if that one small light is from God, the source of all light, then the block warden's words are true: One small light can change everything. Is it any wonder that we are instructed by Jesus to "let your light so shine before men, that they may see your good works, and glorify your Father which is in heaven" (Matt. 5:16)?

ELLIE GREEN

JUNE 4

In the Firing Line

Inasmuch as ye have done it unto one of the least of these my brethren, ye have done it unto me. Matt. 25:40.

The summer of 1993 was a very busy one in our home. Friends came for an extended visit, our sons had student friends to stay, and never less than nine lived in the house at any one time. Other friends arrived and departed every few days, and although it was a job to keep track of the comings and goings, we had great fun.

In the midst of it all, my husband, who works as a volunteer for an international disaster relief organization, left to drive a truck full of supplies to Croatia. Having to run our business while he is away keeps me quite busy, so I was looking forward to his return.

His phone call to say they had safely delivered his load came one Friday evening. After telling me how the trip had gone, he paused, then asked, "How would you feel about my going into Sarajevo?" He explained that there was a warehouse filled with food in Zagreb, but they needed someone with a foreign passport and a truck to take it in. He and his friend Bob were willing to go. How did I feel?

My heart skipped a beat as I contemplated the implications of his risking the dangerous journey into that beleaguered city. However, as I looked at our extended family, their happy faces, and our tableful of food, I knew I could give only one answer. "We will pray every day for your safety," I told him.

It was three weeks before we heard from David and Bob again, and with great joy we welcomed them safely home. The plight of the citizens in that once lovely city has tugged at David's heartstrings ever since, and he has made a number of return journeys.

Two weeks ago their convoy got caught in a crossfire. The truck has five bullet holes, but fortunately no one was injured. When one compares the incident against the terrible suffering being endured by the people of Sarajevo, it pales into insignificance, and the drivers had no hesitation in delivering their load, leaving, and going back in again. They are brave men who demonstrate their Christianity in a very practical way.

Not all of us are capable of performing heroic deeds, but we can all do *something*. By collecting food, organizing fund-raising activities, and praying earnestly for those on the "front line," we can fulfill Christ's commission to look after those less fortunate than ourselves.

AUDREY BALDERSTONE

JUNE 5

God to the Divorced

For your Maker is your husband, the Lord of hosts is His name; and your Redeemer is the Holy One of Israel. Isa. 54:5, NKJV.

Grace's husband died of a heart attack before she was out of her 20s. It was the first condolence letter I felt compelled to write. Somehow I discovered Isaiah 54:5: "For your Maker is your husband." What else could I say to a childhood friend in her grief and her loneliness?

Fifteen years later my own home broke up, and the text came back to comfort me. "For your Maker is your husband." Using the concordance, I found the chapter in which it appears, and also found strength for the particular problems that every divorced

woman faces. Those of you who have walked this path know them:
A tremendous loss of self-esteem
An overwhelming loneliness
An acute sense of rejection
An awareness of an unfair and overburdening responsibility in the rearing of partially estranged children
The ever-present problem of making ends meet
The certainty that she is the subject of ungenerous gossip among her friends
The loss, often, of beautiful and comfortable surroundings
The possibility of danger to her person

I discovered that Isaiah 54 was addressed to the "afflicted one, storm-tossed, and not comforted" (verse 11, RSV). That surely described me. I found at least one verse in the chapter that offers hope for each of these problems.

Loss of self-esteem—"You . . . will not remember the reproach of your widowhood anymore" (verse 4, NKJV); "with great mercies I will gather you" (verse 7, NKJV).

Loneliness—"Your Maker is your husband" (verse 5, NKJV).

Rejection—"For the Lord has called you like a woman forsaken and grieved in spirit, like a youthful wife when you were refused" (verse 6, NKJV).

The responsibility of rearing children—"All your children shall be taught by the Lord, and great shall be the peace of your children" (verse 13, NKJV).

Financial problems—"My kindness shall not depart from you" (verse 10, NKJV).

Unfriendly gossip—"And every tongue which rises against you in judgment you shall condemn" (verse 17, NKJV).

Loss of attractive home—"I will lay your stones with colorful gems. . . . I will make . . . all your walls of precious stones" (verses 11, 12, NKJV).

Physical danger—"No weapon formed against you shall prosper" (verse 17, NKJV).

How does God fulfill all these promises? I found it to be through friends, through counseling, and through the insight He gave as I studied His Word and prayed. As Jesus said, "I will not leave you desolate" (John 14:18, RSV). RUTH ANNEKE

182

The Raspberry Picker's Parable

So I say to you: Ask and it will be given to you; seek and you will find; knock and the door will be opened to you. For everyone who asks receives; he who seeks finds; and to him who knocks, the door will be opened. Luke 11:9, 10, NIV.

A man, feeling that his life lacked a certain sweetness, went out to pick raspberries. As he walked along, juggling his plastic containers, he thought of the heat of the sun, the prickles of the raspberry canes, but especially of the fragrance of the fruit. Nearing the raspberry patch, he noticed that many other men, besides women and children, had the same idea. He placed his empty containers in a patch of shade, then looked about him, hoping to see an unpicked area where his efforts would be richly rewarded.

As he watched, he noticed that some pickers walked beside the rows of canes, picking off a berry here and there, but it was late in the season, and the topmost berries were few and small. These pickers complained loudly, and their faces showed that the berries they tasted were not sweet. Soon they walked away, carrying few berries and mumbling, "Raspberry picking is a pain!"

Then, as he still considered the situation, the newcomer, standing beside his empty containers, saw other pickers. They called loudly to one another, inquiring as to where they could find the most luscious and juicy berries. And he noticed that these people made much noise and stirred up much dust in running to and fro, but did not find much satisfaction anywhere. Presently they too trudged up the hill, hot and dusty, with half-full containers and cross, frustrated faces. As they passed, they warned, "Don't bother, mate; they're not worth picking!"

The man wondered if it was as they said, but noticed that a few were not grumbling and rushing to and fro. Plants usually hid them, just a movement of the leaves showing where each one worked. As the man waited beside his still-empty containers, one of these pickers came up the hill toward him. The individual carried many containers, all full, and had telltale signs of enjoyable eating around the mouth. As the person passed, he paused in the shade and proclaimed, "There are plenty remaining. Just choose your row, get down on your hands and knees, and look up!"

So the man, taking great encouragement and all his containers, went to the nearest row, where he knelt down and looked up. And he found great sweetness and abundant satisfaction.

Now consider the parable, for the moral is not for raspberry pickers only.

GWEN PASCOE

JUNE 7

To Train a Doll

Each man should give what he has decided in his heart to give, not reluctantly or under compulsion, for God loves a cheerful giver. 2. Cor. 9:7, NIV.

*I*f I never heard another sermon for the rest of my life, I'd still enjoy attending church. Now don't misunderstand me. I'm very happy with the quality of sermons presented in my church. They hold my interest and challenge my thinking. Then why am I willing to relinquish the sermons? I'm not, really. It's just that so many other good things take place there that I'd find it well worth the effort to attend each week even if I heard no sermon.

Here are but a few of my special joys: watching the young father/son deacons working in pairs as they collect the offering, noting the seated person reaching over to welcome the latecomer, and seeing the pastor shaking the child's hand even before greeting the parent.

I absolutely love watching the small children bring in their special offerings. In our church, a large gold-sprayed chest sits front and center at the foot of the pulpit. While the offering plates pass down the pews, small children are encouraged to bring their own offerings to the chest designated for the church building fund.

I doubt that many toddlers have a clear picture of how their offerings get spent. Are they concerned about tax deductions, receipting procedures, or audit control? Not one bit. They give for the sheer joy of giving. Some skip uninhibitedly down the aisle, poise over the open chest, hold their gift up high, then drop it and wait to hear it *clink*, releasing each coin individually to prolong the pleasure. Others start out slowly toward the chest, panic midway, then wait for a friend to accompany them. And some will tiptoe timidly all the way, quietly slip in their gift, then race back to proud parents.

Recently I witnessed a new approach to joyous giving. A very shy little 3-year-old cautiously approached the chest clutching her doll after most of the toddler traffic had cleared. As she stood before the chest, she secured her doll in the crook of her arm, opened her purse, and took out her offering. Carefully, she lovingly tucked the bill into her "baby's" hand and helped her drop it into the chest.

A cheerful giver? This little toddler was more than that. She had cheer enough to share. Can one so young experience such joy in giving? Can such a tiny tot already feel the maternal instinct pulsing within her? A cheerful giver, indeed! A sermon in itself.

LORABEL HERSCH

JUNE 8

My Best Friend

A friend loveth at all times. Prov. 17:17.

I was early for a 1:00 appointment, so I popped in to visit my friend. It never entered my mind that I might not be welcome. I knew that even though it was 11:45 a.m. on Sunday, I would find a welcome here. Knocking, I heard the familiar words "Come in!" Harriet was curled up on the couch with an afghan, and her happy smile told me she was glad I had surprised her with my visit. We spent an hour in pleasant conversation. It was wonderful to go to her house because she is my friend.

The word *friend* brings to mind thoughts of sharing confidences, laughter, and having a faithful ally. A friend is a pal, one with whom you enjoy doing different activities. Friendships last through thick and thin. Years spent apart never affect a true friendship. The memories friends share are special.

Friends are people with whom you feel a special bond and share similar interests with. They support you and do things for you without a thought of remuneration or reward. When we meet friends we have not seen for several years, it is easy to continue our friendship on the same plane as before. Friends are loyal and true.

Friendship is like a rope that holds us together. Mountain climbers depend on the rope to bind themselves together for safety and progress. Friends employ the rope of friendship to link their lives together, trusting in one another.

I have many friends. Some of my friends dwell just down the road. Others live farther away. The friends I cherish the most are those of my family: my husband, my children, my daughter-in-law, and my grandchildren.

But I have a very special Best Friend. He has all the qualities of a true friend. His faithfulness to me is unsurpassed. Although I forget to spend time in communication, neglect to thank Him for His love, or act in ways that are not pleasing to Him, yet He is forever the same. He cherishes me and cares for me as no other ever has.

This Friend gave His life for me with unconditional love. He is ever willing to forgive and continue loving me. And He loves to communicate with me. I can share my innermost thoughts with Him and know that He understands and cares. He asks so little of me and gives so much. He is Jesus, my special friend. — EVELYN GLASS

JUNE 9

Give It What You've Got!

Two small birds cost only a penny. But not even one of the little birds can die without your Father's knowing it. Matt. 10:29, EB.

About a decade ago Trivial Pursuit came on the scene as a major pastime for the Saturday night crowd. I recall a group of college students sprawled on my living room floor inviting me to join in playing this new and fascinating game. They probably figured that at my age I must have accumulated lots of trivia. Questions like the following entertained us into the tender morning hours: "Who took the first balloon ride?" "What team won the World Series in 1958?" and "What country produces the most seedless grapes?"

As I staggered off to bed, my head spinning from the fragments of information bumping into each other in my brain, I wondered what all this trivia was worth. What good were such bits and pieces of knowledge?

Sometimes I feel like a bit of trivia myself, of little or no value to anyone. I might wallow in the thought that I'm "just ordinary." And I know others who share my gloomy view at least on occasion. We haven't done anything exceptional, we aren't outstandingly beautiful, we don't garner much adulation, and invariably have "Murphy's Law days" when everything that can go wrong does. Sometimes our lives take on the semblance of "trivial pursuit." We are only a minuscule portion of life's game—and we're not even on the winning team!

That's when we need to remember that with Jesus nothing is trivial.

Once when He was teaching, the usual large crowd gathered. Time slipped by too quickly, and by lunchtime most of the audience, while enthralled by Jesus' message, could no longer ignore the gnawings of hunger. But what could they do? They had no buffet lunch, no caterers, not even the Palestinian version of McDonald's anywhere nearby. Probably they became restless and grumbled while their stomachs protested.

Jesus' disciples knew they had to do something to appease the masses. After all, there were at least 5,000 men present, never mind the women and children, who weren't important enough to even be counted! Then one of the disciples spotted a little boy with a little lunch. With amazing faith and foresight, he brought the youngster to the Master.

You know the rest of the story. One small child who didn't matter enough to be numbered among the 5,000, with five loaves and two fish that couldn't have been very large, made the difference.

We're not trivial to God. He multiplies our efforts. With God, anything can happen. What little we have may be precisely what He needs to work a miracle. With God at our side, life is no longer a game of trivial pursuit. LILYA WAGNER

JUNE 10

Here Comes the Bride!

Is anything too hard for the Lord? Gen. 18:14, NIV.

I was more than depressed—I was beside myself with grief! I knew I could not afford a brand-new $3,000 wedding dress. The astronomical prices of wedding dresses did not fit our budget, and I was so discouraged that I cried. Looking at *Modern Bride* and other bridal magazines did not make shopping for a gown any easier for me.

Eventually I prayed a very simple prayer that I still remember to this day. I said, "Lord, if Leonard is the right man for me, and I am 100 percent convicted that he is, please provide the gown for me. Amen." No sooner had I finished my prayer than I felt a strong impression to call a bridal salon I had visited a year before Leonard proposed. Out of all the gowns I saw, there was one in their huge collection I really liked.

Instantly I rushed to a telephone and called the bridal salon. To my surprise, one of the salespersons told me that they had kept my name, address, phone number, and the style number of the gown I had seen the year before. Naturally I started to get excited. The woman then told me the gown was being discontinued and had been discounted more than half price. I was ecstatic. God solved my problem!

Since I could not afford to let this bargain pass by, I rushed to the store to place a deposit on the gown. The salesperson I spoke with was even kind enough to let me put it on layaway for six months. My total costs for a glamorous wedding gown that looked expensive, with alterations, came to only $262.50. When I share this story with people, they usually react in shock.

Whenever I am tempted to forget the thousands of ways God has in providing for my needs, I remember this experience with a smile.

CAROL ANN FRASER

JUNE 11

Why Not Ask?

Ask, and you will be given what you ask for. Seek, and you will find. Knock, and the door will be opened. Matt. 7:7, TLB.

Shopping completed and bills paid, I was ready to leave the city for my quiet home 10 miles away. Then, as I deposited my packages on the car seat, I discovered my handbag was missing. Quickly I retraced my steps to the store of my last purchase and spoke to the salesperson. She hadn't seen the bag, but directed me to the lost-and-found department. "Leave your name and phone number, but I doubt you'll ever see it again," she told me.

On the way home I chided myself for being careless while feeling grateful that I had used most of the money before losing the purse. My credit cards were my real worry, and I called each place as soon as I got home to stop purchases on them. Now it was almost 3:00 p.m., and I hurried to the hospital for work.

Entering the hospital, I remembered an admonition I had learned as a student nurse: "Leave all your troubles at the door as you enter. You may pick them up when you leave." Good idea, I decided. It proved to be one of my busier days, and after work there seemed to be no time or energy for problems.

The next morning, after a good sleep, I sat with my Bible in hand and thought again of the handbag. *Maybe it's witnessing,* I thought, remembering that a picture of Christ would be the first thing anyone would see on unfolding my wallet. What would a thief think on opening it to see the loving eyes of Jesus looking at him or her?

I said a prayer for that thief while marveling at my resignation of the day before. Why would I accept the prediction "You'll never see the purse again" when God says, "Ask, and you will receive"?

Before I began reading, I asked Him to impress the thief to at least return my credit cards and license.

Halfway through my second chapter, the telephone rang. A woman spoke, hesitantly, "I have your purse. Will you please pick it up? I have no way to bring it to you, and my conscience won't let me keep it."

At once, two Scripture texts came to mind: "While they are yet speaking, I will hear" (Isa. 65:24). Certainly His answer had come quickly. The second one: "Ye have not, because ye ask not" (James 4:2). Would the woman have called if I hadn't prayed about it? I think not. How many blessings have I missed because I failed to ask God's help?

The lesson is one I shall always remember. My Father is interested in all that concerns me. He wants to help whatever my need may be, and no matter how major or minor the problem be, I *shall keep asking.*

ALYCE PICKETT

JUNE 12

Homeland

It was a better country they longed for, the heavenly country. And so God is not ashamed for them to call him their God, because he has prepared a city for them. Heb. 11:16, TEV.

*Y*ou would like Marina. She is young, lively, and ready to laugh. Her eyes sparkle when she talks, and she listens with intense interest. Marina has a rewarding job and attracts many friends. Often traveling abroad, she is involved in planning international events. You may think that Marina has almost everything a young woman could want. But she is missing something very dear to her—the homeland of her ancestors. You see, Marina is a refugee.

Marina is a Greek Cypriot who in 1974 had to leave her homeland in northern Cyprus. Many Turkish Cypriots living in southern Cyprus suffered a similar fate. Marina told me how her family had to flee. Remembering the old house lived in by her grandparents and their parents before them, she longs to go back and see it and the trees around it again, to feel like she is really home at last. But she can't. Now armies and barbed wire divide Cyprus. Marina is a refugee in her own country.

When Marina talks about the "Cyprus problem," her emotions

bubble over. She is frustrated with the politicians who talk about solving the problem but seem to accomplish nothing.

As I listen to her story, I begin to feel some of Marina's pain. Sadly, she is not hurting alone. Millions on earth are refugees.

And I am a refugee too. Perhaps not in the same sense as Marina, but just as surely. You are also a refugee. We all are refugees from the Garden of Eden. We belong in a perfect world, not in this world of pain, sorrow, and death. But our predecessors changed loyalties from God to the invader. They were forced to leave, and so we all lost our homeland.

But the story has not ended. We have the promise of getting our homeland back! Negotiations are going on now. Instead of our being dependent on the choices of fallible and ineffective politicians, we can choose our own destiny. This same world we walk on now will be cleansed and remade (Rev. 21:1-5). The air, the trees and flowers, the lakes and the creatures, will all be as fresh as they were Creation week. Perhaps Adam and Eve will recognize a vine or a bush they tended long ago. Maybe they'll tell us stories of the happy times they spent on their homeland—our homeland.

Marina wants to go home. So do I. JOYCE NEERGAARD

JUNE 13

Promises, Promises

People who promise things that they never give are like clouds and wind that bring no rain. Prov. 25:14, TEV.

*E*d McMahon's likeness beamed at me from the outside of the envelope. "Gina Lee is our new $10,000,000 winner!" read the copy. But when I ripped open the envelope, I found it was nothing but a come-on. Good old Ed promised that I would hear those words only if my assigned numbers matched the numbers drawn in a sweepstakes.

TV and the magazines make so many promises today—promises that are seldom kept. Advertisers assure us that their products will make us popular and happy. Politicians offer us bigger, better social programs, along with lower taxes, of course! Alcohol and other drugs promise instant happiness and instead leave people numb or hurting.

People who should keep their promises—police officers, schoolteachers, doctors—often betray the public trust. Even more devastating are the promises broken among families—the promises between husband and wife that end in a bitter divorce. Or the promises between parent and child that end with a battered baby in a lonely hospital room.

Promises are easy to make and even easier to break, but there is Someone who keeps His promises—our heavenly Father. And what promises He makes—promises to heal our lives and our souls, comfort us in times of trouble, and offer us the miracle of hope! Instead of promising us a mere $10,000,000, He offers us a much bigger prize—eternal life. The price has already been paid through the blood of Jesus Christ.

Among an oceanful of empty and broken promises, the promise of salvation shines out like the welcome beacon of an old-fashioned lighthouse. While mere human beings fail to keep their promises, Jesus stands forever true to His holy Word.   GINA LEE

JUNE 14

Not a Drop to Drink

Ho, every one that thirsteth, come ye to the waters. Isa. 55:1.

Young, enthusiastic, and idealistic, my husband and I found that answering God's call in our lives had led us to establishing a new mission school in New Guinea. The work was by no means simply a "spiritual" experience, as it required everything we could muster down to the last physical muscle to clear jungle and erect temporary bush material buildings to start classes in.

Our seating arrangements in class were simple. Logs felled on the property set in neat rows served as benches. We had no desks, but we did have blackboards, chalk, and a few textbooks. A stream provided bathing facilities, and the cafeteria consisted of a thatch roof supported by poles.

However, enthusiasm was not lacking. After the morning classes teachers and students worked together to clear more jungle and plant gardens to provide food for the school family. Because education was a luxury, students treasured a place in the school.

Our budget had to spread in many directions, but we did have four 1,000-gallon water tanks for drinking and cooking. Fortunately the stream provided for other needs. Then the weather turned unseasonably cruel and the dry season refused to end. The skies remained brilliant blue day after day while the levels in the water tanks dropped drastically, even with rationing.

My husband and I prayed. All the teachers prayed. The students prayed. Morning and evening we joined in special prayer, but still no rain fell. Although the gardens were languishing, the students believed God would send rain and decided that if the school could give them a ration of one cup of dry rice and four cups of water a day, they would stay. After all, wasn't it God's school?

Finally, sadly, the staff decided that if no rain fell in the next 24 hours, we would have to close the school, as the stream had just about dried up, three water tanks were empty, and the one at our house had only a little water left.

After an earnest prayer meeting that night, my husband knocked on the side of the water tank. Three and a half rungs of water remained. The sky was starry. But surely God would send rain.

He didn't. The next morning things were as dry as ever. Feeling confused and dejected, my husband, out of habit, knocked on the side of the water tank. Three, four, five, six. Excitedly, he climbed on a stool and continued counting. The tank was full! God had answered. The school stayed open, and we kept on praying.

In two days the rain started, and our cups were running over, both literally and spiritually. He has continued to fill them, and we still drink deeply. I urge you as well to drink of the water of life today, and you will never thirst again (John 4:14).   URSULA M. HEDGES

JUNE 15

The Innocuous Fly

He sent divers sorts of flies among them, which devoured them.
Ps. 78:45.

I know a horsefly when I see one: long, gray, wings laid back along that sausage body, planning soon to fill itself with my lifeblood. But not if I can help it! A slow, smooth approach of the hand and *wham!* One more contribution for the compost heap, and one more rescue for me from a bite that can itch for days.

A trainee in my new career as a horticulturist, I set out to weed a border in the rose garden. Hot July sun rays bounced off the centuries-old brick walls, redoubling the temperature. I had a major college assignment to keep a detailed horticultural diary, so I observed everything—including an innocuous fly that settled lightly on my forearm. It reminded me of a burnet moth—black with neat yellow patches on its abdomen and attractively mottled wings. Its eyes shone an amazing neon red. I was talking kindly to it when *ouch!* It stabbed me! I batted at it, but it jetted off. And I had a nasty itching bite for days.

I looked the beast up in a field guide book that identified it as: "*Chrysops relictus.* Horseflies. Tabanidae. Stoutly built, fast-flying. . . . Eyes large and often brightly colored. . . . Most females [sorry!] are voracious bloodsuckers, attacking large mammals, inc. man, with their bladelike mouthparts" (Michael Chinnery, *Collins Guide to the Insects of Britain and Western Europe,* p. 200).

As I smoothed soothing baby cream, aloe lotion, and witch hazel gel on my itching skin, I thought ruefully of several lessons I might learn from this incident. First, I don't know everything—about horseflies, or the enemy's attacks. I need to learn more, to be better prepared, in both fields.

Second, I will never know everything; horseflies and satanic attacks do not always come in the same recognizable form. I might learn all the biting flies in Britain, but never all demonic tactics. So I need a close personal friendship with my Guardian, God, who can supply my deficiencies in knowledge with His infinite wisdom.

Third, I notice that evil, like the Chrysops when compared to an ordinary horsefly, is a *lot* faster in getting about these days, harder to kill, noisier, and more blatant in its attack. So now I rub on oil of citronella to keep horseflies of all descriptions off me. I need to reapply it at least twice daily—more often in hotter weather.

And I need, similarly, the oil of the Holy Spirit's presence in my life daily—at least twice (morning and evening) a day, and more often as life's situations become more heated. In fact, I need this healing, soothing, and protecting oil constantly.

Come, Holy Spirit, come! Make my heart Your home.

APRIL DUNNETT

JUNE 16

Fatherless

Sing to God, sing praise to his name, extol him who rides on the clouds—his name is the Lord—and rejoice before him. A father to the fatherless, a defender of widows, is God in his holy dwelling. Ps. 68:4, 5, NIV.

I was having lunch at a restaurant with my husband and daughter when the people at the next table caught my attention. Then I sat watching them in rapt silence. A young woman about my own age was sitting with an elderly man. They were deep in discussion, and I found myself straining to catch parts of their conversation.

"Look," I remarked to my husband after a while. "Aren't they cute sitting over there like that talking?" My husband glanced their way, unimpressed. I continued on. "I'll bet that is a father and daughter. I wonder what they are discussing."

My husband looked up from his meal. "They are trying to decide what the man should give the mother for Christmas." That made me want to leap up from my chair and tell them what a special time they were sharing. I wanted to urge the young woman to cherish every moment she had to spend with her father.

Then I thought of my own father, now dead almost seven years. I was only 27 when he died, but he had been ill for several years before his death. Before that I had been away at college. We had never had time for personal luncheons with just the two of us. As the youngest of six, I usually shared my parents with at least one other sibling during any activity. My heart longed for that special interaction I knew I would never have with my father. Instantly I looked at my own daughter now deep in conversation with her father, discussing the ever-growing concerns of a 2-year-old. *Someday,* I mused, *that could be the two of you.*

The voices of the father and daughter rose slightly, and I heard her insist on paying and meeting again when he could treat. Maybe she did realize just how special it is to have a father to take to lunch. They stood up to leave. As I watched them go, I felt a lump in my throat. If only more fathers and daughters realized their opportunity to share such a special relationship.

I said a silent prayer of thanks to the One who is a father to the fatherless, for even as an adult, being fatherless is sometimes difficult to bear.

"I will be a Father to you, and you will be my sons and daughters, says the Lord Almighty" (2 Cor. 6:18, NIV).   CAREL CLAY

Father's Day

O Lord, you are our Father. Isa. 64:8, NIV.

*T*he third Sunday of every June is a time when people in many different countries celebrate fatherhood. They recognize a biological or an adoptive father, a stepfather, or a father figure—some person who took the time to be a role model and to influence their lives in some special way. Father's Day provides the impetus to honor and respect our fathers and father figures.

Spokane, Washington, was the first place to officially honor fathers with a special day. Louise Smart Dodd wanted to honor her father, William J. Smart, on his birthday—June 5. Her mother had died during childbirth with her sixth child, and Mr. Smart had raised Louise and her five brothers all by himself. The actual celebration didn't materialize until the third Sunday of June in 1910. President Richard Nixon signed a congressional resolution in 1972 assuring recognition of Father's Day on a continuing basis.

For years I celebrated Father's Day, taking for granted that my dad would always be there. And now he isn't—though his love lives on within my heart. To paraphrase King George IV of England, his leaving has left a great blank in my life.

When a baby arrives in the family, unfortunately no mandatory "Fatherhood 101" study course accompanies it. Men probably receive even less formal preparation for their roles as fathers than do mothers. Studies show that most men are almost as excited about becoming fathers as women are about becoming mothers, but that men rarely have any concept of the real impact a baby will make upon their lives, marriages, and responsibilities.

Fathers have a tremendous effect on the lives of their children, grandchildren, and great-grandchildren. Some of their many roles are breadwinner, disciplinarian, authoritarian, friend, and protector. It takes years for children to begin to understand their fathers—30 at least—and these years are a time of growth and change for both fathers and offspring.

Although we now understand that motherliness and fatherliness are both attributes of God, we are perhaps most familiar with the Bible metaphor of God as a father. This is comforting to those who have experienced the love of a wonderful father. For others, who have not known this love, the metaphor can seem strange, unappealing, even frightening. Christ says, however, that if we love Him, we will in turn be loved by the Father (John 14:21). This is a promise we can all cling to, especially those who have not experienced wholesome fathering.

Father's Day can be an occasion for warm remembrances and a time to realize anew that "Our Father, which art in heaven" will parent and/or reparent us according to our need. ARLENE TAYLOR

JUNE 18

The Greatest of These Is Love

And now abide faith, hope, and love, these three; but the greatest of these is love. 1 Cor. 13:13, NKJV.

September 1992 my best friend, Joseph, and I married after a 2½-year courtship. That December he was in a near-fatal auto accident that left him paralyzed below his shoulders. After eight days in ICU and with no hope of recovery, he was transferred to a rehabilitation hospital whose specialty was weaning people off respirators. By the grace of God, after five months he was off the respirator and ready to come home.

The advice of many was to place Joseph in a nursing home and "get on with your life." My love for him dictated differently. Being the newlyweds that we were, we wanted to spend as much time together as possible, so I chose to bring him home. The rehab hospital trained me in physically caring for my husband, and I made it a point to learn every detail. After he arrived home a whole new life began for us, with the hands-on and spiritual support of our parents.

Now, two years later and still quite happy in my marriage, people (even our parents) often remark that they just don't see how I do it. My response is simply that I don't do it. It's the love that God placed in me that does it all! Try love. It works!

BONITA DUDLEY-SCOTT

JUNE 19

Thoughts on a Number of Things

Are not two sparrows sold for a penny? Yet not one of them will fall to the ground apart from the will of your Father. And even the very hairs of your head are all numbered. So don't be afraid; you are worth more than many sparrows. Matt. 10:29-31, NIV.

*O*ur life on this planet truly can be "summed up." One's whole existence can be told in a few seconds by bits of magnetism on a computer tape.

To our employer, we are 910-64-3456 and live in the 500 block of 48th Street in zip code 19146 and answer all calls at (215) 847-6251. To our friends, we are 5'6", 150 pounds of 36-36-36. To the physician, we are patient 9748 with blood pressure of 130 over 88. Still other series of numbers identify us to the department stores and filling stations.

Even the church is not free from the "numbers racket." We sit in the third seat of the fourth pew and sing three verses of No. 191 instead of "Love Divine" and reach our offering goal of $5 per week.

In recent years two more numbers have been added to the growing list—68 and 55. These are not ages for retirement, but figures for our thermostats and speedometers.

This would seem to be but another step in the dehumanization process to further remove the image of God from our personalities. We can query with the psalmist, "What is man?" (Ps. 8:4).

Constantly being identified with numbers can lead us to regard ourselves as nonentities. The desire for noninvolvement and widespread apathy do not improve our self-image.

This process can be reversed only as we seek a oneness with God and recognize His Trinity. The Ten Commandments become our rule of life and the 66 books of the Bible, our guide. Then the millions for whom Christ died become souls we seek to bring to His kingdom, where no one can be "numbered" (see Rev. 7:9).

JAYNE DOSWELL DARBY

JUNE 20

A Promise Is a Promise

Have no fear of sudden disaster or of the ruin that overtakes the wicked, for the Lord will be your confidence and will keep your foot from being snared. Prov. 3:25, 26, NIV.

I shouldn't have been surprised. It was Friday. Everything happens on Friday! However, this particular Friday was going smoothly, and I was feeling quite smug about it. I had dried and put away three loads of wash. Clean sheets all around and fresh towels in the bathrooms. I'd mopped the kitchen floor, baked a cake, and made sure salad stuff was ready in the frig. I'd even spent two hours at my desk, and it was only 4:00 in the afternoon. Not bad.

"Now," I told myself, "to town—the post office, bank, and the cleaners. Then to the grocery store."

I pulled into the flow of traffic on the main road to town behind a smart little red Mustang. It was "riding the bumper" of the car in front of it—an elderly model driven by an elderly man at an elderly pace.

At the corner, I watched the slow car to see if it would go straight ahead or turn right. Whatever that driver did, I would do the opposite. The older car did not turn right. *Marvelous!* I thought. I shifted into second and turned right. Immediately my car began to slide to the right toward a pile of rocks and a big pine tree.

Now, believe me, I didn't *mean* to overcorrect; I just did. And now I was sliding to the left toward *two* trees and someone's front door! Instantly I realized my peril, and my call for help was immediate.

"*Lord!*" I shouted in my mind. His answer came in a soft and well-modulated voice. "Let go," He told me. In much less time than it takes to tell you this happy little story, I actually looked into my lap at this point and my hands were now resting peacefully there. My car was moving slowly and driving into the driveway of the house with two trees. Then it stopped nicely and waited for further directions. I sat there a couple of minutes to gather myself together.

Many passages of Scripture came into my mind about God's faithfulness, but I think perhaps Proverbs 3:25, 26 says it best for me right now: "Have no fear of sudden disaster . . . for the Lord will be your confidence."

My trusty little car and I drove out of the driveway as though nothing unusual had happened. All the way down the hill to town I praised God for His love and direction. I thanked Him for delaying the oncoming traffic that was now a steady stream and for telling me what to do.

No, I take that back. I praised God for *doing it for me.* He told us He would help us in times of trouble, and after all, a promise is a promise is a promise.   Virginia Cason

The Dog Who Came to Church

I was glad when they said unto me, Let us go into the house of the Lord. Ps. 122:1.

*T*humper must have been curious about what happened to his family every week. We lived on a mission compound about a mile from the church. Imagine our surprise, right in the middle of Ralph's sermon, to see him come marching down the aisle, tail wagging, barking with delight as he made his way to the platform. At last he had solved the mystery!

How he had found his way through the busy streets choked with army trucks, taxis, and bicycles I will never know. But I smothered my smile when I noticed that our Vietnamese members were not amused. Mortified now, I got hold of his collar, dragged him under the pew, and held him until the service was over.

The following week I put Thumper in the backyard. High compound walls surrounded it on two sides, and a five-foot-high decorative inside wall made of staggered bricks with open spaces between them enclosed the rest. When he arrived triumphantly at church, I realized that walls could not fence him in! Too ashamed to hold him under the pew, I led him outside and stowed him away in our microbus, carefully lowering the windows so he would not smother in the stifling heat. At the end of the service we found Thumper hanging out the window by his hips, vigorously scratching the door. His plight became permanently etched in our memories!

Next week I found a more humane solution by attaching a chain to his collar and a tough rope to the chain, which I securely wrapped around a tree in our front yard. Now he would have shade and enough mobility to be comfortable.

Chagrin, chagrin! Thumper strode into church dragging the chain and part of the rope behind him. Bypassing the chain, he had chewed through the heavy rope with a cut so neat it looked as if a machete had slashed it. I meekly led him out of the church, inwardly marveling at his intelligence.

All week long I racked my brains as to what to do next. Then I came upon the perfect solution. I drove out of the garage, opened the front door of the microbus, and called, "Come, Thumper." Thumper loved to ride by me on the front seat. He joyfully jumped in and sat tall as he looked expectantly out the windshield. I reached behind him and closed the door, backed into the garage, and imprisoned him there. That day he didn't make it to church.

When I think of all the excuses some people give for staying home from church, I think of Thumper. He is a real testimony to those who often miss out on the blessing of worshiping God with fellow believers. Would that everyone had his joy in overcoming obstacles and making it to church!　　　　BEATRICE S. NEALL

JUNE 22

Only a Daisy

Jesus said, "I tell you the truth, this poor widow has put more into the treasury than all the others. . . . She, out of her poverty, put in everything." Mark 12:43, 44, NIV.

Growing world poverty threatens the health of millions of women throughout the world as they struggle in harsh economic and social conditions. They rise each morning to begin the day's toil of seemingly endless duties in order to survive. Their multiple roles include health-care provider, water and firewood gatherer, tiller of soil or factory weaver, market merchant, and provider for the household. The World Health Organization estimates that in developing countries three quarters of the women produce 50 to 90 percent of the food. Often they work with simple tools and receive little training on new methods and improved technology. Although women are major contributors to the economic and social society, often they are the least rewarded. Many cultures pass women by because they do not see females as important. Thus no one may ever notice them as they succumb to the perils of everyday life.

What can make a difference? Leadership training to help women realize their potential. Loan credit programs, along with community-based support and technical skills training, enable them to begin projects that will successfully earn them a living. Literacy skills and a knowledge of health and child-spacing and child care improve the quality of life, and will help break the cycle of exploitation and self-degradation. A glimpse of hope can bring a ray of sunshine into any life. And most of all, Christ can lift the burdens.

I remember a simple Indonesian village woman clad in tattered clothing. Her income was small, and she worked long hours to feed and support her family. What impressed me most was her bright smiling face. A face that told stories of toil and hardship, but reflected her love toward others and Jesus.

When I left her country, she was among the group who said goodbye. She offered me a daisy as tears fell from her eyes. I hugged her, and wept. This gift was worth its weight in gold. It told of our friendship and respect for each other. We lived very different lives, but she taught me much about the value of life.

Jesus did not tolerate human bondage. He brought healing and hope to the women who came into His presence. As Jesus acknowledged the widow's mite, He showed His acceptance. It was not the gift in her hand that was of value, but rather the gift in her heart. Although these women may fall like the sparrow, or fade like the lily, the Lord remembers them as His jewels.

Remember your fellow sisters from around the world who suffer adversity. Pray that they will hear the good news of Jesus' love and will live in the earth made new.　　　　　　GAIL M. ORMSBY

JUNE 23

Rescued

For the Son of Man came to seek and to save what was lost. Luke 19:10, NIV.

*J*t was early summer in our Pennsylvania countryside, and the winter wheat outside our window was changing to a soft shade of gold in the early-morning sunshine. Looking out the window, I discovered a deer and her fawn starting through the wheat field, and called my boys to come look. As we watched, she exited the other side without the fawn and strolled into the woods. I explained to the boys that mother deer often leave their babies in a safe place while they go in search of food.

A week or so later, a large combine, tractors, and trucks converged on the field to begin the reaping process. For most of the morning Ryan and Cody watched the combine work its way up and down the field, leaving neat rows of straw in its wake. Suddenly one of them called excitedly that a deer had come out of the woods. Why was it out here in the heat of the day, in full view? It almost seemed to be searching for something. When it dawned on me what she was hunting for, my heart sank. Had she left her fawn in the wheat field again, hiding it among the golden stalks of grain, not knowing that today was harvest day? Had the combine run over it? Or had it been frightened so far away by the mechanical monster that she would not be able to find it? We watched with heavy hearts as the doe picked her way up the hill and out of sight.

I went back to my unfinished chores, but one of the boys stayed at the window, watching. "Here she comes!" he called several minutes later.

"Does she have anything with her?" I asked anxiously as I raced to the window. A cheer went up as we saw her bounding toward the woods with, not one, but *two* speckled babies racing behind her. Yeah for Mom! She heard the noise of the tractors, sensed that her babies were not safe, and risked her own life to come to their aid.

What an object lesson of our Saviour! He did not consider His own safety when He came to our rescue. Nor did He wait for us to call for help or for us to come looking for Him. Instead, He left heaven and searched for us. Can you imagine the heavenly hosts cheering as He accomplished His mission? Praise Him, He found us! Do you feel helpless like those fawns? About to be run over by life? Jesus is beside you to lead you to safety—believe it, and follow Him.

LINDA MCCABE

JUNE 24

Future Fortune

There are many homes up there where my Father lives, and I am going to prepare them for your coming. When everything is ready, then I will come and get you, so that you can always be with me. John 14:2, 3, TLB.

*C*an a fortune cookie be trusted? I believe so. Foolish, you say? Let me explain. I've gotten my share of silly cookie predictions: "A favorite relative will be visiting you soon" (my nearest relatives are 1,000 miles away and would never drop in unexpectedly). "Trusting your intuition will boost your business this week" (I'm not in business). But after a Chinese dinner lately, I broke open the complimentary cookie and read, "You will be traveling soon and coming into a fortune." Why do I believe this one? No, I have no plane tickets in my purse, or any wealthy relatives on their deathbeds. But I do have a Friend who has made me a promise.

Jesus has promised to come for me soon. What a journey we will take together! This tour of the universe, guided by its Creator and Mastermind, will include a fascinating array of people, places, and information. Awaiting me are gala events to attend, scientific phenomenon to observe, thrilling adventures to participate in, and riveting revelations to receive. All this, and no jet lag, illness, or exhaustion to interfere with my enjoyment.

At the end of the journey a fortune awaits me. Jesus died so that I could inherit a share of His vast estate. He is preparing a home just for me—one I can't wait to see! He knows me so intimately and loves me so much that with His impeccable taste, masterful creativity, and unlimited resources, I know it will be a dream house that's uniquely "me."

Jesus has set this dwelling in a planned community. The Master Designer has overlooked no need or desire of its future residents. He has made provision for physical, mental, social, and spiritual fulfillment. Here is a fortune with no estate tax, accounting headaches, or investment worries. Better yet, Jesus has promised to provide perfect health, continual happiness, and an eternity to enjoy this inheritance (see Rev. 21 and 22).

Jesus asked me to invite my friends to come along on the journey and share His wealth. Won't you come with me? He's even promised to help us get ready for the trip (see Ezekiel 36:24-28 and Philippians 1:6). You may not trust a fortune cookie, but you can trust my Friend's promises.　　　　　KATHLEEN STEARMAN PFLUGRAD

JUNE 25

Be Distressed for Nothing

Be careful for nothing; but in every thing by prayer and supplication with thanksgiving let your requests be made known unto God. Phil. 4:6.

I went to São Paulo on a weekend retreat and was planning to return on Saturday evening. Sunday morning my husband would be returning from a 12-day, 1,200-mile trip. However, the church program extended into the evening, making my return that Saturday night impossible. I began to feel anxious because I wanted to be home to welcome my husband. I thought he might arrive home before I did and go alone to the college to visit our daughters. I prayed to God about my concern.

The first bus would leave at 7:00 a.m. and the second at 9:00 a.m. Because I was dependent on the couple in whose home I was staying for transportation to the Tietê bus depot, I thought it would be more considerate of me to leave at 9:00.

Purchasing my ticket, I went to the boarding area. As I approached it, I saw someone coming in my direction and could hardly believe my eyes. Could it be true? There was my husband. My bus seat was number 3 and his was number 2. Happily we returned home together!

What a privilege we have of casting all our concerns on our heavenly Father, knowing that He cares for us! The secret of a life of peace resides in making known to God our petitions, not only for our well-being but for everything.

When the apostle said "in every thing," he excluded nothing. It is not enough to tell our problems to God, or even to show Him how deep our pain is. We must put everything in His hands without reservations. We can be certain that He has the best solution. In everything let us be thankful. — MEIBEL MELLO GUEDES

JUNE 26

Questions for God

He will take great delight in you, he will quiet you with his love, he will rejoice over you with singing. Zeph. 3:17, NIV.

This morning I added a question to the list I keep in my prayer journal. It's a list of questions for God. Things I want to ask Him when I get to heaven. Nothing big or heavy—just little things I think about. For instance, "Do all singing birds sing well, or are they like people, some singing wonderfully, some just ordinary, and some not well at all? Does one canary sing so beautifully that all the other birds stop to listen, while another makes its fellow birds wish the singer would close its beak?" Another question on my list is "What are cats thinking when they purr?"

One of the questions that I ponder a lot is the second one on my list. I wrote it quite a while ago. Isaiah 62:4 says: "For the Lord delights in you" (NKJV). Zephaniah goes even further: "He will take great delight in you." And I really want Proverbs 8:30 to be true: "I was daily his delight." So someday from my list of questions, I want to ask God, "Did I ever bring You joy? Did You ever smile just at the thought of me? Did You ever call me Your 'delight'? I hope that is how You think of me! Lord, did You ever say to Yourself, 'I want to spend lots of time with (put your name here). She enjoys being with Me so much!'"?

Today I again read Zephaniah 3:17: "He will take great delight in you, he will quiet you in his love, he will rejoice over you with singing." What a picture—God singing over me! My question for God today is "What do You sing over me? Is it a song You made up just for me? Does it have my name in it? Is it the same song each time? When the angels hear it, do they know it is 'our song'—that it is me You are singing for and over and because of? Is it a happy song because I try so hard to bring You joy? Will You sing it to me when we go for our first walk together? And will I recognize it in some part of my heart because You are so much a part of my life?"

What's on your list of questions for God?   GINNY ALLEN

JUNE 27

Knowing the Signs

Study to shew thyself approved unto God, a workman that needeth not to be ashamed. 2 Tim. 2:15.

A few days ago I walked into the drivers' license bureau to renew my license for the next four years. The test consisted of a combination eye test/sign identification exam. Having drilled myself on the shapes and meanings of the signs, I passed with flying colors, so I was surprised and chagrined to find my hand shaking as I signed my name.

The first time I applied for my license I was an eager teenager. I had spent hours poring over the manual, but when I walked into the examining office I was shocked to see the pencil trembling in the hand of an older man working on the written section. Horrified, I thought that if it made him so nervous, I would surely fail! Relief flooded over me as I began reading the questions and knew that my study had paid off. Then the behind-the-wheel part was easy. I only had to drive around a traffic-free block in my small town.

Years later my husband and I moved to a different state and had to get new licenses. Again, I studied until I felt confident enough to take the test. My husband, taking a more casual approach, had only scanned the book. A large, stern-looking patrolman quickly went through our completed tests, wadded them up, and tossed them into the wastebasket. Then he looked at me and, without smiling, said, "You read the book. He didn't!" In spite of that, we both passed the test.

Reading the book; studying the signs. The test is coming, but the reward will not be a license, but a crown. Not for four years, but for all eternity, never to be suspended or revoked. We have the Book, and we have the signs. Are we diligently preparing for that final examination?

Dear Father, open our minds and hearts to the signs You give us that point to the soon coming of our Lord and Saviour to take us to our eternal home. MARY JANE GRAVES

JUNE 28

Blessed Assurance

And we desire that every one of you do shew the same diligence to the full assurance of hope unto the end: that ye be not slothful, but followers of them who through faith and patience inherit the promises. Heb. 6:11, 12.

*D*uring the Great Depression in America in the 1930s, I was a young woman out of school looking for employment. No office jobs were available. I was fortunate to find a position caretaking an elderly woman invalid while her husband worked during the day. My salary was $25 a month.

Because her home had no room for me, I found a double garage in back of a house several blocks away for $8 a month. My "sink" was a faucet of cold water over a dishpan on a table. I hung monk's-cloth curtains on a wire from floor to ceiling around the bed. The remaining space was my "living room." The bathroom was in the house next door.

A kerosene heater kept me warm on winter evenings and an electric hot plate was my stove for cooking. A live morning-glory plant grew from outside into the side of my window for a special "decor."

As a new Christian I leaned heavily upon the Lord for my happiness, and Bible study with faithful new friends meant a lot to me.

One day when I returned from work to my "apartment," I found a box filled with all kinds of canned foods. It had no note with it, but the box did contain a song sheet, "Blessed Assurance." Later I discovered who the donors were: a doctor and his wife, members of my church who felt impressed by our Lord to bless me. I thanked Him and them.

Our Lord was giving me assurance He had something better planned for my future. I enjoyed waiting on His promises. "Blessed assurance, Jesus is mine!" LEILA GILHOUSEN

When God's Desire Became Mine

You are my hiding place; You shall preserve me from trouble; You shall surround me with songs of deliverance. I will instruct you and teach you in the way you should go; I will guide you with My eye. Ps. 32:7, 8, NKJV.

I don't want to go to Siberia! Do I have to go, Lord?" My husband was excited about spending our vacation doing evangelism deep in Siberia. Our oldest son would assist him. They could manage without me. But I found no happiness saying no to Jesus. For years we had prayed for people in Communist countries. Now we had the rare opportunity to share Christ's love and hope of His soon return with them. But fatigue and fear were holding me back. The deadline for visa applications loomed, forcing a decision.

I called my sister, who patiently listened to my dilemma, then said, "Well, you could ask God to give you the desire to go if that's His will for you."

Stubborn resistance surfaced. "But I can't do that! He might give me the desire, and then I'd have to go!" The truth was out—I hadn't surrendered to His will.

The next morning a little courage came, and I prayed, "Lord, if You want me to go to Siberia, please give me the desire." Then the Almighty Creator and Redeemer tenderly reached down and stirred within me positive thoughts about the trip. They grew into enthusiastic feelings about Russian evangelism and mushroomed into an excited desire to share my husband's adventure on the Siberian frontier.

Joyful memories now tumble over each other: people coming night after night to get hope and help from God's Word, children swarming around me, little hands reaching out to receive gifts from America, bonding in love to the patient, faithful believers, answered prayers, transformed lives, and joyous baptisms in the river.

Oh, I would have missed so much if I had not gone! I wouldn't have known Valentina, Vera, Lily, Natasha, and the pastor's wife—beautiful, strong Siberian women who hold family and church together. I would not have met Alexander, who knew enough English to help me with the children's meetings. His words ring in my heart—"Before you came I was depressed, since my wife and son left me. But now there is a fire in my heart and purpose for my life. God is giving me a new family."

My loving Father didn't want me to miss this enriching, spiritually strengthening experience, so He gave me the desire to serve Him in Siberia. "God never leads His children otherwise than they would choose to be led, if they could see the end from the beginning, and discern the glory of the purpose which they are fulfilling as coworkers with Him" (*The Desire of Ages*, pp. 224, 225). LILA LANE GEORGE

Snuggly Moments

How often I've ached to embrace [you], the way a hen gathers her chicks under her wings, and you wouldn't let me. Matt. 23:37, Message.

*A*fter 17 years we had rediscovered each other. Kim and I spent five years of our early teen years attending church school together. Five years may seem a short time to some people, but they were significant years for me. Growing up as a "military brat," I moved frequently. Finally I had established some roots. But after tenth grade I lost touch with my classmates when my family transferred to another part of the country. No roots again.

Now 17 years later our paths had crossed. Thumbing through our yearbooks, we laughed and reminisced the afternoon away. Roots. I had roots again. We had a shared history and a shared love for Jesus. Such a warm, homey feeling.

During my next visit I got better acquainted with my friend's husband and their 18-month-old daughter. Talk about roots—little Breanna had them, but they seemed totally centered in her mother. Even a friendly look would send her running to Kim. As the weekend progressed, Breanna finally started warming up to me. I hadn't forced myself on her, but waited till she became comfortable with my presence. Eventually she was sitting in my lap, and then snuggling in my arms.

I loved that snuggling time. No pretenses, no barriers, just complete trust from this child. My husband and I have not been able to have children yet, so I treasure those snuggly moments. It also gives me a fresh picture of God.

How must God enjoy those moments of warm snuggly time I spend with Him. He treasures the tranquil union, the complete trust. For me, those times impart the warm, homey feeling of roots. But the blur of life and muddled priorities rob me of this peaceful time. And not only me, but God feels the loss. Jesus yearningly exclaimed, "How often I've ached to embrace [you], the way a hen gathers her chicks under her wings, and you wouldn't let me."

I'm awed by that thought. Jesus looks forward to our times together, and He misses me if I don't show up. When life rushes those moments, His heart longs to calm me with the peace I'm too busy to receive. Lord, nudge me to spend that warm snuggly time in Your arms. Help me to be continually drawn to my roots in You.

HEIDE FORD

JULY 1

Remembering

He put out His hand and touched him. Luke 5:13, NKJV.

Quietly I stepped into the hospital room. She lay there with her eyes closed, this woman who several months before had received the verdict of "inoperable cancer."

I had seen little of her in recent weeks, but the reports went like this: "Confused, cannot feed herself." "Her eyesight is affected so she cannot see." "Very confused, calling out frequently." "Eating very little, nauseated." "Talking incoherently."

The pillows were arranged just right to keep the pressure off an aching back. The overbed table was placed where she could reach the tissues by feel. The cane she had once used to adjust her covers still hung over the head of the bed, not used anymore. The old favorite blue cloth was no longer there. She no longer needed it to protect her eyes from the light.

Hesitating as to whether to awaken her or not, I stepped up to the bed, laid my hand on her arm, and waited. It took a few seconds for the reaction to come. Her eyes did not open, but a half-smile lit up her face as if a light shone through from somewhere. The wrinkles showed plainly, and a net corralled the bushy black and partly gray hair. But an inner light cast a glory around the sallow, emaciated features. Her words, even though slow and hesitant, fairly glistened. "I know who you are; I can tell by your touch. You are the nurse who kissed me. I remember that day . . ."

A chill ran down my spine. Standing there amazed, listening, I too remembered that day. She was a new patient, and I was a new nurse in that hospital. Everything had gone wrong for her, and she had come to this place to spend her last months. Things had gone wrong for me too, but I was alive, healthy, and had much to be thankful for.

I remembered arranging her comfortably in a chair, then bending over and kissing her forehead near the lump that was an extension of the malignancy. The act was impulsive. She needed the affection, and I needed to give.

Through that confused mental state, how could such an ill person tell the identity of a nurse just by the touch of the hand? How could that damaged brain recall such a small incident three months before? I do not know, but I cannot forget.

The same God who said, "I will never leave you nor forsake you" (Heb. 13:5, NKJV) also said, "Inasmuch as you did it to one of the least of these My brethren, you did it to Me" (Matt. 25:40, NKJV).

MYRTLE HICKS

JULY 2

Ants and Sugar

Taste and see that the Lord is good. Ps. 34:8, NIV.

Have you ever sat and watched ants when they find something sweet to eat? They seem to go crazy with excitement as they rush around it, then go tell other ants of their fortune. Soon many ants help to carry the treasure away.

When I was in my early teenage years I had a violent temper, so much so that my mother used to tell me that the man who married me would either kick me out or kill me. One day as I was in a violent outburst, my father called me out to the front porch. Calmly he asked me to sit with him and watch the ants. Angry, I wasn't interested in watching the ants, but I had no choice. I sat there next to Dad with my arms crossed and anger flashing from my eyes as I waited impatiently.

Dad placed a drop of lemon juice and a clump of sugar side by side on the concrete porch. Soon a solitary ant appeared and investigated the lemon, but left it alone. The ant then found the sugar and excitedly ran around it. It left as fast as its little legs would carry it, and soon returned with many more ants who helped carry the sugar away.

In a soft voice Dad said, "You see, darling, if you want to attract friends and be liked, you must be like the sugar. No one wants to be around someone who is always bitter and angry. Happy, positive people have many friends, and they sweeten the lives of everyone they come in contact with."

I never forgot the lesson I learned that day, and the Holy Spirit has used it to speak to me through the years, and to help me gain the victory over my temper.

I knew Dad was right, but I didn't immediately understand how to overcome my temper. Through the years, as I studied my Bible, I found that the only way to experience victory is to surrender to God completely every day, every time I am tempted.

If you need victory today, turn your feelings, your anger, over to Jesus. He's promised to give us victory. And if your teenagers are going through those same turbulent feelings, show them the experiment and let the Holy Spirit drive the lesson home to them.

CELIA MEJIA CRUZ

JULY 3

The Gift

For by grace you have been saved through faith, and that not of yourselves; it is the gift of God. Eph. 2:8, NKJV.

*C*arning had been hospitalized for the umpteenth time for asthma at Manila Sanitarium and Hospital. For 25 years she had been an off-and-on patient. I had met her during a previous hospitalization and had realized that she was a committed Christian.

That afternoon we had a lovely chat as I made my regular rounds as a chaplain to the newly admitted patients. I had shared encouraging promises with her and had offered a prayer for her rapid recovery.

As I was getting up to leave, she said, "Just a minute. You have shared with me. Now I want to share something with you." She picked up the devotional booklet *Daily Bread* that she had been reading that morning. "Here it is!" she said, turning to a marked page. "Just this morning I found this little quotation that I like so much."

"'Salvation is a gift to be received, not a goal to be achieved,'" she read. With a radiant smile she added in her own words, "It's priceless and not to be sold!" I could tell by her expression that Carning had received that greatest gift of all.

"Carning, that is beautiful," I exclaimed. "What an apt way to express how salvation comes to us." I quickly told her goodbye, going straight to the chaplain's office to write down the words while they still rang in my ears.

The salvation formula is so simple that a child can understand, yet we sometimes try to make it complicated. No amount of striving will gain it for us. Jesus did that part. We can only joyfully accept it and walk in the light of His love. A renowned scientist was asked what his greatest discovery had been. "That Jesus loves me!" was his answer.

Thank God for the free gift of salvation in Jesus. It's based on what Jesus did and not on what I do. A woman author stated, "We are not to be anxious about what Christ and God think of us, but about what God thinks of Christ, our Substitute. Ye are accepted in the Beloved" (*Selected Messages*, book 2, pp. 32, 33). — FELICIA PHILLIPS

When God Prunes Our Branches

I am the true vine, and my Father is the gardener. He cuts off every branch in me that bears no fruit, while every branch that does bear fruit he prunes so that it will be even more fruitful. John 15:1, 2, NIV.

*H*ow does this spiritual pruning process work? What is it? Does God stand by the vine, ready to whack off any branches that are not growing properly on His trellis? Or is God tenderly trimming, training, and cultivating new growth? I have often pondered these and many other questions in times of emotional pain. What is this celestial Gardener doing to me? Fortunately, the text offers as many answers as it creates questions. It offers more hope than hopelessness and gives us encouragement and reassurance.

The idea of God as a gardener appears throughout the Bible. In 1 Corinthians 3 Paul refers to God as the gardener and us as His field. The Lord tenderly cultivates every new growth and gently removes the undesirable weeds. He causes us to produce the fruits of the Spirit. Let's look again at the text and think about this pruning process.

"He cuts off every branch in me that bears no fruit." What does that mean in spiritual terms? *Whack! Zap!* You are not good enough? Not at all. The branches He cuts off are the ones that are not truly a part of Christ. They are the ones that are not accepting the life supplied by the Root and Vine—Christ. He said, "Apart from me you can do nothing. If anyone does not remain in me, he is like a branch that is thrown away and withers" (John 15:5, 6, NIV).

"Every branch that does bear fruit he prunes so that it will be even more fruitful." God trims off the undesirable offshoots of our character. Everyone knows that if we allow a vine to develop on its own without trimming and training, it grows wild. God does not let that happen to us. And when we do experience His pruning, it can be a source of encouragement rather than discouragement. If God has bothered to prune us, it is because we have been fruitful! He is training us to bear even more fruit. Now, that is encouragement!

MINDY RODENBERG

JULY 5

The Paper Kite

Thou wilt shew me the path of life: in thy presence is fulness of joy; at thy right hand there are pleasures for evermore. Ps. 16:11.

What was the happiest time you can remember?" my husband asked. We had gathered together for family worship, an event increasingly rare since our children had grown. They had families of their own, their own shared experiences, their own happiest times. But now we were together again in the house where they had grown up, the surroundings comfortable and familiar.

"What was the happiest time?" the question echoed. After only a moment's thought, our oldest son, Harold, volunteered, "The happiest time I remember was the day we flew the kites."

His answer was unexpected and surprising. I had already come up with my own list, not only for myself, but for the others. It hadn't included kites.

My husband, an accomplished sailor, would be thinking about a perfect sailing day—the winds fresh, the seas calm. Our son John, also a sailor, would be right there, trimming sails. For them, nothing was better than being on the water.

Mary would probably be thinking about her tour of Europe when she was 16—the romance of Paris, the beauty of Switzerland, the pageantry of England.

And Harold might recall hours spent with his amateur radio, transmitting through the night to a world far away—Pitcairn, Africa, Antarctica.

The happiest time? Harold's response was a complete surprise.

"It was the day we flew the kites," he repeated, and the others agreed.

I remembered it clearly. It was summer. A Sunday with a breeze blowing. Somebody—I don't know who—suggested that we make kites. My husband, dauntless in such situations, organized the crew. We folded newspapers, glued them around sticks, and attached long rag tails. And then everyone scrambled out to the hills behind our home to see if the kites would actually fly.

The warm California wind caught the kites and sent them soaring high above the city. They danced and fluttered in the breeze. It was amazing that some newspaper, sticks, and string could create so much joy that nearly a quarter century of time couldn't erase it.

"What was there about that day that was so special?" I asked.

The others thought for a moment.

"It was one of the days I remember when we had Daddy all to ourselves," Mary replied, and the other children agreed.

My husband's schedule left very little time unspoken for. He had meetings, evangelistic series, unending travel. Having him all to ourselves always seemed like a rare treat, of which the kites had become a symbol. Daddy was home.

So, too, are the ordinary events of our lives made special by knowing the presence of our heavenly Father. The joys. The sorrows. Each care made easier. Each load lighter. God forever with us. Abba. Father.

Every day should be the happiest day of our lives.

MARY MARGARET RICHARDS

JULY 6

Ye Are the Light of the World

And who knoweth whether thou art come to the kingdom for such a time as this? Esther 4:14.

I used to be employed as a security guard in the palace of the king of Jordan. My work gave me the opportunity of meeting many of the soldiers and members of the security forces assigned there.

Being a Christian in a predominantly Muslim workforce gave me wonderful opportunities to witness for Christ. I would give them Bible texts to support my position and sometimes compare the Bible verses with passages in the Koran, the Muslim holy book. It seemed to surprise them that I could defend my faith with such conviction. When requested, I supplied Bibles and tracts in Arabic. I also gave out health lessons and encouraged a number of soldiers to stop smoking.

One day the general commander of the palace guard called me into his office. He told me he had heard a lot about me from the soldiers and other guards, how they considered me as a mother and counselor. "Therefore, I want you to direct me," he continued, "because I know nothing about either Christianity or health."

He asked many questions and seemed to be pleased with the answers. "We Muslims don't know much about these subjects," he commented.

With a quick prayer heavenward for guidance, I asked, "Sir, would you like to know more?"

"With pleasure!" he replied.

I gave him some tracts, health magazines, and a copy of *Patriarchs and Prophets*, by E. G. White. When he couldn't understand something, he would send his driver for me so I could help with explanations. I prayed hard during those car journeys that God would give me the words to speak.

One day he said, "The one who wrote this book, *Patriarchs and Prophets*, must have been inspired of God. The stories are presented in such an interesting way, and I have been greatly influenced by them. Imagine! I have read the story of our father Joseph three times, and still I cry each time I read it. I promise you that I will keep this great book and read it all. I want you to help my family, too, because we know so very little about Christianity and about health. Especially the way you have presented it to us."

Sometimes we do not have an opportunity to see the results of our labors, but I am convinced that God put me in the palace for a very good reason. I pray I will find friends from there in heaven someday.

TURKEAH NIMRI

JULY 7

One Hundred Dolls

Eye hath not seen, nor ear heard, neither have entered into the heart of man, the things which God hath prepared for them that love him. 1 Cor. 2:9.

The advertisement in the magazine read "100 dolls for $1." It fascinated me. I liked dolls very much, but I had only a few. Imagine having 100 of them! My 8-year-old heart beat with joy at the thought of all the things I could do with 100 dolls.

But one whole dollar was a lot of money for a little girl with a 25 cents per week allowance. Several months passed before I had the whole amount in hand. With all the care I could give it, I wrote my name on the order blank in round, wriggly letters, addressed the envelope, and tucked the order and money inside. With something this important, I could entrust the mailing to no one else, so I personally dropped it in the mailbox.

One hundred dolls would soon be mine! I wondered how they would arrive. Would they be in one huge box—or in many smaller boxes? What would they look like? Where would I put them all? Each day I watched for the mailman to bring my 100 dolls.

Six weeks later a small box addressed to me arrived in the mail. I wondered who had sent it and eagerly tore it open. Inside I found 100 tiny figurines of pink molded plastic. Not one of them was more than an inch tall, and they were not at all attractive. I cried!

Since then I have been disappointed many times. I have had to learn that things in this world are often not as great as they sound. But "eye hath not seen, nor ear heard, neither have entered into the heart of man, the things which God hath prepared for them that love him."

I'm glad I serve a God who will never let me down!   JANET EVERT

JULY 8

Thank God for a Dirty House

But a woman who fears the Lord is to be praised. Give her the reward she has earned, and let her works bring her praise at the city gate. Prov. 31:30, 31, NIV.

I get up in the morning to an array of clutter and to the sounds of a busy young household. Two of the children are already arguing over a toy, which wakens the baby, who begins to cry. Her wails start the dog to barking. In dismay, I look around and wonder what to do first. It is only 6:45 a.m., and already the vicious circle of dirty laundry, dirty dishes, an unkempt house, and fussy children has begun. And the discouraging part is that by 4:00 this afternoon I will have it all in order only to see the same disorder tomorrow morning.

But then it comes to me—this disarray is truly my greatest blessing from God, and I love every messy bit of it. I smile and look at things from a totally different perspective. Those noisy sounds represent life, family, and happiness. The stacks of dirty dishes represent a family of six that I truly love to take care of and cook for. I say a little prayer of thanks to God for those hungry mouths to feed, and that He has provided us with plenty for them.

What a blessing to have four beautiful children to pick up after. As I wipe up the spilled milk dripping down the sides of the cabinet, I pause to hug a little 3-year-old angel who was only "trying to help mommy."

It seems I mop those floors continuously, but I am reminded that those muddy footprints represent a healthy young son running in and out, playing and also helping his dad outside. The daily clutter in the bathroom represents my firstborn daughter. So lovely, and growing up so quickly.

Then comes the never-ending piles of laundry! Mounds and mounds of dirty work clothes now become a labor of love for the man who struggles so hard to provide for our family. And there seems to be no end to the stacks of diapers and other little articles of clothes to launder. But they only remind me of the newest joy of my life—the baby girl who greets me each morning with large brown eyes and a toothless smile.

With a catch in my throat, I can only pause for a moment in the midst of it all and pray, "Dear Lord, I *love* this disarray! And I thank You for the family that creates it. I thank You for the health You have given me to work and care for them. Most of all, Lord, I thank You for the opportunity to be surrounded in love by husband, children, and neighbors who need me. And thank You, Lord, for this dirty house."

BARBARA SMITH MORRIS

JULY 9

Universal Health Insurance

Beloved, I wish above all things that thou mayest prosper and be in health. 3 John 2.

*P*ain—who needs it? It chips away at our good humor and makes even the smallest tasks seem insurmountable. Every drugstore in the land trumpets our desire to live pain-free lives with its shelves full of bottles and tubes promising quick, soothing relief. But did you ever stop to think that pain is one of the most invaluable senses we have?

What would it be like without our pain sensors? My dad, a paraplegic, received third-degree burns on his leg while working on a car, and has experienced injuries to his feet without knowing it. He would tell you that at times the ability to feel pain has its advantages! Pain is the body's response to a stress, injury, or trauma, and ignoring it is like unplugging your smoke alarm because it is noisy, or putting tape over the trouble lights on the car because they shine in your eyes at night.

Recently I read a study that asked people about their health. The majority of people surveyed considered themselves to be in good health, yet further questions revealed that these same people found it necessary to use a wide variety of medicines regularly because of their body's attempts to tell them that something was *not* right. Evidently they assumed that heartburn, constipation, headaches, lack of energy, indigestion, and other assorted aches and pains were normal by-products of life. Strange as it may seem, they had become so accustomed to a certain level of pain that it had become inevitable and acceptable to them.

The mind has warning symptoms just as the body has, informing us of an overload or trauma. Unfortunately, many people know less about their mind than they do about their body. Some of these warning symptoms are depression, apathy, anger, hopelessness, unrelenting guilt, relationship or family problems, a wall between self and God, or just a nagging sense that something is not right. All can be signs of mental and emotional pain. Mental and emotional "painkillers" such as workaholism, food, and materialism may not be sold in colorful packages at the drugstore, but many use them to mask the real problems. Unfortunately, the bill for denying or ignoring pain will eventually come due—often with interest and penalties added.

God's goal for us is nothing short of a more abundant life in which we can "prosper and be in health." The Great Physician is ready and waiting to diagnose and treat the root causes of our pain. "He knoweth our frame; he remembereth that we are dust" (Ps. 103:14). "I am the Lord that healeth thee" (Ex. 15:26). Everyone can afford Him, He is always taking new patients, and He even makes house calls! Now, *that's* health assurance.   LINDA McCABE

JULY 10

Room to Grow

A man scatters seed on the ground. Night and day, whether he sleeps or gets up, the seed sprouts and grows, though he does not know how. All by itself the soil produces the grain—first the stalk, then the head, then the full kernel in the head. Mark 4:26-28, NIV.

*M*anslaughter. It happened in Hyogo prefecture, Japan, in 1990. Every morning at precisely 8:30 a teacher closed that school's large iron gates, keeping out all latecomers. Every morning at precisely 8:30 he set the heavy gates rolling. Never did he look up to see if anyone was coming. He prided himself on keeping the rule perfectly. And then it happened. The swinging gate crushed a teenage girl. An outraged community questioned the teacher. It was her fault, he replied. If she had not been late, she would not have died.

Events like this give us a chance to reevaluate our own legalism. If we view God as a cosmic schoolteacher, closing the gates at exactly 8:30 regardless of who may be crushed, we may feel a constant pressure to be perfect. Even worse, we may translate our struggle with our own faults into intolerance, especially for the faults of young people.

Jesus Himself had to remind His disciples to let the little children come to Him. The disciples wanted only to protect their Master from mundane interruptions. But Jesus showed them He valued children. And so should we. They are our future. But we cannot reach our children until we let God reach us. If we can catch a glimpse of the infinite patience of God, it will release us from the constant pressure to be perfect. We can allow ourselves room to grow when we realize that God always does.

Although we can cultivate the soil and weed the garden, only God can make it grow and only on His timetable. As a child I thought *When I am 10, I will be big. When I am a teenager . . . When I finish college . . . When I get married . . . When I have children . . . When . . .* I looked at adults I admired and longed for the day I would reach their level. Then came the realization that we never really do "arrive." We just keep growing. But we can be what God wants us to be at each step, and we can enjoy the pleasures that each stage brings.

KAREN LINDENSMITH

JULY 11

The Power of God

Acknowledge and take to heart this day that the Lord is God in heaven above and on the earth below. There is no other. Deut. 4:39, NIV.

I was standing next to my alarm clock when the Northridge quake hit my southern California home. In a split second the power went off, and I found myself knocked to the floor. Generally I am the type of person who keeps cool in emergencies. While everybody else is running around screaming, I always have a carefully planned routine to follow. I knew right where my flashlight was, and I had enough bottled water to last several weeks. Having been in many smaller earthquakes, I knew how to protect myself. So what did I do?

If you guessed that I got to my feet and tried to run down the hall while my trailer rocked back and forth so violently that I got slammed against first the left wall and then the right and then the left again, you guessed right. I stopped running only because I hit the linen closet at the end of the hall and couldn't go any farther. Then I huddled against the closet in the pitch black and heard a huge explosion. Instead of calmly thinking about fetching a flashlight and checking for gas leaks, I kept thinking only one thing: *This is it. This is it. It's really happening.* I thought that it was the end of the world.

Only it wasn't. I discovered that I was still breathing—quite heavily, in fact—and I had to get on with the business of living. As the days passed and the authorities restored power and communication, people took comfort in sharing their stories of survival.

If the earthquake had happened a few minutes later, I would have been in the shower and would have tumbled through a glass door instead of merely falling on the floor. One woman told of getting up for no apparent reason to pick up her baby just seconds before falling debris destroyed the baby's crib. Over and over I heard tales of people waking up and moving out of harm's way just before the quake hit. The angels must have been busy that morning!

As I looked at scenes of the city struggling back to normalcy, I thought of how great God is. Even the most hardened cynic knows that we have a greater Power to call on when the very ground we are walking on is shaking. Many found God in the midst of that terrible disaster. Only the intervention of an omnipotent God can save us when we cannot help ourselves. Our God is stronger than earthquakes, floods, and tornadoes. He is Lord of all!   GINA LEE

Reaching Higher

Lord, how are they increased that trouble me! many are they that rise up against me. Many there be which say of my soul, There is no help for him in God. But thou, O Lord, art a shield for me; my glory, and the lifter up of mine head. Ps. 3:1-3.

Something happened recently in my life that troubled me greatly, and I felt as if an enemy were literally pursuing me. Distraught, I needed some time to think and pray. As I walked and talked with the Lord near my home, I was so discouraged and downhearted that I felt the sweetness had gone from my life, and I wondered how it would all end.

I thought about Job, as I am reading a book about him right now, and how the Lord had brought him through, although not without suffering.

Doing some deep breathing while I walked, suddenly I smelled the sweetest scent in the air. I looked down and found some white clover at my feet, and thinking that was where the smell came from, I picked a few pieces. Further inspection convinced me it was not the same fragrance that had been in the air a moment before. Coming to some pink clover, I picked some of that. Still not the right smell! But I felt as though the Lord was trying to tell me that there was still some sweetness in life.

I got to the end of the road, and turned to head for home. All of a sudden I detected that smell again. Glancing to my right, I saw a beautiful tree all abloom with small white blossoms, similar to a "chain of gold" tree, but pure white. I knew I had found what I was looking for, and needed some of those blossoms to take home. However, I had to really stretch to get some, and it was then that I realized the Lord was trying to tell me that the "sweetness" was still there. I just needed to reach a little higher to find it!   CRISS KRAMER

Shelter in the Time of Storm

The Lord will roar from Zion and thunder from Jerusalem; the earth and sky will tremble. But the Lord will be a refuge for his people. Joel 3:16, NIV.

I have never been so terrified in my life," my daughter told me when I returned home. While I had been at work a small tornado had torn through the area where we lived in northern New Jersey. Though it wasn't a large tornado, it was a damaging one.

The pilot of a small airplane reported that he had tracked the tornado's path as soon as it was safe to do so after the storm. "Everywhere the tornado had swept through, it had damaged every house and building," he said. "Several animals were injured or killed. But on this one farm right in the middle of the storm's path a little house didn't have one shingle missing. Trees were torn up all around it, branches everywhere, telephone poles leaned ominously, and lines were down, but this little house stood as firm and untouched as the Rock of Gibraltar."

That little house was in the direct path of the tornado. My daughter saw and heard the storm roaring and screaming as it approached. The cloud shelf rolled rapidly along—low in the wide field straight toward the house. All the fury of unleashed demons seemed bent on total destruction. Trees began to fall, branches whipped the ground. Parts of the shed roof flew off and soared away. Lawn and playground furniture sailed out into the field far from the house as if some gigantic hand had thrown them.

Fear for her little son gripped her with panic. Since the cellar door was on the same side of the house as the storm, she knew she couldn't get to it in time. She shouted over the deafening noise to her 7-year-old son, "Honey, we're in trouble!" Immediately, they dropped to their knees and asked for the Lord's protection.

Reaching the house, the storm suddenly split and went around both sides of it, twisting and tearing out trees as it raced across the front and back yards and sweeping onward to less-protected areas. Animals died on the next farm as the tornado destroyed a barn. Out on the freeway a truck overturned onto a small car.

Yes, the little house stood firm, for it was built not on the Rock of Gibraltar, but a more substantial Rock. While not elegant, it is a house where God is honored and praised at least twice daily when we are all together for worship. His watchcare during that storm and many times since have constantly renewed my faith that He is ever present in times of trouble.   GRACE JOHANSON

Be Still and Know

Be still, and know that I am God. Ps. 46:10.

*M*y husband's premature death the week before had left me with many perplexing concerns. Could I make the payments on the home we had purchased the year before? Would my income cover the taxes and insurance involved? Should I remain in my present enjoyable employment where I had built up some retirement benefits? Or should I seek a position with greater remuneration? And many, many more questions! "What shall I do, Lord?" I prayed.

It then occurred to me that possibly this was really not praying at all. In my frustration I was repeating those four words again and again and saying nothing more. I ceased my prayer, and as I continued kneeling by my bed, I began to sense the worrisome questions fading from my mind.

Then, quietly but clearly, although I knew it was not a human voice, I heard the words "Be still, and know that I am God" (Ps. 46:10). Nothing more.

The worrisome thoughts did not return as I went to bed and, still free of concern, performed my office duties the next day. When I arrived home that evening, it occurred to me that I should begin sorting through my husband's personal effects. Soon I ascertained that the university would appreciate his professional library. Then I went through the tools in the garage. At the same time I found opportunity and adequate composure to make realistic financial calculations and a projection of what course the future should take.

A real estate agent oversaw the sale of the property, and within two months I had accomplished everything I needed to do. Established comfortably in an apartment, I found myself enjoying my work responsibilities.

God bids us cast our burdens on Him (Ps. 55:22), but He also suggests that we be still (Ps. 46:10), because sometimes His answer comes as a still small voice (1 Kings 19:12).   LOIS E. JOHANNES

No More Sea

And I saw a new heaven and a new earth; for the first heaven and the first earth passed away, and there is no longer any sea. Rev. 21:1, NASB.

*H*e trusted me to wake him up. The alarm was set for 5:30 a.m. My husband, David, needed to get up early that August morning so he would be on time for the Rockland bird-watching boat that sails out into the Gulf of Maine. But David sleeps hard despite alarms, so he asked me to be sure he woke up.

I love the ocean. Growing up an hour's drive from the seacoasts of Massachusetts and Rhode Island, I had learned to enjoy the rhythms and complexity of life along the ocean. We spend time every vacation walking over sand, seaweed, and rocks, gulping salt air, hearing the music of surf and shorebirds, and picking up shells. So it was strange to wake up over and over with nightmares.

I couldn't sleep with those mental images of David's bird-watching boat sinking far offshore. All the protection psalms I recited seemed worthless. After all, people who love God experience horrors every day.

When I woke David on time, I did not mention my nightmares. All day I stayed afraid despite repeated prayer for calm and for his safety. Thoughts kept running through my mind: the sea separates continents and people. Gentle waves become violent walls of water during storms. Oceans are metaphors for all the chaos and unexplained destruction on earth.

So I walked to a cove nearby. Herons fed in the tidal flats. Clams clung to rocks near a marine railway. Eelgrass rippled in the waves. And I remembered. Even in chaos one finds underlying order. God does control wind and waves. Destruction has its limits, or else Denver, Colorado, would be a seaport! The birds David boated to see thrive at the edges of order and chaos.

I felt better, but not enough. For the first time, I think I understood why John the fisherman, friend of Jesus, and writer of Revelation sounded so excited about the sea near God's throne being clear glass so people could stand on it, and in the new earth, no sea at all.

Until then I had always thought no sea would be no fun. No seabirds, no seashells, no soothing waves, no dunes, no swimming.

But no sea will also be no separation, no drowning, no hurricanes or tsunamis, no hurt or destroyed whales or puffins or harp seals.

I don't know what God has planned for the new earth. But I am sure it will include delights that fear or grief or pain will never spoil. I can hardly wait to see. — CAROL JUNE HUTCHINS HOOKER

JULY 16

Constructive Thoughts

In my Father's house are many rooms; if it were not so, I would have told you. I am going there to prepare a place for you. And if I go and prepare a place for you, I will come back and take you to be with me that you also may be where I am. John 14:2, 3, NIV.

*I*t is a nightly routine. All the steps are familiar, and I cannot leave any of them out without causing discomfort. Bathe children, dry their hair, brush teeth, get a drink, good-night hugs, read a story, say a prayer, tuck them under the covers, one last kiss.

The pink lamp on the nightstand is a leftover from another house in another state with another color scheme. It casts an incongruous light in the red, white, and blue decor and gives the place a cartoon-like look.

"Mommy," the innocent speaks, "when are our houses going to be done?" Jaime's almost-5-year-old voice is quizzical.

"What houses?" I shift my attention from the pink misfit lamp in the patriotic panorama to the wide eyes and begging-to-be-kissed cheeks of my daughter.

"The houses Jesus is making for us [the tone adds "of course"]. They should be done by now!"

"Oh, *those* houses. Well, I don't know. What makes you think they should be done?" I probe for more of her thinking.

"It's been a long time!"

She's done it again. Without even trying she's shown me that things are so simple and straightforward, so basic and beautiful through the eyes of a child. I know how long it takes to build a house on terra firma. We did it once. I sketched the plans on graph paper and took them to an architect. Although we hired out some of the more complicated pieces of the work, otherwise it definitely qualified as a do-it-yourself project. I learned to wallpaper. My father signed on for the project, much to our delight. And thanks to my husband's ability to turn ideas into reality in wood, a plethora of creative and functional touches made it a mansion in our eyes.

It had taken four and a half months. Then we moved in, happy but exhausted.

Yes, even with the help of experts, it takes some doing to construct earthly mansions.

But how long does it take to build houses in heaven? Are they all done—just waiting for their owners to take up residence? Has Jesus saved the landscaping for those among us who love puttering around in the garden? And is the landscaping completed for those who despise yard chores?

If I spend more time contemplating celestial homes, will heavenly thoughts always be as real to me as they are to Jaime?

Yes, it's been a long time. Come quickly, Lord. I'm ready for moving day.

SHEREE PARRIS NUDD

JULY 17

Even in the Dark

The angel of the Lord encampeth round about them that fear him, and delivereth them. Ps. 34:7.

I never have especially liked the dark. Each morning at worship we asked our angels for protection, but somehow I wasn't sure that protection extended to outside that circle of light after dark.

Each evening I gathered the eggs the hens had laid during the day. That meant going outside the circle of light if I put off doing my chores until after dark. Most of the time I didn't procrastinate, but one night somehow the sun went down before I did my work, and my mother told me I must go. I could see to the gate of the chicken yard in the light, so armed with a flashlight and a basket for eggs, I walked slowly toward the gate.

Even with my flashlight it was dark. The chicken house door squeaked as I opened it, and the chickens made strange noises shuffling around getting comfortable for the night. I stepped inside and went over to the nests.

Soon I finished in the henhouse, but I knew I had to go over to the cow barn to finish, for we had a few old hens who liked to lay their eggs in the manger there. Sliding back the cow barn door, I walked inside and bent over the nest. Then I heard a sound that still petrifies me when I hear it—a *raaattttlllle*. Knowing that I was close to a rattlesnake, I backed slowly toward the door, then almost flew to the light and the house.

My white face and speed told my parents that something had happened. Dad grabbed a hoe, and together we went back to the barn, with him leading the way. He walked through the door first with the flashlight on and urged, "Come on, Connie." Reluctantly I followed. The *rattttllllle* sound came again.

He shone the flashlight, and a rattlesnake lay in the nest with three eggs. My dad took the hoe, removed the snake, and chopped off its head.

"Get the eggs, Connie," Dad urged me. Shakily I picked them up. I wasn't sure the snake might not have a friend somewhere nearby.

As we knelt for prayer that evening, we said a big thank-you for the protection of God's angels even though I had put off doing my chores until after dark. That night I learned God's protection isn't just when we are doing what is right. How grateful I am that God loves us and takes care of us, even outside that "circle of light" when we procrastinate. CONNIE NOWLAND

JULY 18

"It Is I; Be Not Afraid"

Be of good cheer: it is I; be not afraid. Mark 6:50.

*A*fter a busy day with the multitude, Jesus was tired and needed rest. He sent His disciples into the ship while He dismissed the people. Then He remained on land, and the ship drifted out to sea.

Night descended, and the winds became fierce. The disciples struggled to keep the ship afloat, but they were having difficulty. Jesus saw their struggles and walked out on the water to them. The disciples did not recognize their Master, and reacted with fright. They cried out, "It is a spirit!"

Calmly Jesus spoke to them, "Be of good cheer. It is I. Don't be afraid." He went into the ship with them, and immediately the wind ceased. Amazement overwhelmed the men. Sadly they had already forgotten the miracle of the loaves they had witnessed earlier that day.

The disciples had been disappointed because of Jesus' unwillingness to become king (John 6:15-20). But in their distress on the storm-tossed lake they suddenly awakened to their dependence on Christ.

At times God sends storms into our lives. We forget His leading in our past experiences and express doubts that He is in control now. Perhaps we even speak discouragingly of the outcome. But in the midst of the storm, Jesus appears and reassures us.

Dora's life was one of turmoil, yet her face always radiated peace. By all counts, she had every reason to be sad. Her sister and brother-in-law, along with their six children, had moved in with Dora. The three-room house already housed Dora, her husband, and their five children.

The sister's children contracted chicken pox. They had fevers and runny noses, and cried all the time. Dora's five children became infected with the disease. With 11 children moaning, scratching, crying, and having runny noses to wipe, the needs were urgent. How could anyone cope in a situation such as this? someone asked Dora. Smiling through her weariness, she said, "I get up at 4:30 every morning. I sit at the kitchen table with my Bible. I read and pray. God gives me strength."

Though the storms rage around and within, we can find peace through communion with God. If you are troubled or distressed, take a moment now and listen to God's voice speak to you. Just as He stilled the raging tempest, He offers to bring peace to your troubled heart. MABEL ROLLINS NORMAN

JULY 19

Waiting but Coming

Like as a father pitieth his children, so the Lord pitieth them that fear him. Ps. 103:13.

Girls," Daddy spoke at the breakfast table, "be ready right after lunch, and we will go to town to shop."

"Oh, goody!" exclaimed 6-year-old Vicki and 5-year-old Winnie. They loved going with their parents to the shops in Kingston, Jamaica.

After a hastily eaten lunch, Daddy said, "All right, girls, get on your sandals. I'm ready to go."

The girls liked walking barefoot on the cool tile floors. Hurriedly they left the table. Daddy and Mommy went to the garage. Only Vicki appeared ready.

"Where's Winnie?"

"She can't find her sandals, but wait for her, Daddy. She wants to come," the girl pleaded.

Winnie came running. "Wait for me, Daddy. I can't find my sandals."

"Winnie," Daddy said, "we have told you again and again to keep things where you can find them. This will have to be a lesson to you. If you can't find them, we will have to leave without you." Daddy's tone was firm.

"Oh, no, Daddy! Please wait for me," she wailed as she ran back to look again.

"Daddy, wait," Vicki begged. "I'll go help her look." Shortly Vicki raced back. "We have found one, Daddy. Please wait."

"I'm leaving," Daddy said as he put the car in reverse.

"Wait, Daddy, wait!" Now two girls were crying.

Dashing back to the house, Vicki looked in closets, under beds, in the toy basket. Daddy was inching ever so-o-o-o slowly toward the gate. Vicki was beside herself. She knew Daddy meant what he said, and she also knew Winnie wanted to come. She couldn't bear to see her left behind.

Again she ran to the car. "Wait, Daddy, wait." Then back to the house, frantically, tearfully, searching. Finally two sandals appeared, and smiles replaced the tear-stained faces. Daddy was just going through the gate as the girls quickly hopped into the car.

How often when I think of that incident I am reminded of this text. I know my heavenly Father has told me to be ready because He is going to take me with Him. I am excited about going, but have I misplaced my wedding garment? Is it under the clutter of cherished sins?

So He waits. He could come quickly, but "like as a father pitieth his children," He slowly inches toward the gate. He is hoping I will clear away the clutter and find the shining white wedding garment.

ELIZABETH "BETTY" WOODMANSEE HOEHN

JULY 20

In the Dark

For now we see through a glass, darkly; but then face to face. 1 Cor. 13:12.

We were living in Fiji at the time. My husband, principal of a Christian college, was overseas for two weeks, but my teaching duties kept me on campus.

I have never pretended to be one of those women who carry on as well when their husbands are away. I hate that lonely house at night when I have no one to talk to, so I tend to work or read until late, then hope when I go to bed that morning will come quickly.

The college's electricity generator shut off at 10:00 p.m. as usual, and this night I had worked by battery light for some time before praying and sliding between the sheets and falling asleep.

Suddenly, I awoke with a start. At first I just lay listening. Soon I detected a furtive movement outside the bedroom window. Not a ray of light shone into the room. Silence. Perhaps I had imagined that sound. *I should relax, turn over, and* . . . But there it was again. It was moving, whatever or whoever it was.

My imagination began improvising graphic scenarios until I was breathless with terror. The movements were audible again, and I was sure I could detect heavy breathing. A touch against the mosquito netting of the open window horrified me.

Calm down, I told myself. *Pray. Take control of yourself.* I found praying the easiest of the three as I scrutinized the darkness at the window.

Then when the sounds seemed to move toward the adjacent bedroom, I became brave enough to slide into my slippers and robe and peek under a corner of the curtains. Yes, something was out there. A heavy shadow flickered in the hazy, gray light. I held back more of the curtain, and grinning into the darkness, shouted at the monsters.

Two large black cows lifted their heads from my garden, rolled the whites of their eyes, and stumbled off down the hill to the village. I was still in the darkness when they left. Reality had not changed much, but my fear had fled.

Often since then I have remembered the black cows. They have become symbols of unnecessary worry and fear when I cannot see through the darkness of situations. And although now "we see through a glass, darkly," we can look forward to seeing things plainly when we see Jesus "face to face."   URSULA HEDGES

The Long-awaited Day

When the Son of Man comes in his glory, and all the angels with him, he will sit on his throne in heavenly glory. Matt. 25:31, NIV.

We were all excited. After all, we had waited for this day, and it was finally here! My boys and I were part of a large group of autograph seekers standing in line to meet Alan Shepard, one of the astronauts from the early United States space program. The line moved relatively quickly, and after waiting an hour and a half outside we finally got into the building. In just a few minutes we would see the person we had been anticipating meeting all morning.

Then the news came: Mr. Shepard would sign only a copy of his book—nothing else. We didn't have a copy of his book—only post-cards. To say the least, we were very disappointed.

As my children and I drove home, the car was quiet. When I turned off the engine, I asked the boys to remove their hats so we could pray.

"Jesus," I began, "You know today our feelings of disappointment. We had waited to see this special man, and though we saw him, it was not what we had expected. We are looking for that day when You will return, and we won't be disappointed! Help us keep watch and be ready for that day. Amen."

I am waiting with great longing for my King to return, and I know I will not be disappointed. MOIRA BARTHLE

JULY 22

Something Pretty

Neglect not the gift that is in thee, which was given thee by prophecy, with the laying on of the hands of the presbytery. 1 Tim. 4:14.

*P*aul is specifically speaking to Timothy regarding those spiritual gifts that made him a useful tool for God. But could we, like Timothy, be neglecting our gifts too? Let me share a little story with you, and you draw your own conclusions.

Little bare feet, brown from many side excursions, beat a staccato rhythm upon the littered sidewalk as the child made an attempt to catch the adult with whom he was supposed to be walking. One grimy hand clutched his too-big pants while the other knotted into a fist and pumped vigorously to speed him on his way. His bright eyes, however, were free to roam—ever seeking the interesting, tantalizing attractions of his surroundings.

Finding nothing of interest in the squalor of a near-slum street of this large Midwestern city, I wanted to hasten into a better neighborhood, but this sharp-eyed lad arrested my attention, and I paused.

Poor little urchin, I mulled. *How terrible that you have to trudge barefoot through this filth! You need someone who cares enough . . .* It

231

seemed as if he could read my thoughts, for the boy shot a defiant glance my way. He seemed to dare me to have pity for him. His feet paused as he studied me carefully but hurriedly.

Then glancing aside, his eyes fell on a shrub in the last stages of bloom. Only a few blossoms clung tenaciously to the shrub for life. Many littered the ground, in all stages of decay. The lad, still clutching his jeans, reached a tender hand out to touch those on the bush in wonder. He fondled several before he spied those on the ground.

Quick eyes sought the brightest and least wilted. Little fingers cupped one fallen blossom protectively. Still looking at the blossom, the child called to his patient caretaker, "Wait, Candy. I've found something pretty for you."

Candy turned and accepted the offered token of love. Her expression of returned love lifted them both above the squalor of their surroundings. They soared above the filth.

As I went on my way, I reviewed the incident—insignificant perhaps, and yet a parallel to my Christian experience. How often I lag behind the leading of my God. I examine the many attractions along the way, soil my feet with the dust of my surroundings. Then, spying a talent lying uncared for and unused, I pick it up and rush ahead with, "Wait, Lord, I've found something pretty for You!"

He lovingly turns, smiles a welcome to me, and accepts my gift.

WILMA ATKINSON

JULY 23

Sources

And Jesus said unto them, I am the bread of life: he that cometh to me shall never hunger; and he that believeth on me shall never thirst. John 6:35.

*A*head lay the mountain. The track led through thick bush, freshly washed and alive with birdsong. Yesterday's clouds had gone, the sun shone, and the breeze was gentle. It was a beautiful morning for a walk.

Presently I heard a waterfall, and the many voices of running water joined the music of the morning. There it was, cascading into a dark valley, gliding and foaming over rocks, then dropping into still pools, black in the shadows, silver where a sunbeam shone.

Our track continued to the head of the falls, and here, very close to the path, the water ran strongly, chuckling and gurgling to itself, fringed with ferns. It invited us to stoop and drink. But wait! A sign caught our attention: "WATER UNFIT FOR DRINKING!" In a New Zealand National Park?

For weeks we, from drought-ravaged Australia, had reveled in the splendors of majestic glaciers, rushing rivers colored with rock flour, powder snow, serene reflecting tarns, gentle rain, and even pounding hail. But this was the first time we had seen such a sign. True, the water looked a little gray, but heavy rain had fallen yesterday, and that could have discolored it.

Sometime later we understood the reason for that permanent, unequivocal sign. We came to a region of sulfur fumes and multicolored rocks, stained by minerals and encrusted with crystals, where the wind clutched and twisted curtains of steam. A place of gurglings and hissing, a frightening place where the earth seemed to quiver, and dark blue-gray liquid sloshed in holes or was thrown up by fountains of steam. Here was no "river of [the] water of life, clear as crystal" (Rev. 22:1), but a fierce chemical solution, wholly uninviting.

When we returned down that sundappled track, we had no difficulty in understanding the sign, for we had been to the source. But it did make me think about our own lives—for the things we see, hear, even taste, have sources too.

Jesus wants us to choose the best, to come to the Source that never disappoints and is not destructive or hurtful. He is the Water of Life and promises that "he that believeth on me shall never thirst."

GWEN PASCOE

JULY 24

Sweet Cheeries

A happy heart makes the face cheerful, but heartache crushes the spirit. Prov. 15:13, NIV.

J was on my way to town and passed one of the many corner fruit stands that frequent Fresno streets during the fruit season. "Sweet Cheeries," the misspelled hand-printed sign announced. A smile spread over my face, and I couldn't repress the giggles as I thought about "sweet cheeries." Then I did a quick check on my attitude of the moment. Was I a "sweet cheery," or a sour and unhappy person?

Shortly after this experience, a friend told me about her struggle to accept a move when her husband was transferred to another city.

They had just bought a home and had it decorated and finished the way they wanted it. Having settled in and made friends, she didn't want to move, and she was angry, upset, and very resentful over the fact that she had to.

While house-hunting in the new area, she attended church. Inwardly she wanted this new church to show her it was a warm and friendly place. Outwardly she took her "I don't want to be here" feelings with her, along with the chip on her shoulder.

The greeter at the door welcomed the family and asked where they were visiting from. The person handed a church bulletin to them, but no one offered a dinner invitation or welcome of any other kind. "See!" she told herself. "It's not a warm and friendly place!" She knew she was going to hate it there, and now she did.

But before the move took place, she recognized she needed an attitude adjustment toward what she was going to find at this new church. The next time she attended, she determined to go in there smiling, saying hello to everyone, rather than waiting for someone else to approach her. She left the church that day feeling it was a much warmer and friendlier place.

It might do us all good from time to time to take a "sweet cheeries" attitude check on ourselves. Yes, our hearts get heavy with daily stress, tasks to be completed, and new problems to deal with constantly. But dwelling on the heartache of life will only crush our spirit. A cheerful face is easier to look at than an unhappy one and a lot prettier, too. Someone has observed, "If you're happy, notify your face."

We make infinitely better witnesses for God when we cheerfully carry life's burdens rather than allowing them to crush us. Let's do an attitude check and resolve to be filled with "sweet cheeries." Grab a handful of "cheeries" today and pass them on.   NANCY VAN PELT

JULY 25

The Protection of Praise

By the rivers of Babylon we sat and wept when we remembered Zion. There on the poplars we hung our harps, for there our captors asked us for songs, our tormentors demanded songs of joy; they said, "Sing us one of the songs of Zion!" How can we sing the songs of the Lord while in a foreign land? Ps. 137:1-4, NIV.

J have often wondered why so few of the captives returned to Jerusalem when freed from Babylonian captivity. Perhaps these verses hold a clue. The songs of the Lord vibrate with victory and the knowledge of God and His leading. By failing to sing those songs and focusing instead on their misery, the exiles lost their sense of God's presence and leading and failed to pass on to their children their heritage. Had they sung those songs, it would have protected them from being overcome by their environment.

Many times during my life music has provided a lifeline that has helped keep me from being overwhelmed by my circumstances. As a lonely child I always felt better after singing those little Jesus songs. Learning to play hymns on the piano and organ often eased my turbulent teenage years.

The first few years that I had rheumatoid arthritis I was in constant, excruciating pain. I spent all day in bed alone in the house. Listening to a religious music station was the only thing that helped me keep my sanity. I didn't have the energy to read or think or pray. Reality was too frightening to contemplate.

Singing the "songs of Zion" helped me through the first few years after my divorce as I began to heal and put my life back together. Somehow, music helps my heart to hear the message in the words and changes my mood from one of despair to hope.

I have had numerous trips to the hospital for surgery and found, again, that singing helped to ease the fear and pain. Today I find it extremely frustrating that I can no longer play an instrument because of hand deformities, and worse yet, I cannot sing because of paralysis in my throat. I just have to sing in my imagination.

But I still fill my days with Christian music. I want to keep in practice, singing the songs of Zion in this foreign land so that I will keep in touch with my heritage and be ready to return to my homeland when the time comes. LUCILE FREEMAN-KIME

JULY 26

Love in a Doll's Shoe

The Lord hath appeared of old unto me, saying, Yea, I have loved thee with an everlasting love: therefore with lovingkindness have I drawn thee. Jer. 31:3.

$\mathcal{I}$t was just a little thing, and it didn't cost very much. But it made my whole day brighter.

A few springs ago my husband drove my sister and me to the Blue Mountains not far from our College Place, Washington, home. We parked on the edge of a mountain with a view of a lush valley. A cold wind blew, so Hugh walked farther up the mountain alone. He returned with a bouquet of wildflowers neatly placed in a doll's shoe. With a boyish grin he presented me with his yellow and purple gift.

Suddenly time turned back 50 years. I worked in the business office of a small college. Hugh, a theology major, had access through a friend to my office. Morning after morning flowers appeared on my desk—lavender crocuses, purple violets, and pink wild roses. No note accompanied them, but in my heart I knew the giver. And when I very shyly thanked him, he gave me that same boyish grin so familiar to me now.

Today that little Cabbage Patch doll's shoe sits on my kitchen window sill. I glance past it, and I see a rosebush full of pink-petaled flowers. "God is love" is written on each fragrant blossom, on each dewy leaf.

That rosebush is a constant reminder of a heavenly Father's love just as that little shoe is a constant reminder of a husband's love. Someday a little girl may say that doll's shoe belongs to her. She may remember she lost it on that windy mountain top, but she will have a hard time reclaiming it! A bouquet of spring flowers in a Cabbage Patch doll's shoe didn't cost much. It was just a little thing, but it brightened my whole day.

What can I do to brighten someone's path today? What about you?

MARGARET I. CAMPBELL

JULY 27

Tie a Knot and Hang On

Where can I go from your Spirit? Where can I flee from your presence? If I go up to the heavens, you are there; if I make my bed in the depths, you are there. If I rise on the wings of the dawn, if I settle on the far side of the sea, even there your hand will guide me, your right hand will hold me fast. Ps. 139:7-10, NIV.

*W*hen I was a teenager I often heard the popular saying "When you get to the end of your rope, tie a knot and hang on." I didn't pay much attention to it. My whole life was itching to happen. I didn't need a rope to hold on to. Any problems I had God was sure to solve them for me.

Life got busier and busier. I moved across the world, got married, had a family, found a job, and then went back to school. Now I knew what they meant by "tie a knot and hang on," but I discovered that rope doesn't give you much freedom. You can climb up. You can climb down. You can swing, or you can hang. But that's about all.

God was pretty limiting too. Sometimes He didn't even seem to be there. Maybe I was too busy, or maybe I thought I was Superwoman and could do it all on my own. But I couldn't. I tried not to think about it.

A couple months ago I found myself standing on top of a 150-foot-high bungy jumping tower. It was horrifying to realize that I was expected to fling myself over the edge, and worse yet, with only a flimsy piece of elastic string wrapped around my ankles to keep me from plunging to my death.

Stressed out and prematurely aging though I was, I wasn't quite ready to leave the rat race. I desperately wished I had my old rope again . . . so I could climb back down, go home, and hide under the bed.

But too many people were watching for me to back out. My pride was at stake. So I jumped. And fell (oh, where's a rope when you need one?) . . . and fell (where is God when you've just done something stupid?) . . . and fell and . . . was suddenly snatched away from the rapidly approaching ground by that strong elastic cord gripping my legs.

Adrenaline surges have a way of clearing your head. I discovered that the limiting rope of my childhood had been replaced by a strong, supportive cord that could stretch with my doubts, carry me through fears, and bounce me away from death on the rocks below.

God's promise to us in today's text reminds us that He will hold on to us. I don't think I'll forget again.   TRUDY RANKIN

Toby

The eternal God is your refuge, and underneath are the everlasting arms. Deut. 33:27, NIV.

Toby, a 4-year-old black pedigreed pug, came into our lives after his elderly mistress had to move into a nursing home. I begged my husband, who is very much a "cat" man, to let us adopt him. The dog was a cute little fellow with a shiny, satinlike coat, protruding eyes set in his funny, pushed-in, wrinkled face, and a little tail that curled tightly over his back.

Although officially the family pet, Toby and I soon developed our own special "love affair." I took him to obedience school. I usually fed and groomed him. While the family was away all day at school and work, we were close companions. If ever a larger, menacing-looking dog threatened him while we were out on our walks, I always scooped him up into the safety of my arms.

Once while enjoying a beach holiday, our family lived in an old cabin consisting of three adjoining rooms. Two were quite large, and one was not much bigger than a storeroom. Afraid of what roaming town dogs might do to our little pet, I insisted that we bring Toby in for the nights, and so we made him a little bed in the storeroom.

One night when the children and I were already in our beds, my husband was left to put Toby in the storeroom. This particular night, however, the little dog had other ideas. He decided that he didn't want to be locked up and gave my husband a merry chase round and round the two main rooms, dashing in and out under the table, chairs, and beds.

To Christopher, Cathie, and me the pantomime was great fun, but eventually Father became tired of the chase and a little annoyed. Toby started to have second thoughts, and to our utter surprise and amazement, mustered all his strength, took one mighty, desperate leap over the end of my bed, and literally flung himself onto my bosom. Had he, like Balaam's donkey, actually spoken, he could not have more clearly pleaded, "Save me, Mother; please save me!" Even my husband joined in our hearty laughter.

While it was an amusing family experience, that naughty little dog reminded me of today's text. When in trouble do we try to face it alone or do we flee to Jesus, the one who knows and loves us best? Even when the trouble is sometimes of our own making, He is always ready with His powerful arms outstretched to save. IRENE POWELL

My New Purpose

And we know that all things work together for good to them that love God, to them who are the called according to his purpose. Rom. 8:28.

*D*ear Lord," I prayed desperately, "here I am shattered as the result of an accident. Six weeks ago I was actively engaged in Christian service. Now with limited use of one arm, I can't even type. I'm 90 years old and in a retirement home. I need an answer. Why did I survive?"

"You can write letters, and you have a small lending library," was the silent reply.

With the answer to my prayer came the impression that I should write to a special friend. A paperback story of mission service in a distant land accompanied my first letter. When he returned the book, I sent another, then another.

In April, as I slipped the lending card into the pocket of still another book, I saw $5.00 stuck between the pages. Now came a happy thought! *I'll mail this money to Pastor Robert Spangler for Russian evangelism and ask him to send the receipt to my friend. It will help tie him to the church.* The next book had a similar gift.

The first Sunday in June my phone rang. "We baptized your friend yesterday. His brother attended the service," the local pastor informed me.

There was singing in heaven and joy in my heart. Now family and friends participate in my joy by keeping me supplied with an abundance of stationery and stamps. "Enough to last until Jesus comes!" my daughter exclaimed after my ninety-second birthday.

MYRTLE A. POHLE

Who Found the Keys?

Ask, and it shall be given you; seek, and ye shall find; knock, and it shall be opened unto you. Matt. 7:7.

'd like to know . . . Someday I'll ask."

I needed to unlock one of the interior doors to the library where I worked as a college reference librarian. But I could find no keys in my purse, pockets, or desk drawers. Mechanically I started retracing my steps to other desks and areas in the book stacks. Where had I been during the past two hours?

Feeling uneasy, I decided that I would leave the library long enough to go home and look for the keys. Losing them was especially traumatic, for if we lost the keys, we would have to change all the locks in the library.

At home I frantically searched every logical place where I could have laid them down, not forgetting pockets in the clothes I had worn the day before. No keys. As I left to go back to work, my father, who lived with me, said that he would continue to search.

I dangled at the end of my rope for the rest of the morning. At noon I again left my desk to go home. My colleague, relieving me at the reference desk, said as I turned to go, "I'll be praying for you."

Driving into the garage, I jumped out of the car, looked down, and at my feet lay the ring full of library keys. Overjoyed, I ran into the house. "Dad, I found the keys on the garage floor!"

He looked puzzled. "But I searched over the garage floor carefully after you left. *They were not there!*"

Someday I want to ask my guardian angel where he found the keys and why he put them on the garage floor. BARBARA H. PHIPPS

JULY 31

The Fragrant Gift

Now there are varieties of gifts, but the same Spirit; and there are varieties of services, but the same Lord; and there are varieties of activities, but it is the same God who activates all of them in everyone. 1 Cor. 12:4-6, NRSV.

o you have a gift? For many years I was unaware of one of mine.

I was brought up in a very poor home in Belfast. Then I moved to England to work. My church had a very special woman who designed the floral arrangements for the sanctuary. Eventually I went to work in the same office she did, and I would admire the exquisite bouquets she placed every week on the reception desk.

One day, for my birthday, she gave me a bowl, a piece of

chicken wire, and a pinholder, then told me to "get on with it"! I had never had a flower-arranging lesson. In fact, I had never seen an arrangement done. Nevertheless, each Friday I would buy flowers in the market and do a little bouquet for our home.

The time came for Auntie Peg to retire and move away. Our congregation placed me on the church schedule to arrange the flowers. My first attempt was pretty pathetic, but gradually, as I gained confidence and dedicated my offerings to God, I grew more proficient.

Sometimes I find it hard to fit this task into my busy schedule. Yet I know that as soon as I bow my head in church and ask God to guide my hands, His Spirit will calm me, and great blessings will flow. For me doing the flowers is an act of worship, and as with all acts of worship, there is a continual flow of blessing from God as He accepts my humble offering.

I know that my flower arranging is a gift from God because I am not naturally artistic—I can hardly draw a stick man! Gifts are for sharing, and I am so thankful that Auntie Peg released the gift in me. In turn, I try to pass on my gift to others.

Have you found your gift yet? If you have, pass it on. If you haven't, search diligently—we all have at least one!

AUDREY BALDERSTONE

AUGUST 1

Grandma's Standards

Let this mind be in you which was also in Christ Jesus. Phil. 2:5, NKJV.

How I envied the other passengers on the big Greyhound bus that day so many years ago. They did not feel the embarrassment that clutched the back of my 10-year-old neck with hot stinging fingers. And yet well-ingrained duty bade me rivet my eyes and ears to the source of my discomfort.

The diminutive Black lady in the out-of-fashion black dress stood on the bus platform singing for all to hear "Jesus Wants Me for a Sunbeam." Her partner in crime was a small, homely, pigtailed girl clinging to my grandmother's hand and making up in enthusiasm what she lacked in tonal quality.

I prayed silently that the bus would hurry on its way, unless by some good fortune I could die first. I would gladly have traded this unusual farewell for the conventional hugs and kisses. The incident is one of the many vignettes that characterize my memories of Grandma.

Mary Hill Towler was first and foremost a lover of Jesus Christ. Five minutes in her presence left no doubt of that fact.

Though born a slave, she had managed to fulfill her drive for education. She taught for 50 years in the rural schools of the Virginia public school system. When she retired at age 70 she opened a school in her home, dispensing the four R's to the neighborhood children: "Reading, 'Riting, 'Rithmetic, and Religion." Her companion on that faraway ignoble day was one of these little pupils.

She encouraged her own eight daughters and two sons to give of their best to the Master in emulation of their little mother. Daily worship and Bible school were as integral to their development as wresting a livelihood from the uncooperative soil.

Much later, during my own growing-up years, a letter bearing the Richmond, Virginia, postmark always meant a treatise on the love of God and His will for me. The letters were not always received with joy, but I never doubted where Grandma's loyalties were.

Mary's dog-eared Bible bore mute testimony to its usage. She read it from cover to cover more than 50 times and made its principles her own. Her relationship with her personal Friend left no doubt in her mind as to the place she was to fill on this earth. God instructed—she obeyed in love. Mary Towler was called to be a "sunbeam" for Him, and she was.

We can be one too. It is only by daily, personal, intimate relationship with Jesus that each person can know beyond doubt what He expects in each of our lives to fulfill our individual missions.

JAYNE DOSWELL DARBY

AUGUST 2

Jujitsu

And he said, Let me go, for the day breaketh. And he said, I will not let thee go, except thou bless me. Gen. 32:26.

It was 1942, World War II raged, and my husband, Franklin, drafted by the United States Army, was stationed at Fort Francis E. Warren in Cheyenne, Wyoming. We lived in a one-room apartment in that crowded wartime city, whose population had swelled to almost double its previous 20,000 size.

Being a noncombatant, Franklin's earliest training included a series of lessons in jujitsu—an art in weaponless self-defense that employs holds and throws to subdue an opponent. Eager that his young wife should also know how to defend herself, he came home each evening and shared what he had learned that day.

"If someone should come from behind and grab you around the waist," he would ask, "how would you break their hold?" He was determined that I learn what he had been taught. "By using your opponent's weight to your advantage," he explained, "you could actually flip him over your shoulder!" To me the idea was preposterous, but eager to please him, I went along with his instructions.

Again and again my husband—acting as my assailant—patiently showed me how to break his hold. Each time I tried to flip him over my shoulder, but not one pound of him would budge. The secret of success was in the timing. And I couldn't get it right!

"OK, that's all," he finally said after an evening of fruitless practice. "We've tried long enough." Though I was not convinced it could work, I hated to give up in failure.

"Let me try just once more," I pleaded. This time everything clicked. Wide-eyed, I flipped him over my shoulder like a toothpick, and to my utter horror, I watched him fly through space and land providentially on the couch on his back—hands and arms waving in all directions.

Bursting into tears, I knew I had injured my soldier-husband for life. Then I heard his shouts of victory. "It worked! You did it!" And I knew I had learned what he had been trying to teach me. Oh, how thankful I was for that last try!

How often as I have encountered spiritual struggles I have at the same time wrestled with an overpowering temptation to give up. Time after time I fail. But when with His help I persevere until I have gained victory, what a wonderful feeling of gratitude sweeps over me.

Told that we "let go of the arm of the Lord too soon" (*Early Writings,* p. 73), we are admonished to press our petitions to God's throne and hold on by strong faith because His promises are sure. Sometimes, though, we are obliged to wait for the Lord's perfect timing. In His wisdom God may delay His answer, but what a glorious victory is ours if we continue to pray and wait.

LORRAINE HUDGINS

To See and to Care

And when Jesus went out He saw a great multitude; and He was moved with compassion for them. Matt. 14:14, NKJV.

*B*ertrand Russell, the English philosopher known for his studies in logic and mathematics and his essays and lectures on philosophy, wrote in his autobiography of three passions, simple but overwhelmingly strong, that governed his life. The first two were a longing for love and a search for knowledge. Then he elaborated on his third passion—pity for the suffering of humanity. Even the echoes of its cries were enough to create in him unbearable pity.

These same echoes also reach our ears, whether only occasionally or in a steady stream, but perhaps we've lost the capacity to hear them. We who aren't crying from pain may have become so desensitized that we suffer from a classic disorder called "boilermaker's deafness." This describes individuals who have worked in that trade for so long that they become selectively deaf to the sound frequencies that surround them constantly.

Christian ears and hearts shouldn't suffer from this disorder. Our hearts should be a better echo chamber for the cries of suffering humanity than all the valleys of the Rockies. In this we have Jesus as an example. When He was on earth, He went to the cities and villages, teaching in the synagogues, preaching the gospel of the kingdom, and healing every sickness among the people. But when He *saw* the multitudes, He was moved with *compassion* on them.

The two words *saw* and *compassion* sometimes don't get enough attention. It's so easy to become engrossed in our personal lives and daily affairs that we notice little else. Jesus was undoubtedly busier than we are, but He was never oblivious to the needs of others. He saw and was moved to compassion by pain, sorrow, hunger, and loneliness, and He acted on those feelings of compassion.

Stephen Grellet, an obscure nineteenth-century Quaker from Pennsylvania, would have remained an unknown had he not penned these memorable words: "I expect to pass through this world but once; any good thing therefore that I can do, or any kindness that I can show to any fellow creature, let me do it now; let me not defer or neglect it, for I shall not pass this way again."

Jesus knew His time on earth was short. He showed great kindness and compassion because He saw and acted. Women are natural nurturers, caring about the needs of others. Yet sometimes maybe even we suffer from a crisis of insensitivity. I've resolved that I want to model my passage on this earth after my Great Example, who *saw* and had *compassion*.   LILYA WAGNER

AUGUST 4

The Wrong Number

And it shall come to pass, that before they call, I will answer; and while they are yet speaking, I will hear. Isa. 65:24.

The phone rang for the tenth time that Saturday evening. "Hello, this is Pastor Campbell's residence." No sound came from the caller. I tried again. "Were you calling the pastor?" A hesitant voice answered. "I must have the wrong number." Then she added slowly, "Do I hear children's voices?"

"Yes," I answered. "We have two little girls. They're playing here in the hall."

"Oh, how fortunate you are." A note of interest appeared in her voice. "Love them! They grow up so soon." I sensed her wistful longing to talk.

"How many children do you have, and where do they live?" I asked.

Her story was a sad account of children she loved, and who had loved her. But all had left home with bitter feelings. "They never call or write," she added dejectedly. "I don't know where any one of them lives. No one cares for me."

"Dear Lord, help me say the right thing," I prayed. To her I said, "But God loves you. You are precious to Him."

"You mean He cares for even me?" The voice sounded incredulous.

"Yes, Jesus loves us all. He died for us all. And He is coming again." Our conversation grew lengthy. She was hungry for friendship. Finally I said, "I would love to have your address," thinking we could be of more help.

But her reply came quickly. "Oh, no, lady."

Then I ventured, "My husband is away this evening, but we would love to visit you sometime."

"Oh, please don't," she insisted with the same urgency. "My brother sits in the doorway with a gun and threatens to shoot anyone who comes here."

We talked again. She seemed to want to hold on to the moment. Finally after a long sigh, she confided, "I'm so glad I called your number by mistake." Did I detect a tinge of hope? "This was to be my last phone call before turning on the gas in my kitchen. Thank you for saving my life." Her voice broke into a sob as the receiver slowly slipped into place.

I thank God too that she had dialed the wrong number. I praise Him for allowing me to be an answer to her prayer before she even called on His name. How wonderful is our ever-attentive, loving Father!

MARGARET I. CAMPBELL

Only Two Cases!

For whoever wants to save his life will lose it, but whoever loses his life for me will find it. What good will it be for a man if he gains the whole world, yet forfeits his soul? Matt. 16:25, 26, NIV.

Each day of our lives we confront situations in which we have to make choices. Sometimes the choice is an easy one, but often they're very difficult.

It was April 7, 1994. My husband told me to begin packing because the Rwandan president had been killed the night before and an evacuation of foreigners would begin at any time. I spent the morning calmly ironing and started to pack our clothing that afternoon.

Then we received word to pack a single suitcase for each family member and be ready to leave the next day. There were four of us, and I set out things that would fit into four suitcases. Later, however, the evacuation organizers informed us that they had no room for luggage. We would be leaving in the few personal cars on the college campus. Each family had to wear most of the essentials. That presented a big problem! Wasn't everything I had prepared essential? Surely! But these items wouldn't fit into the two small cases we could take with us.

I would put in one thing . . . take it out . . . put it back again. I struggled so many times over what we really "needed" that it left me exhausted. Eventually I sat down and prayed. Finally, real priorities led me to make choices as I packed: a Bible, a church hymnal, a Bible lesson book, important papers, valuable letters and diplomas, the children's correspondence course books, and some clothing (three outfits and two pairs of shoes for each member). The cases filled to capacity. Nothing more would possibly fit inside them.

The choices were very painful to make, but the situation gave me a great spiritual insight. We will soon be transported to our true homeland—the New Jerusalem. What are the essentials we will bring with us? Our character will be our passport. We will definitely need that. And let's not forget to bring our children along. They are our greatest treasures.

Yes, an escape from the problems of this world is inevitable. Let's get ready without delay!   JEANNE D'HARIMALALA RASOANINDRAINY

AUGUST 6

A Tribute to Children Born in Poverty

Let the little children come to me, and do not hinder them, for the kingdom of God belongs to such as these. Mark 10:14, NIV.

One morning as I worked in the child survival clinic, a mother brought in her dehydrated, malnourished child. The child weighed about 17 pounds and had severe diarrhea. The body was limp and nearly lifeless. Folds of skin could be plucked up easily from the child's stomach, and they did not spring back into place as they should.

The clinic nurse administered intravenous fluids to rehydrate the child as quickly as possible. We feared brain damage had already occurred because the child had gone too long without treatment. Then we took the child by vehicle more than 12 rough miles to the hospital. Days later the child died. Help came too late.

Every day thousands of children perish from preventable childhood illnesses. Many die just because they have only polluted water to drink.

Many young girls, because of their family's economic need, seek work in the cities, but they end up on the streets or are sold into prostitution. I have seen poor families sell their daughters because they desperately needed food. Unfortunately, the girls become victims, caught up in the vicious cycle of economic and social survival. Their story usually ends tragically as many become slaves to industrial workshops or contract AIDS or other sexually transmitted diseases. All of them lose their self-worth.

It cuts you to the core when they look at you and ask for help. They did not choose to be sold into this form of slavery. Now they seek some way to escape the snare that holds them, but they have no voice.

We often become critical or blame them for their actions, but this does not solve the problem. We need to extend a hand of friendship, love, and compassion, just as Jesus would. By establishing income-generating projects, we help them obtain worthwhile ways to earn a living.

Jesus never turned the children away. Instead He blessed them and reassured their mothers. He saw them as "heirs" of the kingdom, and He still encourages us to influence a child's impressionable mind for divine purposes.

Maybe today you can help one of these children, whether they live in your own neighborhood or in some distant land. You could pray for them, or get involved in a Community Services center, or send funds to a development and relief agency that works on behalf of the vulnerable poor. Become involved in practical Christianity, as Jesus did.

GAIL M. ORMSBY

AUGUST 7

Its Own Way

Love does not insist on its own way. 1 Cor. 13:5, RSV.

T was a young mother when the Revised Standard Version of the Bible was first published. While I was reading 1 Corinthians 13 in this version, it took on new meaning, and I made a chart.

Love Is	*Love Is Not*
patient	jealous
kind	boastful
	arrogant
	rude
	irritable
	resentful

Love Does	*Love Does Not*
rejoice in the right	rejoice at wrong
bear all things	insist on its own way
believe all things	end
hope all things	
endure all things	

I put my little chart above the kitchen sink. One day I looked up at my Love Chart to discover "Does not insist on its own way" neatly underlined in red. My husband had used this quiet method to give me a badly needed reminder.

But the chart also reminds me every day that God is love. He is patient and kind, and never jealous, boastful, arrogant, rude, irritable, or resentful. What glorious good news! I'm so glad we have this text to describe to us how God is and what we should strive to be as well.

RUTH ANNEKE

AUGUST 8

Linked by Love

Therefore do not worry about tomorrow, for tomorrow will worry about itself. Each day has enough trouble of its own. Matt. 6:34, NIV.

For the past six months I have been planning a massive fundraising event for the charity for which my husband is a volunteer. We set out to collect boxes of food for the people of Sarajevo and enough money to transport them to their destination. As the culmination of our "Boxes for Bosnia" appeal we planned a magnificent Festival of Flowers in our church, where we would highlight the organization's work throughout the world.

As is often the case, the whole thing snowballed, and I found that orchestrating the appeal, planning the festival, studying for my university final exams, coping with the family business alone for two weeks while my husband was in Sarajevo, and keeping the home running was almost more than I could cope with.

I was having to exist on very little sleep each night, so I needed what I did get to be deep and restful. However, I found that as soon as I would lie down, my mind would begin to work overtime. I knew that in my own strength I would be unable to accomplish all I had to do, so I learned to rely completely upon God. I began to ask Him each day for just enough strength for that day, and He gave me the passage from Matthew 6 as my motto.

Each day I could feel the power of God in my life as the prayers of my friends mingled with my own. My strength was just enough for each day. The few hours' sleep I managed to get were deep and refreshing, and God sent me human help when it was most needed.

The appeal and our Festival of Flowers were a great success, as many people joined together to demonstrate their Christianity in a very practical way. We collected food and funds in excess of £10,000 sterling, but I am humbly conscious that everything we did we accomplished only through God's strength.

Most of us spend needless energy worrying about future plans or present difficulties, and I am no different. I am praying now that I will be able to incorporate the lesson I have learned over the past few weeks into my daily life, for it is sometimes all too easy to rely on God when the going gets tough and then neglect Him once things return to normal.

The title of our festival was "Linked by Love," and I have been made aware that while I have a close link with God, He also enables me to be linked to my fellow human beings. Only as I keep that first link strong will He be able to give me the strength I need for each day.

Let us pray today that in our prayer lives we all will be "linked by love."

AUDREY BALDERSTONE

AUGUST 9

Following His Pattern

For we are His workmanship, created in Christ Jesus unto good works, which God hath before ordained that we should walk in them. Eph. 2:10.

Needlework is something that I enjoy, and I like to give the completed designs to those I love. Whenever I begin a new project, I make sure I have the correct tools, and often shop for hours in stores and leaf through catalogs for just the right materials. Most important, I read through the instructions. They tell me the supplies I need, the new stitches to learn, and the pattern to follow.

If the project is a knitted sweater, I choose the color and style, then measure carefully to ensure a proper fit. Or if I want to make an afghan, I select the pattern and cast on the stitches, following the design closely. And if I am doing a piece of embroidery, I sort out the different colored threads according to their charted symbols, referring frequently to the colored photograph of the finished picture.

But sometimes the yarn tangles. The thread twists up in a knot and breaks as I try to pull it through the cloth—always on the front side. The sweater just does not fit, no matter how carefully I measured. The afghan is the wrong color for that housewarming and totally clashes with the decor. Or I memorize the instructions and forget to refer to them anymore, and discover that I really didn't know them as well as I thought I did. Then comes the tedious task of untangling the yarn or ripping out the mistakes. But the finished product is always worth the effort.

When I begin my day, I make sure I have the materials to work with, the correct tools, and I study the instructions. My tool is a prayer for God to take the material of my life and do with it as He wills. His Word contains my instructions. When my life tangles or my "thread" is in danger of breaking, I hand everything over to Him, and He straightens it out. He always refers me to His instructions. Then He wraps His sweater of love around me, and it is always a perfect fit.   DEBORAH BILBY

AUGUST 10

Facing Fear in Siberia

Fear not, for I am with you; be not dismayed, for I am your God. I will strengthen you, yes, I will help you, I will uphold you with My righteous right hand. Isa. 41:10, NKJV.

The knocking on our door broke the stillness of the Siberian midnight. A peek outside revealed two lurking, shadowy strangers. The local pastor had warned this might happen. My husband, oldest son, and I had come to this city on the eastern Siberian frontier to share the gospel and the promise of our Saviour's soon return. Many came to the evangelistic meetings hungry for God's Word, but others opposed our work with negative advertising and harassment. Had these intruders come to intimidate the first American evangelist ever to preach there? If so, they would be disappointed, for Ben is not easily frightened or distracted from his mission.

But I am familiar with fear. My thumping heart echoed their pounding on the door, as Ben, Dave, and I huddled together on our knees. We had no phone to pick up and dial 911, but we had a hot line to heaven, and we asked our all-powerful Father to handle this situation for us. Persistent knocking kept us pleading for an angel of light to frighten the men away. That must be what happened, because all became quiet, and we eventually went back to bed with grateful hearts.

But sleep eluded me. I thought about fear—that confusing emotion that's a friend urging caution when needed, but sometimes an enemy robbing me of peace, joy, and courage. It had almost kept me from coming to Siberia, but the Lord was holding my hand, helping me move beyond fear.

We had reason to be afraid on some of those wild taxi rides when we were inches away from injury or death. Guardian angels protected us with split-second precision. My faith was growing. But my fear of entering the ancient, dark, and narrow elevator several times a day was less logical. Loaded with evangelistic equipment, supplies for children's meetings, and Dave's guitar, the three of us, the local pastor, and the translator quickly jammed into that dreadful elevator before the doors slammed shut.

"Here we are again, Lord. You know I am afraid of dark, tight places. Has anyone ever checked the cables on this old hoist? I am powerless over this. Please uphold us with Your righteous right hand as we go down these nine floors."

It was challenging to face all my fears far from the familiar and comfortable. Public speaking is scary to me, but every night as I looked into the faces of nearly 200 children, love did cast out fear, and I delighted in the opportunity to teach them about Jesus' love, His life, and His promise to return and take His children to heaven.

In Siberia I learned beautiful lessons in trust. My loving Father wanted me to face my fears. He put me in a place where I was utterly dependent, and I threw myself with abandon upon Him—finding Him totally trustworthy.   LILA LANE GEORGE

AUGUST 11

I'm His

How great is the love the Father has lavished on us, that we should be called children of God! 1 John 3:1, NIV.

Oh, Lord, You know how much I want that job . . ." As I finished praying, a thought intruded my mind: *I had better have a nice, long devotional time this morning.* Immediately I laughed at myself. Was I thinking that if I was good, God would reward me? Like getting a lollipop after seeing the dentist or lots of presents from Santa if nice all year?

It amazed me how a faulty understanding of God could slither into my mind when I know full well that God's love is unconditional. After all, He sends sun and rain on the just and the unjust (Matt. 5:45). In no way can I earn His love, nor does He give points for good behavior or long devotions.

Contemplating my mental slipup, I felt reassured by the thought that God loves me simply because I'm His daughter. Just like my mother loved me at birth, not because I did anything great (I screamed and made dirty diapers!), nor for something great I might become, but simply because I was hers, so God loves me just because I'm His.

God, our heavenly Father, created us, gave us birth. He spent months planning for our arrival. Then just before we were born, He prepared the baby room and created a whole zoo for our playroom. He did this, not because we had done anything for Him, but just because we are His. Then when we got lost wandering out of our yard, He put up everything He owned as a reward for our safe return. All this because He loves us—we're His children.

I marveled at the thought as peace and security caressed my heart. *Thank You, Lord, for this reminder of Your free and lavish love. You are an awesome God! Yes, I still want that job, but Lord, I want to spend time with You even more.*   HEIDE FORD

AUGUST 12

Reliable Glue

There are friends who pretend to be friends, but there is a friend who sticks closer than a brother. Prov. 18:24, RSV.

*W*hatever happened to glue? Plain, ordinary glue? The only thing that really sticks anymore is the glue used to fasten labels onto jars. Where else can one find glue that really performs its intended function? Rarely on envelope flaps, stamps, or most address labels or package tapes—except those approved by the United States Post Office.

At one time an ordinary white flour and water mixture formed a paste that poor people could afford, and it actually worked!

Sticky situations also call forth another type of glue—loyal friendships, the kind that persevere through trials, through hardships, beyond grief, and over the sometimes rough terrain of personal relationships.

While working one evening in my classroom, I heard a knock on the door leading to the outside. I admitted a student who seemed eager to talk with me. She appeared upset about a malicious rumor circulating in the women's dormitory regarding me.

"I'm tired of hearing this gossip, so I have come to get some information from you—just enough to put a stop to it," she said. "Enough is enough. I do not believe what I have heard, and I want to refute this misrepresentation of you."

While I appreciated her loyalty and sincerity, I reassured her that if rumors are untrue, sometimes the best way to counteract them is to do nothing and not try to "chase the devil's rabbits." One's life can prove what really is. And bad rumors will soon die. Nevertheless, I thanked her for the straightforward approach and loyalty she exhibited.

Today we sorely need the good glue of loyal friendship. Good glue, reliable glue, sticky enough to enable one to remain steadfast, true to biblical principles of truth, persevering enough to stand for right despite ridicule, contempt, and threats.

Reliable glue sticks fast. It cannot easily be removed.

Yes, there is One who "sticks closer than a brother." His name is Jesus.　　　　　　　　　　　　　　　　　MARILYN BROWN

AUGUST 13

Our Private War

Let us throw off everything that hinders and the sin that so easily entangles. Heb. 12:1, NIV.

We fight a constant battle with very real enemies for over five months each year. They come in mass, trying to conquer our five acres in northern Idaho. By diligent work with the rototiller, the hoe, and our aching backs, we can almost win in the garden. But we fight a losing battle everywhere else. Who's winning our private war? The weeds!

Some come up front, like the thistles. We recognize them by their thorns. With a whack of the hoe or a strong pull, they're gone. While we can see the prolific knapweed, it's the snaky yellow salsify that's so hard to conquer.

It goes by various names, including yellow goatsbeard and meadow salsify. When it begins to grow, its long linear leaves come to a point, just like grass, where it hides until it blooms. The flower buds look like a long beak, pointed and green, a perfect camouflage. What's worse, when the yellow flowers do appear, they close up before noon. So unless I start the war early in the morning, I haven't a chance of finding my enemy.

This giant-sized dandelion soon develops into the most spectacular flower head. You can't miss the large, round ball of fluffy seeds, each attached to a tiny parachute. A puff of wind will dislodge the feathery seeds and carry them a great distance. As I wage my early-morning battles and gather these two-foot-high weeds, the milky sap drips on my clothes and causes ugly stains I can't remove. I dare not throw them down, for that's where they would grow again. I go to great trouble keeping the seeds from spreading, carrying them up the hill to later haul them to the dump. Now you understand why I don't like salsify.

But it's taught me a lot about sin. Salsify often sneaks in among our shrubs and flower beds, hiding behind their beauty. Time after time I've walked right by a large plant and never seen it, only to look out the next day and watch the wind spreading that ball of seeds over our ground. It grows very fast, so I must be diligent every morning or the plant will bloom and go to seed before I find it. Covering five acres takes time, effort, and a watchful eye. Even then, I miss a lot. What's worse, the wind shares our neighbor's seeds with us.

Will I ever win the war against salsify? No. Will I ever conquer sin? Yes, but not without my Friend. He knows how to deal with a sneaky enemy. He can spot any camouflage. Always on the job, He can detect even the sins that look as innocent as grass. My job is to stay very close to Jesus, who has already won my war with the enemy.

EILEEN E. LANTRY

AUGUST 14

Jesus and Breakfast

Jesus said to them, "Come and have breakfast." John 21:12, NIV.

As a wife and mother I spend a good portion of my time fixing meals. One job that demands attention early in the day, most times while the other members of the family are still in bed, is fixing breakfast. Is it by instinct that I consider what my family would enjoy, what is good for them, what they need?

Jesus once invited His disciples to a breakfast He Himself had fixed. The menu included fresh fish and toasted bread still hot on the burning coals. In contrast to performing a miracle from available loaves and fish for supper for thousands, this time He Himself tended the fire and turned over the fish and the bread to keep them from burning. He served nothing fancy or exotic—just a meal His friends would appreciate because it was familiar food and because it was hot. After a night on the sea and catching nothing, one forgets the discomfort and disappointment while savoring a hot meal.

You remember the circumstances that brought the disciples back to the lake (John 21:1-14). After the Crucifixion, when they faced a bleak future, to what could they turn to but the past? Peter's fishing instincts revived, and he announced, "I'm going fishing." Instantly the fishers of men became just fishermen once more.

The night without a catch dampened their spirits more than the seawater could. But in the morning Jesus, unrecognizable in the distance, greeted them and commanded them to cast the net on the right side of the boat. It resulted in a catch more than sufficient to make them forget the futility of the night's efforts, to restore confidence in themselves, and to recognize that "it is the Lord!" (verse 7, NIV).

When the meal was ready and the disciples had hauled the miracle catch in, Jesus could have announced, "The food is ready. Come and help yourselves." But a fisherman's work uses up much heat and energy, and the seven fishermen were tired. So "Jesus came, took the bread and gave it to them, and did the same with the fish" (verse 13, NIV). Could He have expressed His love more eloquently?

It amazes me that the Lord, in the last days before His ascension, would choose as one of the ways to demonstrate His love to His friends a humble domestic task: fixing and serving breakfast. I like to think that as I work in the kitchen at an inconvenient hour, deciding what is best for those I love, He understands all I feel because He has done this task before.   BIENVISA LADION NEBRES

AUGUST 15

Be the Answer to Someone's Prayer

Men ought always to pray. Luke 18:1.

*B*e an answer to someone's prayer today! Once I wondered if we could really do that. Then I realized that of course we can. Many times we do it without even knowing it. But just once in a while God may reveal it to us.

All of us pray for ourselves—to receive forgiveness, to be given health and strength, for our own daily needs. We also pray for others—for the care and protection of those we love and for guidance of those who lead in our churches and in our country. But have you ever prayed that you would be the answer to someone's prayer?

God mysteriously draws people together to fulfill His purpose in their lives. I pray each time I have a vacancy at our retirement center that God will direct me to the one who needs to come. And I know that He has sent each one. I have had the wonderful experience of seeing it evidenced again and again. A little elderly woman will clasp my hand and say, "Oh, your call was truly an answer to my prayer!" Or a concerned son will say to me, "Surely God led my parents here. I did not know what more I could do to help them, so I just prayed for guidance."

You too may have also had the wonderful experience of writing a letter or making a telephone call and been told, "I really needed someone to encourage me today" or "I prayed for someone to share my anxiety, to cheer me today and help me not feel so alone."

I believe that if we pray for the experience, it will come. We truly can be an answer to someone's prayer.

"My life shall touch a dozen lives before this day is done, Leave countless marks for good or ill ere sets the evening sun; So this the wish I always wish, the prayer I ever pray, Let my life help the other lives it touches by the way"—(Strickland Gillian).

BARBARA SMITH MORRIS

AUGUST 16

𝒜 Little Patience

Patient persuasion can break down the strongest resistance and can even convince rulers. Prov. 25:15, TEV.

When I was in fifth grade my family moved, and I had to get used to a new school where I had no friends. Being unbearably shy, I had little hope of making friends in the remaining months of the term, and I faced the prospect of a bleak and friendless summer.

Most recesses we spent playing four-square, a game of skill in which each of the four players stood in her own giant square and tried to bounce a ball into someone else's square in a way that the person there couldn't return it. If you missed the ball, you were "out" and had to take your place at the end of the line, waiting to get "in."

Since four-square was one of my few talents, I scouted out the games until I found the hardest one on the playground. However, I soon found out that the group of tough sixth-grade girls playing it did not welcome strangers, especially fifth-grade ones.

Every time I was in, three of the girls would team up against me. They would bounce the ball gently among themselves and then twist it or slam it into my square. I played with them every day despite their hostility. They were the best players, and I was determined to be one of the best.

A funny thing happened during the last week of school. Another girl from the fifth grade tried to get in the game, and the sixth graders used the same strategy to get rid of her. Finally, she asked them why they kept hitting her out, and they told her the game was only for sixth graders.

"But you let her play!" the irate girl said, pointing to me.

"Oh, her?" one of the big girls said casually. "That's different. She can hold her own. She's one of us."

I've grown older now, and I no longer feel a great need to persuade people of my athletic ability. But I find that patient persuasion still works when I try to share the good news of Jesus Christ with the people whose lives I touch. The changes may be gradual, but they are there, and I know that a little patience can overcome any obstacle. GINA LEE

AUGUST 17

Stars or Weeds?

Praise the Lord from the heavens, praise him in the heights above. Praise him all his angels, praise him, all his heavenly hosts. Praise him, sun and moon, praise him, all you shining stars. Ps. 148:1-3, NIV.

*A*nd praise Him, hurried and harried mothers—all of us who need 36- or 48-hour days to get accomplished what we have to every day.

Some days I have to encourage my two children from their cozy early-morning nests, pour them into wearing apparel for the day at school, pump them full of some breakfast nourishment, and load them into the pickup truck for a half-hour drive to the highway where the school bus is waiting for them only to repeat the process in reverse later in the day, after I had completed umpteen other chores during that time. This schedule was not always conducive to a cheerful attitude, until one day . . .

We sped along the remote road, my two children and I. We were living at that time in northern Nevada, where the desert country presented no spectacular scenery. It was cold and frosty this particular morning. Nita sat next to the window and seemed very pensive as the never-changing panorama slid across our view. Craig was more interested in the jackrabbits that popped out from under bushes. Every so often a tiny cottontail would scurry across the road. I would swerve the pickup from one side of the road to the other, trying to miss them. That annoyance and the sandy ruts, often veering into or aside chuckholes, sometimes made us later than usual meeting the school bus. This caused me to do some under-the-breath muttering. My inaudible complaining came to an abrupt end as Nita spoke suddenly.

"Oh, Mama," she breathed rapturously, "look at the stars in the weeds!"

In a moment wonder replaced monotony. The countryside changed as if touched by a magic wand. As we passed each sagebrush, the rising sun's rays transformed its frozen stalks and bracts into an upside-down chandelier. Icy branches became prisms of refracted light as glittering pinpoints twinkled on each end. It was as if we had driven off into another realm. Each morning from then on we saw something delightful.

That experience taught me more than one lesson. All my life's roads can appear different if I just take a little time to ponder them. As I experience what I might call "weeds"—unkindness, heavy burdens, loneliness, criticism, failures, mistakes, etc.—I know I need to take a closer look. When I present them all to my personal Saviour, something wonderful happens. Without exception, these weeds become prisms of light for me when transformed by the Son's rays.

GRACE JOHANSON

AUGUST 18

Be Ye Grateful

Bless the Lord, O my soul, and forget not all his benefits. Ps. 103:2.

"Madam, do you remember me?" he asked as he paused in front of my desk.

Did I remember him? I puzzled silently. He was not one of the local merchants from whom I bought hospital supplies. Neither was he one of the men who delivered the goods I purchased. In fact, he wasn't dressed like any of those men.

His clothing. That was the clue! It was that worn by the men in the interior desert states, and since the only people I knew from the desert had been patients, I made the rather obvious observation, "You were a patient here." The response pleased my visitor.

From the folds of his voluminous garments he extracted a hand-loomed shoulder bag and laid it on my desk. "When I returned home," he began, "I told my wives [he apparently followed the allowable custom of plural marriage] about the woman at the hospital who helped me so much."

Still perplexed, I didn't clearly remember this patient, the circumstances of his hospitalization, or anything I might have done for him personally.

"They were so pleased you helped me so much," he continued, "that they decided to make a gift for you." He removed a piece of embroidery from the bag and spread it out on my desk—two 10-inch identical medallions consisting of a series of concentric circles solidly embroidered in brilliant shades of cerise, yellow, chartreuse, blue, and orange, and joined together onto a jagged piece of tomato-red cotton by rows and rows of delicate chain stitches.

I could envision those women sitting cross-legged on the smooth mud floor of their simple desert home, working tedious hours on the complicated pattern, all in appreciation of some very small consideration from an unknown woman. "And this is my gift to you," the man indicated, placing his hand on the shoulder bag. "You helped me so much."

In bewilderment I expressed my appreciation for the thoughtful gifts and wished God's abundant and continued blessings on him and his family. Then he was gone.

The "help" he had been thankful for? I thought that might qualify as the "little, nameless, unremembered acts of kindness and of love" that William Wordsworth classified as the "best portion" of a person's life. And might this be included in Jesus' response to those who also were unaware of any little acts of kindness and love (Matt. 25:37)?

Those unexpected gifts of appreciation from loving people moved me to focus my thoughts on my own expressions of gratitude, particularly my gratitude to God for health, family, friends, opportunities for service, and much, much more. Most of all, gratitude for the assurance of eternal life Jesus made certain for me on Calvary long ago. With a humble, but very thankful heart, I vowed that daily I would "forget not all his benefits" (Ps. 103:2).

LOIS E. JOHANNES

God's Storehouse

Bring ye all the tithes into the storehouse, that there may be meat in mine house, and prove me now herewith, saith the Lord of hosts, if I will not open you the windows of heaven, and pour you out a blessing, that there shall not be room enough to receive it. Mal. 3:10.

*I*t was shopping time again for our two little boys, who seemed almost to outgrow their clothes before we got home from the store with them! We were bargain hunting, for we lived on one salary—my minister husband's rather meager one.

Four-year-old Tim was with his dad, looking at clothes in his size range, while Ted, Jr., and I cruised the aisles for size 8. Tim suddenly appeared beside me, holding up a beautiful little sport coat, his size, made of the finest material. I was sure we couldn't afford it, but we checked the tag and found that the price had been cut several times, until it was unbelievably low even for that time—$1.98. We bought it on the spot!

A few years earlier my husband and a fellow minister were to be ordained to the gospel ministry. We went shopping for a new suit, hoping that at least he could make a good outward appearance. Then we found it—a handsome charcoal-gray suit on sale for a ridiculously low price. It was the only one at that price and that size.

Another time when 9-year-old boys just *had* to have gold pants for school, I felt that they were too expensive to be practical, but we went looking anyway. You guessed it—in the stack we found one pair the right size, on sale at a price reasonable enough to justify buying them for school wear. Again, a happy boy and a happy and relieved mother. I have experienced many other instances of the windows of heaven being opened in blessing, as promised to those who return the tithe to God's storehouse.

Are we trying to buy God's blessings? Of course not. We are not "paying" tithe. It is the part that already belongs to God, the part He asks us to return to Him. God does not need our money—it is that we need to have a part in the support of His work in the earth, not only in returning the tithe, but in giving additional offerings for such projects as missions and the support of the church. When we do it, He has promised to open the windows of heaven and pour out more blessings than we have room to receive.

They will not always be as obvious as a little sport coat or a pair of gold pants. We receive untold rewards that have nothing to do with material needs. Prove Him, and be ready for some delightful surprises!

Mary Jane Graves

Moving

Blessed is the man who trusts in the Lord, whose trust is the Lord. He is like a tree planted by water, that sends out its roots by the stream, and does not fear when heat comes, for its leaves remain green, and is not anxious in the year of drought, for it does not cease to bear fruit. Jer. 17:7, 8, RSV.

More than 10 years ago a friend gave me a ficus tree that she knew wouldn't survive her cross-country move. I was thrilled in part because it was a beautiful plant, but mainly because it was a reminder of her friendship.

As time passed, many leaves dropped, few replacements grew, the trunk began to look brittle, and guests in the home joked about my stick in the corner. Obviously, my tree was dying. Having no horticultural skills, I sought advice, but nothing helped.

Walking by the church one spring evening, I noticed a dead-looking ficus tree just outside the back door. Guessing that someone was trying to save it, I began routinely checking on the tree's condition. One evening I noticed small green leaves growing on several branches. Racing home, I wrestled the container containing my ficus tree out to the patio. No immediate miracles took place, but by August the tree had many new leaves. Watching hummingbirds, chickadees, and several goldfinches flit in and out of the tree's branches one afternoon, I was struck with not only the new life in the tree, but how it was sharing itself with others.

Settled and secure, we often must look as barren to the Lord as my little tree. To help us grow spiritually, He may draw us from our sheltered existence into circumstances that make us feel more vulnerable. Such situations, though sometimes painful, teach us dependency on God and give new skills for ministering to others.

When God moves us from shelter to the patio, we need to be like the tree planted by water that doesn't fear when the heat comes and that bears fruit even in the year of drought. He will be with us as we experience both the rain and sunshine.

Cherie Smith

Heavenly Treasures

Happy are those who claim nothing, for the whole earth will belong to them! Matt. 5:5, Phillips.

*L*ooking around Catherine's tiny, crudely made adobe brick home high in the mountains of western Mexico, I feel a sacredness in that moment. No refrigerator or electricity make her cooking easier. She has the only wood-heated shower I have ever seen—in her kitchen. In the living room, guests sit in reed and tar Indian chairs. The wall decoration is a map of the mountains where she lives with the Huichol, whose tribal history goes back more than 1,000 years.

Catherine's bedroom is a minimalist's dream: a bed made of sawhorses and boards, a small cupboard, a tiny closet holding a few dresses, an old tape recorder playing Mozart, and a candle to light the way across the room to one of the only flush toilets in the Sierra Huichol. Outside is a tiny balcony facing a mountain vista of such beauty that it strikes visitors silent.

I look at Catherine now—almost 90, far too thin, feet and hands curved with arthritis, one eye nearly blind, recovering from a broken hip. Her possessions give few clues to the life she once had. Her crude bathroom shelves, holding little other than medicines, soaps, and brushes, don't reveal that she was once a New York beauty magazine editor and an advertising manager for Helena Rubenstein. And her food supply, chosen for nutrition, not pleasure, belies that she once wrote advertisements for Campbell's Soup. Only the photo lovingly placed over her bed of her late husband sitting astride a horse hints at her previous life.

Where is that New York executive now? Transformed by God's grace, her life has become a study in simplicity and service. At age 62 she was a retired widow with "rugged health and a restless disposition" who decided to simplify her life and seek a challenge. She sold her house with the English garden, giving away the Oriental carpets, silver, and antiques. Packing a few books into her VW, she said goodbye to her children and set off for Mexico.

Seeing the villagers' need for medical care, she began devouring medical texts, until she learned enough to serve as a practical nurse. Catherine then moved to the mountains and began treating the sick in her tiny adobe house, or traveling by mule through the steep canyons to reach them.

Her recognition of the importance of education in the Huichol's struggle for tribal survival has led her to help 15 Huichol boys obtain a higher education. Living on little other than her modest Social Security check, she sometimes goes without firewood or home repairs so she can "help her boys through school."

I meditate on the blanket she holds out to me for approval. It is strong, simple, and durable, like her life. If it is true that "a woman's wealth consists not in the abundance of her possessions, but in the fewness of her wants," then surely this woman is wealthy. I have learned much this morning.   KAREN KOTOSKE

AUGUST 22

Miracle of the Visa

I will say of the Lord, "He is my refuge and my fortress, my God, in whom I trust." Ps. 91:2, NIV.

Several years ago my husband was scheduled to speak in South Africa. Soon after the invitation came, we listed the countries we were to visit on the way to and from South Africa, then made our way to the passport office at the city postal department. We gave them our itinerary, and they gave us the necessary passports and visas.

Upon our arrival in Israel months later, we were confirming our flight to South Africa when we learned that we would need a visa to enter that country. In the United States we had been told that we did not need a visa for South Africa. Now a tiny mistake created a *major* problem.

As soon as the vice consulate's office for South Africa in Tel Aviv opened its doors that Monday morning, we were there to apply for a visa. The vice consulate told us that he felt it was impossible to get a visa cleared in three days. With a prayer on our hearts, we pleaded for the office to try. We hurriedly got our pictures taken and completed the necessary papers. The information was sent to South Africa, and we phoned there as well to tell them our story.

The office in Tel Aviv closed at 4:00 p.m. Wednesday. The only flight out to South Africa was at 2:00 a.m. Thursday. Therefore, the answer had to arrive from South Africa by 4:00 p.m. Wednesday. We returned to Jerusalem and prayed and waited. With our suitcases already packed, we received the call at 2:00 p.m. that our visas had been cleared. Thanking the Lord, we raced to downtown

Jerusalem and hired a taxi, arriving in Tel Aviv at 3:50 p.m. My husband hailed another cab to the vice consulate's office, leaving me sitting on the curb in this strange city with our luggage. I prayed that my husband would arrive before the office closed and that he would once again be able to find me. After an hour he returned with our visas. How we rejoiced!

We learned upon our arrival in South Africa that it usually took approximately six weeks for a visa to be cleared for a minister coming from the United States. The Lord had performed an incredible miracle in our lives. Despite a clerk's error, an impossible human situation was made possible through God.　　　　JUNE LOOR

AUGUST 23

Answered Prayers

Before they call I will answer; while they are still speaking I will hear. Isa. 65:24, NIV.

*I*t is good to know that one doesn't have to be among the heroic or the persecuted to receive specialized attention from heaven.

It was 1990, and my husband and I were nearing the end of our holiday, going home to Cape Town, South Africa, with chunks of the Berlin Wall in our bags. Our 4:00 p.m. train to Zurich was waiting on Platform 21 of Munich Station. Since it was only 3:30 p.m., Louis left me in a compartment with our luggage and strolled off to buy soft drinks for the journey.

Upon returning, he heard people calling out and train doors closing. Wondering why the train was leaving earlier than scheduled, he sprinted for the nearest door, sprang aboard, and set off to find me. Glancing through the window as the express glided away, he watched with horror the number 23 on the rapidly receding platform. He raced through the carriages until he found a guard and an obliging passenger, who translated that the train was on its way to Dortmund, 300 miles away. From there my husband could take another train back to Munich.

My husband had no money, no documents, and no ticket. "Lord, please stop this train so I can get off," he prayed.

Moments later an announcement came over the intercom. Once again the passenger translated: "The train will stop for just a few seconds at the next local station. You must get off very quickly." Louis found himself at Dachau Station and took the train back to Munich. By 3:50 p.m. he realized he was not going to make it. He prayed again, "Lord, please get Ivy off the Zurich train before it leaves."

It was about this time, waiting for my husband on the Zurich train, that my growing anxiety produced my *first* prayer for someone strong and English-speaking to help me. Immediately a large German man entered our compartment. He spoke a little English, so I explained my predicament and my plan.

He placed our three suitcases beneath the window in the corridor. Should Louis appear in time, I could jump back on the train. If he didn't, the man would pass my bags through the window at the last possible second, which he did. I was not concerned that he would leave with our luggage. I knew that God had sent him.

Now came my second dilemma. Louis must be in serious trouble. My first impulse was to hunt for the police. But if he returned while I was away, he would assume that I was on my way to Zurich. So I carefully formulated my second prayer: "Lord, if Louis is safe, please bring him here by 4:30 p.m. If he's not back by then, I'll go and look for help." At 4:24 p.m. I watched awestruck as he came running up the platform. We hugged and gave thanks to God.

A series of lucky coincidences? No way! In a secular, cynical age, we were once again convinced that God lives, He cares, and He acts.

IVY PETERSEN

AUGUST 24

His Eyes Are Watching Us

For the eyes of the Lord are on the righteous, and His ears are open to their prayers. 1 Peter 3:12, NKJV.

"Margie, put your book away," the chapel speaker, Frank Gillen, spoke from the podium. The height of embarrassment flushed my cheeks as sheepish tears came to my eyes. My sister Beth, seated next to me, also felt for me as she stifled a sob and reached for a Kleenex to wipe her eyes.

We were attending a small academy called Hylandale, nestled and protected among the hills near LaCrosse, Wisconsin, during the 1950s. Every day we had a chapel period with a religious talk. Studying seemed more important to me that particular day as I kept my nose in a book instead of directing my attention to the speaker, who was also my teacher. Looking up embarrassed, I quietly closed my book as I felt 60 pairs of eyes staring at me.

This experience was humiliating to me, but it has taught me a very valuable lesson. We should give our full attention to the speaker. I know there are times when it is difficult—nigh impossible when children or grandchildren are vying for attention. But try to put yourself in the speaker's place. Think how they feel when they have prepared a talk, and the audience isn't paying attention. There is an even more important relationship we should honor and protect. Does Christ have to allow us to embarrass ourselves sometimes when He wants to get our attention? If we focus our eyes on Him, however, we won't have to hang our heads or shed tears of embarrassment because we have cut ourselves off from our relationship with Him. — MARGE LYBERG MCNEILUS

AUGUST 25

No More Pain

And God shall wipe away all tears from their eyes; and there shall be no more death, neither sorrow, nor crying, neither shall there be any more pain: for the former things are passed away. Rev. 21:4.

Benjamin is my treasured grandson. A 4-year-old blond-haired, bright-eyed, bouncing bundle of energy who never seems to want to stand still for one minute.

I well remember the excitement at his birth. My son and his wife were so happy with the result of their first attempt at procreation. They brought him home, and we all fussed over him and offered to baby-sit to give us just that bit longer to hold him. I have to admit that he felt like mine. I loved him as if I had borne him.

Yet things didn't seem to be going right at all. To my nurse's eye, he was definitely not well. But what was wrong? We couldn't put our finger on it. Eventually, at 8 days old he was admitted to the hospital. I can still remember the coldness in my heart the day that one of the nurses told me they had done two sweat tests on Benjamin, and both were positive. They were running one more to be absolutely sure.

Cystic fibrosis! My heart cried out against it. Not us, not Benjamin. My whole experience with CF had been in nursing teenagers to an untimely death and comforting their devastated parents. How would my son and daughter-in-law cope? How would we cope? Benjamin spent the next eight months in hospitals. We prayed, cried, and pleaded with God.

Benjamin takes his medication like a man, wolfing it down in the first few mouthfuls of food so as to enjoy all the rest. He endures the "pat-pats," his daily doses of physiotherapy, and has learned to sit quietly on a lap while someone injects drugs into his lungs. Soon he will be going to school and will start to realize that not all children endure these things on a daily basis. Eventually he will learn about his illness and his prognosis.

When we were called to work in Cyprus, my first thought was of Benjamin. We had been the "respite care" to give his parents much-needed breaks. What if he got sick? Our son and daughter-in-law might need us in those circumstances. Would we be able to be there for them?

My eldest son and his wife have become the "respite caretakers," and thank God, Benjamin seems to be in good health. Everyone is coping. I get to thinking sometimes that if I as his grandmother feel such pain, what must his mother and father be going through in the silence of their hearts? They don't like to talk about it.

We have come to admire the fortitude and inner strength of cystic fibrosis children and their families. And we have learned to lean on God for our support—we have no strength in ourselves. But we long, yes, absolutely long, for the time when all thought of death is put away, and the pain and anguish that we feel will be gone forever. To see Benjamin with a whole body and an endless future in the new earth. Oh, come, Lord Jesus, quickly come.　　　VALERIE FIDELIA

AUGUST 26

Way of Escape

There hath no temptation taken you but such as is common to man: but God is faithful, who will not suffer you to be tempted above that ye are able; but will with the temptation also make a way to escape, that ye may be able to bear it. 1 Cor. 10:13.

*M*y husband and I admired the 4-day-old colt in a pasture along our walking route. Brown like his mother, he had a lopsided-to-the-left white blaze marking his forehead. Already his long, wobbly legs had gained strength, and he bounced about playfully.

As our brisk, gravel-crunching steps approached, the colt suddenly jerked his head toward us. Then, tiny tail in the air, he bolted toward his mother.

"Look at him go!" my husband exclaimed. The colt fairly flew the few feet to his mother. He galloped around her and came to an abrupt, four-footed halt on her far side. There he stayed, tight against mom, till we were gone.

"Well, I've learned something this morning," I mused.

"What's that?" my husband questioned.

"How to respond to the devil. Just like that colt. At the first sign of danger, he took off like a shot and stayed beside the one he felt safe with. We couldn't have gotten to him without dealing with his mother. At the first hint of temptation, I need to make sure I'm beside Jesus."

Later I read: "Live in contact with the living Christ, and He will hold you firmly by a hand that will never let go. Know and believe the love that God has to us, and you are secure; that love is a fortress impregnable to all the delusions and assaults of Satan" (*Thoughts From the Mount of Blessing*, p. 119).

Jesus is my way of escape today.

HELEN HEAVIRLAND

AUGUST 27

Let Go of the Rope

But when he saw the wind, he was afraid and, beginning to sink, cried out, "Lord, save me!" Immediately Jesus reached out his hand and caught him. Matt. 14:30, 31, NIV.

I was very excited one summer day in 1979, for this was to be my first waterskiing adventure. My father strapped my life-jacket around me, and I plunged into the cool water. Bobbing in the water with the skis on my feet pointing up, I gathered the rope that would take me on the ride of my life. I had visions of myself skiing gracefully back and forth, waving to my proud parents and jealous sisters. Then I hollered to my father. I was ready. Or so I thought.

I skied about nine inches before plummeting face forward, smacking my entire body against the hard water. The skis ripped off my tiny feet in an instant as my body whipped along the water's surface. I knew the correct thing to do at this point was to let go of the rope. Yet somehow I could not trust the life preserver that had kept me buoyant just moments ago. I was afraid of drowning. Of course,

I knew that I would drown anyway if my father did not very soon look back to see that he was dragging my soon-to-be lifeless body across the lake at breakneck speed. But I figured that with the occasional spurts of air I was receiving from being jerked along the surface of the water I would live a few minutes longer. Well, it sounded logical to my 12-year-old mind.

My father finally did look back and repeated his instructions that when I fell I was to let go of the rope! The second try was a success.

Let go of the rope. That's sound advice in the spiritual as well as the aquatic realm. We're always told, "When you get to the end of your rope, tie a knot and hang on." Good advice—sometimes. And sometimes the best thing we can do is to let go of the thing that's dragging us around.

How many times do we want to hold on to our own lives, to control things ourselves, to swim without the Life Preserver who keeps us afloat in the waters of trouble? It doesn't seem logical to any mind, whatever the age, yet we still want to hold the rope.

I still want to hold on to the rope. At times I don't trust Jesus, my life preserver. I think I can control every aspect of my life better than God or anyone else can. And I'll do it, too—even if it kills me. But I also have learned that when you trust the only One who can save you from drowning, then you won't be dragged perilously through the waves. In our distress, we too can cry out like Peter, "Lord, save me!" And we can have no doubt that He will reach out His hand to catch us.

MERRI LONG

AUGUST 28

The Language of Love

Above all, love each other deeply, because love covers over a multitude of sins. . . . Each one should use whatever gift he has received to serve others. . . . If anyone speaks, he should do it as one speaking the very words of God. If anyone serves, he should do it with the strength God provides. 1 Peter 4:8-11, NIV.

One of the delights of visiting other countries is observing the different ways of doing and saying things. It was while I was luxuriating in my collection of French phraseology that I realized it had something to say about today's text.

The French really excel at the kindly approach in their public notices. On a boat I read, "Tips are not required, but are very welcome."

At a campsite a sign declared, "Your faithful friends must be kept on a lead." A beach notice declared, "If you love the radio, do not impose it on those who wish to forget it." In a tropical garden a sign announced, "I am a real orchid; I am not plastic. It would be kind if you did not touch me." And on the door of a little campsite shop: "No bread is delivered on Monday; please remember this on Sunday."

It seems to me that this is the kind of approach that builds people up, and I thought how much you and I need to cultivate this talent, this gentle touch, in our day-to-day encounters with people if we are to be like Jesus.

I found food for thought, as well as a real challenge, at a bridge over the Dordogne River. No matter which side you approached it, the signs indicated that traffic coming from the opposite direction had priority!

Is it that important, in the helter-skelter of everyday living, to take that much care for other people? Our text today says it is. We can offer them all that the Bible promises: forgiveness for the past, hope for the future. But even heaven itself will have very little appeal if we haven't first offered them our love and shown them that following in Jesus' footsteps has given us His sensitive awareness of their needs.

The French word for the sunflower is *Tournesol*, literally, "turn to the sun." And that is exactly what huge fields of sunflowers seem to do. Wherever the sun is, that's the direction they face. Whether it's morning or evening, they face the sun.

And it's the only way you and I are going to be able to practice the gentle approach and build up our families and friends, colleagues, neighbors, and acquaintances. We must take time daily, and at all points of the day's journey, to turn to the Son, the source of all spiritual energy. Only from Him comes the strength, the inspiration, and the capacity for caring.   PEGGY MASON

AUGUST 29

The Hearing Ear and the Seeing Eye

The hearing ear, and the seeing eye, the Lord hath made even both of them. Prov. 20:12.

As I have struggled to learn God's direction for my own life, I have considered this verse and others, wondering if I really could see and hear what is important. Jesus said,

"Who hath ears to hear, let him hear. . . . Therefore speak I to them in parables: because they seeing see not; and hearing they hear not, neither do they understand" (Matt. 13:9-13).

When we really search and ask for the gift of hearing, sight, and perception, God will answer us. And if we are hearing and seeing, we should be bearing the fruit also—wisdom. The book of Proverbs, especially chapters 1-4, is full of admonition against rejecting wisdom. And it stresses the benefits of obtaining it.

So where does all of this leave us? Are we listening to God's wisdom? Do we learn when we read and study? Are we just repeating words we have heard again and again but have not put into our heart?

Looking for God's guidance cannot be a superficial, instantaneous action. In our current society of fast food, instant replay, and 24-hour access to money at the bank, we want our guidance quick and easy! If ever there was a time for us to take time to listen, it must be now.

Here are my ears, God. Help me to listen. JULIA L. PEARCE

AUGUST 30

Arise and Walk

"Do you want to get well?" . . . "Get up! Pick up your mat and walk!" John 5:6-8, NIV.

A paralyzed man lies helpless by the Pool of Bethesda on God's special day. It has been suggested that the name Bethesda means "house of mercy," but for him there has been no mercy. For 38 years he has lain there, hoping to be the first one into the pool. He believed that if he could only get there first when he saw the water moving, he would be healed. But even though kind people would carry him to the edge of the pool, he was never first. And he never came to realize that the waters were only natural springs with no power to heal. His persistent effort to be first in the pool was wearing away the little strength he had left.

The man looks at the decaying bodies of his companions in suffering. Then he glances at the pool. Today is God's special day, but for him it is not special. For him there is no Temple worship, no hymns of praise, no celebration—just helpless despair and groans of agony.

Suddenly he looks up to see a compassionate face bending over him. He clutches his shabby blanket in a futile attempt to cover his broken body. The Stranger reaches down and touches his bony shoulder as if to say, "It's OK, I accept you the way you are." Then

272

He asks, "Do you want to be healed?"

The man thrills with hope. "Sir," he pleads, "I have no one to help me into the pool, and someone else always gets in ahead of me."

"Get up!" Jesus says to him. "Pick up your mat and walk."

The man relaxes. He does not try to reach the pool. At the command of Christ, he gets up. He walks!

We too often find ourselves lying paralyzed at the pool at Bethesda. We burn up our energy trying to be first into the pool only to find that its murky waters have no power to heal. Even those who do beat us to the pool still lie there with us—soul mates in suffering. We have learned that love is based on achievement, but our best achievements are never enough. So we lie paralyzed by fear. Fearing failure and rejection, we push toward the pool, but find we cannot move.

Then Jesus asks each one of us, "Do you want to be healed?" We try to cover our brokenness from His searching gaze. But it is no use. He sees everything as He reaches down to touch us. "It's OK," He says. "I love you, but do you want to be healed?"

"Yes, Lord! Yes!" we respond. Fear gives way to love—despair to hope. We quit striving toward the pool. And He says, "Arise and walk." Suddenly we are free. It is God's special day, and we celebrate with hymns of praise.   KAREN LINDENSMITH

AUGUST 31

Following Dreams

And my God will meet all your needs according to his glorious riches in Christ Jesus. Phil. 4:19, NIV.

*M*en must follow their dreams, so the saying goes. Whatever provokes them to cross continents, try bold new adventures, plan large endeavors, or labor at all hours is sometimes incomprehensible. But dream they will, and they'll follow their dreams with utmost intensity. But alas, although we wish them God's blessing, it is sometimes hard for us women to follow their "dreamers."

It so happened that a few years ago I saw one such dream arising in the mind of my young husband. It seemed like a reasonable and heaven-commissioned dream, so I encouraged him to follow it. Sometime later I watched him go out the driveway on the way to a "follow your dream" interview. I could manage being stranded at home in the country with my baby for five days without a vehicle. Five days *would* pass.

He liked the opportunity, and the employer liked him, so he was hired. We headed north from our pleasant country home in green and rolling Mississippi. It had been a nice place for our family.

As we neared our destination, the countryside was neither green nor rolling. The landscape became flatter, the trees were much fewer, and the winding roads disappeared. When I envisioned living in the midst of a treeless cornfield, I felt like crying. But somehow I managed dry eyes and bravery.

At last we left the main road and dipped down by the river. Then we turned up a dirt road that wound its way up a little wooded ravine. Finally, we rounded the corner into the driveway of the country parsonage. It was by a flat cornfield, but roses bloomed by the front door, and down in the ravine it was woodsy and green. It was what *I* had dreamed about.

Yes, men will follow their dreams, but the eye of the Almighty is surely open to the needs, wants, and even dreams of mamas and little children.   JULIANNE PICKLE

SEPTEMBER 1

God's Beloved Child

And a voice came from heaven: "You are my Son, whom I love; with you I am well pleased." Mark 1:11, NIV.

*J*esus heard these words at the beginning of His ministry. Can you look back to a time in your walk with God when you believed and felt and reveled in God's love for you? Perhaps at the beginning of your own ministry. You don't have to be a church pastor or a chaplain to have a ministry. When God called you to value yourself and bless others, He summoned you to your ministry. These God-spoken words applied to you then, and they still do. "You are my child, whom I love; with you I am well pleased."

Does it seem presumptuous to take to yourself the words spoken to the Saviour? God has no trouble saying them to you. He allowed Jesus to live and die so that you may be able to know and claim, "I am God's child, whom He loves. God is well pleased with me." But the voices of those around us and in our head tell us the opposite.

Late in Jesus' ministry, things were going poorly for Him. Many had rejected Him. His work seemed ineffective. At that low moment, once again those words from God penetrated His discouragement: "This is my Son, whom I love" (Mark 9:7).

Let these words break through the negative noise around you today. You, with all your inadequacies, all of your mistakes, all of your rejections, even with all of your sins—you are still God's child, God's beloved. With you He is well pleased.   PENNY SHELL

SEPTEMBER 2

Sunshine in My Soul

How good it is to sing praises to our God, how pleasant and fitting to praise him. Ps. 147:1, NIV.

*I*t was the first week that my friend was back in church in her regular seat since she had lost her husband. They had been sitting together in church for almost 50 years and were planning their fiftieth wedding celebration in a few months. She looked at me and said, "I can't believe 'There's Sunshine in My Soul Today' is the opening song. How can I sing this song? Why did they choose it for me to sing today?"

I realized it was painful for her to sing about sunshine when the sunshine of her love was resting in the ground. My heart went out to touch her pain. Slipping my arm around her, I silently observed as she turned to the hymn, stood up to sing, and the words flowed out, "O there's sunshine, blessed sunshine . . ."

We were able to smile at each other, realizing that God's love in our souls is the real source of sunshine, and it will peek through even on the dark days. We saw it and felt its warmth in our hearts.

When you feel discouraged or depressed, invite God to fill your life with His love. May you bask in the sunshine of His love today.
                                                                LORRINE PHILLIPS

SEPTEMBER 3

Fatal Shooting

The thief comes only to steal and kill and destroy; I came that they may have life, and have it abundantly. John 10:10, RSV.

"urglar Accidentally Shoots Himself" the headlines read. A subheading further explained, "Intruders flee when home-owner returns, and the gun one man is carrying goes off, fatally wounding him." There is something strange in such a report, something twisted. More often we hear of the homeowner either becoming the victim or doing the shooting. In this case it was the perpetrator who did himself in.

Perhaps you've heard the expression "shooting yourself in the foot." At least, unlike this man, the shooting isn't usually fatal. And the cliché is metaphorical. Yet there is a message here in the news story that many of us might consider.

Sometimes some of us seem quite frightened of success. It may be in our career, relationships, goals, or any number of areas. If we get too close to our goal, we either consciously or unconsciously do something that keeps us from reaching our ideal. We "shoot" ourselves.

Jesus said that He came to give us a full and abundant life. Through Him we have the potential to live successfully. If we've been in the habit of "shooting ourselves," we don't have to continue the self-destructive habit.

May I encourage you to ask yourself today what abundant, full life means to you? How do you define true success? Then talk it over with Him. You may be surprised at the opportunities that will then open up to you. And you can avoid the headline "She Fatally Wounded Herself."

BEULAH FERN STEVENS

SEPTEMBER 4

Love Is Being Together

I will . . . receive you unto myself; that where I am, there ye may be also. John 14:3.

hen I was a student missionary, my boyfriend and I kept in contact through letters. Sometimes they came frequently enough to keep the communication going, but other times we almost felt as if we had forgotten each other. I was involved with my work, and he was adjusting to his new job, so we were kept extremely busy. It was hard to write as often as we wanted to. Nevertheless, while reading his thoughts, experiences, and emotions, and feelings through his letters, I could sense our togetherness, almost as if he were right there with me. Sometimes that really comforted me. But I realized that there was so much more in store for us when we would actually be together again.

When Jesus had to leave His friends, He sent His Holy Spirit so that His friends would continue to feel His presence here on earth. And His presence is real. But there are still so many things that get between God and His people. We often get distracted with the struggles of this world, and we look to heaven for relief from our suffering.

While God's second coming will soon bring an end to our suffering, He has an even greater purpose for returning. He longs to have His children in heaven with Him so there will be no more separation. The Lord wants nothing to come between Him and us.

In the last phrase of today's text I sense such profound love. God's purpose of preparing a place for us is so that, as Jesus said, "where I am, there ye may be also." God longs to have His children with Him. His is a love too great for us to comprehend even through His love letter to us in the Bible. He wants to tell us all about it. In person. At home. CINDY SUMARAUW

SEPTEMBER 5

Another Form of Talking

Everyone should be quick to listen, slow to speak. James 1:19, NIV.

*J*n sorting through my files the other day, I came upon this American Indian proverb: "Listen or thy tongue will keep thee deaf." I placed it near my phone to help me remember. It's not easy to be a good listener, especially if one likes to talk—and I do. But because it is one of the most important forms of communication, it is a skill we all need to understand and practice.

Listening is a way of learning. A child who has been taught at an early age how to listen is fortunate indeed. Learning to listen carefully will stand any young person in good stead, both in future jobs and home relationships. "More failures in academic and social growth can be traced to an inability to listen than to any other single aspect of the language arts," declares Professor Mark Neville in *Listening Is an Art*.

Whenever I follow God's admonition to "Be still, and know that I am God" (Ps. 46:10), when I take time to listen to my spouse, when I quietly give my children their mother's full attention, I am talking, for listening is a form of conversation that says "I care about you. You are important." Alice Duer Miller has said it well: "Listening is not merely not talking . . . it means taking a vigorous, human interest in what is being told us. You can listen like a blank wall or like a splendid auditorium where every sound comes back fuller and richer."

My friends include many good listeners. All of them have in common the following characteristics:

1. They have a basic interest in people.
2. They never interrupt, but patiently hear me out.
3. They respect my right to express my opinion.
4. They are interested in comparing their point of view with mine.
5. They are interested in broadening their viewpoint rather than defending their position.

Naturally, I enjoy being around such friends. Their unselfish listening helps me understand myself better and find the solution to some of my problems. By their example they are teaching me how to become a better listener, and for this I am grateful. "He who has ears, let him hear" (Matt. 11:15, NIV).   EVELYN VANDEVERE

SEPTEMBER 6

God's Child

Rejoice, because your names are written in heaven. Luke 10:20.

"Who are you?" In the 1950s Loretta Young, the actor, posed that question on one of her weekly television shows. She suggested that most people would first say their own names. "But," she persisted, "besides your name, who are you?" In the program that followed, she dramatized important concepts of relationship and values that affect self-esteem, thereby shaping our lives.

What we are called and what we value has an influence on what we become. Our names then become synonymous with our very personalities, characters, and reputations. Unlike the rose, which by any other name remains a rose, a human being by another name would somehow be different.

In the film *A Patch of Blue* Sidney Poitier plays a young Black man who befriends a blind White girl named Selina. Her father carelessly blinds her, then leaves. Her mother and grandfather seem cynical and uncaring, addressing her roughly as "Sleena" or by other coarse epithets. The young man sees her sitting under a tree in the park and courteously engages her in conversation. When he calls her "Selina," she replies softly, "Nobody never said my name that purty way before." From him she learns about loving relationships.

Isaiah and other Bible writers remind us that our heavenly Father tenderly calls us by a new name (Isa. 62:2). Again and again in Scripture God assures us of our worth to Him: "He that toucheth you toucheth the apple of his eye" (Zech. 2:8) and "Behold, I have graven thee upon the palms of my hands" (Isa. 49:16).

When people speak our name roughly or mispronounce it, it affects us, sometimes cuts us to the heart. God is also sensitive to how we speak His name, our tone of voice, the names by which we address Him. It's about joining a relationship. When God wrote, "Thou shalt not take the name of the Lord thy God in vain" (Ex. 20:7), He was not being petulant. He wanted to preserve a special relationship between Himself and His children. Jesus took time to teach His disciples to call on God by the name He loves best of all "Our Father." As a loving Father He knows all about us, even how many hairs are on our head. He has recorded our names in His family register.

Loretta Young closed her show that day by declaring, "If you identify yourself as a child of God, you have discovered a priceless identity." RHODA WILLS

SEPTEMBER 7

Longs Peak

For with God nothing shall be impossible. Luke 1:37.

I'd just begun my senior year at a boarding high school in Colorado. Every morning I watched from my dormitory window as the sunrise tinted Longs Peak a lovely pink. Something within me longed to experience that glorious moment myself.

That's why I joined a hikers' club. At our first meeting the leader announced, "We have something special planned for you. Early September is a good time to climb Longs Peak. How many of you would like to climb it next Sunday?"

My hand shot up, but inwardly I heard the words that had been drilled into me for years. I could hear my mother's warning: "Remember, rheumatic fever has caused leakage of your heart valves. You can't do what other kids do. You must be careful and never overexert yourself."

"It's a tough climb! Many turn back at the Keyhole," he continued, "but if you'll follow my guidance, you'll make it."

God, You know how much I want to prove I'm normal like other kids, I thought to myself. *Would You do for me what's impossible for*

me to do alone?

I didn't tell my mother. The next Sunday at 2:00 a.m. we left the school and drove to the trailhead at Rocky Mountain National Park to begin the 15-mile round-trip climb. As we hiked through the dark forest we could see the flashlights of other hikers winding along the tundra trail in the predawn morning.

At about mile six we came to Boulder Field. The trail disappeared in a maze of pup tent-sized rocks. Never surefooted, I realized how easily I could sprain an ankle jumping from boulder to boulder. Gradually we ascended toward the Keyhole, a huge rock with a hole big enough to walk through.

Beyond the Keyhole I gasped. Could I navigate that narrow trail with cliffs of almost vertical drops? I felt encouraged when I saw embedded steel posts from which cables were stretched. Several, however, turned back, exclaiming, "Looks too dangerous!"

I didn't dare look down as I crossed the ledges. Using both hands and feet, I crawled up the large boulders, careful of the loose rocks. Fear made my mouth dry. I followed our leader's directions across the Narrows, clinging to the vertical side of the footwide trail, which dropped several thousand feet.

Finally we came to the last 300 feet to the top, a sharp incline of 45-50 degrees. Looking for cracks to use as finger- and toeholds, I inched my way to the summit—14,255 feet—and dropped exhausted beside my friends.

No one but God knew the extreme joy I felt. I belonged! A normal 17-year-old, tough enough to have made it to the top. God helped me achieve an impossibility. While the others exclaimed about the beauty of the view—60 peaks that reached 14,000 feet— I thanked God that He gave me the strength and drive to endure.

He'll give you the strength you need in whatever "mountain" you have to climb, but you can't be a quitter and still conquer.

EILEEN E. LANTRY

SEPTEMBER 8

"Ye Shall Receive"

And all things, whatsoever ye shall ask in prayer, believing, ye shall receive. Matt. 21:22.

*D*addy," my daughter said, "I need a piano."

"I know you do, Jenny," he replied. "God knows you need a piano too. Why don't you ask Him for one?"

Jenny enjoyed her piano lessons and, even at the age of 8, showed uncommon musical talent. She practiced on the school piano before and after school. Given a choice, she would rather practice her piano lesson than play with the other children or eat her lunch. Jenny had been "practicing" on the kitchen table, careful to use the correct fingers on her make-believe keyboard. An occasional "oops" escaped her lips as she mentally made a mistake.

Carl and I were so impressed by Jenny's talent that we decided to buy a piano for her. We checked the classified ads for a couple weeks and one day saw a piano advertised in a garage sale that weekend.

At 7:00 a.m. Friday Carl rang the doorbell at the address listed in the paper to inquire about the piano. A woman called to him from a second-story window, informing him that the sale began tomorrow. He apologized, but explained why he was interested in the piano. Her heart was touched by a little girl's need, and she invited Carl in to look at the piano.

The piano had belonged to her grandmother, and even though it was old, it was still in good "practice" shape. However, the price was quite a bit more than we felt we could afford to pay. The owner said that if the piano didn't sell in the garage sale on Saturday, she would give us a call. Sunday and Monday came and went, with no word about the piano.

It was Thursday when the phone rang. The woman on the other end of the line said, "The piano didn't sell. You can come get it for the little girl."

"And how much do you want for it?" I asked.

"Oh," she said, "nothing! My grandmother would have wanted the little girl to have it!" And our prayer-answering God wanted her to have it too, in answer to her prayer of faith.   MARLENE ANDERSON

SEPTEMBER 9

I Need the Prayers of Those I Love

Pray for each other so that you may be healed. The prayer of a righteous man is powerful and effective. James 5:16, NIV.

J can still recall the incident clearly. I was visiting a friend who, only days before, had received word of her husband's death in an accident while he was overseas on church business. Between her tears she mused, "I used to wonder why people always say in a situation like this, 'I'm praying for you.' Now, I realize just how important it is to know that there *are* people praying for me, because I'm too numb to pray for myself."

Soon after, at a prayer meeting, I found myself singing James Vaughan's hymn "I Need the Prayers of Those I Love," which served to deepen the impression my friend's words had made. Needless to say, many prayers rose on her behalf, not only that evening but on many other occasions also.

Some two years later, however, I tasted firsthand the comfort of the phrase "I'm praying for you"—so much more uplifting than the well-meant platitude that, at first glance, it seems to be. A close family member had been diagnosed with a life-threatening illness. Again and again came the words: "I pray for him every morning and evening." "I'm praying that God will heal him, and I'm praying for *you* too." "I'm praying for all of you as a family."

As the days turned to weeks and months, those pray-ers hung in there, more diligent in prayer on my family's behalf, it seemed, than I was myself. Many were close friends, others I scarcely knew, and some were very special—such as the elderly widow who had health problems herself and whose own granddaughter lay desperately ill in a hospital miles away. Yet she could spare an extra thought, an extra prayer. My family and I needed the comfort and support of those prayers. Many times I found that my thoughts just couldn't seem to form themselves into words to God. I was often tired, and confused, too. I didn't know what to pray for. For healing? For courage to accept the worst? For both at once? Or what? I thank God for the support and persistence of those praying friends as I echo Vaughan's words:

"I want my friends to pray for me, to bear my tempted soul
    above,
And intercede with God for me; I need the prayers of those
    I love."   JENNIFER BALDWIN

SEPTEMBER 10

Dressed to Live

Come, let's talk this over! says the Lord; no matter how deep the stain of your sins, I can take it out and make you as clean as freshly fallen snow. Even if you are stained as red as crimson, I can make you white as wool! Isa. 1:18, TLB.

The woman sat across the desk from me, trying to focus her bloodshot eyes. Her pockmarked skin bore the ravages of 23 years of drug and alcohol abuse. She looked more like she was 66 than 36 years of age.

As we filled out the forms that would enable her to qualify for social service benefits, she swore. When I said that I did not use such words and would prefer she didn't use them in my office, she shook her head in disbelief. Her alcohol-demented mind could not grasp that fact. In amazement she declared, "You've never cursed? You sure must be an angel! You must be going to heaven!"

Quietly I asked, "And when I do go to heaven, will you go with me?"

Sitting upright, she looked me in the eye and said, "Of course I'll be there. But, you see, I'll be so clean and dressed up and looking like new that you won't know me!"

Shocked at this response, I saw in it a challenge. A challenge to see all people as precious, special, loved of God, and candidates for heaven. A challenge to love them no matter what their circumstances or physical condition.

This intoxicated woman had taught me a great lesson: in every heart resides hope for something better. She also impressed on me the fact that each day I can learn to love the unlovely and seemingly unlovable. Why? Because each day I also am loved of God.

MAUREEN O. BURKE

SEPTEMBER 11

A Clean Heart

Create in me a clean heart, O God; and renew a right spirit within me. Ps. 51:10.

$\mathcal{M}$y husband and I were getting ready for church one morning. I made sure that my dress was appropriate for the service, shoes and handbag matched, and my hair was combed nicely. My husband wore the right color tie with his suit. We were ready.

As I looked in the mirror for the last time before going out to the car, the thought hit me: *What have I done to prepare my heart for going to God's house? Are my thoughts appropriate? Have I cleaned out everything that has no place in church? Is my heart ready to fellowship with my God?* Sometimes I'm so busy fixing the exterior that I forget the interior of the heart and mind.

All through the week, every week, I have to ask the Lord to renew the right spirit in me. Then as I go to church, I can pray with the psalmist, "Send out thy light and thy truth: let them lead me; let them bring me unto thy holy hill, and to thy tabernacles. Then will I go unto the altar of God, unto God my exceeding joy: yea, upon the harp will I praise thee, O God my God" (Ps. 43:3, 4).

ANNA JOHANSEN

SEPTEMBER 12

In God's Time

Man plans his journey by his own wit, but it is the Lord who guides his steps. Prov. 16:9, NEB.

$\mathcal{G}$rowing up in rural Australia, my mother, a trained nurse, was my role model. Like her, I wanted to be kind, cheerful, always hospitable, helpful to my neighbors, and thoughtful of others. Always working, many times under trying circumstances, she cared for us five children and my father. Mother often read mission stories to us. It was during those times that the seed was sown in my heart to one day work for the women of Africa.

At 18 I left the farm. World War II was in progress, and I needed to do something to help. I went to Sydney Adventist Hospital for a year, gaining experience in the kitchen, and then to the Sanitarium Health Food Café in Sydney as second cook. This experience became significant years later. Unknown to me, the Lord was guiding my every step.

Three years later I commenced my training at the Sydney San. Four years of general nursing and an additional year in midwifery training passed quickly. During that final year I received a call to mission service in Kenya. Gladly I responded, "Yes! At the conclusion of the three remaining months of training." Then the wait. How time dragged!

Eventually a letter came stating I had been released from my call because someone was needed sooner than I was available. The bottom had fallen out of my world, my dreams shattered. Yet the Lord was still leading.

After 18 months as a practicing midwife, I was invited to work at Carmel College on the western seaboard of Australia. As I bid my parents farewell, I remarked, "Next stop will be Africa. Only the Indian Ocean between." I still had my goal in view. Two years as matron and school nurse gave me more invaluable insight into working with students and staff, disciplining and rostering experience, and practice with the culinary skills I had learned earlier in my life.

Another day, another call to Africa. Yes, the very place offered four years before. Rejoicing filled my heart. This time my dream came true.

The Lord had been preparing me in spite of my disappointments. He knew the training needed and placed me in situations where I gained the skills necessary to face with joy and gladness my two four-year terms of service at Kendu Mission Hospital, ministering to the women of Africa. Those years of service proved to be the happiest and most rewarding days of my life.

Like Moses, I felt I was ready to go, but the Lord knew better and prepared me in His own time and way. When it seems as if God is closing doors in your face, remember that He is ever equipping you for His work—in His time. Let us daily rejoice in His leading.

VERYL DAWN WERE

SEPTEMBER 13

A Woman Named Ruth

Intreat me not to leave thee . . . thy people shall be my people, and thy God my God. Ruth 1:16.

*I*t was a scorching summer, and I remember the beads of sweat dripping off my brow. Although I was only a small child, it was expected that all the family work in the hot dusty rows of walnut trees. We were gleaning the fields. Poor and in need of food, we all worked diligently. Gleaning fruit fields was natural to us. It was a way to survive. Furthermore, we wanted to do it.

We sensed our parents' struggles and their love for us as they kept us fed each day. Yes, at times we complained and found it a difficult task. Under the discomfort of the sun, exhausted, we would squabble with each other as children do. How could we go on and make it each day? Yet somehow we did.

Obstacles often loom large for many of us as women. Yet God has graced women with strength and wisdom. The awesome story of Ruth speaks to our hearts about this. After 10 short years of marriage her husband dies. She is a childless widow. The only family left is her mother-in-law, who is old, bitter, and tired. Ruth faces multiple losses and an uncertain future.

She comes to a fork in the road of life. Which way should she go? If she chose to leave Naomi, she could justify it with any number of excuses: "Someone else can take care of this forlorn, aging woman," or "I'm still young. I have my whole life ahead of me," or "I want to marry again. Staying with an elderly woman might lessen that prospect." We know Ruth's response. She gracefully chose to stay with her mother-in-law. In a spirit of love she decided to join Naomi's people and Naomi's God.

When she decides to go to Bethlehem, she knows she must find work, for who will support them? She does find a job—one usually reserved for the poor: gleaning the grain fields. Gleaning was a humble, lowly task. After working all day in the hot sun, Ruth joyfully returns home with her small harvest. She never complains or swerves from her purpose.

Ruth was a woman capable of rare friendships. She loved Naomi, and in spite of their difficult life together, she was able to turn the older woman's sourness into sweetness. The basis of her friendship was love. Love overcomes all. This touching story has influenced many people's lives. One reason may be the exquisite expression of love and devotion that shines through. God grant us this love that is self-forgetting, this love that overcomes adversity and conquers all!

RAMONA PEREZ GREEK

SEPTEMBER 14

To Please My Father

I delight to do thy will, O my God: yea thy law is within my heart. Ps. 40:8.

*A*nd please remember to bring me my good suit," he softly says as I leave him in the room which he shares with two other extended-care residents. It has been his plaintive plea for the past two visits, and although he cannot wear the suit because he has no place to go, I agree to honor his request. That is the least I can do for him now.

My father has convalesced in a nursing home since his series of strokes a year and a half ago. Initially our family thought he would not survive these episodes, for they rendered him extremely weak and frail. Rather than dying, he lingered on, gaining minimal strength, and simply enduring. Unfortunately his mind had not fared so well, for he had already been diagnosed with Alzheimer's disease.

Since our family felt his condition was terminal, I chose to have him reside in a facility near my home, because I am the social worker in the family, and I know the procedures for placement in a skilled-care setting. But time dragged on, days turned into weeks, and weeks turned into months. Initially I appreciated having the opportunity to care for him since our relationship prior to his illnesses had been rather dysfunctional. I perceived him then as selfish, exacting, and uncaring.

The strokes have mellowed him and perhaps me as well, for I have begun to see him as a precious little person, weak and needy, reduced by life's circumstances to just a shell of a man. He is frail, confused, and totally dependent for all his care. My father cannot feed himself, bathe himself, or even tend to personal needs. At times he can barely speak and make his thoughts known. I can do nothing to restore him to what he once was. So during my visits my hope is simply to bring him some cheer, give him some comfort, and honor his requests.

Lately, however, continually seeing him this way is wearing on me. "How long, Lord, must he go on like this?" I find myself frequently praying. "Who is benefiting, Lord? What can be gained from this? How are You being glorified?" I want to know. Perhaps they are questions that will receive answers only in heaven.

Yet there is a lesson I am learning now. It is that I must find pleasure in granting the simple requests of my earthly father, while delighting to obey the "simple" request of my heavenly Father when He says to me, "Honour thy father and thy mother: that thy days may be long upon the land which the Lord thy God giveth thee" (Ex. 20:12). Yes, Lord, give me pleasure in obeying both of my fathers.

ELIZABETH WATSON

"Dollar" Kindness

Love ye therefore the stranger: for ye were strangers in the land of Egypt. Deut. 10:19.

*T*he trip had been a long one. I was traveling more than 1,000 miles alone with my children, ages 5 and 2. Although they had done really well the first day, today was trying their patience. But they had my sympathies, for I was tired too. Then up ahead I saw the sign for the last toll booth in Oklahoma. Half to myself and half to the Lord I prayed, "Lord, I don't want to pay another toll!"

As I slowed down, I pulled out my money. Upon arriving at the booth, I dutifully held out my money. To my surprise, the attendant told me that I didn't have to pay. "You see that fourth car way up there?" he said. "The lady in that car paid for the next four cars after her." I told him that I didn't know her. He said that he didn't know her either, but that is what she had done. I thoughtfully put my dollar away and solemnly, joyfully, continued my journey.

Who was that woman, anyway? Was she a Christian? Most likely she wasn't an angel, but what a great influence for good her $4 had made. Just $4! Unmerited kindness to a total stranger. She does not know the effects of her deed, but it surely cheered the rest of my trip and has brought me many happy thoughts since then.

She had given me $1. It didn't cost a lot, but it meant a lot. Can we also give "dollar" gifts? Perhaps there is a neighbor, church member, or even a total stranger who would benefit greatly from one thoughtful "dollar" act done in kindness. The giver and the receiver will most likely each receive more than was spent. "Freely ye have received, freely give" (Matt. 10:8).   JULIANNE PICKLE

The Last Time

Seek ye the Lord while he may be found, call ye upon him while he is near. Isa. 55:6.

*L*ittle did I realize as I got out of our faithful pickup that it would be the last time I would ever ride in it. It had been a wonderful truck, taking us countless miles through every kind of weather and all kinds of roads and conditions, running smoothly and quietly, keeping us warm or cool as needed, and never complaining or needing repair.

We could scarcely believe our eyes some 45 minutes later when we walked out to the parking lot, and there was no pickup. We looked, disbelievingly. Perhaps we had forgotten where we parked it. Perhaps it was only a bad dream. But very soon we knew that someone else had claimed our gallant "horse" and taken away a part of our life.

After calling the police, we gladly accepted the offer of a kind stranger to take us home. We were still in a state of utter shock. How could such a thing happen in a busy parking lot in broad daylight?

The last time . . . when will it come? Will we be expecting it, or will it be a complete surprise? When we kiss a loved one goodbye, will it be the last time? When we go to sleep at night, will it be the last time?

To neglect is to reject. If we reject God's plea for our hearts, reject His love letter to us in the Bible, will there be a time for us to change our minds and give up conflicting interests before it is too late?

What solemn words: the last time! When Jesus comes, will we be surprised? How tragic if we have rejected His yearning, loving plea to give our lives to Him—the last time.   PAT MADSEN

SEPTEMBER 17

Solution for My Stress

When you pass through the waters, I will be with you; and when you pass through the rivers, they will not sweep over you. Isa. 43:2, NIV.

*A*s a receptionist in a busy social service agency the rewards of my duties generally outweighed the pressures. However, during my subway commute to work I began to notice an increasing amount of tension in my body the closer the train approached my destination.

For a while I managed to shrug off the persistent tension in my body, telling myself that what I felt had no direct relationship to my job. But little by little, the wall of denial I erected in my mind began to crumble. Job-related stress was the primary source of my problem. Face-to-face with reality, I realized that my only recourse was to quit the job. Red flags went up at every turn. Quitting work was not an option for me. I prayed for help.

Months passed without any directive from God. Then one Sunday afternoon my sister called from Virginia, excited about the position my brother-in-law had been offered at a university in upstate New York. Enthusiastically she concluded, "We flew to New York and found a house. We love the area. Have you thought about leaving the city? Come up and look around. We'll be moving next week."

It took a few weeks for me to realize that God was using family members to answer my prayers. I requested two personal days of leave at work to drive upstate, search for an apartment, and seek employment. I found a lovely apartment the day I arrived. The following day I left résumés and drove back to the city.

Returning to work, I announced my plans to relocate and gave my two-week notice. "Do you have another job?" my director asked.

"No," I replied. "But God will provide one for me."

The day before I was to leave the job, I called the university in upstate New York to follow up on the résumé I had submitted. The woman politely told me, "The position you applied for has been filled. To be perfectly honest," she continued, "things are extremely competitive here. You have about a 1 percent chance of working at this university."

Hanging up the phone, I swallowed hard and did some fast thinking. Perhaps I should reconsider this move. Play it safe. Ask for my job back. Then the thought came to me that if God had opened the Red Sea for Moses and the Israelites, He could certainly open a position for me.

I moved into my new apartment in good faith on November 1 as scheduled. On November 8 I was hired at the same university that gave me a 1 percent chance for employment. God still works miracles! His solution for my stress was sure. It required only my belief.

IRMA LEE

The Cover-up

Blessed are they whose transgressions are forgiven, whose sins are covered. Rom. 4:7, NIV.

was 17 and in my senior year in high school. As part of an office education program, I'd hop a bus headed for downtown San Antonio after lunch. One afternoon I got off at my usual stop—one of the most congested downtown intersections and surrounded by tall buildings. The pedestrians had the light, and, schoolbooks and folders in tow, I began to cross in front of the bus I had just stepped from. Suddenly I lost everything in a gust of wind swirling between buildings. There went my English folder, protecting my vital term paper notes on Shakespeare (at least 50 index cards!). The cards flew, and so did I—in hot pursuit.

After what seemed like an eon, the cards finally plummeted onto the street. In disbelief, I scurried to gather my far-flung notes. Then, horror of horrors, the light turned green! In my mind's eye I saw the monstrous bus and the 100 cars behind it stampeding over my hapless index cards. But when I turned to the bus, I saw the bus driver through the giant contact lens-like window patiently smiling down at me. Somehow I was able to gather my wits and Shakespeare notes, and I made my way to the other side.

Needless to say, the bus and the cars lined up behind it missed the light. Because the bus "covered" me, they never saw my theatrics. Perhaps some wondered why traffic wasn't moving, but being the location it was and the lunch hour, no one honked or hollered.

Psalm 32:1 also reiterates, "Blessed is he whose transgression is forgiven, whose sin is covered." Through my traumatic high school experience, although comical to me today, I am reminded how Jesus looks down, smiles, and patiently covers us with His love and care in our times of great distress. ROSALYNDA "GINA" KOSINI

SEPTEMBER 19

Am I a Stranger?

I am become a stranger unto my brethren, and an alien unto my mother's children. Ps. 69:8.

Sunday morning I picked up the phone to call a family I know. It was for purely selfish reasons. My husband was out of town, and the weeds were growing more quickly than the flowers. I needed a strong young man to do the work, and the family had two teenage sons home from college for the vacation, hence the call.

After greeting the father, I stated my request and asked if the young men could come that morning to look at the work and discuss the terms of payment, then return another day while I was at work to do the job. He explained that it would not be possible because they were moving and needed the boys to help them. We agreed to talk later.

When I hung up, I started to think a bit. Why had I not known that they were moving that weekend? We worship in the same small church and work for the same organization. Their family has always been helpful to me since my arrival here in Cyprus. What was happening to me that I appeared to be so out of touch?

Oh, yes, I greet people at church, ask how they are—the usual platitudes. But when did I last take a real interest in other people, their joys, and their problems? Perhaps I have been a bit bogged down lately getting a daughter ready for school abroad, preparing for the visit of a treasured son and daughter-in-law, planning a trip back home, and keeping abreast of my job. All these things are good, I reasoned with myself, but I had to admit that they ought not to crowd out my interest and concern for those around me.

That evening my sister-in-law called from Canada, inquiring about family news. After the conversation I realized that I hadn't given her a real thought in weeks. She got covered in the prayers, but apart from that . . . I felt ashamed.

The mirror God held up for me the next morning showed me someone I didn't want to see, and no amount of external applications would change that. It would be purely cosmetic. God wanted me to undergo a total face-lift. A real bit of surgery. He wanted to take out the selfishness in me and replace it with the contours of His love. I am praying for the transformation. The mirror won't show it, but my thoughts and actions will. VALERIE FIDELIA

SEPTEMBER 20

The Last Bus

Now is the accepted time; behold, now is the day of salvation. 2 Cor. 6:2.

I was sitting in a bus station one evening, having nearly an hour wait for the bus that would take me home. As I enjoyed watching the people come and go, I noticed the efficiency of the young woman at the information booth.

While I sat there, I was impressed by the number of people who asked, "When is the last bus to—?" or "What is the latest time I can leave for—?" It seemed that so many wanted to wait until the last possible minute, to stay in the city and have a good time as long as they could while still making it home.

Now, if those people in the city get back to the bus station on time, they are quite likely to get home. But they are taking a chance when they wait for the last possible opportunity. What if they should become absorbed in what they are doing and not realize how late it is? What if their watches should be a few minutes slow? What if the bus should be so crowded that it wasn't possible to pack in everyone who wanted a ride? They could not wait for the next bus, as there would be no next bus! Instead they would just be left behind.

Isn't that what many people do in life? They want to catch the last bus to heaven. Sure, they do want to go, but they want to stay in the world and have a good time just as long as they can. "When is the last chance for me to turn to the Lord and be saved?" they ask. "How long can I remain with the pleasures and sin of the world and still get to heaven?"

Aren't we taking chances when we wait for the "last bus" to heaven? What if we should get so absorbed in the cares of this world that we forget to turn to the Lord until it is too late? What if our timepieces do not agree with God's? We may think we have a few years of life ahead of us, then have them taken away unexpectedly!

Why not play it safe and take the very next bus—the very next opportunity—to turn to the Lord? We can do that right now by telling the Lord that from this moment on we are ready to do His service, and we will forsake everything not pleasing to Him. Let's not take a chance. The bus is pulling out now. Get on board.

LAURA DROWN

Being Grateful

Praise ye the Lord. O give thanks unto the Lord; for he is good: for his mercy endureth forever. Ps. 106:1.

Lucy, an elderly friend of mine, lives in a small apartment and manages on an even smaller income. Her granddaughter, working in a distant town, asked Lucy if she could help a student friend.

"Karen has to go to the city and sit for two important exams a week apart," she wrote. "She has never been away before, and she is nervous. And she doesn't have much money. Could you put her up, Gran? I'd be ever so grateful. Karen's awfully quiet and won't bother you any."

Lucy replied that she'd be glad to help. She met Karen at the railway station and paid for a taxi to take them home. Fussing over the girl as she would her own granddaughter, she provided tasty meals and gave up her own bed to sleep on a borrowed mattress under the table—the only spare space left in the tiny apartment.

On days when the girl had no exams, Lucy took Karen to see the city sights. They traveled by train or bus, and Lucy paid all the fares and entrance fees. Although disappointed by the girl's lack of response, she reminded herself that Karen was a country girl and obviously very shy.

The last day came. Karen packed her bags and carried them downstairs to the taxi that Lucy had ordered for her. Wordlessly she climbed into the taxi and settled back.

My friend could stand it no longer. "Haven't you forgotten something?" she asked.

Karen looked surprised and hurriedly checked her bags. "I don't think so."

"Yes, you have," Lucy smiled. "You've forgotten to say thank you."

The girl blushed. "I don't know how," she stammered as the taxi slid away from the curb.

How sad that some people do not know how to express appreciation. Gratitude and giving thanks are such highly prized virtues that they are mentioned many times in both the Old and New Testaments.

The Psalms are full of injunctions to praise and thank the Lord for His mercy, goodness, and other attributes. Psalm 92:1 says that "it is a good thing to give thanks unto the Lord, and to sing praises unto thy name, O most High."

Paul often admonished believers to give thanks. "In every thing give thanks: for this is the will of God in Christ Jesus concerning you" (1 Thess. 5:18). "Be careful for nothing; but in every thing by prayer and supplication with thanksgiving let your requests be made known unto God" (Phil. 4:6).

God has made this beautiful world for us to enjoy. Let us thank Him for it. When our fellow men and women help us in some way, let us thank them. Giving thanks costs nothing, but it brings much happiness. GOLDIE DOWN

As a Child

Unless you become as trusting and harmless as this little child, you cannot even be admitted into God's kingdom. Matt. 18:3, *Clear Word*.

*M*ommy, why do you have that ugly face on?" I was shocked at my 4-year-old daughter's question. I had just finished speaking on the phone with an irate caller. By taking slow, deep breaths and maintaining my tone of voice in a calm demeanor, I'd managed to convey a polite and courteous persona.

Until, just as in the story of the emperor's new clothes, the innocent query of a child exposed my "nakedness." My irritation showed on my face despite my polite tone. I couldn't fool my child.

A child doesn't worry about political correctness or appearances. When she hurts, she cries. When she's hungry, she eats—regardless of the fat content. And when she needs a hug, she crawls onto your lap and snuggles in.

Where had I learned to hide my true feelings? When did I learn to "show a happy face, despite the pain," or "don't tell the truth, because you might hurt someone's feelings"? Where did I learn that if I ask for help, I may be seen as weak? Or if I stay home to raise my children, I may be seen as unfulfilled? Or if I ask my husband for more of his time, I may be seen as nagging?

Who creates these intelligent, fashion-conscious, educated wives, mothers of 2.5 children, presidents of companies, church leaders, community activist women? Are we victims of society or are we afraid to become "real"? To share with somebody our deepest needs and feelings?

Jesus, my example, was real with His feelings. In the middle of a joyous celebration He begins to weep over Jerusalem (Luke 19:37-41). His pain is great. He is misunderstood, and no one seems to be listening. The people milling around the Temple mount are His children, and He wants to love and protect them, to gather them under His wings. He is here for them, in person, to heal, advise, comfort, and they turn Him down.

I have to wonder, am I "real" with my Friend, or are my prayers a polite list of needs and fix-its with a few thank-yous tossed in? How is it with you? We must learn to be honest with the Lord in our prayers, to show our true feelings, for He is the only one who could ever really understand us.

Don't be afraid to tell Him that you sometimes feel abandoned by Him, that maybe He doesn't really understand your hurts. That trying to juggle a busy career, be a loving wife, a wise mother, and comforter of friends makes spreading His gospel to the world a bit overwhelming at times. When you're overburdened and just plain tired of trying to fool the world, be willing to look at Him, show Him your "ugly face," and say, "I need Your help!" JANIS VANCE

SEPTEMBER 23

Remember

Remember now thy Creator in the days of thy youth. Eccl. 12:1.

I was a freshman in high school when I first became familiar with this text. Our choral group was preparing for the first concert of the year, and our instructor had chosen a piece of music based on Ecclesiastes 12. As we sang, I thrilled to the majesty of the music and the words.

The phrase "Remember now thy Creator in days of thy youth" made a very deep impression on me. Very conscious of living a life that would rightly represent the God I had chosen to serve, I decided that this was an excellent verse for me to adopt as my motto, for it expressed so well what I wanted for my life. I was His child, and He cared for me. The least I could do in return was to remember Him and to value myself as He did.

The years have gone by, and I am no longer considered a "youth" in many people's eyes. Yet I feel young in my heart, and the verse is still my favorite Bible text. Each morning as I begin my day with God, I realize that in His eyes I am still young. He guides me as I grow ever so slowly to be more like Him.

There are so many things to know about Him and His glory and majesty. I am continually learning to praise Him more, to lean upon my own understanding less, and to rejoice in His love. Each new day is an opportunity to exercise faith anew, to trust Him as the storms sweep into my life.

Shall I let my "youth" fade? No. It is my decision to remember my Creator in the days of my youth and to enjoy each moment of the learning experience here on earth with Him by my side. Life's slippery paths are easier to traverse with Him by my side. To rejoice with Him and in His goodness is a new experience each day.

EVELYN GLASS

Joy, Like a Red Fox

Do not grieve, for the joy of the Lord is your strength. Neh. 8:10, NIV.

J think that joy is like the red fox that lives near our house. My husband has seen him (or her) around for two or three weeks. Bright eyes in the driveway reflect the lights of his car, a fleeting glimpse across the lawn in the evening, and at about 6:00 p.m. a strange yipping sound. But I always miss these furtive encounters.

Then one early November morning, sitting in my prayer room overlooking a scene of sunlight upon golden trees and swirls of leaves flying about, I do see the fox! He is just a quick flash racing through the woods—an impression of something moving among the trees. There is no detail in this impressionistic view—only a fox-like shape and a glint of sunshine on red fur. The creature does not stand still so that I might study his sharp nose and long tail. The trees and bushes that it weaves through are also a barrier to a clear view of the creature. He speeds away, leaving me to contemplate what a fox looks like when seen properly.

I have been reading in my Bible about joy. We often strive for Christian joy as if it were something we could manufacture and wonder why we don't constantly have it in a Christ-centered life. But at times we experience it in a special spirit-filled way in a church group or other inspirational gathering.

During the summer I attended a prayer retreat and enjoyed the company of a most loving group of Christians. It was the kind of mountaintop experience that one cherishes for a long time—perhaps forever. Now fall is here, and I wonder if the rest of the group still remembers. I even question if the feelings of love I shared with those people were real or just a transitory emotional high generated by the music, praise and prayer, and fellowship.

Perhaps that lovely summer interlude was like the glimpse of the fox. The retreat sped through my life one week and gave me an impression of what heaven would be like. It did not stand still for me to experience it fully, and the bushes and trees of our differing ideas occasionally got in the way. Nonetheless, it was beautiful and spiritually moving.

It had been only a temporary experience, but that doesn't mean it was not real. I know the fox still exists even though I don't see him every day, but I expect to catch glimpses of him again. I believe that

Christian joy exists, now expressing itself in our human feelings like a small, quick fox running through the woods of our lives, but we will know and observe it in living detail in the eternity to come.

ELLA RYDZEWSKI

The Hurting Parent

Thus saith the Lord; Refrain thy voice from weeping, and thine eyes from tears: for thy work shall be rewarded, saith the Lord; and they shall come again from the land of the enemy. And there is hope in thine end, saith the Lord, that thy children shall come again to their own border. Jer. 31:16, 17.

The world is full of hurting parents. I am one of them. Children are our heritage. We love them and seek to train them to live lives of integrity. Most of all, we want to teach them to know God, and we want to be good examples to them. I know I did my best, but even so, that was not good enough. It all happened after the teenage years, during the changing lifestyles of the 1960s.

Whose fault is it if we fail? One pastor told me that some blame the establishment, the schools, the church, their associates, even God! Who is really to blame? God has made each person a free moral agent. Really, we can blame ourselves only for our own choices. As our children mature, they too need the Holy Spirit's guidance as never before for their choices. But ultimately they are responsible for their choices.

God's marvelous grace, along with uncondemning, heartfelt prayer and loving kindness, seasoned with hope, will sustain us through these heartbreaking trials as parents.

God was so patient with Israel when they forsook Him. In Jeremiah 31:3 He says, "Yea, I have loved thee with an everlasting love: therefore with lovingkindness have I drawn thee." Let's ask Him to give us wisdom to treat our wandering children the same way.

May God's Holy Spirit comfort us all. May we trust His promises. I am convinced our children, for whom we have done our best to be an example, will come again to their own border and to God.

MARGUERITE V. KNAUFT

A New Name

I will also write on him my new name. Rev. 3:12, NIV.

While attending a conference for Christian nurses last June, I felt the appeal of a theme song by D. J. Butler. "I will change your name," it declared.

During a night Jacob spent in prayer, Someone attacked him. That encounter changed him forever. He left it broken and limping, but a new person with a new name. (Even I would trade the name "Heel" for his new name, "Winner.")

What a deal! Like exchanging filthy rags for shiny new garments. Where do I trade my worn-out threadbare clothing? Bullocks, Saks Fifth Avenue, Emporium, K Mart? Would a clerk officially change my name from "Loser" to "Saint"? Not hardly!

My God is a God of hope. Jesus longs for the "gift" of my broken life, even if it is full of pain or damaged by my own poor choices or those of others. Having purchased the option to buy at Calvary, He longs to hold the title free and clear. He wants to put His name on me so I will be His personal property. Even now He covers me with His sparkling life of joy and peace, changed in beautiful ways as only He can even in the midst of chaos and turbulence. When He rebirths me with His own new and wonderful life, He selects a new name for me.

For you this transformation might be a dramatic and sudden occurrence as it was for Jacob. For me it is a continuing and gradual process of regressions mixed with growth spurts. Perhaps the metaphor of the fetus developing in the womb fits me best. But however the new birth takes place, we will come forth with a new name—one given us by God Himself. May I wear it proudly for Him today.

GINY YOUNGBERG LONSER

The Comfort of My Sisters

I long to see you so that I may impart to you some spiritual gift to make you strong—that is, that you and I may be mutually encouraged by each other's faith. Rom. 1:11, 12, NIV.

I had grown accustomed to the joys of having sisters—six of them. Then death began to claim them, far short of old age and in far too rapid succession—two just 12 days apart. By the time the doctor suggested that the family come to bid farewell to our mother in June 1994, I was down to just two sisters.

For the next six months my sisters and I spent a lot of time on the phone, trying to bridge the Maryland-Michigan distance between us. I called my mother every day at lunchtime. When my mother stopped struggling to talk ("I've said everything I have to say."), I called her and sang. During those days even the promised resurrection of the righteous did not console me. Neither could my sisters.

In September my husband, Ed, brought home *A Gift of Love,* the 1995 daily devotional for women. "Beautiful," I told him and put the book on the shelf "until next year." But I repeatedly caught sight of the cover through the glass bookcase where I also stored *The Listening Heart.*

I don't know when I began leafing through the next year's devotional. *Just to see what the reading for today's date is,* I thought to myself. September 27. I read it through, then instantly thought, *Ah! Grief turned into joy!* It was enough to start my day with a feeling that had been too long uncommon: a hopeful attitude. Even on my darkest days the light shone through the writing of my "sisters." Each day these unseen sisters provided for the needs of my heart, especially the day of the phone call that I had so long dreaded.

It was now November 28. After the funeral Ed and I had flown to Texas with our older son and stayed for the Thanksgiving holidays. Today I was due back at work, but I couldn't bear the thought of facing lunchtime—the time of day that I had always called Mama. The alarm clock went off. I turned it off. Ed reset it. It sounded again. I could not force myself to get up. Then my mind's eye caught a glimpse of *A Gift of Love,* the daily comfort from my worldwide sisters.

"Dove's Wings, Eagle's Wings, God's Wing's" the title ran. "Perhaps you may be feeling as David did," Maria Vicente had written, "an intense need to escape to a faraway place . . . life often wounds us, and we are left without motivation or enthusiasm." But "if even with this promise [Isaiah 40:31] you still feel incapable of believing that strength will be given to proceed . . . 'under his wings you will find refuge.' . . . Courage, dear one!" *Thank you, Maria!* I thought, and in my journal I wrote, "Thank You, Lord, for Maria."

I have had many good friends within the church, but I had

never grasped the concept of "the family of God" until that September 27 when I began to rest in the comfort of my sisters.

FAITH JOHNSON CRUMBLY

SEPTEMBER 28

Bottles of Tears

Put thou my tears into thy bottle. Ps. 56:8.

I'll be back tomorrow," she said to her son. Her words took me by surprise, as I had driven three hours to Washington, D.C., to pick up my elderly friend. I had thought I wouldn't have to return her at least until Sunday. Perhaps she didn't realize that the Virginia I lived in was not just outside D.C. But location didn't matter. She wanted to visit me, to be able to return to Michigan and report that she had stayed with me. I silently packed her bag, and we headed toward southeastern Virginia.

The next morning she was up bright and early. As we drove across the James River, I mentally computed the additional, accumulating miles. My companion, however, was taking in the tremendous expanse of water that seemed more than just a river. She meticulously jotted down the names of places, landmarks, and even the rivers and streams.

The next day we prepared for the return journey. After dropping her off at her son's home, I promised that on her next trip we'd visit the ocean and various historic sites. She seemed hesitant, admitting that she hadn't known I lived so far away.

A year later she was dead. I thought about our short, exhausting Virginia weekend and of the many days I, as a graduate student, spent with her in Michigan at her business, and then in her home. She had gradually opened up to me, revealing parts of her life story.

The eldest daughter of sharecroppers in Alabama, she had been married twice, yet raised four children alone. When I met her, she was sole owner of a thriving nursing home, even as she limped with an arthritic knee.

From all the conversations we shared, the words which struck me most were: "I'm not saying that my pillow wasn't wet many a night." In spite of her seemingly successful life, she too had shed tears. She too had a "bottle."

Little did she realize that in relating this story, she was fulfilling the command in Titus 2 that elder women be teachers (Titus 2:3). She was teaching me that I could indeed go on, that my trials and adversities, weighed against hers, were small. She had endured—so would I.

I can look back and be thankful—feel honored—that I had the opportunity to spend time with my friend and teacher, to observe her reveling in God's creation, to show her I had indeed "made" it. And when more tears fill my own bottle, I know that others have experienced the pain of life, have shed tears. Yet God, who seeing, knowing, and understanding, records those tears and sends people into our lives who need guidance and encouragement.

PAULA C. BARNES

SEPTEMBER 29

Ever Had an "Unperfect" Day?

When my heart is overwhelmed: lead me to the rock that is higher than I. Ps. 61:2.

Have you ever had an "unperfect" day? A day that took you further than you wanted to go in physical exhaustion and emotional energy? And you didn't have anything more of yourself to give?

I recently had such a day—more interruptions on my project and extra phone calls with last-minute additions. The end of a week with too much to do and too little time—in all areas of my life. Then during the last few minutes of work, the computer, which most of the time I appreciate, "ate" three documents. When I reconstructed them, the printer wouldn't print, so I had to type everything again to meet a deadline that evening. The capstone to an "unperfect" day!

Somehow I survived an "unperfect" ending to my "unperfect" day, at least until I arrived home to nourish a wounded spirit. But it was Thursday. Company was coming for the weekend. I couldn't stop now.

In the high-tech world of computers we sometimes lose our inner selves. As women, we give much of ourselves. Problem solvers, both at work and at home, we don't let our feelings or needs show. We are courteous, professional, concerned, and too often put ourselves on hold.

When we look to our families or friends for support, they are sometimes there and sometimes insensitive to our needs. And sometimes no one is there for us at all. What do I need? Space, kindness, and people letting me know that they too are human. I especially want affirmation that I am an OK human being, even if I've had an "unperfect" day.

How did I handle the situation at the end of that "unperfect" day? I let some things go that needed doing and took some time to read, asking God for spiritual renewal. Then I sat down at the piano and played some of my favorite music. I called several relatives long distance just to say I cared and missed them. The house didn't get cleaned, but I took time to read, to talk with my God, and to refresh my own soul. I took an overwhelmed heart to the Rock that is higher than I.

As we nourish our own inner selves, we will then have more quality time to give our families, work, and friends. And a sense of inner strength makes an occasional "unperfect" day somewhat less traumatic.

EDNA MAYE GALLINGTON

SEPTEMBER 30

The Blues or the Gold

Though the fig tree does not bud and there are no grapes on the vines, though the olive crop fails and the fields produce no food, though there are no sheep in the pen and no cattle in the stalls, yet I will rejoice in the Lord, I will be joyful in God my Savior. Hab. 3:17, 18, NIV.

I obviously don't understand how to appreciate the blues. Listening to people sing about the terrible trauma they have just experienced and hearing the despair in the song's cadences distresses me. It seems that the singers can see no solution for the problems at hand, and they keep on moaning. But from the other side of the fence, talking, singing, or writing about disaster has to be therapeutic!

Certainly Habakkuk must have felt that was the case. Picture the tribulations of a family in an agrarian culture whose livelihood rested on the promise of the harvest. Imagine the disaster inherent in the prospect of abundant crops withering away along with the cattle. His blues, however, are different. They don't stop with his roster of disaster. He includes a twist of gold.

I reworked the last three verses of Habakkuk with a group of women friends at a seaside retreat:

"Though a husband exists only in my dreams, and I shall be

forever childless;

Though I hit my professional head against the glass ceiling, and my credit rating is shot;

Though I have more tasks than hours in the day, and my health is failing;

Yet will I give thanks to my God, and praise Him for His unshakable love.

"Creator God is my mentor.
My God will show me new goals to strive for,
And I will scale professional, spiritual, and personal heights
I never even knew existed!"

Despite differences in history, geography, gender, or age, one thing remains unchanged. When God's people go through tribulation or suffer from numerous wounds, we know to whom to turn.

This is how we differ from the blues writers. For us, the gold is in ascendance even though we may still be fighting with the blues. While we continue to experience life's trials, we can keep on singing a joyful song. Our problems are merely transient. God is right there beside us, lifting us up to infinite heights. We are ultimately invincible if we follow His lead. When we put ourselves in His strong, merciful, and loving arms, we'll make it through. And that is gold!

GLENDA-MAE GREENE

OCTOBER 1

Do Not Steal Sunshine

A cheerful look brings joy to the heart. Prov. 15:30, NIV.

*W*e have no more right to put our discordant states of mind into the lives of those around us and rob them of their sunshine and brightness than we have to enter their houses and steal their silverware."

I just ran across this old quotation by Julia Seton. Her use of such words as sunshine, discordant, rob, and steal shows the importance of our disposition. We need only to put these four words into our minds, and it can easily change our lives.

We meet or pass many people during the course of our day. What do we leave with them: discord or sunshine? As we shop we can easily become impatient or angry with slow or inept clerks. Last week I was in line waiting while two clerks were talking. A well-dressed woman joined us and said loudly, "Doesn't anybody work around here?" The rest of us were waiting quietly. We all had minutes to spare, and we had no idea what problems the two clerks might be having. The woman's comment embarrassed us, but we all had at sometime or other done the same kind of thing. People deserve sunshine from us.

The next stop was my bank. I stepped up to the teller's window and waited, as she was busy with paperwork. At last she looked up and said, "Oh, I didn't see you. Why didn't you tell me you were here?" I smiled and said, "No matter, I was just resting." We laughed and parted with a "Have a nice day!" Cheerfulness shared beamed in both of us. It brightened our day.

I volunteer in the Boston school system, and each time I enter my school I put a smile on my face. I may not know the children's names, but it is important that I share sunshine with them. I would not deny one child a smile. One of my important roles is to be one more adult to love and care for these children in today's fractured, disruptive world. I am not there as a teacher or parent to discipline—my responsibility is to bless them with smiles and love.

We as Christians dare not bring discord into the lives of others or steal their happiness from them. We must protect the sunshine in people's lives.

DESSA WEISZ HARDIN

OCTOBER 2

A Song of Love

We love because he first loved us. 1 John 4:19, NIV.

Recently I heard a story on the Bakersfield evening news that brought tears to my eyes. A physician told a 7-year-old girl, deaf from birth, that he could give her hearing through a complicated and expensive surgery. The doctor quoted the cost of the surgery to the single-parent mother. Noting the frown on the woman's face, he added, "Don't worry if you don't have the money. I'm sure there are government agencies that can help defray the expenses."

Unfortunately the girl did not qualify for any government funds. Marci's mother fell into one of those bureaucratic cracks where she earned too much to qualify for the aid but not enough to afford the surgery. There seemed to be little hope that the child would receive the operation that could make it possible for her to hear. When a local TV news team heard of the child's plight, they reported it on the Bakersfield evening news.

The little girl's story touched the heart of a man living in Los Angeles. He immediately called the child's physician and arranged to pay for the little girl's surgery. More than most people, the stranger could appreciate the child's desire to hear. The man's name? Ray Charles, the famous blind musician.

The medical procedure was a success. And today the girl hears for the first time the sound of a kitten purring, a bird singing, a dog barking. She can hear her mother whisper words of love in her ear, and she hears laughter and music.

Whether or not the child and her mother appreciated Ray Charles' singing and piano-playing abilities before the surgery, I don't know. But I can guarantee you that for the rest of the little girl's life Mr. Charles will be her favorite musical performer. She'll probably buy every one of his CDs. His raspy voice will be music to her ears and his concerts a celebration of joy. Every song he ever sings will be, to her, a song of love.

The story reminds me of Jesus and His love. He not only restored my "hearing" and my "sight," but my soul as well, by granting me the gift that only He as the Creator could give—eternal life. He forgives my sins and fills my heart with joy. With the psalmist I sing, "I will extol the Lord at all times; his praise will always be on my lips. My soul will boast in the Lord; let the afflicted hear and rejoice! Glorify the Lord with me; let us exalt his name together" (Ps. 34:1-3, NIV).

KAY D. RIZZO

OCTOBER 3

Air Pockets

Wherefore didst thou doubt? Matt. 14:31.

As I was praying one morning, I suddenly realized that I was feeling extremely jumpy and nervous. Continually searching for a way to express myself to God in my private devotions, I felt critical of myself if I made a request that did not follow all the "rules" of proper approach to my heavenly Father.

As I continued to meditate, I recalled a flight I had made from California to South Bend, Indiana. I had approached it with a feeling of apprehension, because previous flights near Lake Michigan had been rough because of air pockets. It was not difficult to remember to pray as I walked that narrow passage to board the plane.

When the plane hit the largest air pocket in the history of my life, I was frozen with fear. I saw soda splash over passengers and drip from the ceiling. The flight attendant lost her balance and dove toward a seat, where she remained. The buzzing "fasten seat belts" sign flashed on. The pilot gave safety warnings over the speaker. I sat tense as the passengers of the plane expressed their feelings in high-pitched voices and nervous giggles.

As the plane continued to pitch, I heard sounds I felt sure were ripping wings. "No!" Placing my hand tightly over my mouth, I stifled a scream. I, a Christian, could not scream, could not dare to be human. What an example of perfect love casting out fear that would be! Yet, in my panic, I felt abandoned by God.

As prayer beads shot between the fingers of some, the flight attendant worked hard at spurts of humor, preplanned for such an occasion. I then thought of Peter.

"But when he saw the wind boisterous, he was afraid; and beginning to sink, he cried, saying, Lord, save me" (Matt. 14:30). Open, honest, blundering Peter could be saved, because he asked for what he needed. "And immediately Jesus stretched forth his hand, and caught him" (verse 31).

Jesus is a personal Saviour. He knows my heart. It is He who will understand if I am concerned about me. It is me He comes to in my fear. It is my hand He holds in sickness. It is the water under my boat He calms.

With a gentle reprimand, Jesus was able to help Peter, and draw my attention, centuries later, to a loving Father. "O thou of little faith, wherefore didst thou doubt?" (verse 31).

SUZANNE DANFORTH BROZNY

OCTOBER 4

No Fear in Love

There is no fear in love; but perfect love casts out fear. 1 John 4:18, NKJV.

Sitting sternly on the desk, our math teacher ordered all of us to come forward for a swat on our palm. We had done something to deserve punishment. Forming a line, one by one we stretched out our little hands for a sharp smack from his cane. Fear gripped me, and I suddenly slipped out of the line. Rubbing my hands together and blowing on my hand at the same time, I pretended to be suffering from the punishment. I thought I had played a rather clever trick.

One boy shouted, "Teacher, this one did not get the beating!" The teacher was kind enough, however, to excuse me, and it made me feel guilty for trying to deceive him.

Fear can lead us to sin. I hope that in a time of crisis I will not be driven to deny my Lord. I understand and pity Peter. When he saw his Master looking powerless in the hands of the soldiers, fear overwhelmed him. The fear that he too might be arrested drove him to deny that he even knew Jesus. Later, when love took control of his life, he had no more fear. He gladly died as a martyr for Christ.

When a crisis arises, what will take control of us: love or fear? If we really love our Lord, we will say, as did Paul, "Who shall separate us from the love of Christ? Shall tribulation, or distress, or persecution, or famine, or nakedness, or peril, or sword? . . . For I am persuaded that neither death nor life, nor angels nor principalities nor powers, nor things present nor things to come, nor height nor depth, nor any other created thing, shall be able to separate us from the love of God which is in Christ Jesus our Lord" (Rom. 8:35-39, NKJV).

God loved us so much that He gave His only begotten Son to die for us. He took our punishment. Though we deserved it, God has excused us. It is His delight to make us happy. He calls us His children, and He wants us to call Him Father. He promises to take us to His home one day, not just for a vacation, but for eternity.

We will all someday face a crisis. We need to love Him more now, to let our relationship with Him grow. Then we shall not need to fear, for "perfect love casts out fear."   BIRDIE PODDAR

OCTOBER 5

God's Surprises

And He shall be the stability of your times, a wealth of salvation, wisdom, and knowledge; the fear of the Lord is his treasure. Isa. 33:6, NASB.

J had viewed my husband's determination to always know exactly where we were going, what time we were leaving, and how to get to our destination as cramping my more casual lifestyle. My suitcase was literally always packed, and I had no problem dropping everything to go off on some adventure, figuring out how to get there while on the way.

When I became a widow, however, I discovered that his need for structure had given stability to the impulsive side of my nature. As a result I decided that the Lord needed to help me with my problem of self-control. Out of a contrite heart I asked the Lord for the ability to think things through before acting, and for the strength to say no to anything that might cause me to regret my actions later.

I was serious about the admonition to "pray without ceasing" (1 Thess. 5:17), to "ask, and it shall be given" (Matt. 7:7), and to accept the fact that God would supply all my needs (Phil. 4:19). Although I tried to be very specific about my requests in every area of my life, still in the back of my mind always lurked the idea that maybe I did not really need the things for which I had asked. My recent track record of choices had not been very good, and maybe I should make some modifications.

I thanked the Lord for the promise in Mark 11:24 that says we should believe that we have received the things we have asked for. Yet I was afraid that I might get what I had requested and that it would be wrong for me. I had experienced enough disaster to last me for the rest of my life.

So I explained to God that I would (1) pray for spiritual growth, (2) pray for family and friends, and (3) give thanks for His blessings. I reminded Him that He knew what I needed before I asked (Matt. 6:8), and I was sure that He would provide. Then, almost as an afterthought, I added, a bit shyly, "But I like surprises, too, Lord, and if You want to surprise me with something nice once in a while, I would really like that."

He has honored that last prayer request many times since then, always in a way that enabled me to recognize it as one of His special gifts. Very happy with this arrangement, I have so much for which to be thankful. Foremost is the fact that I love and serve a God who understands and responds to me as a unique individual, and in a way that is always meaningful to me. I am sure that He must chuckle when He sends me one of His surprises.   SHEILA SANDERS

OCTOBER 6

He Gives Us Inner Peace

Peace I leave with you; my peace I give you. John 14:27, NIV.

Twenty-five years of service as a homemaker in a pastor's home has brought me moments of intense joy and excitement. It has also provided periods of deep reflection over what God has promised or has not promised the pastor's home in terms of joy and pain. At times I've questioned, "Why me?" only to discover God's love shining even more brightly at the end of the tunnel.

It has been said, and truly so, that a family that prays together sticks together. When Satan attempted to bring gloom into our lives, my husband and I never forgot to pray to our God, who instantly and constantly would supply us the strength we needed.

I especially cannot forget those years we spent studying in America. At one point we had run out of funds for our education just as I was also expecting our second daughter. My doctor advised that I quit work. My health became so bad that I could not walk, and my husband had to help me in and out of bed. Without health insurance and with mounting medical bills, I wondered how we were going to make it. Finally I sat down and wept my heart out to the Lord. Then I remembered that the right thing to do was to thank God for bringing us thus far, and that looking at the bright side of life is to face in the direction of victory.

My poor husband worked three jobs and studied full-time, but God gave him ample strength. He had a night job and spent the day at school and at two other work sites. I thanked the Lord that neither his grades nor his health suffered. Words became inadequate to express my joy and thanks to the Lord when our baby girl was born.

I have seen the Lord's blessings. Through prayer God is able to grant us an inner peace that sustains us through any difficulty.

JULIANA AGBOKA

OCTOBER 7

Fast Faith Franchise

I am the Lord; in its time I will do this swiftly. Isa. 60:22, NIV.

The twentieth century has become an age of "fast" everything. We have the Express Oil Change, where they guarantee to change the oil in your car in 10 minutes. "Walk-ins Welcome" appears in the windows of many beauty shops. Weight-loss clinics for "fast fat fixes" have sprung up in every community. TV shows solve murders, love triangles, and other modern problems in a half hour. We expect everything to come, go, and be accomplished *instantly!*

Sometimes Christians expect growth and sanctification to occur the same way. We want faith and patience, and we want it *now!* It isn't as though we can drive down to the neighborhood "Fast Faith Franchise," speak our order into a steel box ("give me a double order of faith, hold the trials and sorrows"), and then drive around to a window where it is neatly packaged and handed to us to carry home. If the Christian life were that simple, we wouldn't appreciate it. Things that come that easy are often worth what we put into them—nothing.

We desire more faith, but faith is like yeast . . . it grows. As it grows, it produces more faith. We want to share it with others because we are so full and excited about it and what it has done for and through us.

Faith that doesn't produce works is dead, like the baker's yeast that settles to the bottom of the bowl and just stays there. Faith that is alive slowly rises to the top, all bubbly and full of works.

If we want fast food, we can go to a fast-food restaurant. But if we want more faith, we must go to God and be willing to go through the experiences we need to receive it. We must pray that He won't withhold anything—that whatever comes with faith, be it sorrow, trials, heartache, or loss, He will give it to us. We must be willing to accept anything, for the faith that He gives us will see us through the "anything."   MARLENE ANDERSON

OCTOBER 8

Amazing Grace
Where sin abounded, grace did much more abound. Rom. 5:20.

The last "good nights" echoed along the half-empty streets as we spilled out of the church after the evening prayer meeting. It was autumn and already dark as I walked along the dimly lit streets, hurrying to reach home.

Suddenly I realized that someone was following me. Changing pace and direction, I tried to throw off my "shadow," but without success. Not daring to look behind me, I hurried toward busier, better-lit streets, but in one quick movement he caught up with me.

I froze, my heart thudding against my ribs so loudly that I was sure he could hear. Towering above me was a convict! Heavily built, with shaven head and stubble-covered chin, he fell into step beside me. Where had I been? he asked. Why? Where was I going? How often did I go to church? What did we do there? His questions were endless.

Still a fairly new believer myself and unsure of my ability to answer his questions, I offered to study the Bible with him. To my surprise, he readily accepted. He suggested he come to my home, but I didn't want him to know where I lived, so I told him it would be better if he stopped by my classroom after school. He accepted this, and when I told him we would meet at school the following week, he left. As he disappeared, I turned and ran for home.

He did not forget our rendezvous, and as the last children left my classroom, he appeared in the doorway, waiting quietly. We talked awhile, studied the Bible together, and then prayed. He knelt on the classroom floor, his face hidden in his hands as tears rolled down his cheeks and his massive shoulders shook with emotion. God's Spirit was whispering a message of love to that hard, calloused heart, changing it before my eyes.

He studied faithfully each week, and after a time he started to attend church regularly. Late in the spring he made his decision to be baptized, and it was then that I heard his story. The son of a policeman, he had drifted into a life of violence and crime and had spent many years behind bars. From his father he had acquired a police truncheon with Queen Victoria's coat of arms on it, and with this, he had cracked many a hard skull. "But now," he said, "I have no further use for this, and I want you to have it." With a broad smile, he handed it to me.

Years have passed since then. The truncheon still hangs on my bedroom wall, a silent reminder that no heart is too hard for God to soften, no human being so fallen that God cannot re-create him/her in His image if he/she accepts the precious gift of salvation so freely offered to all.

REVEL N. PAPAIOANNOU

Our Guardian Angels

For he shall give his angels charge over thee, to keep thee in all thy ways. They shall bear thee up in their hands, lest thou dash thy foot against a stone. Ps. 91:11, 12.

"Mommy, Mommy, save me! Save me!" The screams of our 5-year-old son pierced the roar of the rushing water at Wheelbarrow Falls in Quetico Provincial Park that sunny day in Canada.

My husband and I, along with our four children and their two second cousins, were vacationing in this lovely place for 10 days during the late 1960s. Camping, canoeing, and hiking 150 miles with six children, ages 3-16, may not be your idea of a vacation, but for us it was a wonderful change from milking cows and baling hay during the hot summer months. It had taken six weeks to carefully plan and package meals and supplies for the eight of us. Everyone had a backpack to carry—even the "baby."

This fall day, to save a long hike, we were traveling upstream of the falls by walking alongside the water. We traversed the high rocks, pulling with ropes the canoes laden with our gear and children. My husband guided the canoe in the rear with the four boys while I had the lead canoe with the two youngest children. Suddenly the rope on mine came loose, and the rapidly flowing waters caught the canoe, swiftly carrying our small children on a wild ride downstream. Our sons' screams filled me with terror.

My husband, seeing the canoe begin its rapid journey, leaped from the rock he was on, and miraculously catching the canoe by its bow, rode a wild ride in the water, his own body weight providing sufficient ballast to keep the canoe upright. Thanks to his quick thinking, agile body, and the loving protection of one of those angels who have charge over us, the incident had a happy ending.

Many hundreds of years after God gave this promise in the Psalms, Satan quoted it to Jesus from the pinnacle of the Temple, trying to tempt Him to throw Himself off. Satan sought to misuse a promise which, under normal circumstances, would bring hope, courage, and strength. Praise God that Jesus met Satan on his own ground with the answer "Thou shalt not tempt the Lord thy God" (Matt. 4:7). Defeated again for the third time that day, Satan left Jesus, and "angels came and ministered unto him" (verse 11).

What joy will be mine to someday meet these beautiful, strong, wonderful beings who have charge over us and to gratefully say, "Thank you!"   BETTY BURNETT

OCTOBER 10

His Garment's Hem

Now a woman, having a flow of blood for twelve years, who had spent all her livelihood on physicians and could not be healed by any, came from behind and touched the border of His garment. And immediately her flow of blood stopped. Luke 8:43, 44, NKJV.

She had spent all her money, still she was ill.
Nothing could stop the flow,
Then she heard of a man named Christ
And knew that she must go.

Go find the One who could heal the sick,
Who could make the blind to see.
Her faith was strong as she followed along
That day by Galilee.

The press of the throng kept pushing her back,
But her place she would not yield,
Till she fell at His feet and touched His robe,
And immediately she was healed.

Oh, for the faith of that woman of old,
Oh, for the faith of one of them
That He made whole, both body and soul,
By the touch of His garment's hem.

Physical contact did not make the woman whole. Rather, it was the personal living faith that reached out and took hold of the divine power that made her well, the faith that acknowledged Him as the giver of the blessing that she received.

It is not enough to believe on Christ or about Him. We must believe *in* Him. He calls upon every trusting, believing individual to reveal what we ourselves have felt, seen, and heard. Our faith is strengthened to claim and receive more and more.   ELVA E. SPRINGER

Glimpses of the Rainbow

I have set my rainbow in the clouds, and it will be the sign of the covenant between me and the earth. Whenever I bring clouds over the earth and the rainbow appears in the clouds, I will remember my covenant between me and you and all living creatures of every kind. Gen. 9:13-15, NIV.

Who made the beautiful rainbow? I know, I know; God made the beautiful rainbow, that's why I love it so!"

The children sang these words with gusto, exuberantly waving their wands with the rainbow-colored streamers attached. They looked so happy, enjoying the movement and the music. The teacher had just finished telling them the story of Noah and the ark, and God's promise never again to destroy the earth by a flood. To always remind us of His promise God placed the rainbow in the sky.

As I traveled out west in the wide-open spaces of Australia, a sudden shower spread across the sky. A few moments later a rainbow appeared, reaching in a perfect arc from the horizon to the road on which we were driving. Standing at the foot of a cascading waterfall, I saw a beautiful rainbow appear as the dazzling sunlight illuminated the falling droplets. The colors were so magnificent, the bow so perfect.

Throughout the Bible we catch other glimpses of the rainbow. Ezekiel gave us a description of God when he wrote, "And brilliant light surrounded him. Like the appearance of a rainbow in the clouds on a rainy day, so was the radiance around him" (Eze. 1:27, 28). John the revelator also had visions of other rainbows. In one scene, a mighty angel comes down from heaven, clothed with a cloud and a rainbow upon his head (Rev. 10:1). John also viewed the throne of heaven with a rainbow encircling it (Rev. 4:3). The rainbow surrounding the throne of God is our assurance of His eternal love.

Each view of the rainbow, whether on earth or in heaven, reminds us of God's promises and love. What better way could God have chosen to remind us of His caring than with a beautiful rainbow? Just as the red, orange, yellow, green, blue, and violet blend into one magnificent rainbow, so His promises blend to proclaim His eternal love for the children of earth.   ALMA ATCHESON

It's Up to Us

Think about all you can praise God for and be glad about. Phil. 4:8, TLB.

"T hat person would criticize heaven itself" is a remark I sometimes hear. Until recently, though, I had considered it as just a rhetorical statement, something that would never literally happen. But then I heard of a woman who actually found fault with heaven. She had read about it, and in contemplating it as her future home, she was definitely dissatisfied.

"If everyone in heaven is going to be playing on harps, what an awful racket that will be!" She shivered as she thought of the possibilities. The streets of gold bothered her. "That will be hard on my poor feet—walking on gold pavements all the time," she moaned. Then she asked, "Do all the angels wear halos?" Informed that they probably did, she replied, "What a glare that will make!"

The woman had been sick a long time, and had many aches and pains. But the incident shows that a person can find fault even with something that is perfect if her thinking has a gloomy trend.

On the other hand, we can see good in the most unfavorable situations if our thinking is on the cheerful side. Remember the story of the man who had no shoes and felt sorry for himself—until he saw a man who had no feet? Then he was thankful for his feet, even if they were unshod.

It's really up to us, isn't it? We can be heaven-criticizers, or we can be barefooted thanks-givers. Which shall we choose when tempted to find fault?   LAURA DROWN

Promises

Behold, I come quickly. Rev. 22:7.

S everal years ago my dear friend and occasional roommate, "Rags," left me to move across the country. We had gone through a lot together and had become close through our mutual love of music. Since we would now be living on opposite coasts, I was sure I would never see her again.

When the time came to say goodbye, we both cried and promised to write. Rags also promised me that she would visit me, but my logical mind prevented me from believing this at first. She had no car, and I doubted very much that she could save up enough money for the airfare.

"I'll leave my guitar with you," she told me finally. "That way you'll know I have to come back soon."

Rags did return within a few months, but I expected her to. She had let me keep her most cherished possession—her guitar. When she departed this time, she took her guitar with her. I didn't need it anymore to believe her promise that we would see each other again.

In His earthly ministry, Jesus knew what it was like to say good-bye to His friends. In John 17 He pleads with His heavenly Father that not only His disciples but also those who become His friends through their teaching could one day join Him. He did not leave us with vague allusions that He "might" come back. Instead, the Holy Bible gives us a written contract of His intentions. It is His promise to us, signed with love.   GINA LEE

OCTOBER 14

The Secret of Giving

He gives strength to the weary. Isa. 40:29, NIV.

*J*esus had a secret. One that is available to you when you feel you have no more to give. To learn it, you need to read Matthew 14 and experience a typical day in Jesus' life. Won't you peek with me beyond the narrative of that chapter and enter into the emotions that Jesus may have felt?

It began with the news of John the Baptist's death. Imagine Jesus' pain. The only one who had an inkling of His mission had been bru-tally beheaded. That death and the news that Herod sought His own life must have left Jesus feeling stunned and shocked. Aching for time to grieve for His friend, He yearned for solitude and seclusion.

But the 12 disciples interrupted His thoughts. They had been away scattering God's love, and now they returned like excited schoolchildren. With exuberance and joyous laughter, they told story after story of miracle after miracle. Jesus denied His need to grieve in order to respond to their need to rejoice.

As they talked, He noticed a large group of men, women, and

children approach. Like honey trickling off a warm spoon, the crowd edged closer and closer. Jesus, aware of the disciples' need to rest, urged them to get into a nearby boat. They set sail.

However, the people were not to be daunted. Seeing Jesus in the boat, they ran alongside on the lakeshore, waving and calling out to Him. When He reached the shore of Bethsaida, they were waiting for Him. Complete confusion reigned as hands reached out to touch Him. People tugged at His clothes. Voices screeched out a variety of pleas. Again, Jesus lay aside His need for stillness and time alone with the 12. He met the needs of those around Him.

Later in the day, tired and weary, He fed the people before sending them home. Again He urged the disciples into a boat—this time so that He could replenish His own soul. After waving goodbye, He turned and slowly ascended the hill before Him. Alone with only the gentle rustling of the trees and the rhythmic splashing of the water against the rocks, He talked with God.

Life for Jesus was one of constant giving. He always put aside His own heartaches to heal the aching heart of another. To be able to do that, He had to be filled by God. With a bowed head, open heart, and a spirit willing to achieve God's goals, He waited for God to heal the weariness within Him. It is a secret for us to emulate. In your quiet visits with God, ask Him to take away your tiredness and to put His vitality and freshness within you. Linger with God, and let Him "minister" to you. Then, like Jesus, you too can touch the emptiness in people's lives.   MARY BARRETT

OCTOBER 15

A Blood Pressure Check

Create in me a clean heart, O God; and renew a right spirit within me. Ps. 51:10.

Addi wasn't really her name, but it served to identify our wrinkled, little Aborigine patient.

Entering the hospital, Addi straightened her slight shoulders and without so much as a glance toward the registration desk, passed all the patients waiting their turn to see the doctor, then stationed herself just outside his office door. It was evident she understood that no one enters a doctor's office while he is seeing a patient. When the door opened, she darted in, seated herself by the doctor's desk, and began a vivid description of her infirmities.

An examination suggested that she did have reason to complain, but that the difficulty was not life-threatening. The doctor could correct it by a relatively simple surgery without charge to her. She was to go with his nurse to the supervisor to schedule the surgery.

Addi and the nurse left the doctor's office. Moments later the nurse returned with the information that Addi had gone home, refusing to set up a time for surgery. Before the week ended, Addi, following the same pattern, again sought the doctor's attention and received the same response. After repeating this procedure two or three times a week for a month, the doctor advised her that he was unable to do much more for her until she was willing to schedule her surgery.

Bristling, Addi left the office in a little flash of fury, only to return shortly, plop her arm on the doctor's desk, and demand, "Well, then, you can take my blood pressure!"

Her blood pressure duly checked, she left the hospital seemingly happy.

We all smiled at little Addi's naïveté! But as I considered the episode, I realized that possibly I was somewhat like Addi. How many times I've prayed, "Lord, take away my unpleasant disposition, especially my hasty and unreasonable temper. Please take it away, Lord."

God responds, "A new heart *also* will I give you, and a *new* spirit will I put within you" (Eze. 36:26).

"A new heart?" I ask. "Nothing wrong with my heart, Lord. Why, a new heart might completely change my personality, and one thing is certain, I do want to be me! No, Lord, no new heart. Just take away this disagreeable temper."

But God indicates He really wants to give me a new heart and a new spirit to enable me to walk in His paths with Him. Then, He says, I shall be one of His distinctive people, and He truly will be my eternal God (Eze. 11:19, 20). I can become a totally whole, committed, victorious Christian. Yet I've been insisting on a blood pressure check when I could have had restorative surgery!

"Create in me a clean heart, O God; and renew a right spirit within me."   Lois E. Johannes

Finding the God of Creation

And ye shall seek me, and find me, when ye shall search for me with all your heart. Jer. 29:13.

I searched for God. I trod the hills, the deserts bleak and bare;
Explored the bustling cities; tramped the crowded thoroughfare.
I searched, but could not find Him. In distress I called His name,
Then into my surrendered heart, His soothing presence came.

"Dear child of Mine," He whispered, "I am closer than you know;
The things that I've created all are meant to tell you so.
At night My arms surround you in the splendor of the stars—
Arcturus, Saturn, Jupiter, the Pleiades, and Mars;

"I guide the grunion to its shore, the swallow to her nest,
And hold the beauty of the rocks deep in my treasure chest.
Six thousand years ago I set the pattern of the sun,
Prepared the hawk to fly, and taught the cheetah how to run;

"I knew the friendly chimpanzee would brighten up your day,
And you would find Me as you watched the dolphins in their play.
With manna I sustained a nation—healed them from the quail,
And housed a fleeing Jonah in the belly of a whale;

"Provided Samson with the strength to wield an ass's jaw;
A raven for Elijah, sapphire stone for My great law;
A cave for David in distress, and for the widow, oil;
A net of fish at Galilee, crowned My disciples' toil.

"You cannot ride a comet as it catapults through space.
Not one black hole of mystery in the sky can you erase.
You cannot fashion iridescent wings for butterflies;
Or hold a mountain in your hands to modify its size.

"You cannot cause the sun to cease, or dim the full moon's
    glow;
Construct a beehive, tint a rose, or cause the corn to grow.
But you can walk beside Me, hear My voice, and grasp
    My hand;
And as we talk together, you'll more wisely understand

"My love for you in every violet blooming at your feet;
The peacock's opalescent fan, a soft lamb's muted bleat."
Thus spoke creation's Architect when I took time to pray.
I've learned He's waiting for me at the start of each
    new day.

I've found Him! Oh, I've found Him, in the fresh cool
    morning dew;
In aloe vera's healing balm, in noonday's cloudless blue;
I find Him in the sunsets; watch His fingers brush the sky
With pigments from His palette in extravagant supply.

His brilliant tints of changing color take my breath away
As crimson, yellow, pink, and gold fade softly into gray.
I feel His hand, in soothing breezes, waft across my brow;
In trees He sets in motion as winds stir each tender bough;

I find Him in the robin's song, the lily pure and white;
The moonbeams on my pillow in the stillness of the night;
And so each time I seek expression, as I kneel in prayer,
I feel my quiet heartbeat, and I know I'm in His care!

LORRAINE HUDGINS

Torn Hearts and Smiling Faces

You hear, O Lord, the desire of the afflicted; you encourage
them, and you listen to their cry, defending the fatherless and the

oppressed, in order that man, who is of the earth, may terrify no
more. Ps. 10:17, 18, NIV.

I knew it wasn't going to be an altogether pleasant day. Our
group was scheduled to tour the site of the World War II
Auschwitz-Birkenau concentration camp. We walked reluctantly from building to building to the one labeled "Plunder." It
housed stacks of shoes—thousands of shoes. A whole big heap of
children's shoes. And then there was the hair, mostly women's.
Three tons had been sold before the chaotic final days of the camp,
but two tons still remained—braided, curled, matted, mostly gray.
The guide said some had turned gray with time and through chem-
icals, but most had become prematurely gray through trauma.

On we walked past piles of suitcases with names and home-
towns from all over Europe. Mounds of hairbrushes, eyeglasses,
wash pans. As we entered the "prison" building within the camp,
our guide pointed out the rows and rows of pictures on the walls of
the long central hallway. They were all Polish people. The camps
had taken no pictures of the Jewish prisoners. Most of them had
gone directly to the gas chambers. But the camp authorities had
photographed and recorded each Polish prisoner. Here they were,
rows and rows of pictures, names, dates of arrival and of death.
Usually the two dates were from only two to six months apart.

I had looked at many pictures before I realized that all of them
on the left wall were of women. They had the same shaved heads
and striped prison uniforms as those on the other wall. The only difference was their feminine first names. Then I noticed that many of
the prisoners were smiling. Maybe some of the men smiled too, but
I couldn't take my eyes off the women. Why would anyone, in such
a place, in such circumstances, smile? These people were under no
illusion as to why they were here or what was going to happen.

The whole thing haunted me. It staggers the mind and twists the
heart. How could this all be? And what does one do with the emotions it evokes? Then one remembers those smiling women again.

Life and history have never been what one can really call fair, especially for women, but sometimes we have an opportunity to make
a difference, even if a small one. Maybe today you and I can lift an
unbearable load from someone's heart. Perhaps by a smile. Possibly
by doing something more significant, but we must never allow hate
and fear to overcome us. Until that great day of final liberation, every
smile or act of kindness will make a difference.   ARDIS STENBAKKEN

True Contentment

Not that I speak in regard to need, for I have learned in whatever state I am, to be content: I know how to be abased, and I know how to abound. Everywhere and in all things I have learned both to be full and to be hungry, both to abound and to suffer need. I can do all things through Christ who strengthens me. Phil. 4:11-13, NKJV.

*D*id you ever have to work with someone annoying or with a grossly unfair supervisor? Or have you just been in some situation that wasn't to your liking? Have you ever prayed "God, please fix that person!" or "Lord, get me out of here!"? Well, maybe not in those words, but perhaps you asked the Lord to change the circumstances to something more favorable. Here's how God answered my prayers.

One fellow in my office was, in my opinion, insufferable. I could not stand his way of correcting other people's errors, particularly mine. He was unavoidable, since we were assigned to the same support team. I would complain to God, asking Him to somehow "fix" this guy. Can you imagine the kind of witness I was? Finally my prayer changed to "Please help me to be understanding and accepting." God answered that prayer and changed my heart to see more of what Jesus saw in him. So much so that I began to value his intelligence and discovered more of his appreciable traits.

In another experience, I had an "impossible" job assignment and team leader. When the company assigned me to this task, the client was already displeased with our company and was ready to terminate our contract. I was sent to assist in completing the project and to perform some public relations with the client. The team leader would take the credit for any work done well and blame the rest of us for anything that went wrong. He was a congenial fellow, but was also crude and deceitful.

Again I asked God to "really fix" this guy and to get me out of this mess. I even tried to help by looking for another job. During the job search process, however, I surrendered to God and asked Him to fix me instead. He touched my heart, and I was at peace and more pleasant to people.

It must have been noticeable to others, because not too long after this "change of heart," my department supervisor highly recommended me for a position that included a promotion. Not only did the Lord help me to find contentment under demanding and stressful circumstances, but He also prepared me for a better place.

In other trying times, I focus on how wonderfully God has answered my prayers during my journeys from "state to state." Like Paul, my goal is to be able to say "for I have learned in whatever state I am, to be content."   MARGUERITE THYGESON

OCTOBER 19

Friendship

Two are better than one, because they have a good return for their work: If one falls down, [her] friend can help [her] up. But pity the [woman] who falls and has no one to help [her] up! Eccl. 4:9, 10, NIV.

I need friendship. By friendship, I'm not talking about a greeting and a handshake at the door of the church. Nor do I mean the most hospitable smile and courteous greeting in the foyer by the best of greeters, as important as that is. And I'm not talking about a "friendship time" during the worship service when someone tells us to stand and shake the hands of those around us. Such exercises are excellent icebreakers but can never take the place of personal friendship.

I don't need someone to be friendly to me at church nearly as much as I need friendship outside the church service. I need it during the week when I am struggling with everyday trials. I need a friend I can call to ask for prayer. I need friendship on Saturday night when I know others are getting together. Nothing hurts more than to overhear a group of women talking about getting together for lunch and not be invited to join them. I desperately want and need their acceptance—to feel that I belong to a group of friends who like and care about me.

There are other women out there like me. They also want and need friends to affirm their worth. The trouble with women and their friendships is that we frequently get locked into a circle of those we like and trust and rarely reach beyond our "sacred circle."

Perhaps you have a secure circle of friends in place around you and do not feel the loneliness that others complain about. What I'm asking you to do is look around you, outside of your circle. Is there someone out there who needs your friendship? Someone to whom you might minister in a special way?

Your assignment is to offer encouragement and affirmation to an established friend this week through a phone call or a personal note. Then create an opportunity to make a new friend. Take the first step and invite her to join you for lunch or a get-together.

NANCY VAN PELT

When Technology Fails

Some trust in chariots and some in horses, but we trust in the name of the Lord our God. Ps. 20:7, NIV.

*A*fter first conquering a mountain of bedtime stories, my 3-year-old and I stood poised for bedtime prayers.

"Are you ready to ask Jesus to bless you in the night and to send His angels to watch over you while you sleep?" I asked, reciting the question as predictable as a bedtime story plot line.

"No," he replied through the darkness. "I don't need the angels tonight. I had a chewable vitamin, and I'll be fine!"

Stifling my immediate reaction, I explained that while vitamins sometimes help our bodies stay healthy, angels have a very different job. They work to keep us safe, to reassure us of God's nearness, to comfort us when we fear the dark or the threat of a thunderstorm.

It was a delicate balance between restoring childlike faith and talking my son into a nightmare. But helping children understand the dangers in life is often like that. When I finished, I waited to hear his response. It was aimed at God, not at me. Folding his hands, Alden intoned up to heaven, "OK, God. Go ahead then!"

After a few minutes of laughing in my room, it occurred to me that my son had already absorbed the basis of faith for most of twentieth-century humanity. So did one of my college professors the day the space shuttle *Challenger* exploded. "Once again," he said, "we are reminded that our technology is not infallible."

Indeed, we are reminded more often than we realize. We discover it when power surges destroy computer files, when mammograms miss malignancies, when wonder drugs leave a score of the next generation's women struggling with infertility and cancer. Accompanying each admitted blessing of invention and discovery is a corresponding heartbreak when that technology fails or proves inadequate.

None of this is meant to detract from the gift God has given in the curious, inventive, creative mind. It is one of God's best gifts, particularly as we struggle against the weeds and diseases of a sinful world. The trick is to remember the Giver behind the gift.

David saw Him clearly. The psalmist's song asked his listeners, "I lift up my eyes to the hills—where does my help come from?" (Ps. 121:1, NIV). Perhaps they envisioned a mighty army swarming down those hills to assist the king's troops. But David saw the Giver behind this great gift. "My help comes from the Lord, the Maker of heaven and earth" (verse, 2, NIV).

This day, determine to focus your faith on the Giver of all good gifts. Every time technology touches your life, remember the Creator of discovery. Pray also for the ability to discover the simple, yet unceasingly marvelous gifts, like sleepy little children who make us laugh.   SHELLEY CURTIS WEAVER

OCTOBER 21

Asking for Help

Carry each other's burdens, and in this way you will fulfill the law of Christ. Gal. 6:2, NIV.

J awakened with a heavy sense that time had run out. Our daughter Robyn had been home nearly two months, but in less than 12 hours we'd say goodbye again. When she first arrived from teaching in China the eight weeks she'd be in the States had seemed fairly long. But they'd passed in a heartbeat.

I'd decided to go on to work that day. There was no real reason to stay home, for Robyn would be putting the finishing touches on her packing and didn't need my help. She was a seasoned traveler and excellent packer with her own way of fitting a year's worth of clothing, books, and personal items into two suitcases and a carry-on. Her father and I would work till midafternoon, then pick her up and go on to the airport.

At the office, I settled down to handle some routine matters. I wasn't up to any problem solving or creative thinking. About mid-morning a young coworker stopped by. When she mentioned coming by that afternoon I told her I wouldn't be in. "Oh, yes," she said, chuckling. "This is the day your tears start, isn't it?"

I brushed off her remark. She had no way of feeling what I felt—the joy and pride I had in my daughter, the weight of sadness at being parted again. She left and I sat quietly, thinking. Suddenly I knew what to do. I got up and hurried down the hallway to see

Carol. Only weeks before she'd left her college freshman daughter at school, a whole day's drive away. Our college freshman son had chosen a school twice as far in the opposite direction, and we often compared notes on our kids. Carol would understand.

I didn't even say hello, just went straight to her desk and said, "I'm feeling awful and I need some sympathy. In less than four hours we're going to take Robyn to the airport. I won't see her for a year, or maybe more, and I think I'm going to die."

"Oh!" she gasped. "Has time passed this fast? You must feel *awful*. I don't know what I'd do if it were Sherri. I can hardly stand having her 500 miles away. What would I do if she were leaving for Europe? Are you going to be all right?"

Another friend joined our conversation, sharing how she'd felt when her son and his family moved across country; how she'd missed them even though she was glad they were doing well. My friends asked for details about Robyn's work and said that it takes special people to respond to God's call to work so far from home. What they said wasn't all that significant, but what they gave me was beyond price. They gave me empathy, their understanding of my mixture of happiness and despair. Something wonderful happened that September morning. Out of their experience, they comforted me.

Over the months I've pondered the fact that if I had not asked for help, my friends could not have helped me. I could have spent the morning in an abyss of depression, and no one would have known the difference. And this, I think, is the most important thing I learned.

We don't often share our emotional traumas with people, and there are good reasons for keeping those boundaries in place. But I have learned that sometimes it is all right to ask for help. It's OK to tell a friend, "I feel dreadful right now. Do you have time to let me tell you about it?"

God didn't mean for us to carry our burdens alone.

PENNY ESTES WHEELER

OCTOBER 22

Suffering for Christ's Sake

Our struggle is not against flesh and blood, but against the rulers, against the authorities, against the powers of this dark world and against the spiritual forces of evil in the heavenly realms. Eph. 6:12, NIV.

ong day at school?" I asked my young daughter as she walked in the door. Her broken smile betrayed her weariness. "Pretty hard day, huh?" She nodded as her eyes filled up with tears. "What happened?" I asked, bracing myself for whatever was to come next.

"Mom," she said, "those boys keep bugging me."

"What did they do this time?" I asked.

Two weeks before, "those boys" had been teasing her about being "just like her mother." I didn't know what that was supposed to mean, but trying to be lighthearted about the whole thing and somehow ease her pain, I had jokingly said, "Well, is that really so terrible?"

"Oh, Mom!" she had giggled, and then together we both had had a good laugh.

Now "those boys" were at it again. This time they had gone too far! They had torn down my reputation in front of her and had made some false accusations against me. Not only that, they had said that I was a hypocrite because of the way I dress, etc. I was not really a "true" Christian, they had told my daughter.

"You didn't really do that, did you, Mom?" The pained look on her face mirrored my own expression. My heart sank. Then instantly anger boiled up inside me. Their words had caused her to doubt my integrity.

"O God," I silently screamed. "How can this be happening? We came to this church to work for You. I've poured my heart and soul into Your work, and this is the thanks I get!"

The next morning I angrily related the whole ugly incident to my pastor-husband as I sobbed bitterly in his arms. He patiently listened and tried his best to comfort me. Then suddenly, imitating a TV evangelist, he raised his arms up in the air and belted out, "Blessed are ye, when men shall revile you, and persecute you, and shall say all manner of evil against you falsely, for my sake. Rejoice, and be exceeding glad: for great is your reward in heaven: for so persecuted they the prophets which were before you" (Matt. 5:11, 12).

His words startled me and were such a surprise that my tears vanished into uncontrollable laughter. His laughter met mine and filled the room. We couldn't contain ourselves. Once again in the midst of tears and pain the Lord had used my spouse to turn my sorrow into joy (John 16:20).

We are called to suffer for Christ's sake, and it won't always be easy. But "rejoice, and be exceeding glad: for great is your reward in heaven"! KATHY JO DUTERROW YERGEN

The Obedient Ear

Whether you turn to the right or to the left, your ears will hear a voice behind you, saying, "This is the way; walk in it." Isa. 30:21, NIV.

I wish you could meet Shona Allie as she shimmers, bubbles, and brims over with the love of Christ. She grew up on the Cape Flats—that sandy, arid, dumping ground for communities dispossessed, uprooted, and fragmented by South Africa's infamous Group Areas Act. Like many others, she possessed little education, money, or hope.

Though raised a Christian, she married a Muslim and was an enthusiastic convert to that faith until she heard an imam preaching on Christ as a lesser prophet. Rising to her feet in the mosque, she declared the divinity of Christ to a stunned audience, and marched out, never to return. From that moment her life has been under His control, and she moves at His direction.

Walking in Cape Town one day in 1993, she was instructed to go to the luxurious Sun Hotel. Reluctant for several reasons, she nevertheless obeyed, and in the foyer found Muhammed Ali and a huge entourage. She walked up to him, and they exchanged names, hugs, addresses, and tracts—his on Christ as a prophet, hers on Christ as the Son of God.

Her special ministry stems from the time her son became involved with the gangs that infest most Cape Flats townships. Now painfully aware of the problems of the youngsters and their families, she began walking the streets at night, armed with her Bible and a huge faith.

"Aren't you afraid that we'll rape and kill you, mama?" gang members asked.

"No. Just listen to what Jesus says here, and you'll know why I'm not afraid of you," she would reply.

When a desperate mother appealed to her to visit her son in jail, she began a long career of prison visitation. Her work came to the attention of Raymond Ackerman, owner of the largest supermarket chain in the country. His support includes supplies of intercity bus tickets, and she is able to visit major jails in other cities, including death row in Pretoria. Her down-to-earth admonitions and liberal distribution of Bible correspondence school enlistment cards have led many men and women to the feet of the Saviour. It would take a book to chronicle all she has achieved.

She has no office, not even a home telephone. To facilitate her work, the church has granted her a special missionary license. But with or without earthly backing or credentials, Shona marches on, guided by the personal inner voice of the Holy Spirit. IVY PETERSEN

OCTOBER 24

Something "New"

Because of the Lord's great love we are not consumed, for his compassions never fail. They are new every morning; great is your faithfulness. Lam. 3:22, 23, NIV.

New"—the word carries with it exciting connotations: new toys at Christmas, a new car. "New" also suggests challenges, the unknown: a new job, a new relationship, a new season. Let's look together at how the Bible uses the adjective "new."

The most common use of "new" is in relation to "wine." "New wine" appears 44 times. In most cases, the new wine is one of a group of three items: wine, grain, and oil. Together, they represent the bounty promised by God to His people (Deut. 11:13-15 is an example). David could sing: "You have filled my heart with greater joy than when the grain and new wine abound" (Ps. 4:7). The prophet Joel prophesied of Israel's restoration: "In that day the mountains will drip new wine, and the hills will flow with milk; all the ravines of Judah will run with water" (Joel 3:18).

Yet, along with the promised blessing of new wine, comes the responsibility of recognizing the source of the bounties they received. Among Nehemiah's reforms was the payment of tithe of the new wine, grain, and oil—long forgotten by Israel (Neh. 10:37; 13:5). Thus God's people were to openly admit that the blessings came from God above.

Jesus spoke of "new wine"—He made it a symbol of His new teachings, which could not be put in old vessels. There could be no mixing of old anad new, of truth and error, of the divine and human tradition (Matt. 9:17, 18).

Another major use of the description "new" is in the phrase "new moon." The Scriptures mention the religious celebration 24 times. We have given up this special festivity, but Isaiah prophesied that worship on the New Moon day would be a part of God's creation (Isa. 66:23).

The phrase "new song" appears nine times in the Bible. The "new song" denotes a new experience, and the adoration evoked by that experience. The psalmist extols God for having heard his cry, for having delivered him "out of the slimy pit, out of the mud and mire," for giving him "a firm place to stand," and for putting "a new song" in his mouth (Ps. 40:3). All God's children are encouraged to proclaim God's salvation, to "sing to the Lord a new song" (Ps. 96:1, 2) "for he has done marvelous things (Ps. 98:1). In heaven, a "new song" celebrates the victory of the Lamb, who is worthy of adoration because by His death He redeemed human beings (Rev. 5:9). Only the redeemed, those purchased from among men, who follow the Lamb everywhere (Rev. 14:3-5), can learn this new song of praise.

Scripture repeatedly brings a new covenant to view. The prophet Jeremiah describes this covenant in chapter 31. Different from the old covenant, it will be in the hearts and minds of God's people. Forgiven, their sins will be remembered no more. They will become God's only possession. Jesus tells His disciples that the new covenant is His blood, spilled for them (Luke 22:20). In Hebrews we are told that Jesus is the mediator of the new covenant, that His death has set us free so that we may receive the promised inheritance (Heb. 9:15).

As part of the "new covenant" God promises a "new heart" and a "new spirit" (Eze. 18:3; 36:36)—a "new attitude of mind" (Eph. 4:23). The "new self" is "created to be like god in true righteousness and holiness" (verse 24). Buried to sin, resurrected with Christ, the Christian lives a "new life" (Rom. 6:4).

Along with this "new covenant" comes the "new command"—to love one another (John 13:34). The beloved disciple points out in his epistle that although Jesus called this command new, it is not really new. However, its implementation is the sign that God's kingdom has come (1 John 2:7, 8). The distinguishing mark of God's community is embedded in this command: "By this all men will know that you are my disciples, if you love one another" (John 13:35). By obeying the "new command" to love one another, Christians do away with divisions among themselves. The "new man" (Eph. 2:15) is reconciled to brothers and sisters, and to God. Hostility and separation are not part of the "new creation" (2 Cor. 5:17): "If anyone is in Christ, he is a new creation; the old has gone, the new has come!"

Yes, the word "new," as used in the Bible, speaks of God's love— not new at all, but existing from before Creation—which wants to create in each of us individually, and in us as a body, "something beautiful, something good"—something "new." God wants us to realize that He is in the business of the "new." "His compassions never fail. They are new every morning."   NANCY JEAN VYHMEISTER

A New Vision

Before they call, I will answer; and while they are still speaking,
I will hear. Isa. 65:24, NKJV.

I need a change!" My work was beginning to feel humdrum, and I wanted to do something to boost my energy level and spirit. A few former classmates, then teaching at a college in the Far East, invited me to visit Asia for a few weeks during the summer.

Things worked out quickly. I obtained my passports, visas, physical examinations, and specified injections. One month before my departure, though, my mission friends were transferred to a new location in a nearby country. They asked me if, instead of just visiting for the summer, I would consider going there to teach their children on a permanent basis. Almost immediately I answered yes. Because of my previous preparations, I completed the final arrangements in only a month.

School started with five children, which soon grew to seven. One of the fifth-grade boys could not read at all and was at the second-grade level in math. It looked as though he was having trouble seeing things on the page. Pulling from my prior teaching experience with dyslexic and learning-disabled children, I designed a special program for him. We were able to arrange for him to receive an eye examination—a difficult journey to the nearest city—and he obtained glasses. By the end of the school year he was able to complete three grades of reading and was experiencing success in most subjects.

At a parent-teacher conference his parents explained that they had been praying diligently for someone who could help their son. They felt that God had indeed answered their prayers—through me.

Stunned, I stared at them. I had gone there to help out some friends and find a change for my own life, but I was changing another person's instead. Before these parents called, God was already planning a solution for them. Although my agenda had been totally different, God had used me to answer someone else's prayer. He was using me to help others without my being aware of any part of the process.

As long as we are willing to be who God created us to be, and if we place our talents and lives in His hands, He can employ them to answer the prayers of others. Although you may never perceive it, you may be the answer to someone's prayer today. And every day.

LORNA LAWRENCE

OCTOBER 26

The "Undo" Feature

For God shall bring every work into judgment, with every secret thing, whether it be good, or whether it be evil. Eccl. 12:14.

*R*ecently I made a great discovery on my computer: the "undo" feature. With it I could easily edit out my misspellings and typographical errors with a single keystroke. I could delete all the wrong commands I had fed into the computer and replace them with the right ones. Everything could be corrected and come out perfect so that no one would ever see the flaws. The "undo" feature would work wonders!

I have often wished I had an "undo" feature in my life—that something I'd done could be completely blotted out as if it had never occurred. The wonderful truth we as Christians have is that we do have an "undo" feature. The blood of Jesus will erase and blot out all our transgressions. How thankful we should be for the wonderful sacrifice that our Saviour made. It is a priceless gift!   PAT MADSEN

OCTOBER 27

Bitter Sweets

But rejoice that you participate in the sufferings of Christ, so that you may be overjoyed when his glory is revealed. 1 Peter 4:13, NIV.

*I*have two kinds of chocolate in my house most of the time. One round container contains Hershey's candy kisses. I will eat them by the dozens if I can get to them before my children do. In another small brown box I keep Hershey's baking chocolate. The first ingredient to go into hot fudge sundaes, I use it in chocolate pie and in many other delicious treats. While it is the same chocolate, I never eat it straight from the box. Although it smells wonderful, it is bitter and horrible in taste. I never have to compete with the children for baking chocolate. Even they won't touch it!

Since the two kinds of chocolate are basically the same, what makes the difference? When I ask this, some people tell me, "The baking chocolate is bitter." That is true, but so is the chocolate in the candy kiss. The processing does not remove the bitterness. The difference is the addition of sugar, which covers up the bitterness and makes the kisses not only palatable but desirable.

Life can be like that. In this life we have many bitter experiences: the loss of a job, the loss of a good friend, a failing grade on an important exam. If we insist on taking life in its bitter form, we become bitter and unpleasant too. But God wants to add the sweetening to our lives that will make them palatable, even desirable. He will not protect us from all the unpleasant experiences, but He will use them along with other experiences to make our lives more beautiful and richer than we could imagine.　　KATHLEEN STAUBACH

OCTOBER 28

"Go, and Sin No More"

Woman, where are those thine accusers? hath no man condemned thee? She said, No man, Lord. And Jesus said unto her, Neither do I condemn thee: go, and sin no more. John 8:10, 11.

The woman of old who was taken in sin
Was brought before Jesus to see.
He pitied her human weakness,
And He longed to set her free.

Her accusers gathered around her,
Those who condemned in conceit,
They quickly left when seeing their sins
In the sand at Jesus' feet.

"Who now, is here to condemn thee?"
Christ's words fell on her ear.
"No man, Lord," she tremblingly said
As she knelt at His feet in fear.

"Go then, and sin no more,
For neither do I condemn you."
She heard His words in astonishment
And knew that they were true.

She lifted her eyes to Jesus,
Confessing her sins in bitter tears,

And steadfastly followed her Saviour
In devotion and love through the years.

Today Jesus longs to forgive us,
But we must do our part:
Confess and then forsake our sins
With a broken, contrite heart.

Sins forgiven, no condemnation, no guilt. How can it be? Jesus said it and He meant it—and it is ours. Believe it, accept it, and thank Him for it!   ELVA E. SPRINGER

Not My Load

Come unto me, all you that are weary and are carrying heavy burdens, and I will give you rest. Matt. 11:28, NRSV.

My TV paraded scenes of babies with matchstick limbs and swollen bellies, mute evidence of starvation. Little girls and boys, with tear-streaked faces, held out empty bowls and cups, pleading for something to eat. Teen and adult bodies lay strewn in alleys and streets, victims of violence. Their only guilt? They belonged to the wrong tribe or ethnic group or were in the wrong place at the wrong time. Such scenes haunted me.

I read many books and articles claiming to have an answer to the question racing round and round in my mind: "Why do innocent persons suffer?" I don't mind telling you that *all* the explanations made no sense to me. My prayers for understanding went unanswered until a recent morning.

Happy, my little schnauzer, and I walk for an hour while the day is fresh and beautiful. As we walk I talk to God. This particular morning I told Him again of my frustration and inability to understand, and how the answers given seemed like excuses, not reasons. I explained that I needed to know "why."

And then I heard Him. His voice was as soft as a gentle spring zephyr tugging at the corners of my mind. "My child, I can see this really perplexes you. Listen carefully, and I will tell you how it is.

"Your understanding is human, not divine. You can't comprehend everything. *But you don't have to understand!* All you need to do is know that I understand, then just trust Me."

In the awesome quiet that followed His message of love, a great peace washed the troubled thoughts away and left magnificent freedom and total joy!

BARBARA ROBERTS

OCTOBER 30

Lesson From a Pig

Justice and judgment are the habitation of thy throne: mercy and truth shall go before thy face. Ps. 89:14.

On our way home from a shopping trip, my husband suddenly remembered he had forgotten to purchase something. Parking the car on the side of the road, right near a garbage dump, he shouted over his shoulder that he would be back soon, then raced off. While I waited for him, a pile of garbage spilling over from its container caught my attention. In fact, there seemed to be more garbage around the container than in it. A huge pig with a number of piglets was scrounging for tidbits of food.

Every now and then one of the piglets would go near the mother and try to nurse. Each time, the mother hit the piglet hard with her snout, and the poor little thing, squealing in pain, hurriedly retreated. I felt sorry for the creatures and thought "mama pig" was very cruel indeed. After a while the mother pig lay down and grunted for the piglets to come for dinner. They all left what they were doing and made a beeline for mama and contentedly suckled until their stomachs were full. Looking at the piglets, I changed my mind about the cruel mother and realized that she was fair and wise. No little one was allowed to get undue advantage over the others. It amused me to think that an "abominable" animal like the pig could teach a Christian mother a lesson in justice and fair play!

BIROL C. CHRISTO

OCTOBER 31

Muddy Shoes and a Greeting

See! . . . The rains are over and gone. Flowers appear on the earth; the season of singing has come, the cooing of doves is heard in our land. S. of Sol. 2:11, 12, NIV.

*T*tiptoed out of the house, quietly closing the door behind me, planning to return before my family awakened. Carefully choosing where I stepped, I walked in the roadside weeds. The cool wetness of the tall grasses swished against my bare legs, sending shivers up them.

Raindrops clung to the grasses and shrubs, sparkling like diamonds in the early morning sunlight. The dazzling brightness reflected the colors of the rainbow. I couldn't resist expressing my appreciation in song. "How great Thou art," I sang.

An elderly man approached, clutching a small parcel close to him. Head down, he muttered to himself.

"Good morning!" I spoke.

Scowling, he snapped, "What is so good about this morning! And what are you so happy about?"

"Everything looks so clean and pretty after last night's rain," I responded.

The man briefly studied my face as though he questioned my sanity. Then his gaze shifted to his feet, and raising his right foot for my inspection, he complained bitterly, "Can't you see how muddy the road is? Why don't they fix this street, anyway?"

Suddenly a faint smile gradually eased the tension on the old man's face. "I guess you're right," he conceded. "Thanks, you just taught me a lesson. I'll remember that." The elderly man shuffled away, head up, and smiling.

How easy it is for us to get so caught up with our daily routines and annoyances that we fail to notice evidences of God's love all around us. Right now, pause or step outside. Notice the majesty of the trees. Listen to the singing birds. Admire the beautiful flowers. In even the most dismal city you will find some of His handiwork that He gave us to enjoy. Praise Him for it.   MABEL ROLLINS NORMAN

NOVEMBER 1

The Heart of the Matter

But store up for yourselves treasures in heaven. . . . For where your treasure is, there your heart will be also. Matt. 6:20, 21, NIV.

*T*he word *heart* evokes a wide range of emotions. Webster's dictionary has devoted a whole column of definitions to it. The English language contains all manner of coined expressions in relation to the importance of the heart in maintaining life:

"the heart of the matter," "well at heart," "have a heart," "all heart," "no heart."

My mother underwent open-heart surgery a few years ago. Hundreds of miles away we waited anxiously by the telephone for news of her condition. Finally it rang. After she had spent 10 hours in the operating room, her heart had started to beat again without the aid of the heart-lung pump. What a relief to hear that her *heart* was working again!

What is this heart that beats within each one of us? It pumps about 70 times a minute for as long as we live, or about 37 million beats every year. It can beat much faster if an emergency arises. Scientists still have not been able to construct an implantable "machine" that is as efficient as the heart itself.

One reason the heart can go on for years is that the muscle cells have brief, regular rest periods. While one section is contracting, the other is relaxing.

The efficiency of the heart depends upon the condition of its contracting muscles, as well as how well the valves are functioning. The heart muscle needs a regular supply of oxygen. Anything that damages the heart muscle, coronary arteries, or valves can result in decreased efficiency and eventual heart failure.

An old English saying declares, "Absence makes the heart grow fonder." While we can be close to God mentally and spiritually, we are physically absent from our heavenly Parent. Does the absence make *our* hearts grow fonder? Is God in our hearts and in our thinking so that we really yearn to be physically present with our heavenly Parent? Even as we sense each beat of our physical hearts, let us take heart in a spiritual way. Let us hold on to God in our hearts and in our minds. Let us yearn to be with our heavenly Father. And let us store up our treasure in heaven—because there our hearts will be also.

ARLENE TAYLOR

NOVEMBER 2

Best Foot Forward

My foot standeth in an even place: in the congregations will I bless the Lord. Ps. 26:12.

It was our first visit to the church in Port Alberni, British Columbia. Knowing that first impressions are often lasting ones, I dressed carefully, then glanced at my reflection in the mirror. I liked the way I looked in my new navy and white dress. Finally I slipped on navy blue shoes.

One step, and I knew something was wrong. They didn't feel right. I looked down to see a square toe on my right shoe and a pointed toe on the left one! Instantly I checked the heels. One was high, the other low. I started to walk across the room and burst out laughing. What a sight I'd make hobbling into church one side up and the other side down.

"At least they're not both for the same foot," my husband Ron laughed.

"Small comfort," I responded.

"Go barefoot," he suggested.

I gave him a hopeless look and called to my hostess. "Carol! Look what I did!"

She chuckled, then headed for her bedroom. "Let's see if anything I have fits." Nothing did.

"I'll go like this," I said bravely. "Maybe no one will notice." But I knew they would. What a first impression! Carol called up a friend. "Ann has a size 8," she said. "Think that would work?"

When we got to Ann's house, she had several pairs lined up for me to try. I put on a navy blue pair and took a few steps. "A little tissue in the toes, and they'll be perfect," I said. "Thanks, Ann, you've saved my day!"

A few minutes later I walked proudly onto the platform to give my talk, glad for the solid feel of balanced shoes on my feet. Thanks to Ann, I was able to put my best foot forward after all. (However, I'm sure the women of Port Alberni will remember me as "the preacher's wife who borrowed Anne's shoes.")

Occasionally life gets out of balance, and I feel as though I'm hobbling along on mismatched shoes. Sometimes I'm up and sometimes I'm down, and I make my ungraceful way along, doing the best I can, but knowing it's not good enough.

Then Jesus, my friend, offers to let me wear His "shoes." I accept His offer of love and stand on even ground once more. His "shoes"—His righteousness—is what it takes to stand solid, firm, and secure. In His "shoes" I can always put my best foot forward.

DOROTHY EATON WATTS

Don't Talk—Act!

If anyone has material possessions and sees his brother in need but has no pity on him, how can the love of God be in him? Dear children, let us not love with words or tongue but with actions and in truth. 1 John 3:17, 18, NIV.

Last fall my husband and I joined an evangelistic series in what used to be Stalingrad. Going into a provincial city in Russia felt like traveling backward in a time machine. Everything slowed way down. We were deeply affected by what the people in this nation have endured. Imagine spending your whole life standing in long lines for anything worth getting, and then often not obtaining it; putting up with erratic electricity and water supplies, or none at all; never even having a telephone, a washing machine, a car, or even a decent iron; or accepting menial jobs just to survive.

Our exposure to such raw human needs creates a paradigm shift in our values. Suddenly we see with new eyes. Our cozy mobile home looks like a lavish palace. Our second car has become an indulgence. Our bulging closets and drawers remind us that we have an adequate wardrobe for years to come. Even our granddaughters are deciding that instead of asking for yet another new doll, they'd like to send one to a Russian child.

"Don't talk—act!" John says, and he is right on. We've always given generously to the church, helped the missionaries, and tended the local needy at Thanksgiving and Christmas anyway. But these days we happily search for ways to save a little more here, a little extra there. This day-to-day involvement with human need brings God's love to life in a vivid and personal way. And that warm glow in our hearts, as we think of the joy and blessings our little "extra gifts" might provide, must be a glow straight from heaven!

AILEEN LUDINGTON

NOVEMBER 4

Under His Wings

Wondrously show thy steadfast love, O savior of those who

seek refuge from their adversaries at thy right hand. Keep me as the apple of the eye; hide me in the shadow of thy wings. Ps. 17:7, 8, RSV.

*I*t had been a hard day at work—many needs, little time, troublesome experiences. When I got home, the evening news wasn't any better: trade wars, political wars, religious wars, drug wars, and more. The commotion of the holiday season loomed before me. I also had house guests arriving in a few days.

Too tired to think, read, or do anything, I decided to worry later and went to bed early. During the middle of the night, sounds of a storm outside wakened me. *That fits*, I thought as I turned over and pulled the covers a bit higher. But sleep was elusive. Yesterday's events marched across my mind only to be interrupted by plans for the day ahead.

Then from somewhere in the deep recesses of my memory came a very old song, one I had often heard as a child. In my mind I sang it and felt better. In case you may be feeling buffeted about today, I'm sharing it with you. If it's familiar to you, I invite you to sing it aloud. If it's not, enjoy the words.

"Under His wings I am safely abiding;
Though the night deepens and tempests are wild,
Still I can trust Him; I know He will keep me;
He has redeemed me, and I am His child.

"Under His wings, under His wings,
Who from His love can sever?
Under His wings my soul shall abide,
Safely abide forever."   BEULAH FERN STEVENS

NOVEMBER 5

God Needs Love Too

We love Him because He first loved us. 1 John 4:19, NKJV.

*T*hrough the years I've often heard of God's love for me, and the concept that I would love Him in return seemed a logical response. But it never crossed my mind that the One who has everything could really need *my* imperfect gift of love. Only through the maturity of years and the varied circumstances of life have I really appreciated the positive impact that appreciation, kind words, and expressions of love and support can have.

Because I want to become more comfortable in receiving and giv-ing love, I practice a mental visualization in the morning that helps to make Jesus the close, personal friend I desire Him to be. I imagine going with God to one of my favorite sites of nature. As we converse I share my concerns, successes, and failures. He listens, encourages, and supports me with a warm hug, a bit of advice, or the mere strength of His presence. We have walked arm in arm through pine-scented forests, splashed in the ocean waves as they broke around our feet, or felt the cool breeze on our faces as we cycled on a country lane. Sometimes I invite someone else along on our excursions, some-one I know needs to have Jesus especially near at that particular time. We share the moment, passing the love along, leaving ourselves in God's care, and together thanking the Lord for our friendship.

"When my life gets busy and the world is crowding in,
I'm thankful for the times of quietness
When I talk to You, Lord, and listen for Your voice.
Grateful praise to You I must express.
You thought of me, Lord, I was in your plan.
Thanks for accepting me the way I am.
You will supply all my need.
By Your Spirit You will lead.
Take my life today.
Thanks for loving me.

"Then I hear Him gently say, 'I'm glad you took the time
To read My word and talk to Me in prayer.
When we walk together, I'll keep you in my love.
Believe the promise of My special care.
I thought of you, child; you were in My plan.
Loving, accepting is the way I am.
I will supply all your need.
By My Spirit I will lead.
I gave My life for you.
Thanks for loving Me.'"

DEBBY GRAY WILMOT

NOVEMBER 6

Reflections on Failure

Commit everything you do to the Lord. Trust him to help you do it and he will. Ps. 37:5, TLB.

*A*s a child I was terrified of failure. I attended the elementary school next to the University of Colorado in Boulder. All the smart kids went there: kids who had parents who were university professors, nuclear scientists, published authors, or mathematicians from the nearby Bureau of Standards. They talked about things I had never heard of before and seemed so much smarter than me.

I remember in second grade my teacher announcing that if *all* of us got perfect scores on the spelling test each Friday, she would give us each a lollipop. That meant if I missed one word, I would keep the entire class from being rewarded. The pressure caused me to become physically ill. For weeks I threw up every morning before leaving home, and my last words to Mom were, "How do you spell . . . ?"

In third grade I just couldn't seem to understand long division, but was far too shy to admit it by asking a question in class. Instead, I'd go home and ask Mom. But when the teacher announced a quiz later that day, I stayed in the restroom the entire recess period waiting for my cousin Sharon, who was in another class, to come in so I could ask her how to do long division.

During my fifth grade the teacher would go down one row and up the next, asking each student to stand and read aloud to the class. I feared this more than anything I had ever experienced in my life. As my turn came closer, I began to count which paragraph would be mine so I could read it to myself first. By the time it was my turn, my palms had turned sweaty, my voice shook, and I could hardly focus my eyes. One day as I began to read I came to the word "where," and my mind went blank. I stumbled and stammered and finally ended up crying.

I've failed many times since elementary school, but I've also learned a few things. First, the fear of failure is usually worse than the real thing. Second, when you feel like a failure, you're often the only one who sees it that way.

I've also learned that failure is only failure if you believe it's failure. And it helps to have family and friends stick by you through the tough times—in fact, the more emotional support, the better. Words of encouragement help to change perceived failure into the belief that the experience is merely a stepping-stone to success. We all need to hear words like: "I am sure that God who began the good work within you will keep right on helping you grow in his grace until his task within you is finally finished on that day when Jesus Christ returns" (Phil. 1:6, TLB).   KAY KUZMA

To Love You

Love does no harm to its neighbor. Therefore love is the fulfillment of the law. Rom. 13:10, NIV.

*S*queak! *Squeak! Squeak!* Someone's little joggers crossed the
floor outside my bathroom.

"Who's there?" I asked absently, checking the time.

"Yo," answered my 3-year-old in Spanish, the language we still
used most with the four children who'd joined our missionary home
the year before. I didn't reply or turn from the mirror as I hurriedly
brushed my hair. Loysi would express her need without prompting.
Besides, I was busy reminding myself that she was far from ready to
leave for church.

"I'm here," declared Loysi from two steps behind me.

"Ah," I answered, "and why are you here?"

Her matter-of-fact answer bounced back. "To love you."

All my concern and rush disappeared. I found myself in the typical jungle squat I'd used during our children's first days with us. My
arms enveloped the little tyke, as she'd known they would. We both
luxuriated in the happiness of our mutual love—love first given in
the midst of crisis and struggle, now freely returned.

She made me an instant and intensely pleasurable memory that
day—one I'll treasure always.

With that memory comes a question: How often have I heard
another Voice two steps behind me saying, "I'm here"?

When in my worry and hurry I have heard and responded, "Ah,
and why are You here?" Christ's answer has come back in ever different ways. Each tells me, "To love you."

Soon, not just in imagination, but in eternal reality, I plan to
step up beside His throne and say softly, "I'm here."

His response, filled with the pleasure of anticipation, will be,
"Ah, and why are you here?"

I'll say, "To love You."

PAMELA BAUMGARTNER

Taught by a Bird

He shall cover thee with his feathers, and under his wings shalt thou trust. Ps. 91:4.

*B*aby quail this time of year?" My husband, Erling, looked in the direction I was silently pointing. A father California quail, black plume bobbing jauntily above his head, pranced down the concrete gutter of the roadway before us, leading nine tiny babies of yellow fluff. Behind them came Mrs. Quail, her stubby black bill poised gracefully above a brown breast speckled with white.

When father and mother quail spotted us, they quickly ran across the road, hopped up the six-inch curb, crossed the sidewalk, and disappeared into the brush growing on a vacant lot. Nine little babies tried to follow.

"Kyuu, kyuu, kyuu," called mother quail, which probably meant "Come, come, come" in quail language.

The babies, try as they would, just couldn't make it to the top of that curb. Their little legs were just too small, and their little wings were not big enough to help them.

"Kyuu, kyuu, kyuu," mother quail kept calling from the bushes. Father quail added his "Chee, chee, chee." Again the baby quail tried with all their might to follow their parents.

I walked over to help the babies. They scattered and ran down the road farther from their parents. "Don't run away," I said gently. "I just want to help you." But they raced faster.

"Leave them alone," Erling said. "They don't know you want to help them. They're afraid of you." Then he added, "Let's walk farther down the hill away from the babies." We quietly backed away. The babies turned and headed up the hill toward their parents. Mother quail came out of the brush, hopped down into the gutter, and gathered her babies under her wings. The "peep, peeps" of distress immediately changed to "peep, peeps" of contentment.

Erling walked slowly and quietly toward them. The mother ran up the hill in short spurts, followed by her brood. About a hundred feet up the street was a driveway. Mrs. Quail and her little babies raced up the drive, across the sidewalk, and into the brush. They were now all together in the safety of their refuge.

I thought about how much more God loves us. He will calm our fears and keep us safe under His wings if we will only trust and follow Him as the baby quail followed their parents. ELLIE LUKENS CALKINS

NOVEMBER 9

"Señora, Culebra!"

Trust in the Lord with all your heart, and lean not on your own understanding; in all your ways acknowledge Him, and He shall direct your paths. Prov. 3:5, 6, NKJV.

We were working at the Nevati Mission Station in the Amazon. It was the last week of July. July 28, Peru's Day of Independence, was the most exciting part of our year. Teachers brought people from schools and villages near and far for camp meeting, teachers' meetings, and a big fiesta.

This year had a sad addition. Measles broke out in a group of about 27 very primitive Campa Indians. They had moved onto the Nevati Reservation, a distance from the main village, where they could observe and decide if they wanted to become Christians. Measles can be extremely deadly for these people.

Juan, our translator, accompanied me daily as we took food and medicines to the group and directed the care of their sick. Because of the meetings, one day Juan could not accompany me. Maria, the wife of a teacher from a faraway school, spoke Spanish and Campa. She offered to go with me.

A big problem was that she did not know the trail, leaving me to "break trail" without that marvelously trained eye of the native. As I stepped down over a tree root, I heard the movement of something hurrying away in the fallen leaves along the path simultaneously with Maria's cry, *"Señora, culebra!"* I turned to see a very pale companion. She explained that it was a poisonous snake coiled exactly where I had stepped down and that my dress had flipped onto the snake. Instead of striking, it had fled.

Since I could not take antivenins, I went on the small path only when I was needed. Then I depended on God, who had sent me there to care for others, to protect me. In a miraculous way, He did!

It is good to contemplate God's care for us in the past and to renew our gratitude to Him and our faith in His protection. God is constantly at our side.   WALOMA BENNETT FEHRENBACH

China

And the Lord said unto me, Behold, I have put my words in thy mouth. Jer. 1:9.

T was halfway around the world. The city was Chongqing, in the country of China—the land that had been behind a bamboo curtain for so long.

World trade is the predominate thing in China now. Because English is essential for businesspeople to know, American teachers are in demand.

There were four of us in Chongqing. We knew the Lord had sent us to be ambassadors in this atheistic country, but how would our students respond to us? The first day of school arrived, and we had feelings of trepidation and concern. Would the students be happy to see us as we had been told, or would they resent Americans as people do in many parts of the world? We did not know.

Before going to breakfast in the university guest dining room, I opened my Bible for some encouraging words from the Lord. My joy knew no bounds when I read the first chapter of Jeremiah. Verses 7 and 8 say, "Whatsoever I command thee thou shalt speak. Be not afraid of their faces: for I am with thee to deliver thee, saith the Lord."

How gracious of the Lord to send those verses to me just when I needed them. It was easy to stand before 25 glowing, vibrant, intelligent university students the next morning when I knew the Lord would give me words to say. All year I saw black hair and black eyes, but I forgot they were Chinese and I was American.

Part of the class was spent just letting them listen to an American speak. They had only heard Chinese teachers, and some of them didn't speak English at all; they taught only grammar and writing. It was amazing the variety of subjects I found myself talking about. God truly did give me words to say.   VERNA WHITE

NOVEMBER 11

Loving Arms

And he took them up in his arms. Mark 10:16.

*W*hat a friend we have in Jesus,
        All our sins and griefs to bear."
        Softly Brian Costa sang in the background. Someone had put my husband's favorite tape on before I got there. I set it to repeat continuously and sat down to spend the last hours of my husband's life with him.

Around 6:00 p.m. our middle child and his wife came. Tearfully they said their last goodbye and left at 8:00. About 9:00 our older son, our daughter, and her children came from the airport. We sat quietly listening to my husband's even, labored breathing. Every two hours his faithful nursing assistant would come and tend to him. At 1:00 a.m. our daughter and her children went home. Finally, at 2:00 a.m. our son left for some much-needed rest, and I was alone with my husband. It was the first peaceful night I had spent with him in years. Before his final two years in nursing homes, his Alzheimer's disease had made nights anything but peaceful.

> *"Can we find a friend so faithful,*
> *Who will all our sorrows share?"*

The clock on the wall marked off the minutes. My husband's eyes jerked from side to side, stopping occasionally to focus on my face. Memories of 44 years together flooded my mind. I quietly shared some of the memories. Some brought tears to my eyes, but it was the happy times that stood out. They lasted to the very end. Even when he could do nothing for himself because of the Parkinson's disease, he retained his sense of humor and would laugh with the abandonment of a child.

I sat repeating Bible passages and talking softly to my husband about a better time to come when his sick brain would be well and we would be together again. With us would be Jesus, our special friend throughout our marriage. I sang along with the tape as it came again to that special song. As I sang I felt the warmth of the loving arms of Jesus around me.

Daylight came. The sky was overcast. No beautiful sunrise greeted us. But someday . . .

Suddenly, it was over. My husband took his last breath. I kissed him goodbye, then turned off the tape player. It would be a long, lonely life ahead. Through the window I watched my son drive up. He walked into the room, and I fell into his strong, loving arms.

> *"In His arms He'll take and shield thee,*
> *Thou wilt find a solace there."*

IVADEL PETERSON

Gifts From God

Every good gift and every perfect gift is from above. James 1:17.

S ometimes God gives us unusual "gifts." The key is to see whatever the Lord gives us as a gift from Him for us that we can use in His service or to glorify Him with. Such is the case with our special son Matthew, our "gift from God."

My husband and I are the parents of four boys ages 6 to 13. Life at our home has always been busy and noisy. To complicate matters, having a child with special needs is a never-ending challenge. It is something that I feel my husband and I, as well as the children, have dealt with in our own lives fairly well. But the daily reminders and challenges are sometimes overwhelming: how to put a 7-year-old in preschool, getting one of our schools to allow him to attend, making arrangements so that he can go on field trips, helping him to partic-ipate with his classmates and be accepted by them for who he is.

We have learned to take things a little slower, to have a wide va-riety of expectations, and to enjoy whatever we can accomplish. We have also learned what an impact this has on life. I know of many people who have said to me what a special effect Matthew has had on their lives or on their children.

Matthew is a child who loves God, and when he was baptized two years ago, it was a big decision for us. We questioned his young age. Yet in talking with his teachers, pastor, and grandparents, we came to the conclusion that it was the right time for him. It was a special event in our lives. His grandfather, who had baptized me and performed our wedding ceremony as well as the dedication of our four boys, baptized Matthew. I know of one of my son's peers who was so affected that he too asked for baptism.

Yes, life as a family with a person with a disability in it is more complicated. But it has rewards that only a loving heavenly Father could give. We are thankful for our gift of Matthew.

CARLENE R. WILL

Help for Tightrope Walkers

The eternal God is your refuge, and underneath are the everlasting arms. Deut. 33:27, NKJV.

*O*n a sunny October day the members of the graduate class I attended at Western Michigan University went on a field trip to Pretty Lake Adventure Camp. Most of us were apprehensive, having no idea what would happen. After we filled out a medical information sheet, complete with the name of the person to contact should we be injured or killed and the name of our medical insurance carrier, we *really* wondered why we had come.

Our facilitator then took us to the first activity. Twin thick wire cables hung suspended about two feet from the forest floor. Two people at a time were supposed to walk the cables and keep in constant physical contact. That wouldn't be hard at the beginning, but in the middle of the course the wires spread far apart. There were also two trees between the cables. At those trees, the couple would have to release hands one at a time and support and balance each other with the other hand. Each of the two participants had five support people on the ground who constantly stayed within two inches of their bodies to catch them if they started to fall.

Several times I functioned as a support person. Support people gave not only a feeling of physical safety, but verbal encouragement and directions along the way. They could see the angle of lean in the couples' bodies and encourage them to lift their hands up or down to increase their stability. We said things like, "You're doing it!" "You can make it!" "That's right, great!" The support people were almost as elated as the couple who finished the course.

I couldn't help thinking that's what God wants the church to be—people supporting each other verbally and physically along the hard challenging places of life. Because I had my support group around me as I walked the tightrope, I could concentrate on my relationship to my partner on the other cable. I could focus on the task I had to accomplish. Arms waited to catch me if I fell, and voices would encourage me if I faltered. Ideally, that is the church. *Always* that is God, for "underneath are the everlasting arms."   ALBERTA HACK

Thank You, God, That I Am Poor

Be satisfied with what you have. Heb. 13:5, TEV.

*H*ave you ever thanked God that you are poor? I must admit that the concept was new to me until my 10-year-old son wrote a prayer.

The children in his class at school had been given a little exercise that required them to think of things for which they could thank God. You can imagine the responses. Some thanked God for food, some for their bicycles, some for rollerblades and other toys. They obviously had much for which to be thankful!

As an extension of their ideas, they were then asked to write their prayer in the form of a letter to God. The teacher shared my son's with me. It went something like this:

Dear God:
I thank You that we are poor, because if we were rich,
my mother wouldn't spend so much time with me.
Yours faithfully,
Lynden

Like any mother, I shed a private tear when I read his prayer. I had been given one of those rare glimpses into the hidden, uncomplicated thoughts of a child.

"Thank You, God, that I am poor." I had never interpreted lack of material wealth in quite that light. Instead, I have complained because the budget didn't stretch quite as far as my need. Or I have become anxious because I couldn't afford a new pair of shoes for my daughter or a new bicycle for my son's birthday. I have worried away precious hours of time by focusing on the things I haven't got.

How incredible that a child should have the insight to show me how rich I really am. God has not given me things. He has given me time. He has given me people to love. He has given me memories—a source of wealth that can never be taken away. He has given me love that is unconditional and that never ends. And He has shared with me a new view of life through the eyes of a child.

Dear God, I thank You for all that is beautiful in my life and all that can become beautiful. Help me to be satisfied with what I have. I thank You that I am "poor." ADELLE ROCHFORD

When Days Are Terrible

Cast all your anxiety on him because he cares for you. 1 Peter 5:7, NIV.

I was in a bookstore once and saw in the children's section a book entitled *Alexander and the Terrible, Horrible, No Good, Very Bad Day*. I felt like I was having a day like that, so I picked up the book and started reading. That poor kid! Everything that could possibly go wrong did, and on top of everything else, he got in trouble. "I think I'll move to Australia," he kept saying.

I can relate. I've had some really, really awful days that have stretched into weeks. And it was during one of these bad days that I finally had enough and started complaining to the Lord about it. I was so frustrated, worried, and angry that I asked Him, "What did I do wrong? Don't You love me anymore? If You love me, then why do I feel so bad?" Boy, was I feeling sorry for myself!

Calling a friend, I tried to drag her into the misery. She finally said, "Why don't you get some exercise or something and pull yourself out of this thing?" Good suggestion. So I went for a walk. During it the Lord tenderly spoke to my heart in spite of my bad mood.

I passed by a small pond in which ducks were swimming and bobbing upside down for food. Busy little squirrels scurried among the tall trees at the side of the path, shaking their bushy tails behind them. Birds sang melodiously overhead, and a cool, gentle breeze brushed past my face as I stood gazing at a brilliant sunset that tinted softly floating clouds with shades of crimson and violet. Suddenly I felt ashamed of myself as the warmth of the Holy Spirit glowed in my heart, and I came to the realization that I was surrounded by the evidence of God's love for me. All I had to do was open my eyes and look at it.

I asked the Lord to forgive me for my complaining. Why hadn't I come to Him before I became so frustrated? Why hadn't I shared every little disappointment with Him before they all piled up into one huge seemingly insurmountable problem? And I purposed in my heart that I would no longer allow my circumstances to discourage me, for I was surrounded by the love of God. Wouldn't you know, the situation turned around a few days later. What a difference attitude makes! As the song says: "Why worry when you can pray?"

The next time I start to have a "terrible, horrible, no good, very bad day," rather than moving to Australia, I'm going to go and talk to Jesus right away. And I'm going to let Him love me right out of it. HEARTSONG

Another Answered Prayer

And all things, whatsoever ye shall ask in prayer believing, ye shall receive. Matt. 21:22.

We had purchased tickets for a musical program. The proceeds were for a certain charity. Although we really couldn't afford to go, the program was supposed to be good and the charity a worthy one. Going to a public concert was a rare treat. All during the week the children were excited.

On Sunday morning I looked for the tickets in the place where I had put them, but I was surprised when they were not there. I asked the children if they had seen the tickets. We searched frantically for them in every place we could think of. If the missing tickets did not turn up, we couldn't attend the program. The children and I were upset.

As I continued looking through the morning, I remembered that we hadn't asked God to help us find the tickets. I called the children together and said, "Let us ask God to show us where the tickets are." We quietly knelt and earnestly asked our heavenly Father to help us as we continued our search.

As I stood up, a voice told me to go and look for the tickets where we threw our garbage. Being careful that no one was watching me, I went alone and poked around the dumpster among the papers and kitchen leftovers. And there, almost on top of the pile, I saw the unsoiled tickets. It was as if someone had carefully laid them on top of the garbage.

Running home, I excitedly told the children that God had answered our prayer and that we could go to the program after all. We knelt together again and thanked God for sending His angels to go through a pile of rubbish and locate our tickets. I have discovered that God loves to surprise us by answering prayers that don't seem very important!   BIROL C. CHRISTO

A Merry Heart

A merry heart doeth good like a medicine. Prov. 17:22.

*A*s I finished reading a story to my 3-year-old daughter, she looked up at me with a big smile on her face and said, "Mama, let's just sit here a while and laugh." Her suggestion caught me by surprise. Sit and laugh? About what, I wondered. I had a mountain of work waiting to be done. On second thought, however, I decided to stay with my daughter and have a chuckle. Surely we could find *something* to laugh about!

As I've spent more time laughing lately, the words of Gladys Taber come often to mind: "The truly happy person is one who realizes the happiness of that moment, or that hour."

Perhaps you've seen the bumper sticker that asks: "Have you had a good laugh today?" Even the medical world is realizing the healing significance of humor. A nurse friend of mine serves on a "humor committee" at her hospital. Their purpose is to brighten the lives of both patients and hospital personnel through the use of appropriate humor.

A popular song tells us not to worry, but to be happy. Despite the many disasters occurring in this world, we really do have much to be happy about, because we know that God is in control. That is not to say that we shouldn't do what we can to relieve suffering and discomfort, but we shouldn't worry about situations because God really is in ultimate control of them.

If we truly trust God, we won't worry our lives away. We will take instead the good medicine of a merry and thankful heart. "The most wasted of all days," says Sebastien Chamfort, "is that in which we have not laughed." So how about it? Would you care to join me for a good and healthy laugh?   BRENDA FORBES DICKERSON

NOVEMBER 18

Refocusing

"Then neither do I condemn you." . . . "Go now and leave your life of sin." John 8:11, NIV.

*R*ough hands grabbed her. The voices, so hushed, hurried, and evil, were triumphant. The plot had been successful. The sunlight and the eyes of the plotters, the crowd, and of Jesus hit her simultaneously. She shrank from being the center of attention.

One shove placed her within touching distance of Jesus.

Somehow she managed to focus on the spokesman as he declared menacingly, "Teacher, this woman was caught in adultery, in the very act . . ."

She needed to hear no more. In an attempt to endure the last remaining elements of her life, she reveled in inward anger. "Where is he who seduced me? Why was he not called to suffer the consequences of his action? Will someone see the whole picture and stand up for me?"

Then she snapped back to reality. Women did not count in her world!

Adrenaline poured through her. She expected to hear "Guilty," but instead Jesus answered, "'Then neither do I condemn you.' . . . 'Go now and leave your life of sin.'"

Did she really hear this? Relief rushed through her as she realized that her accusers had dispersed. The Saviour's own words publicly declared He did not condemn her. Instead, He admonished her to leave her sinful way of life.

Was Jesus addressing only the sin of adultery? It seems unlikely, as this was a trap set for Him. It is conceivable that Jesus was also referring to the kind of obsession in which our focus becomes fixed on our emotional pain. Often such self-focus creates a mental state of helplessness, rendering a potentially creative individual impotent and helpless.

It's possible that Jesus recognized that problem in the woman caught in adultery. As this victim focused on her feelings, she saw herself as of no value to her family, her society, or her God. And as she lived out her self-image, she became prey to lustful, selfish men.

I can imagine Jesus saying, "Go, My daughter, and stop focusing on your pain. Focus on what I can do and have done for you. Focus on My gift of love, on My forgiveness. The more you focus on My power, the smaller your emotional problems will become. I will personally show you My love. I will fill your mind with joy and peace and forgiveness so that your scars will be healed. You were too weak to come to Me of yourself, but circumstances forced you here. Doesn't My Father work in mysterious ways? Go now, My child, and leave your life of sin." NORMA JEAN PARCHMENT

God Cares

How excellent is thy lovingkindness, O God! Ps. 36:7.

*I*t would be a long drive to my school reunion, and I didn't relish the thought of driving alone. However, the desire to see family and friends took precedence, and I was soon on my way.

When I drive alone I frequently talk to God about my concerns, my joys, and my sorrows. This day as I drove through the spectacular Columbia River Gorge, I thanked Him for the beauty that surrounded me. Majestic mountains, cascading waterfalls, and the mighty Columbia wending its way to sea.

Then came the "why" questions. "Lord, why didn't You heal my husband? Why did he have to suffer so long? Why have You closed the doors I wanted so much to be opened? Why didn't You work some miracles for me?" The "whys" kept tumbling over each other until I remembered the birds.

Longing to have goldfinches share my backyard, I bought a special feeder, filled it with thistle seed, and hung it where it could be seen easily from my kitchen window.

Day after day I watched and waited for the little birds to arrive. "Just be patient, and they will find you," friends told me. More than two months passed, and still no goldfinches. It seemed hopeless! They just weren't going to find me!

One morning, noting the still-empty feeder, I prayed, "Lord, You know how much I want some goldfinches. Please, please send me some."

Later that same week, as usual, I peered out the window. I could scarcely believe my eyes! In the feeder, enjoying a thistle breakfast, were some long awaited goldfinches. I danced for joy and could hardly wait to share the exciting news with my daughter. There it was! A miracle of God's love and care just for me.

Tears blurred my vision as I pondered the past 14 years. I realized God had been working miracles for me all along the way. He gave me loving friends and family who had never ceased praying for us during my husband's ghastly 12-year illness. I remembered miracles of financial and physical help just when it was needed most. The list was endless.

Sometimes God's answer to our petitions is no, because in His great wisdom He knows what is best for us. One day He will answer all the "why" questions, and we will be satisfied.   RUTH WALL

The Attitude of Gratitude

Were there not ten cleansed? But where are the nine? Luke 17:17, NKJV.

*O*ne of my earliest recollections is skipping happily and repeating the memory verse for the next week all day one Sunday. Musical and rhythmic then, it has definitely grown poetic now: "Were there not ten cleansed? But where are the nine?" (Luke 17:17). The lesson my mother taught during that week and that my primary class teacher later reinforced during the lesson study was that of being grateful. She stressed the importance of saying "Thank you."

Benefactors, philanthropists, and persons of otherwise generous means invariably react in negative ways to an ingrate. Parents, foster parents, and extended family members carry emotional scars to their graves because of the ingratitude of children who disrespected them.

Teachers, social workers, medical practitioners—all those who give of themselves daily—will readily testify that a genuine expression of thanks gives them a lift of spirit that no paycheck can ever achieve.

Jesus highly commended the attitude of thankfulness. I like to call it "the attitude of gratitude." He called attention to the single man out of 10 healed of the dreaded disease, leprosy, who returned to say thanks. Of greatest significance is the man's nationality. The Bible says he was a Samaritan. He belonged to a race generally ostracized by the Jews.

Because of my involvement in Community Services and my experience as a teacher and principal, I have often met the "Samaritans"—those whose activities and lifestyle definitely go against the norm. Such persons, however, have always expressed and demonstrated great appreciation and "returned" to give thanks when they had some great need met or their children did well in exams or they achieved something that gained them recognition. Most people, however, take the attitude "After all, that is what you are paid to do."

Each day provides us with opportunities to say thanks. We receive innumerable blessings. Among those we should be grateful for are:

Relatives, for concern most true,
Friends of long standing and those new,
Colleagues whose experiences we share,
And neighbors who are always there.

We should also remember
To give thanks for blessings we sang of as children,
For health and strength and loving care
And all that makes the day so fair.

This world would indeed be a better place
If each of us could be persuaded
To adapt such an attitude,
That our lives may be pervaded
By a sense of gratitude.

Thank God, I say, for the "Samaritans." They make my day. May you and I endeavor always to take a leaf out of the Book of the Samaritans.

SUDLYN ELDER

NOVEMBER 21

The Miracle Plant

Have mercy upon me, O Lord; consider my trouble which I suffer. Ps. 9:13.

To try to cheer my husband, who was confined to a bed in the hospital, I bought a small gloxinia plant for him. It had two small red velvet blooms on it. The color was fascinating, and the price was right—only $3. It was pretty, and he enjoyed it even if it was small!

Later when Everett could leave, we brought the plant home. Soon the few blooms dropped off, and we put it aside. Occasionally I watered it, not knowing whether it would ever bloom again. Then one day we saw buds ready to flower. Perhaps it had four or five bright blooms. We enjoyed them.

Surely this would be the end of the small plant. But a few weeks went by, and we discovered a good amount of buds again. This time we delighted in seven or eight flowers. It was winter, and the scarlet blooms brightened our hearts as my husband and I suffered together over his serious illness. Was the Lord trying to bring comfort to us through the plant kingdom? We were most appreciative.

More time went by, and I scanned the leaves to see more buds starting. Could it be that it would blossom again? Yes, indeed! This time we counted 14 flowers on it. In fact, the blooms were so thick they could scarcely find room to open.

How we praised Him who had spoken words of joy to us through

His creative power. We who had so little happiness at the time had something to be joyful about! He surely knew how we both loved flowers and perhaps chose to speak to us in this unique manner.

The Bible declares, "So then neither is he that planteth any thing, neither he that watereth; but God that giveth the increase" (1 Cor. 3:7). We had witnessed a fulfilling of this verse as we had been blessed by our small, blooming gloxinia. JEANNE CALKINS

NOVEMBER 22

Hope for the Depressed

Why are you downcast, O my soul? Why so disturbed within me? Put your hope in God, for I will yet praise him, my Savior and my God! Ps. 42:5, NIV.

I grew up believing that Christians are always cheerful, that it is a sin to feel discouraged. So whenever black feelings overwhelmed me, I simply convinced myself that I did not feel that way and forced myself to appear cheerful and act as if nothing was wrong.

I guess I must have been a pretty good actress, because for years I fooled myself, as well as everybody else. Even today I suspect that all but two or three of my closest friends would be totally amazed to learn that I have a problem with depression. My husband of 37 years, who should know me pretty well by now, still finds it hard to believe. But then, he's one of those cheerful, optimistic persons who always sees the bright side.

Eventually, I reached the point where my depression became so severe that I could no longer ignore it. By pretending I did not have such feelings, I had only been making the situation worse. I began to understand that not only do I have the type of temperament that sees risks and dangers with great clarity and finds it difficult to be lighthearted and optimistic but I also have a heredity of depression. As I learned to acknowledge and cope with it, I gradually gained a new perspective on feelings of sadness and discouragement. I came to realize that the Bible does not condemn or deny the existence of sorrow.

For the first time I really identified with those psalms of David that nakedly display his pain and distress. "I am worn out from groaning; all night long I flood my bed with weeping and drench my couch with tears" (Ps. 6:6, NIV). For the first time I really noticed those verses that show God as a loving Father who understands our grief and promises comfort. Isaiah prophesied that God would send His Son "to bind up the brokenhearted, . . . to comfort all who mourn" (Isa. 61:1, 2, NIV). And Jesus Himself said, "Blessed are those who mourn, for they will be comforted" (Matt. 5:4, NIV).

God does not accuse me of sin when I am sad and become discouraged. It is because He loves me and wants to help me that He encourages me to count my blessings and not to dwell on negative thoughts. But when I find this difficult to do, He understands. He is, after all, "a man of sorrows and acquainted with grief" (Isa. 53:3, NKJV). With Him I can feel safe expressing my true feelings, no matter how dismal they may be. But first I must admit that I hurt before I am willing to go to Him for healing.　　CARROL GRADY

Entertaining Angels

Do not forget to entertain strangers, for by so doing some people have entertained angels without knowing it. Heb. 13:2, NIV.

Four of us bustled around in Mother's kitchen—Pat, a teenager who had just joined the church partly because of my mother's friendship and careful nurturing; Louise, another young girl who had stepped out alone to find fellowship with the church; Dovie, a church school teacher who lived with my parents; and me.

It was another of my mother's special get-acquainted meals. She had invited four single senior women in the church home for dinner. Mother found some of her greatest happiness in entertaining, especially those who could never return the favor. We had left church immediately to rush home and help with the last-minute preparations for the sumptuous meal mother had prepared.

The dining room was festive. Crystal candlesticks flanked a colorful bouquet of flowers from the garden. The artistic place settings, the maple ladder-back chairs, and the maple-framed picture on the wall gave a homey aura of warmth and caring. That day the picture held special significance. It depicted a medieval family preparing to sit down around a humble table. It included one extra chair for the "unseen guest."

"Donna, get another place setting on the table, quickly!" Dovie urged as she gazed out the dining room window at mother's car disgorging its passengers. "Your mother has evidently invited a man I don't recognize to join us. He's standing by the back of her car."

Louise also peered through the corner window that looked out on the street. She too was excited about the kindly man holding the door open for the women. I was busy gathering up the necessary place setting. At the same time I was wondering who this unexpected guest might be.

As Mother and the women walked through the front door, Dovie asked, "Where is the gentleman you brought with you?"

"Gentleman?" Mother queried. "There was no gentleman with us."

"But I saw him, and so did Louise!" Dovie declared vehemently.

Mother suddenly grew exuberant. "Ladies, do you suppose we might be entertaining angels today? Isn't that thrilling?"

We left the extra place setting on the table, and through the excited chatter of that meal, we felt the presence of that heavenly guest.

O Jesus, as I try to carry on my mother's tradition of hospitality, I pray that my guests will also sense the presence of You and Your angels as we fellowship together. DONNA LEE SHARP

"Now Ye Are Clean"

"Now ye are clean." John 15:3.

$\mathcal{M}$y young friend and I finished our supper and were doing dishes. I washed; she wiped. We talked, and the washing went fast, perhaps too fast, for suddenly I felt a little tap on my shoulder. I turned to see her holding a plate and pointing to an area on it.

"What's wrong?" I asked. "I don't see anything."

"Feel it," she suggested. I did. The plate looked clean, but it wasn't.

I recalled Jesus' statement at the time of the Last Supper. "Ye are clean, but not all" (John 13:10). The plate seemed clean, even as Judas did to the other disciples. Neither were. I wondered if I could be like that—seemingly clean, but not.

Immediately I breathed a prayer, "Wash me thoroughly from mine iniquities" (Ps. 51:2).

As I rewashed the plate and again handed it to my friend, I heard her say, "Now it's clean." I want to hear Jesus say to me, "Now you are clean." JUANITA SLACK

The Lost Pictures

And I will do whatever you ask in my name. . . . You may ask me
for anything in my name, and I will do it. John 14:13, 14, NIV.

*I*n November 1993, while en route to visit my mother, my husband and I stopped overnight at a motel. We carried to the
room a small bag of necessities for our stay. Carefully we arranged the remaining baggage out of sight under the canvas shield.
Since we parked under a bright light in view of our second floor room,
we felt that all would be well. But it was a false sense of security.

During the night someone broke into our vehicle, taking a coat,
jacket, pair of gloves, and a bag of pictures. Thanking God that the vehicle and our luggage was still intact, we realized we should have taken
everything into the motel. I was devastated over the loss of the photos.
They were pictures of a recent overseas trip. Also in the bag were photos of the beautiful flowers and family members taken at my grandmother's funeral. Nine months earlier she had celebrated her 100th
birthday. These recorded memories were what I cherished most.

I was feeling quite depressed. My husband reminded me to pray
and leave it in God's hands. As I prayed about those pictures, I asked
God (1) to let someone find those pictures and (2) to return them to
us by December 16. We were planning to travel again over the holidays, and I hoped to have the pictures to take along on this trip.

Several weeks passed. No word. Although I had set a date, I reminded myself that God knows best when and how to answer our
prayers. One morning my husband received a call at his office. He
learned that a construction contractor had found our photos on the
shoulder of a highway while working at that site. He discovered so
many pictures that he put them in a grocery bag. The kind man's
wife and daughter laid the damp pictures out to dry in every available space on the floor of their home. Of the dozen or so photo envelopes, only one had our name and phone number—and he found
that particular envelope!

We thanked God for answering the first part of our prayer and
mailed the man a reward. On December 14 a neatly packaged shoe
box arrived—just two days before the date I had mentioned in my
prayer. Every picture was there. The dampness had damaged the
glossy finish, but other than that, the pictures were perfect.

Isn't it wonderful that God still answers prayers? Each time I
look at these pictures, I am reminded of His goodness and of His

love for me. If He can protect and gather lost pictures, how much more will He protect and gather His children! MARIE H. SEARD

Ice Crystals

And you He made alive, who were dead in trespasses and sins. Eph. 2:1, NKJV.

We awoke to a world of wonder. Looking out our picture window, we saw artistic splendor that no human sculptor could match. During the night nature had performed a delicate miracle of beauty covering all living things. With infinite care, God had used frost crystals to transform every twig, weed, blade of grass, and leaf into fancy, glorious designs.

All this grandeur free—in our own yard! What a surprise gift from our Father, who loves to lavish His best on His children. Hurriedly dressing in warm clothes and boots, we stepped out into the frosty morning. The beauty overwhelmed us.

Slowly we walked down our trail from our house, stopping often to examine the variety of designs on the pine and fir needles. Intricate ice crystals decorated the branches of each bush. The dried wildflower plants looked even more beautiful now than when they were covered with summer's blossoms. Six-sided, hollow columns of ice formed fantastic shapes sticking out in all directions.

Suddenly we noticed an unusual phenomenon. Only living things were covered with frost. Rocks, dirt, fallen pine needles, and dead, dry wood were all untouched. They still looked bare and ugly, a stark contrast to the beauty surrounding them.

I imagined I heard God speaking to us that morning. "My child," He seemed to say, "I want to change you into My likeness, transform you with My glory. If you choose to live apart from Me, you are dead in sin. But you can be alive and beautiful if you will allow My life, My Spirit, to dwell in you. Please let Me use My creative power to make you into a new person, gracious and lovely like the frost."

God will keep His promise to make us, who were dead in sins, beautiful like Him when we allow Him to cover us with His magnificent robe of righteousness, even more glorious than the frost.

EILEEN E. LANTRY

You Must . . .

But seek ye first the kingdom of God, and his righteousness; and all these things will be added unto you. Matt. 6:33.

*Y*ou must desperately seek,
  before you will find.
You must acknowledge blindness,
  before given spiritual sight.
You must claim victory,
  before waging war.
You must know peace within,
  before surrendering all.
You must share,
  before you have a share.
You must be patient,
  before you are gracious.
You must walk meekly,
  before you boldly run.
You must harmonize,
  before singing psalms.
You must shed tears,
  before rainbows you'll see.
You must trust,
  before you can impart.
You must be lowly,
  before you are holy.
You must reflect,
  before you shine.
You must be born again,
  before you enter in.
You must have strength,
  before enduring the pain.
You must serve,
  before you reign.

DEBORAH SANDERS

Thanksgiving Peace

My peace I give you. . . . Do not let your hearts be troubled and
do not be afraid. John 14:27, NIV.

*A*t Thanksgiving I heard a man say, "I am grateful for 12-
step programs." Many Christians are not acquainted with
the biblical basis for 12-step programs, the first of which,
Alcoholics Anonymous, was born in the mid-1930s.

The first three steps address the need for us to repair our relationship with God.

STEP 1. We admit that we are powerless over our dependen-
cies, that our lives have become unmanageable (Matt. 9:36; Ps. 6:2-
4). This step hits at the issue of control.

STEP 2. We come to believe that a Power greater than ourselves
can restore us to sanity (John 6:63; Mark 9:23, 24). This step
teaches that we must transfer our dependency upon an outside substance, behavior, or person to God.

STEP 3. We make a decision to turn our will and our lives over
to the care of God as we understand Him (Eph. 2:8, 9; Ps. 91:1-4).
This step involves renouncing whatever we have allowed to usurp
the place of God in our lives.

Steps four through six motivate us to heal our relationship with
ourselves.

STEP 4. We make a searching and fearless moral inventory of ourselves (Gal. 6:3-5). This step requires absolute honesty with ourselves.

STEP 5. We admit to God, to ourselves, and to other human beings the exact nature of our wrongs (James 5:16). This step marks
the end of personal isolation as we learn to share who we really are
with God and with trustworthy human beings.

STEP 6. We become entirely ready to have God remove all our
defects of character (Eph. 4:22, 23; Col. 3:5-8). This step requires
us to be willing to allow God to remove specific character flaws and
patterns of dysfunctional behavior.

Steps seven through nine teach us how to heal relationships
with others.

STEP 7. We humbly ask God to remove our shortcomings
(Matt. 18:3; 1 John 5:14, 15). This step involves asking God to
transform our lives from defective personalities into effective instruments for Him and others.

STEP 8. We make a list of all persons we have harmed and become willing to make amends to them all (Matt. 5:23, 24, 18:35; John 13:34, 35). This step involves acknowledging that we have made mistakes that have hurt others, and that we are willing to set things right.

STEP 9. We make direct amends to such people wherever possible, except when to do so would injure them or others (Matt. 5:23, 24; Phil. 1:9; Luke 6:27-36). This step means taking responsibility for making amends—with discretion.

The last three steps outline a maintenance program for integrating the first nine steps into our daily living and for maintaining a healthy relationship with ourselves, with God, and with others.

STEP 10. We continue to take personal inventory, and when we are wrong, promptly admit it (Heb. 2:1-3; Mark 14:38). This step involves maintaining a healthy relationship with ourselves, including creating healthy boundaries.

STEP 11. We seek through prayer and meditation to improve our conscious contact with God, praying for knowledge of God's will for us and for the power to carry that out (Rom. 8:26-28; John 4:13, 14). This step involves maintaining a daily spiritual relationship with God by slowing down, taking ourselves out of the driver's seat, and seeking God's will.

STEP 12. Having experienced a spiritual awakening as the result of these steps, we try to carry this message to others, and to practice these principles in all our affairs (Mark 5:19, 20; Ps. 96:1, 2). This step involves maintaining relationships with others, and rather than directly proselytizing, living the 12 steps and sharing how God has had compassion on us.

At Thanksgiving let us be grateful for the profoundly simple and immensely practical 12 steps—from which we can all benefit.

ARLENE TAYLOR

NOVEMBER 29

Forgiveness

And forgive us our debts, as we also have forgiven our debtors. Matt. 6:12, RSV.

*E*ager to reach her distant destination, my daughter received a speeding ticket. Upon returning home, she gave me the ticket and money and requested that I send a check to the courthouse. I noted that the due date was a month away and placed the ticket with the monthly bills, where I promptly forgot it.

One evening, sometime later, I picked up the ticket and realized with horror that the court date was the next day. Dire warnings on the ticket warned of the recipient's future if she chose not to be at the courthouse or make payment by the due date. I hardly slept that night as I struggled with what to do. Express mail wouldn't work. I would have to make a four-hour, one-way trip to pay the ticket. My oversight had made the matter a *major* problem. How could I explain my irresponsibility to my daughter?

Early the next morning I called directory assistance for the courthouse telephone number. At 8:00 a.m. I nervously dialed, only to reach a recording stating the office hours. The lump in my throat grew. I deserved any tirade the court personnel went into. Should I just avoid the lecture, leave work, and start the long trip to pay the fine?

At 9:05 a.m. I nervously dialed the number again and stuttered my explanation to the young woman who answered the phone. "Just a moment. You'll need to speak to Carol." Gulp! They had someone designated to deal with offenders!

A gravelly voice spoke: "This is Carol." I began my explanation. Practice hadn't helped. I was still sweating, and nervousness made my voice shake.

"Honey, this is no problem." What? I couldn't believe what she was saying. Put the money in the mail and send it to them? That simple? I hung up, reread the threatening words on the ticket, and panicked again. Surely, it wasn't this easy. I redialed. "May I speak to Carol?" I knew *who* to ask for this time. "I'm sorry to bother you, but my daughter wants to know if delay of payment will go on her record."

Carol's voice was friendly. "Honey, tell her you're sorry for the mistake, but she needs to forgive you. *[Laugh]* We're behind anyway. You could probably take 10 days to get the money here."

It had been a long time since I had understood God's grace so fully. Carol's kindness, her empathy, her forgiveness, and her message urging my daughter to let this one go made me giddy with relief.

Is there someone you can give the gift of forgiveness to today? Forgiveness is God's greatest gift to us. Sharing it with someone will lighten her burden and relieve anxiety. It will also do the same for you!

CHERIE SMITH

For Real

As it was in the days of Noe, so shall it be also in the days of the Son of man. Luke 17:26.

*M*y first and second graders prepared to act out the story of Noah and the ark. Soon Noah and his sons were wielding imaginary hammers and saws in the corner of the room by my desk (the ark). Then the bad guys came marching around them.

"Whatcha doin', old man?" cried one.

"Building a boat 'cause there's gonna be a flood," answered Noah.

"Aw, y'er crazy, Noah!"

More loud jeers, insults, and laughter from the bad guys, until I said, "OK, the ark's built now, and the animals are all in. Noah, take your family into the ark." They crouched behind my desk. I continued, "Now it's one day . . . four . . . six . . . seven. Here comes the rain!"

The bad guys screamed, "Let us in, Noah!" Chad pretended to be drowning. When the screams and howls reached a pitch that threatened to disturb the other rooms in the school, I had to put an end to the role-playing.

Calming down, the pupils took their seats in preparation for a discussion of what had happened and their reactions to it.

"How did you feel about being safe in the ark?" I asked those who had played Noah and his family.

"Aw, it wasn't much fun down in there," Jimmy complained.

"I didn't like it either," Carl said. "We couldn't do anything. I want to be a 'bad people' next time."

"I'd rather be a bad one too," Anna said. "They had all the fun!"

I tried again. "Well, how about those of you who were supposed to be drowning? Wasn't it scary?"

"Naw!" Chad declared. "It was fun."

Josh said, "It was fun being outside the ark. We got to do all those things."

"Yeah!" echoed several others. "Saying all that mean stuff to Jimmy—I mean Noah— *that* was fun."

My students' frankness was disconcerting to say the least. Now I had a real problem. The lesson had not turned out as planned. But after more discussion and many leading questions, most of the students agreed that if it had been "for real," they would have been happier inside the ark.

Is Jesus' second coming "for real" to us? How many of us still are having more fun "outside" than "inside"? How often do we rationalize that the "things" we want and on which we spend much of our money and time are not really all that bad? We tell ourselves, when the time of trouble comes (or, we hope, just before it), we will make the supreme sacrifice and begin to study our Bibles earnestly, spend more time in prayer, be careful about what we watch on TV, stop criticizing, and so on. When it's "for real," we will get ready, we will go in. But is it not "for real" right now?

God said, "As it was in the days of Noe, so shall it be also in the days of the Son of man."

REVA I. SMITH

Grandma's Love

For one who loves them shall lead them. Isa. 49:10, NEB.

The quarter-mile walk to Grandma Brown's house took me back a hundred years. She wore ankle-length dresses and a sunbonnet. Cooking on a wood-burning stove, she lit her house with kerosene lamps and drew water in a wooden bucket from a well. Grandma Brown had an outhouse where the toilet paper was the Sears catalog, much more interesting than the white stuff on a roll at my house.

As a small child I spent many hours with my great-grandmother. Others thought her eccentric, but I loved her dearly and delighted being with her. In her presence I felt cozy, excited, nourished, and accepted.

Grandma's home was cozy in winter. She shut off the rest of the house and heated only her bedroom. In the middle of the room was a woodstove and two rocking chairs with velvet patchwork covers. I'd sit in one chair and she in the other as she told stories of the long ago by lamplight. At night I snuggled against Grandma under a downy comforter and felt safe.

To a 5-year-old Grandma's house was full of excitement. She told thrilling tales of frontier life and the Civil War and had two cupboards filled with boxes of buttons, empty spools, bottles, scraps of cloth, and old pictures. She and her treasures made me feel accepted, belonging to a family that went back many generations.

Her cooking nourished me. She taught me to savor fried pumpkin blossoms, wild blackberry cobbler, and cornbread baked in an iron skillet and smothered with butter and honey.

Grandma nourished not only my body, but also my soul. The beauty of her patchwork quilts, embroidered pillowcases, and fine china captivated me. I loved the smells in her garden: roses, lilacs, azaleas, sage, and mint. All summer her garden contained a profusion of color from lilies, pansies, peonies, and hollyhocks. She nourished my love of the beautiful.

Sometimes I'd like to go back to the security of those childhood visits to Grandma's house, but I can't. However, there are times I experience that same coziness, excitement, nourishment, and acceptance. It's in the presence of another One who loves me. He was Grandma Brown's God. Now He's my God, too.

His treasures excite me, and His handiwork nourishes my soul. I snuggle up to Him and feel safe. He makes me feel accepted, a part of His family. I love Him dearly and delight in His presence.

DOROTOHY EATON WATTS

DECEMBER 2

"I'm Hungry!"

Casting all your care upon him; for he careth for you. 1 Peter 5:7.

One summer day as my 2-year-old, Gene, and I sat down to lunch, it suddenly occurred to me to ask him to say the blessing. He had never done it before, but he readily agreed and bowed his head. Since I hadn't taught him a grace to say, I waited expectantly to hear what words would ensue.

Solemnly he began, "Our Father, which art in heaven." *So far, so good,* I thought. Then, with an abrupt change in style, he continued, "I'm hungry, and I want to eat the food. Amen."

Struggling to keep from laughing, I responded, "That was very nice, Gene. Thank you." But in my mind I pictured God, high in His heaven, also smiling at this first mealtime prayer from one of His babes.

We older ones sometimes get into the habit of repeating set words and phrases that don't really come straight from the heart. Or we use flowery expressions and formal language when what God really wants to hear is the simple, earnest relating of the wants and needs of the soul.

As I reflect upon my little boy's prayer, now recorded in his baby book, I realize it is just the kind God desires. Although Gene offered no words of thanks and made no requests, he expressed his need: "I'm hungry," and his want: "I want to eat the food." It was short, sincere, and to the point. He told God just how he felt.

As one of my favorite authors puts it: "Keep your wants, your joys, your sorrows, your cares, and your fears before God. You cannot burden Him; you cannot weary Him. He who numbers the hairs of your head is not indifferent to the wants of his children" (*Steps to Christ*, p. 100).

Through the years I have studied and meditated on how to pray, and I have tried various methods. But more and more, I realize the value of the simple heartfelt prayer: telling God just how you feel, believing that He cares, and trusting Him to do what is best for you.

VIVIAN PREWITT

DECEMBER 3

Friendship in Times of Trouble

And she said unto them, Call me not Naomi, call me Mara: for the Almighty hath dealt very bitterly with me. Ruth 1:20.

We all dread those times when terrible news comes. Someone, a loved one, a close friend, has died. The call may have been expected—a long illness, a brave struggle, all over. Or the news may bring an awful shock—a fatal accident, a plane crash, a shooting. Tragedy may seem to block out the light of God's love

Naomi had such an experience. She and her husband and two sons had left Bethlehem to escape famine. Times were difficult, but they were still complete, a family. Then came the first blow: Elimelech, Naomi's husband, died. Even so, she had her sons. They would care for her. The boys grew and married girls of Moab. Then came the final blows: both Mahlon and Chilion perished.

Now she was bereaved, and destitute. But she would not mourn in a strange land. She would return to Bethlehem. At such times, the love of human friendship can bring light to darkness. Naomi's daughter-in-law Ruth would not leave her, would not let her suffer through this bitterness alone. Ruth offered herself, and she made all the difference.

We struggle after someone's tragedy to know what to say, what to do. The best we can do is to offer ourselves, as naturally as we know how. Has tragedy struck the home of good friends? Are you hurting too? Then don't put on a facade when you go visit. Take a handkerchief, and offer a warm embrace. Weep if you must, but also remember, you are there to bear the others up!

Are you a close friend? Then you can help with personal details, such as doing some laundry, washing dishes, sweeping or vacuuming to get the house in order. If the family has to leave, getting things organized will make it easier to pack. Should family members be coming, you can offer to bring them from stations or airports. Many times grief wipes out details in a daze, and others must fill them in.

And if you're not a close friend? You can still help. Visit, quietly let the family know you're praying for them, and leave if no extra hands are needed. If you're asked to help, plunge right in, answering the door, taking coats, serving food, or reassuring children. The little things count, and often they mean the most.

What of the other tragedies, though? Death is not the only one. What if the child of a friend is in trouble—drinking, on drugs, unmarried and pregnant? What if the marriage falls apart? What then? Often these are more testing to friendship than death. Losing a mate through divorce or a child to drugs or crime can be a walking death. The loss is final, but the person still lives on as a reminder!

There are no easy answers, but the need for real friendship is just as potent, if not more so, in such cases. Let the hurting friend be your guide—let her talk about the problem when she is able, let her open up at her own rate. You may grow impatient, thinking you have "all the details" already, but you don't have her perspective, so wait! Let her know you can be trusted. Don't make her confidences "common fodder" the next time you're in a wider circle of friends. And if you have some need to "compare notes" with others, let it only be in developing a strategy to help the person.

For example, some parents using the "tough love" techniques with children on drugs tell them, "You have a problem, and you're not willing to face it. But we know it, and we're not going to allow this in our home. You and the problem can't stay, but you can come back when you're clean!"

Where does that troubled kid go? To the home of family friends! The friends know about the problem. They have the emotional and spiritual strength for the battle. Perhaps they may have been through their own battles themselves, and they share the standards and values of the parents. More than anything, they want to help the child get clean and stay clean, and in many cases, they're able to get through to the child. Now, that's real friendship!

Certainly, every case mentioned above may not apply to you, and should misfortune come, you should always ask for God's guidance. He can always be trusted to lead you and your friend through the rough seas of life into a safe harbor. Just let Him use you.

KYNA HINSON

DECEMBER 4

The Stubborn Amaryllis

I would have lost heart, unless I had believed that I would see the
goodness of the Lord in the land of the living. Ps. 27:13, NKHV.

*E*arly in December our boys received a package from their
grandmother Ruth. They tore into the box to find an amaryl-
lis bulb, with instructions to keep it well watered and in the
sun. The promise was that it would bloom on Christmas day.

The boys eagerly awaited the promised bloom of their
Christmas flower. But Christmas came and went. New Year's arrived
and departed. Still no blossoms, as their grandmother had
promised.

We moved it from the table to the window, and finally to the
living room in the hope that the big windows would provide the
missing ingredient. Yet it refused to bloom. We were doing everything the instructions said to do. What could be wrong?

What joyful glee arose through the house when, on the morning of January 3, the long-awaited bright-red flowers appeared.
"Mommy, Mommy!" the boys shouted. "Come see our huge flowers!" Sure enough, two gorgeous blossoms had appeared.

Funny, I thought to myself, *why today?* I had so hoped for a more
significant, triumphal emergence on Christmas Day or at least New
Year's Day, but the third of January?

Little did I know then that within several hours I would hear
that my father had passed away that very morning. Through my
tears, I could see God's love for me.

He had sent me a sign, a promise, for what will bloom again
someday. Yes, He will make us new again, perfect in every way,
without pain and suffering. And the comfort to my heart is that I can
forever remember this day, not for the sadness, but for the hope of
a new life in Jesus Christ.   DAWNA GIEM

DECEMBER 5

Expectation

Now to him who is able to do immeasurably more than all we
ask or imagine. Eph. 3:20, NIV.

373

*T*he mob dashed around the bus, grabbing the tangerines, bananas, and pens that we were handing out. Anger engulfed me as I saw the adults and teens hoarding the handouts, while the children and those less aggressive stood wistfully by.

Turning to the young mother standing beside me, I noticed her look of disappointment as the door of the bus closed, signifying that the handouts were all gone. She had received nothing. I smiled and touched her baby. "She's beautiful," I said in Spanish, trying to take her focus away from her disappointment.

Looking me straight in the eye, she pleaded, "Deme una pluma, por favor?"

I blinked away tears that threatened to spill. Her request seemed so insignificant. A pen! I owned more than I could ever use, yet in this circumstance I was unable to supply even one. My heart ached as I replied, "I am so sorry. All gone. No more." Then my mind raced . . .

Through broken Spanish and gestures, I motioned for her to wait that I had something for her. I was not sure she understood what I was trying to communicate. Would she think that I was running away from her, or that I did not understand her? Was she in for another disappointment? Could she trust that I would come back? The bus was ready to leave, yet she waited.

My handbag, stored under a seat in the bus, contained a bottle of perfume. As I reached for it, I discovered that under that very seat was a grocery bag filled with bananas. I felt a surge of joy. Did my God allow this bag of fruit to be overlooked for this special reason?

How could I give these gifts unnoticed to the waiting mother? The mob had expectantly positioned itself by the door in the event something else would emerge for grabs. Leaving the bag, I retraced my steps. Taking her hand, I led her to the opposite side of the bus. Someone from inside handed me the perfume and bananas through a back window. I slipped the perfume into her pocket and handed her the bag of bananas. Her expression of gratitude, like sunlight bursting through the darkest cloud, will remain forever etched in my memory.

Her meager expectation of a pen and one banana had turned into the reality of receiving a bottle of perfume and a bag of bananas. As we drove away, her expression reflected the satisfaction of a woman who had received a gift suitable for a princess, a daughter of God.

How often have I pleaded with my God for one inexpensive "pen" and "one banana" when His gift for me was a bottle of perfume and an armful of bananas? Lord, continue to remind me that you want to give me immeasurably more than all I can imagine or even think to ask for.

NORMA JEAN PARCHMENT

The Fragrance

Ointment and perfume rejoice the heart. Prov. 27:9.

For most of my growing up years I lived in Miami and Hialeah, Florida. Our houses had terrazzo floors, a mixture of concrete and chips of colored stone. When I was 13, we had a beautiful 10-month-old German shepherd puppy named Lobo, who spent most of his time in our fenced-in backyard. He was, however, allowed in the house when we were there to watch him.

One day we all left the house and forgot to put him in the backyard. When we returned home that evening and opened the front door a beautiful fragrance greeted us. But when Lobo finally showed himself, his tail was between his legs and he slunk away. Following the fragrance down the hallway to my bedroom, I could already guess what had happened. I had left a beautiful new bottle of perfume on top of my dresser. Being a large, curious puppy, Lobo had been exploring in my bedroom. Now my new bottle of perfume lay in pieces on the floor in a puddle of perfume.

I was so angry and disappointed that I cried as I cleaned up the mess. Although I scrubbed and scrubbed the floor, the fragrance lingered for many, many weeks. The odor was so strong and overpowering in my bedroom that it became obnoxious. Even with the windows open, it gave me a headache. I had to sleep in my sister's room for several days.

As I later reflected on the experience, I realized that each one of us is like that beautiful bottle of perfume. God has made each of us unique and special. He has given us a special fragrance all our own. But He has also given us the power to choose what we do with it. We can be a blessing, a sweet fragrance, to the lives of those we touch, or we can choose to waste our lives, and be an obnoxious, offensive, overpowering odor.

By the grace of God, may we each choose to be a sweet fragrance to those around us today and every day.   CELIA MEJIA CRUZ

DECEMBER 7

Yearlong Christmas

When they saw the star, they were overjoyed. On coming to the house, they saw the child with his mother Mary, and they bowed down and worshiped him. Then they opened their treasures and presented him with gifts of gold and of incense and of myrrh. Matt. 2:10, 11, NIV.

Festivals celebrating the birth of Christ have been held annually since the beginning of Christian churches. Children, who often are quite whole-brained (until their particular culture encourages them to develop a preference for processing information in one or the other of the brain hemispheres), love Christmas. With their left brain hemispheres, they don't have any trouble learning the theology of Christmas, and with their right brain hemispheres, they enjoy the stories, music, and symbols of Christmas. Perhaps that is one reason that Christ called the little children to Him and said to the disciples, "Unless you change and become like little children, you will never enter the kingdom of heaven" (Matt. 18:3, NIV). We adults need to learn a lesson from this. We need to approach the celebration of Christmas in a whole-brain style.

One of the most meaningful symbols associated with the Christmas season involves "gifts." Children of all ages love to receive and to give gifts. Their spontaneity is contagious. Sometimes adults get caught up in the hustle and bustle of preparation and forget that gift-giving, while no doubt representative of the singular gifts of the Magi, really has its basis in the most incredible gift of all—the Christ child. That gift was not just a one-time occurrence. It is perpetual.

I recall a story about a woman who received a glass jar from her husband one Christmas Eve. It was filled with 365 colorful strips of wrapping paper, each tied into a gentle knot. The instructions on the jar indicated that she could select one knotted note every day and redeem them anytime.

She found all manner of delightful handwritten surprises. One note, "good for one dish drying," rescued her one evening after a late good night from a group of dinner guests. Another, "good for a walk together," came in handy the evening her best friend called with sad news. Several that read "good for 10 kisses" became the spark for pleasant reminiscences of their courtship days and for a rekindling of gentle touching between them. And so on. This creative and unusual gift stretched Christmas into a year-round celebration.

This is what God did for all of us—stretched Christmas into a year-round celebration through the gift of the Christ child. During the Christmas season, let us rejoice in the Gift that lasts for the whole year. Let us share:

> The spirit of Christmas which is peace;
> The gladness of Christmas which is hope;
> The heart of Christmas which is love;
> And the gift of Christmas which is Christ.   ARLENE TAYLOR

DECEMBER 8

A Christmas I Shall Never Forget

I have shewed you all things, how that so labouring ye ought to support the weak, and to remember the words of the Lord Jesus, how he said, It is more blessed to give than to receive. Acts 20:35.

I grew up in a rural area in western Colorado during the Depression. We didn't have much money, but somehow the Lord seemed to take good care of us during those years.

One Christmas my parents asked us if we would like to give up our own family gift-giving to provide something to our neighbor family. They had 12 children, and the father had been out of work for a long time. The family survived by preserving and canning the summer bounties from the garden and orchard.

I remember how we went shopping and looked carefully for just the right gift for each member of that big family. The thought of how surprised they would be and how much fun it would be to see their faces when they opened the presents was exciting.

The days and weeks went by, and we carefully wrapped each gift and stowed it away. I could hardly wait! Finally my father loaded the treasures in a sack on his back. I will never forget the joyous expressions on their faces as each child received his own gift.

As my dad and I walked home, I felt happy and warm inside. And as I snuggled down in my warm bed that cold night, I thought this truly was the best Christmas I would ever remember.   PAT MADSEN

DECEMBER 9

Embracing Love

Yea, I have loved thee with an everlasting love: therefore with lovingkindness have I drawn thee. Jer. 31:3.

*W*hile we were on a recent trip to New York, our daughter called to say, "Mom, nothing important. I'm here in your home checking on things, and I just wanted to say your house exudes love inside and out. I feel your love all around me, even though you're not here."

Her words made my day! Then I thought about the wonderful God we serve. Although we cannot see Him, we can feel His love enfolding and embracing us at all times.

Love isn't something you can turn on or off like a faucet. It does not come to an end. Once Christ has entered our heart, permanent love is locked in there—love for every human being, regardless of his/her station in life, rich or poor, dirty or clean.

God loves people—all kinds of people—and He left us an example to do as He does: love unconditionally.

The first fruit of the Holy Spirit is love. The others—joy, peace, longsuffering, gentleness, goodness, faith, meekness, temperance—follow in its train.

This day, Lord, let me possess that everlasting love for others that you possess for me.   ETTA MAYCOCK DULEY

DECEMBER 10

The Comforter

And I will pray the Father, and He will give you another Helper, that He may abide with you forever. John 14:16, NKJV.

*G*od is our Comforter.
    The Three. The One.
    My Father "shall give you
    Another Comforter,"
    Our Saviour said.
    Jesus is our Comforter.

"He who has seen Me
Has seen the Father,"
Our Saviour said.
"I and My Father are One."
Our Father is our Comforter.

"The Spirit of truth,"
Our Saviour said,
Will "abide with you forever."
The Holy Spirit is our Comforter.
God is our Comforter—
The Three in One.   ROBERTA SHARLEY

DECEMBER 11

Beauty Spots

Never will I leave you; never will I forsake you. Heb. 13:5, NIV.

I was watching out a window while preparing for Christmas
company. Suddenly, the sun shone in all its splendor
through snow-covered trees. *Spectacular!* I thought. Out
loud, I said, "Praise You, Jesus for coming here and for sharing Your
sunshine with me this moment in my harried day." Then I sang a little praise chorus that escapes from me whenever I think of my Lord.

When I had soaked up all the peace and beauty I could hold, I
noticed how dirty the big window was. It even had little hand prints
from a grandnephew's visit long ago. Puppy nose marks were as
high as she could reach as she tried to communicate with the deer
in the yard. Some deer nose marks were on the outside where an or-
phan fawn looked in to see what we do in this cabin in the woods.

It occurred to me that my life is like that window—not clean! But
if I focus on the sunshine of my Redeemer's love for me, I won't even
notice the smudges I've made or allowed to be made on my life.

For many reasons, women are not always confident in their abilities to serve the Lord. We have a tendency to focus on our dirty-
windowed lives instead of concentrating on the beauty of God's love
for us and His promise to never forsake us. This would free us to be
all that we can be for Him.

Why not bow your head for a moment to focus on our Saviour?
Soon you will find all the spots on your soul's windows will fade away.

MARJORY BUTTON BODI

DECEMBER 12

Daily Bread

Give us today our daily bread. Matt. 6:11, NIV.

Somebody's going to Zambia tomorrow!" When such news reaches our mission compound in Lubumbashi, Zaire, communication lines start to reconnect, typewriter or computer keys click away even into the late hours of the night, envelopes and stamps get pulled out of the drawer. Hopes soar, spirits revive, excitement fills the air. Whenever someone goes to Zambia, besides doing his business, he posts everyone's letters. It also means that on his return he will bring with him incoming mail.

In the mission field, mail is daily bread. One's spirit feasts or fasts, depending on what the mailbag contains. Where we live, we cannot easily phone, fax, or telex, and even mail we have to post and collect at our next-door-neighbor country. Expatriates from the Methodist, Pentecostal, and other missions work together to solve the problem by doubling as mail carriers for everybody when they travel.

One Christmas season nobody went to Zambia. Some of the expatriates were away on vacation or visiting their projects in other parts of the country. No one had business to do in Zambia that would make it worth the trip and expense. The mail that trickled in came by DHL or was hand-carried. But nothing arrived through the mail boxes. Those of us who were left had not heard from families or friends for weeks and months. Day after day the question "Any mail?" received the disappointing response: "Nothing."

Christmas came and went. Fireplaces displayed only a few greeting cards. It took some effort to keep our spirits up.

One day in mid-April someone went to Zambia. He returned with his car packed with the long-awaited letters, Christmas cards, and parcels. When all was sorted and distributed, everyone enjoyed a bonus that only mission life can afford: a Christmas season that extended beyond Easter.

How did our spirits survive the "famine"? Each one received strength through a line of communication that nothing could cut. Day by day prayers ascended, asking God to take care of the loved ones we could not reach and who could not reach us. One letter received said, "When we don't hear from you for long periods, we just have to trust God that all is well with you." We encouraged one another. Some recounted experiences showing that if there were an emergency or some urgent news to send or receive, God would provide for that. Without God with whom we could share our deepest concerns, it would have been easy to give up hope or worry because of the lack of good news from our far countries.

BIENVISA LADION NEBRES

DECEMBER 13

Complete Resurfacing Needed

No one puts a piece of unshrunk cloth on an old garment; for the patch pulls away from the garment, and the tear is made worse. Matt. 9:16, NKJV.

Commuting on winter-ravaged roads is quite an experience! The other day, while driving home from work, my husband and I found ourselves on a road with its asphalt entirely ruined. Cracks and potholes ranged from fist-sized ones to holes as deep as six inches and as wide as two feet. The asphalt appeared to be coming apart at the place where the surface, apparently considered too narrow, had been widened several years before. The road had merely been added to on both sides, rather than being totally resurfaced. The resulting seams were the weak links, and once they began to give, the additional moisture and temperature fluctuations split the road into three jagged-edged areas—the middle section and the added-on side portions. This, along with the abundant potholes, made traveling a guaranteed commuting hazard.

No quick fix, no add-on repair job, will remake us into Christians any more than it will make good, strong, lasting wide roads out of narrower ones. In spite of the fact that we live in an "instant everything" society, this is one aspect of our lives that we can't put in the microwave or buy ready-made off the shelf. When we come to Christ, each one of us needs total resurfacing. We cannot merely patch our old garments with bright raiment, for they will still end up ragged and unfit to wear to the banquet Christ is preparing for His people. Nor can we merely sew a new piece onto the old wineskin, because it will not hold together when put under pressure. There is nothing strong enough, or good enough, or worthy enough in any of us for Christ to even use as a base on which to add His character traits. We may be very good people, according to the criteria of this world, but Christ has a different standard.

The only remedy to our narrow, inadequate lives is a total remake. To have the Great Creator make us brand new is the only way to become strong and resilient enough to withstand the stresses of each day. Only by relying 100 percent on the Lord of our lives can we avoid falling apart at the seams.

Once we are remade, we need to come to our Creator everyday to avoid crumbling again. Ask Him for a fresh remake each day, for the spiritual glue that binds us to Him, and for the strength to meet each challenge. Ask Him to help you withstand the stresses, temptations, and the problems you will face. Thank Him for His marvelous creative and recreative power that can keep us from falling apart like the winter-damaged roads. Ann E. Slaughter

DECEMBER 14

When Mountains Don't Move

If you have faith as small as a mustard seed, you can say to this mountain, "Move from here to there" and it will move. Matt. 17:20, NIV.

*E*ach morning I breathed the same prayer: "Lord, please heal Terry." But my words seemed to bounce off the ceiling. Didn't I have enough faith? Didn't God hear? Was it something I hadn't done? My mind spun.

Six-year-old Terry slept as I prayed, his black hair falling carelessly over his forehead. He was oblivious to my pleadings for his healing from cerebral palsy.

When I read the life of Jesus, each healing incident leaped out at me, especially those involving palsy. I never doubted that Jesus could heal my son. I read about His visit to Capernaum where "the whole town gathered at the door" (Mark 1:33, NIV), and He healed many of them. How I longed to have been there that day. My son would be running like other boys. But I wasn't in Capernaum.

Verses swirled at me. "If you believe, you will receive whatever you ask for in prayer" (Matt. 21:22, NIV), "I will do whatever you ask in my name" (John 14:13, NIV). The promises bounced off the corners of my mind continually. "If you have faith as small as a mustard seed, you can say to this mountain, 'Move from here to there' and it will move" (Matt. 17:20, NIV).

One Friday night I knelt by his bed and prayed with faith inspired by Scripture. Then, knowing I couldn't command God to heal my son, I added, "Nevertheless, Your will be done." I was bitterly disappointed, but as I poured out my anguish to God, He seemed to say, "I have a better plan."

I read Romans 8:28, and the verse provided special encouragement. "And we know that in all things God works for the good of those who love him, who have been called according to his purpose" (NIV).

I'd read that verse before, but that day something clicked, and I knew it was God's message for me. He wanted me to stop begging and start living in His strength. God was answering my prayers but in His way. I wrapped that verse around my shoulders and determined to live one day at a time.

I don't know why God hasn't answered my prayer for Terry's healing. God knows how much I want it—I tell Him daily. Our mountain of cerebral palsy is still here. But I've learned that sometimes mountains are for climbing and developing strength. God has a plan and has promised strength for the day as He leads us ever upward. I don't know the future, but I am learning to trust the judgment of the One who does.

Someday our family will all *walk* together into the New Jerusalem. Then Terry will hold my husband's hand and mine as together with all the redeemed we sing, "Glory to God in the highest."

CONNIE NOWLAND

DECEMBER 15

Words of Pride

Pride goeth before destruction, and an haughty spirit before a fall. Prov. 16:18.

She strutted toward the table in the college cafeteria, chin up, shoulders back, tray held daintily in her hands, extremely conscious that everyone else was very much aware of her grand entrance. Admiring fellows and jealous girls alike stared, eyes following her proud walk. No one denied her beauty. Then she tripped, her foot catching on a chair leg, sending her tray of food crashing to the floor.

Pride goeth before a fall—in her case, a literal one. The proverb speaks more, though, to those who tumble from high places symbolically, falls usually more significant than actual spills.

Our family's trip to the former U.S.S.R. was the most memorable one ever. Its ancient rivers, different language structure, various peoples, and revolutionary history satisfy every tourist's interest. From Peter the Great's tomb in St. Petersburg to Lenin's tomb in

Moscow, the land of the Czars remains a study in contrasts of cultures, ideologies, and religions.

As we waited in the hourlong queue to get our chance to go into Lenin's tomb, a mausoleum in Red Square that displayed his still-preserved body, we noticed several less ostentatious graves between Lenin's tomb and the Kremlin Wall. Our guide, a trilingual university graduate, explained to us that they were the burial places of the previous premiers, such as Khrushchev and Stalin, the best-known and longest reigning of them all.

My husband had heard that the current leaders were downplaying Stalin's significance, so he asked our guide for clarification.

"Yes," she frankly acknowledged, "the school textbooks are being rewritten to minimize his memory." Minimizing his memory. Quite a euphemism for manipulating the past to obliterate the works, heinous though they were, of a man who for nearly 25 years ruled in terror over the largest country on earth.

Now there he lies in a second-class grave, toppled from his pinnacle of power, first by death and now by revised history books. How ironic that he who once dominated history was now being done in by it!

Pride goeth before destruction. It holds true in the family, the church, and the nation. We tend to enjoy these falls from pride, be they the haughty coed or the proud premier, defending our pleasure on the basis that they deserve to be humiliated. Laughing at others, for whatever reason, is a form of superiority too.

But if we laugh too hard or too often, maybe we haven't internalized the essence of the text ourselves. How tragic that those of us who will never be powerful enough to commit the crimes of Stalin should likewise commit the sin of pride. WILMA MCCLARTY

DECEMBER 16

Caught Up With Him

Then we which are alive and remain shall be caught up together with them in the clouds, to meet the Lord in the air: and so shall we ever be with the Lord. 1 Thess. 4:17.

Signs all around us point to Jesus' second coming. In fact, they are so numerous and so frequent that many believe that it is time for Jesus to return. I certainly hope it is. I long to be caught up with Him in the clouds of glory to spend eternity with my Lord.

A little girl once asked, "Mother, who will be caught up with Jesus when He comes?" Perhaps the child expected her mother to answer, "Well, honey, of course there will be you and Daddy and Mamma and Grandmother . . ." But the mother's answer was more profound. "Those who will be caught up with Jesus when He comes," she said, "will be those who are caught up with Him now."

It's easy for the sports fan to get caught up with football, then basketball, followed by baseball. We can get caught up with the soaps and who is in love with whose spouse and who is having whose baby. Some are caught up in the lottery, and they calculate, theorize, and try to beat the odds.

The things I am caught up with may be good in themselves, but the important thing for me to consider seems to be the time element. I enjoy cross-stitch and could involve myself with it very easily. However, I discipline myself and spend only a certain amount of time doing it. If I didn't discipline myself, I could spend many hours every day doing nothing but cross-stitch. But cross-stitch isn't what I want to be caught up with when Jesus comes.

Are we caught up with the one thing that is really important—our relationship with Jesus Christ? To be "caught up" in something requires that we spend an adequate amount of time being "caught up." Let's spend our time wisely, being caught up in the Lord, so that when He returns, we may be caught up with Him for eternity.

MARLENE ANDERSON

Beauty for Ashes

Whereby are given unto us exceeding great and precious promises: that by these ye might be partakers of the divine nature. 2 Peter 1:4.

We were flying in a friend's little plane far above the clouds. It seemed that my heart would burst with the grief that consumed me. The evening before, we had received word that our only son, our firstborn, had fallen while mountain climbing in the Cascade Mountains. We waited throughout the long night, and when daylight brought no word yet, telling us whether or not he had survived, we could wait no longer. We had to go to where the climbing group was camped, hoping for good news at last. Now we were on our way to the airfield nearest the camp.

My heart cried out with the most intense agony, "O God, how can I survive this? I need something to calm me, and I must be strong for the days ahead. Could You please give me a promise that will ease my pain and give me peace?" As I sat there, leaning against my husband, my hands clenched tightly, I listened and waited for something, anything, that would ease my grieving heart.

Then, quietly and calmly, deep in my inmost heart I heard it— a gentle voice saying, "Be not dismayed; for I am thy God: *I will strengthen thee!*" (Isa. 41:10). That was all. But it was enough. Comfort and healing flooded over me with such intensity that tears of joy filled me as I sensed Him there in the plane with us. He was feeling our grief, sorrowing with us, yet giving us the evidence of His love and His presence. I mentally reached out for those words again and again, and then said, "Thank You, Father, for understanding how much I needed Your promise."

All through that long, heartbreaking day, whenever I felt the grief well up inside and threaten to overwhelm me, I claimed that special promise that was mine for the moment, and a feeling of calm flooded my heart. With His love, God gave me the words that quieted my pain.

It was not easy, this bidding goodbye to our 22-year-old son, who was just beginning his adult life, the son who had been such a joy and a blessing to us. But Jesus was there to walk the "valley of the shadow of death" with us. He promised He would strengthen us, and He never failed.

Through the many grief experiences I have known since then, my "tranquilizer" has never let me down. He assured us that He is "a man of sorrows, *acquainted* with grief" (Isa. 53:3). Just to know that is enough. He never asks us to endure more than He has endured. Because of His own experience He can give us "beauty for ashes, the oil of joy for mourning" (Isa. 61:3).

JEAN REIFFENSTEIN ROTHGEB

DECEMBER 18

The Cedar Chest

And with joy give thanks to the Father, who has made you fit to have your share of what God has reserved for his people in the kingdom of light. Col. 1:12, TEV.

The cedar chest was lovingly handcrafted by my grandfather as a gift to my mother. She told me it was the only gift she had ever received from him. I remember her refinishing and polishing it before she gave it to me when I was just a young girl. It was to be my "hope chest." I really thought of it as a "hopeless chest," since I believed Jesus was certainly going to come before its contents filled it or they would ever get used. But its treasures gradually increased over the years—things like hand-crocheted pillow slips and doilies from my grandmother.

I felt honored to be the recipient of such an heirloom handed down from my grandfather, then to my mother, and then to me. Yet, while I valued it, I did not always respect it as a treasure. I remember the time I was taking drum lessons and used the top of the chest to practice my drum rolls on. It still bears the scars.

It reminds me of the way I grew up in my Christian experience, respecting the knowledge of God handed down from grandparents to parents, not realizing the gift's whole value until I really began to know it for myself. It was when I started to explore and learn truth on my own, examining the many facets of God, that I finally came to recognize and treasure this wonderful gospel.

Each of us has to discover, in our own way, the value of God in our life. While we can share certain concepts with one another, it is only by tasting the heavenly manna from the Bible for ourselves that we become truly nourished—and truly appreciative of the gift.

PEGGY HARRIS

DECEMBER 19

Kids' Praise

From the lips of children and infants you have ordained praise.
Ps. 8:2, NIV.

How do children and infants praise? They grin, giggle, belly laugh, bounce up and down, give bear hugs, clap their hands, shout for joy, say "thank you," and whisper, "I love you." And they do it all spontaneously with their whole heart and whole body. Sometimes it's short and sweet. Other times it seems to go on forever. And sometimes it's accompanied by a gooey kiss.

I was a kid once. But too many "settle downs," too many "don't get so exciteds," too many "what will others think?" and too much pain and disillusionment have destroyed the enthusiasm. It is hard to be spontaneous and difficult to do anything with my whole heart. Perhaps you are like me in this way, too. If so, pray with me that God will renew the little child in all of us.

Lord, thank You for using a little child to spark within me the desire to offer my whole being as a sacrifice of praise. Restore in me the ability to respond to life and all the little things it brings my way with that same self-abandonment, that same exuberant gratitude to You that I once had . . . before all the "shoulds and shouldn'ts."

LUCILE FREEMAN-KIME

DECEMBER 20

Keeping Hearts Merry

A merry heart doeth good like a medicine: but a broken spirit drieth the bones. Prov. 17:22.

I recently followed the nurse as she bustled into an examining room, and asked her why I had been called in for a special, unscheduled test. "Is it the same thing you did last week?" I wanted to know.

"Oh, no," she assured me. "This is much more complex. The results of the last one . . ." and she went on to explain that a phenomenon had appeared that prompted more extensive research, since if a certain condition existed, "it could cause sudden death." On that cheery note, she left me to change into a gown.

As I sat awaiting her return, suddenly I was struck with the absurdity of a nurse actually telling a patient that the patient might die suddenly. I couldn't restrain a chuckle. And then more chuckles. It occurred to me that if the nurse or doctor walked in and found me laughing, my sanity might be in question as well as my physical condition! It turned out that I had nothing to worry about anyway, but I still smile when I think of that nurse.

I have read Proverbs 17:22 in several versions, and I find that the New King James (margin) suggests that a merry heart makes medicine even better. When we find ourselves under the care of a doctor, staying cheerful will improve our condition.

The Living Bible says "a broken spirit makes one sick." Haven't we seen that the depressed person is often the one with the most physical problems? We sometimes wonder which condition came first!

But my favorite translation for this verse is still the King James: "A merry heart doeth good like a medicine: but a broken spirit drieth the bones."

I'm thankful that God gave me a sense of humor. The situations in which I find myself are often not amusing. But thinking about them usually shows me some ridiculous aspect of each one. Laughing makes me feel better, and gives me the strength to make the problem right when possible, or endure it when I must.

Thank You, God, for showing me the comical.   LEA HARDY

Two Gifts

On coming to the house, they saw the child with his mother Mary, and they bowed down and worshiped him. Then they opened their treasures and presented him with gifts of gold and of incense and of myrrh. Matt. 2:11, NIV.

My little child
brought me a gift
and watched with eager eyes
as I unwrapped it.
"It's lovely!" I exclaimed,
"Just what I needed,"
while he glowed
to think he'd pleased me.

Although he chose this gift himself
and paid for it with money
I'd given him,
it pleased me nonetheless
because of this—
he'd given because
he loved me.

I cannot give a gift to God
unless I purchase it
from out of God's own bounty.
But as I give with eager hands to Him,
the Father, God, exclaims,
"My child, it's perfect.
Exactly what I needed."   CARROL JOHNSON SHEWMAKE

Tell the Story!

But the angel said to them, "Do not be afraid. I bring you good news of great joy that will be for all the people. Today in the town of David a Savior has been born to you; he is Christ the Lord." Luke 2:10, 11, NIV.

Christmas is a time to give, a time to share, a time to create warm memories. A wonderful way to do this is to share our own personal stories with someone.

My granddaughter, Josie, loves to have me tell her stories of Christmas at my house when I was a child. I am one of 10 children, so you can imagine what my parents went through at Christmas! There was not much money for gifts, so my mother and grandmother handmade most of them: mittens, aprons, scarves. Sometimes we received only paper dolls or a new coloring book. We each had a stocking with a popcorn ball, an orange or an apple, and some assorted flavors of hard Christmas candy. As we gathered around the fire, Father would tell his own stories. Though we were poor in means, we were rich in love!

In the Christmas story, the people of Bethlehem didn't know that angels had filled the heavens that night the Babe was born. Some had been talking together of the promised Saviour throughout the silent hours of the night and praying for the coming of the King to David's throne. "An angel of the Lord appeared to them, and the glory of the Lord shone around them, and they were terrified. But the angel said to them, 'Do not be afraid. I bring you good news of great joy that will be for all the people'" (Luke 2:9, 10, NIV).

Today, I bring you good news of great joy, and this news is for everyone—not just for those who have been good this year! God declares, "Even in darkness light dawns for the upright" (Ps. 112:4, NIV). To those who are seeking for light and who accept it with gladness, the bright rays from the throne of God will shine. That's good news! It brings joy to my heart. Christ is my Saviour, my Redeemer, my Lord, and my soon-coming King!

This Christmas, take the time to share this good news with someone. Pray that God will send someone to you by divine appointment. Joy to the world, the Lord is come! Jesus—the most precious gift of all. HAZEL BURNS

DECEMBER 23

Sheri and the Nativity Scene

Now we see but a poor reflection as in a mirror; then we shall see face to face. 1 Cor. 13:12, NIV.

We were looking forward to spending Christmas with the family. This meant entertaining our 3-year-old daughter, Sheri, and our 4-year-old son, Scott, during the nine-hour car trip. I planned to read lots of books to lessen their boredom. One book was a story about the birth of Jesus. It fascinated Sheri.

Each time I finished reading it, she begged, "Read it again, Mommy." Since she seemed so interested, I began telling her about our plans to attend a live Nativity play at a church near our family home.

Sheri's big, blue eyes sparkled. She asked, "Will I see Jesus?" I assured her that Baby Jesus would be there, along with Mary and Joseph, singing angels, and shepherds with animals by a fire. "Can I pet the animals?" she asked. She squealed and clapped her hands when I answered yes.

Early the next morning I awakened with Sheri's mouth against my ear asking softly, "Is it time to go see Baby Jesus yet?" Periodically throughout the day as we prepared for Christmas Eve, she stopped playing and asked, "Is it time yet?"

At last it was time to leave. She jumped up and down in her excitement. When we pulled into the church parking lot, the spotlights shone on 12 costumed angles standing on a scaffold above the manger. "Joy to the World" blared so loudly that any explanation to Sheri was impossible. A roaring fire with shepherds and many live animals were in front of a manger. A live, illuminated Baby Jesus with multicolor lights swirling in a mist around a Mary and Joseph completed the scene. Sheri was elated! Her face was luminous with joy as she stared motionless at the manger scene. She leaned over and kissed one of the lambs.

Then it was time to go home. Suddenly Sheri began screaming and crying at the top of her lungs. "I don't want to leave Jesus and the angels. Please, Mommy, please don't make me leave Jesus and the angels!" As she wailed at full volume every eye in the crowd turned to look at us. The angels and the shepherds smiled. Mary and Joseph grinned. Her daddy hugged her tightly and hurried to the car as the laughter faded behind us.

Sheri was devastated. We had a difficult time explaining through her brokenhearted sobs that the *live* Nativity wasn't *real*. When she finally understood, she raised her big blue eyes to her daddy and asked, "When *will* we see Jesus?" For weeks she explained to everyone who would listen that Baby Jesus and the angels were *pretend* at the church, but someday in heaven they would be *real*.

Today Sheri is 26, married, and a registered nurse. She still gets excited talking about seeing Jesus and the angels. Someday, soon, Sheri . . . *very* soon . . .   ELLIE GREEN

DECEMBER 24

A Time for Everything

There is a time for everything, and a season for every activity under heaven. Eccl. 3:1, NIV.

I remember Christmas past. The cut trees, piney and pungent. The colored lights in starlike silver reflectors. The angel with the spun-glass aura. And the whole shadowy, tree-lit room.

I remember the excitement mounting throughout December, the delicious curiosity that made me want to know—and not know—the secrets my parents were accumulating under the bed or on the high closet shelf. An early Christmas memory has me standing at the closet door, looking up.

Every year I relived the torture and the ecstasy of sitting on the floor beside the tree on Christmas Eve night. There I would lift and weigh each wrapped present in my hands, spending the most time with the box that said "ma-ma" when I turned it over . . . and over . . . and over.

Should we open presents on Christmas Eve this year? I would agonize, almost beyond waiting. But no. That would spoil Christmas morning. At last I would leave the tree and go to bed.

Christmas morning inevitably came. Very early we'd gather around the lighted tree, Daddy mischievously hinting that he hoped my gift would "fit," Mother bringing the scissors. Though dressed in a warm robe and slippers, I could not stop shivering.

Christmas was much like that until the year I was 9, or maybe 10. The days of that December came and went as usual, stores filling with shoppers and the radio playing "White Christmas." It was time, I knew, for the high tide of excitement to roll in. But I noticed that it didn't come quite as far as usual. Something was wrong. The edge was off the ecstasy.

"For some reason, I'm not as excited about Christmas as I usually am," I confided to Mother, thoroughly puzzled.

Her comment smacked of finality. "You're growing up," she said.

And, of course, I was. In time I would leave the portals of Toyland . . . and teen romance . . . and young motherhood . . . each wonderful beyond measure.

"There's a time of life for everything," Mother often told me from her pinnacle of years. She's resting now. From my own pinnacle, I observe that she was right. As my celebration of Christ's first coming to earth merges with expectation of His second, I sit reflecting in my shadowy, tree-lit room. It will soon be Christmas. But there's more.

Something wonderful is about to happen. A delicious curiosity makes me want to know—and not know—when.

The secret things are on the high shelf.

I am standing at the door, looking up.

ANN BURKE

DECEMBER 25

Reach Out and Touch . . .

But Jesus turned right around and saw her. "Cheer up, my daughter," he said, "your faith has made you well." Matt. 9:22, Phillips.

Perched on the kitchen counter, Melissa was reminiscing about the school Christmas program of the previous week. The highlight for her had been the procession to the crèche—real people acting out all of the parts of the Christmas story. A new mother had brought her 2-week-old son, appropriately wrapped in swaddling clothes, and had laid him in the manger.

"I wanted to go up and touch the baby Jesus," Melissa said with a wistful smile. "The story would be more real if I could touch Him."

"You can touch Jesus any time you want to, Melissa," I answered. "Remember the movie screen in your mind?" She nodded. "Create a picture of the manger scene on your own private movie screen," I suggested, giving her a moment to get the picture in place. "Now see yourself walking up to the manger. Are you there yet?" Eyes tightly closed, Melissa nodded. "Reach out and touch the Baby," I continued. "Can you feel the tiny hand curl around your finger?"

Suddenly her eyes flew open, and she bounced up and down on the counter. "I did it! I did it!" she squealed. "I touched the baby Jesus in my mind. It felt like the electricity when I rub my feet over the rug and then touch the iron rail."

"You can touch Jesus in other ways," I continued. While we ate brunch together, we discussed what it would be like to climb up into His lap and feel His arms around us, to walk down the street holding His hand.

We recalled Bible stories that mentioned Jesus and His touch. The children who climbed into His lap. The daughter of Jairus. The woman from Capernaum who had suffered from a debilitating disease for 12 long years. She felt a thrill of electricity too when she touched the hem of His garment.

All too soon the doorbell rang. Melissa's mother had arrived to drive her back home. As we hugged goodbye, she whispered in my ear, "I am going to touch Jesus every day!" She skipped off to the car, and I breathed to myself, "Thanks, Melissa. You just reminded me again, 'Of such is the kingdom of heaven' [Matt. 19:14]."

Today, every day, I can reach out in imagination and touch Jesus. I can touch my Best Friend as a newborn babe in Bethlehem, as the Miracle Worker of Galilee, as the Great Comforter, as the King of the universe, and as my personal Redeemer. I can touch Him when I feel joy, love, thankfulness, respect, and also when I feel anger, loneliness, sorrow, and pain. God will understand. But I must reach out my hand in faith to touch—and my faith will make me whole!

ARLENE TAYLOR

DECEMBER 26

Grand Performance

I will praise thee, O Lord, among the people: and I will sing praises unto thee among the nations. Ps. 108:3.

My favorite Christmas program happened on the tiny island of Carlos in the Pacific's Marshall Islands. The volunteer teacher, a student from the United States, had drilled her eight grades of students in perfect English. Some of the faculty from Ebeye Island, six miles distant, had boated over for the special celebration.

We, the captive audience, sat on white-painted wooden benches. Soon the elementary choir paraded solemnly through the old abandoned military barracks. Beautiful bronze-skinned girls entered, faces tilted shyly downward. Wire hanger circles shone as silvery, glistening halos above each head of jet-black hair.

Boys in crisp shirts and pants marched slowly, orderly, to assigned positions. Suddenly they began to sing. "O, Come, All Ye Faithful!" followed by "Silent Night" and "Away in a Manger." The youthful leader directed like a pro. I studied the uplifted faces praising Bethlehem's Newborn and pictured angels rejoicing again this day.

Then the Christmas play. In this tropical climate Mary reclined on a palm mat as an angel announced her pregnancy. More angels entered, clad in white and glitter. Excited, forceful tones and much flailing of arms commenced when Joseph was denied lodging. Wise Men in bath towel hoods and shower curtain robes entered. A giant palm frond waved off imaginary insects as the king interviewed the Magi.

A life-sized room of plywood and green foliage housed Baby Jesus under a palm-strewn roof. Nearby a fenced enclosure penned small animals. Pomp and pageantry mingled with poverty as the program progressed. It was professionally acted, as if from their own experience.

We expected to hear "baa, baa" from lambs in the pen. Instead, a rumble of "oink, oink" and unrelenting squeals pierced the holy night. Marshall Islanders' beloved piglets were demanding their freedom.

"Joy to the World!" the children sang heartily in practiced unison. This mini pageant, so perfect, so simple, so majestic, sealed an indelible impression upon my heart. I was blessed by the dedicated efforts of the one lonely teacher in the Pacific, thousands of miles from home. She had taught her students well.

It is inspiring when races and people of all ages unite in grand unison to serve and praise the Lord. Someday the whole universe will celebrate the triumph of that Babe born in the manger. I want to be there, don't you? Not only as a spectator, but also as a participant.

JAN CHAMBERLAIN

DECEMBER 27

Beating Those Morning Blues!

Oh, satisfy us early with Your mercy, that we may rejoice and be glad all our days! Ps. 90:14, NKJV.

*H*ow did you feel this morning when you awoke? Eager, excited, and enthusiastic about the possible events of the day, or did you stagger out of bed depressed about the difficulties staring you in the face?

Perhaps the abrupt ringing of the alarm clock jolted you back into mundane household chores, exhausting conflicts with a strong-willed child, pressures at work, and a never-ending "to do" list. This verse challenges us to experience something different.

Each morning the gentle touch of God can greet us as He fills us with a fresh supply of His love. His love, satisfying and soothing, enables us to sing with gladness and joy. I wonder, however, if we sometimes want to be filled with His love.

Sometime ago I started to refill a hot water bottle, but couldn't get the top off. Although I tugged, pulled, and twisted it, the bottle refused to allow me to release its stale, lukewarm, useless contents. Finally I tossed the bottle aside, frustrated and disappointed.

Every 24 hours God comes to replenish His gift of love to us. Sometimes He too must go away frustrated and disappointed that we do not let Him empty us of the staleness that needs to be cleaned out of our lives.

Because we cling tenaciously to our old ideas, our independence, our stubborn attitudes, He cannot pour His refreshing, renewing, powerful love into us.

But God's promise in Psalm 90:14 is glorious! Why don't you ask Him to remove the debris that accumulates in your life each day so that you can overflow with His abundant love? Not only will you sing with gladness, but you'll beat those morning blues!

MARY BARRETT

DECEMBER 28

Shouting for Joy

Oh, clap your hands, all ye peoples! Shout to God with the voice of triumph! Ps. 47:1, NKJV.

I remember as a little girl standing on a large rock in our field, pretending I was a great singer. It must have been humorous to my guardian angel, since I couldn't, at that age, carry a tune. That didn't deter me at all, however, full as I was with the joyfulness of the young. Fortunately I did not disturb anyone else, since we lived way out in the country with few houses nearby. So I could shout at the top of my lungs as much as I wanted.

I've often wondered what it will be like to stand in heaven and sing the songs of the angels. To have voices like them, to have the joy of eternal life, to have our tears wiped away, to know no more sorrow. It's beyond my comprehension.

I think of my 90-year-old mother-in-law. She still lives by herself, but now she's going blind, and things will have to change.

Change is difficult for all of us, but especially so when you are 90. She is in quite good health except for her eyes, and her mind is very clear. That makes it even more difficult. It is hard to live in an aging body with a young mind.

I think of our little Boston terrier, Penny, whom we had to put to sleep early in December. She had learned to trust us so completely that she submitted willingly to the needle that took her life.

I think of the daughter we had for only 28 years before a rare disease took her young life. Everywhere I look—every newspaper, every newscast—is filled with violence and death.

Yes, I look forward to Jesus' return—to no more tears, no more sorrow, no more death. To be able to stand on a rock in heaven and sing for joy in perfect melody that sin is finally ended. And the whole universe will come to hear us as we the redeemed sing with the wonderful voice of triumph.   LORAINE SWEETLAND

DECEMBER 29

Unity in Christ

I plead with Euodia and I plead with Syntyche to agree with each other in the Lord. Yes, and I ask you, loyal yokefellow, help these women who have contended at my side in the cause of the gospel, along with Clement and the rest of my fellow workers, whose names are in the book of life. Phil. 4:2, 3, NIV.

I have read my Bible through a number of times, but it was only recently, when I began to have disagreements with another woman in the church, that these verses came alive for me.

Paul had many helping him preach the gospel. We always think of Barnabas, John Mark, Silas, and others, but do not realize that women aided him, too. Furthermore, these two had problems in their work, for the verse reads "have *contended* at my side in the cause of the gospel." I looked for various meanings of the word *contend* and came up with the following: battle, clash, fight, struggle, war. The opposites of the word *contend* are surrender, agree, cooperate, ignore.

Could it have been that workers in God's cause were having problems with one another, so much so that Paul pleaded with the two women to agree with each other, and for others in the church to help them? Evidently so, and it can still happen today.

As Paul develops his exhortations to the Philippian believers, he turns their minds to more positive thoughts. Today, it is still our duty to look for the good in others, to help those having difficulties with one another to resolve their problems, and to do everything in our power to become united in Christ. Then we can contend, or struggle, *for* God's cause instead of against each other. We will be fellow workers with our names all in the book of life.   EUNICE MASON

DECEMBER 30

Service With a Smile

Therefore, whether you eat or drink, or whatever you do, do all to the glory of God. 1 Cor. 10:31, NKJV.

"Now what are they doing with that old service station?" I asked, and my husband shrugged. Our curiosity was aroused though, and we kept watching, wondering, and trying to guess. Surely it wouldn't be another service station—the area had three already. A convenience store? No way! We didn't need another one. What about a restaurant? A good idea, but the shape of the building canceled that idea out.

Time went by. Then one day, to our amazement, a construction crew put storage tanks in the ground—another service station. But a strange one—the office area seemed far too big.

We kept watching until shelves showed through the glass windows. A convenience store, too? What a waste! With that idea in mind, we ignored the rest of the building process. One thing for sure, we didn't need what they were going to offer.

A couple months later my husband, Dennis, shook his head one evening and commented, "It's the strangest thing, but today two people told me that we should try the sandwiches at the new gas station."

"They sell sandwiches?" *What an amazing idea,* I thought. "What kind of sandwiches would we get there?" Dennis went on to say how they were reported to be selling "hoagies—full of fresh vegetables on great rolls."

Our friends were right. The owners had put in four tables. And the prices couldn't be beat. But the American Convenience Store became more than great hoagies at a good price. Soon we found ourselves welcomed by friends who cared.

Where else could we find another Joel, always greeting us with a smile and saying, "The usual? Coming right up!" The rest of the crew were great too. Other eating places just didn't compare with the service.

Enough about stores and sandwiches. What do these things have to do with you and your family? I wonder how many people look at you, your family, and even the church you go to (if they are aware of which one it is) and wonder, "Do we really need that kind of person, their family, and their church in our town? Are they any different than the others?"

I've got a challenge for you. It goes like this: You don't have to act like you care—just care enough to act. Think about it. But you'll have to do more than think. Remember, actions speak louder than words.

GINGER MOSTERT CHURCH

DECEMBER 31

What a Sight!

I lift up my eyes to the hills—from where will my help come? My help comes from the Lord, who made heaven and earth. Ps. 121:1, 2, NRSV.

"et's go to Zermatt!"

"It's raining! We couldn't see a thing."

"But maybe on the other side of the range . . ."

We agreed to venture over in the morning. Going by car around the mountains was out of the question, since our days in Switzerland were limited. Out came the map and, yes, we'd take a shortcut through the mountain by putting the car on the train.

We made good connections and after about a 45-minute ride, drove off of the train and headed down the other side of the mountain. But the weather had not changed.

Since no cars are allowed in Zermatt, we parked at the train station in Täsch three miles below, grabbed our suitcases, and hustled on board the train just as it pulled out.

The accommodations board in the station listed 18-20 hotels, and a button for each listing put the caller in touch with the hotel keeper. Which one to choose? Which one would have a view of the Alps we longed to see? Which one could we afford? We selected a button, and to my query, she replied, "*Yah, yah, vie have zimmer frei.*" I knew that meant a room free—"free" as in available.

I asked for one with a view of the Matterhorn and hoped she understood my request. After getting directions, we started walking in the drizzle toward the village to the small hotel. The two-bedroom-with-kitchen was adequate and warm after our dampening walk.

Following a light supper we went to bed wondering what tomorrow would bring.

How I woke up before anyone else is a mystery. I walked to the window and slowly pulled back the curtains. The hesitant peek immediately turned to a jerk of the curtains and a shout of, "Oh, my goodness! Gene, wake up! Come and see this! Bette, Gil, come! I can't believe it! Look!"

There, filling the entire window, was the most exquisite sight I have ever seen. The sloping back of the snow-covered 14,690-foot Matterhorn loomed in a bluer than blue sky that took my breath away. Lord, could You be so good to us? A room with a view, indeed!

Nature speaks to me. I see the pleasure in God's face as He sneaks His surprises. I feel His loving hug in mountain splendor, a purple gentian, a lush field of cattle, a good thunderstorm, or the scent of frangipani, jasmine, or a Tiffany rose. Sometimes nature shouts His love to me. Other times it just peeks through a crack in the curtains.

May the coming new year be filled with God's surprises for you!

HELEN STILES